America's Culture of Terrorism

America's Culture of Terrorism

*Violence, Capitalism,
and the Written Word*

Jeffory A. Clymer

The University of North Carolina Press

CHAPEL HILL AND LONDON

Manufactured in
the United States of America
Set in Bulmer type by
Tseng Information Systems, Inc.

The paper in this book meets the guidelines
for permanence and durability of the Committee
on Production Guidelines for Book Longevity
of the Council on Library Resources.

Library of Congress Cataloging-in-Publication Data
Clymer, Jeffory A.
America's culture of terrorism : violence, capitalism,
and the written word / Jeffory A. Clymer.
p. cm. — (Cultural studies of the United States)
Includes bibliographical references and index.
ISBN 0-8078-2792-4 (cloth : alk. paper) —
ISBN 0-8078-5460-3 (pbk. : alk. paper)
1. Terrorism—United States—History.   2. Violence—
United States—History.   3. Capitalism—United States—
History.   4. Mass media—United States—History.
5. United States—Social conditions.   I. Title.   II. Series.
HV6432 .C59   2003
363.3'2'0973—dc21
2002154608

cloth   07   06   05   04   03   5   4   3   2   1
paper   07   06   05   04   03   5   4   3   2   1

For Christine and Gene Clymer
and for Brandy Anderson

Contents

Illustrations

Acknowledgments

During the several years I have worked on this book, I incurred numerous personal and professional debts. Many people have generously shared their time and ideas with me, and I would like to take the opportunity to thank them here. Cathy Davidson, Joy Kasson, Jan Radway, and Karla Holloway were this project's first readers. Cathy is a true model of readerly savvy and insight; Joy's capacious intellect is only matched by her generous and kind spirit; Jan has a phenomenal mind and always makes penetrating, compelling inquiries and suggestions; and Karla asked substantial questions about the shape of my ideas. Michael Bérubé has been an intellectual inspiration and source of encouragement for many years. Chris Wilson's large expertise, keen critical insights, and unstinting generosity have been invaluable. For their willingness to read drafts of chapters and offer helpful suggestions, I want to thank Steve Hardman, Ryan Schneider, Heather Hicks, John Pauly, Stephanie Brown, Georgia Johnston, Toby Benis, Ray Benoit, and Michael Berthold.

I am fortunate to have an excellent and amusing circle of friends who have both directly and indirectly helped this book along. I have shared much laughter and many good times in St. Louis with Allie Wesson, Dave Lesser, Ken Wu, Scott Stone, Tom Nagashima, Carol Dyer, Didier Hodzic, Paige Canfield, and Mike Streeto. I also wish to thank my parents, Christine and Gene Clymer, my sister and brother-in-law, Beth and Dave McCoy, and my in-laws, Gina and Keith Anderson and Ruth and Tom Oldenburg, for their generosity and kind encouragement.

Sara van den Berg has been a wonderfully supportive department chairperson and a sage advisor. Saint Louis University's Interlibrary Loan office and archivists at the Chicago Historical Society and Washington State Historical Society helped to make my research possible, while Randy McGuire provided much-needed technical assistance on the illustrations. A series of Mellon summer research stipends from Saint Louis University also greatly aided my research and writing. The final touches to this book were completed at the Wesleyan University Center for the Humanities, and I would like to thank the center's director, Henry Abelove, as well as everyone associated with the center, for such a stimulating working environment.

Acknowledgments

I am grateful to my students in graduate and undergraduate classes on literature and terrorism. Their questions, interest, and efforts helped to sharpen and clarify my thinking.

I would also especially like to thank the editors and staff of the University of North Carolina Press, particularly Sian Hunter, whose advice, intellectual rigor, and editorial acumen I have greatly appreciated.

Parts of Chapters 1 and 4 have previously been published as "The 1886 Chicago Haymarket Bombing and the Rhetoric of Terrorism in America," *Yale Journal of Criticism* 15 (2002): 315–44, and "'This Firm of Men-Killers': Jack London and the Business of Terrorism," *Modern Fiction Studies* 45 (1999): 905–31. I gratefully acknowledge the Johns Hopkins University Press's permission to reprint each of these articles.

Most important, I want to thank Brandy Anderson for being so wise, so loving, so wonderful, for making me laugh so hard, and for giving me more joy than one person ought to have. In addition to being a wonderful companion and wife, she always takes time out of her own schedule to discuss the minutiae of American cultural history with me and unfailingly brings her own unique and witty interpretations to these conversations. I am very lucky.

America's Culture of Terrorism

Terrorism in the American Cultural Imagination

I n the penultimate draft of *The Rise of Silas Lapham*'s famous dinner party
scene, William Dean Howells's patrician character Bromfield Corey
gives vent to a shocking idea. "In some of my walks on the Hill and down
on the Back Bay," Corey informs his startled guests, "nothing but the surveillance of the local policeman prevents me from applying dynamite to those
long rows of close-shuttered, handsome, brutally insensible houses."[1] Reading these words in 1885, Howells's editor, Richard Watson Gilder of the *Century*, quickly issued a panicked response to his renowned author. He warned
Howells that "it is the very word, *dynamite*, that is now so dangerous, for any
of us to use, except in condemnation." Gilder then worried that Howells's
fiction might yoke Howells himself to "the crank who does the deed,"[2] as if
writing about dynamite and throwing dynamite are two versions of the same
action. Howells ultimately acquiesced to Gilder's anxieties and substituted
"offering personal violence" for the much more sinister "applying dynamite"
in the American and English book versions of his novel.[3]

Gilder's apprehensions about dynamite suddenly seemed prophetic the
next year when a bomb exploded at an anarchist rally in Haymarket Square
in America's volatile western metropolis of Chicago. The interpretation of
the Haymarket bombing as a terrorist conspiracy is my subject in Chapter 1, but I should also note here that Howells's name was indeed closely
tied to the political violence at Haymarket, albeit in a way that Gilder certainly did not anticipate. Howells emerged after the bombing as the *only*
major American literary figure to publicly condemn the sham legal proceedings accorded the Haymarket anarchists.[4] However, Gilder and Howells's
interaction in *Lapham*'s editing bears significance for reasons far beyond its
implications for Howells's biography. Gilder's case of editorial nerves offers
one important barometer of American culture in the 1880s, which the famous

editor apparently could imagine only as a besieged society subject to cataclysmic terrorist assaults at any moment. His almost visceral response to the massive power and indiscriminating slaughter made possible by dynamite prompted Howells to reach for the seemingly more manageable and smaller-scale notion of "personal violence." Gilder's surprising concern that Howells's mere fictional pondering of a dynamite attack (let alone the depiction of a bombing itself) could somehow tie the author to a terrorist "crank" who actually throws a bomb also exemplifies the frequent disappearance of the boundary between fact and fiction in discussions of terrorism. Additionally, Howells's otherwise inconsequential revision in his most famous novel holds substantial import because the vast difference between his revisionary and original words — "offering personal violence" and "applying dynamite" — is also a key measure of modern terrorism itself. And lastly, in coupling the then-new fear of dynamite with the development of modern capitalism, personified here in the form of industrial magnate and stock speculator Lapham's intrusion into the wealthy enclave of Boston's Back Bay, this scene highlights the concurrent and interrelated trajectories that emergent conceptions of terrorism and the development of modern, industrial capitalism traced out in the United States at the end of the nineteenth century.

Nearly forty years after the editorial negotiation between Howells and Gilder, on 16 September 1920 a massive bomb drawn by a horse cart exploded in New York City. The blast took place directly in front of a United States Sub-Treasury building and across the street from J. P. Morgan's Wall Street offices. Thirty-eight persons were killed, hundreds were injured, and Morgan's offices were heavily damaged by the combined effect of the explosion and the hundreds of iron window weights that the bomb makers had included with the explosive material. Despite years of international sleuthing, and many accusations and admissions of guilt followed quickly by retractions, the person or persons responsible were never apprehended. Striking at the very nerve center of the American corporate economy, this grisly explosion made explicit the ties between the development of American capitalism and terrorism that were intimated in Howells's exchange with his editor. Not only did the bombing wreck Morgan's offices, but, in an eerily dramatic enactment of its symbolic destruction of capital, the explosion also destroyed thousands of dollars worth of paper bonds and stock securities that were in the possession of messengers victimized by the blast.[5]

Along with the (near) appearance of dynamite in the canonical *Silas Lapham*, the virtually forgotten terrorist attack on Wall Street in 1920 marks the temporal boundary of this study. The Wall Street bomb came in the midst of, and perhaps as a response to, the ongoing persecution of "subversives" led by Attorney General A. Mitchell Palmer. Palmer's own home had, in fact, been targeted as part of the round of bombings that occurred simultaneously in several different cities in 1919 (a latter-day version of the fictitious conspiratorial plot woven by Henry James's notorious terrorist, Diedrich Hoffendahl). In response to these bombings, the Justice Department launched surprise raids on the headquarters of radical organizations throughout the country in 1919 and 1920. With the absence of anything resembling due process, the "Palmer Raids" led to the roundup, detention, and eventual deportation of hundreds of leftists. Though the raids came under their own public scrutiny not long thereafter, they left American radicalism, organized labor, and any real alternatives to the consolidation of American corporate capitalism crippled and in disarray for years to come.

The elision of dynamite in Howells's novel exemplifies the intense fear of terrorist violence felt at the turn of the century, and our own contemporary forgetfulness about the horrifically deadly and destructive 1920 bombing demonstrates America's amnesia concerning its history of terrorist violence. But while the Wall Street explosion brought to life Howells and Gilder's worries about the economic politics of dynamite and stands in relief against the backdrop of our present cultural amnesia, the bombing was also discussed at that time in historically significant ways. Officials, the *New York Times* wrote, were convinced "that the bomb was exploded as an 'act of general terrorism,' believed to have been aimed against the Federal Government as well as against American capital."[6] As was so often the case in these decades, mainstream opinion about terrorism conflated violence aimed at drawing attention to the inequities of capital with an outright attack on the American government. Partially, of course, this was because radical Americans, including the men tried for the Haymarket bombing in the 1880s and those members of the Industrial Workers of the World (IWW) put on trial for sedition thirty years later, often coupled their critique of the American economy to a critique of the government structure. But beyond this, those opposed to such radical economic politics surely thought it easier to win the hearts and minds of the public if they could pathologize strenuous objections to the American economy as an assault on law, government, and the very foundations of the American republic itself. As such, a bomb exploding in front of J. P. Morgan's Wall Street office became prima facie an attack on the United States government.

In reporting the blast, the *Times* described the event in a manner that unconsciously combined both older and more modern ways of perceiving such mass, random violence: "The conspirators in large measure failed of whatever direct objects they had beyond sheer terrorization. They evidently timed their infernal machine for an hour when the streets of the financial district were crowded, but they chose as well the hour [12:00 P.M.] when not the captains of industry but their clerks and messengers were on the street."[7] Here the *Times* notes the psychological dimension of terrorism and its production of widespread fear, which came to be seen as the primary purpose of terrorist violence over the course of the twentieth century. The *Times,* though, is not yet ready to imagine the horror of specifically targeting innocent and random people. Instead, the newspaper intimates that there must have been another purpose beyond the strange-sounding "terrorization," perhaps an assassination attempt aimed at a particularly powerful man, such as J. P. Morgan, an idea that would make the random blast more assimilable to familiar paradigms of violence. In much the same way that "terrorism" and "terrorization" coexist in the reportage, the venerable newspaper also uses the older phrase "infernal machine" alongside the more modern-sounding "bomb," thus appearing to be both dimly aware and wary of the possibility of indiscriminate mass violence. While "infernal machine" tied the hellish to technological contrivance in popular notions of terrorists, especially at the end of the nineteenth century, the more neutral and simple "bomb" suggests a culture becoming inured to such cataclysmic violence. Additionally, "infernal machine" registers some of the period's widespread anxiety about and fascination with machinery itself, but the more generic-sounding "bomb" instead focuses interpretive attention and narratives on the perpetrators and victims of a blast, rather than on the surprising and awe-inspiring power of the mechanism itself.

As with any cultural movement, there is not a straightforward line connecting the discourse of bombings in Howells and Gilder's exchange with the terms used to make sense of the Wall Street bombing nearly forty years later. The coexistence of words such as "terrorization" and "terrorism" suggests that a vocabulary for seemingly indiscriminate, mass, and public violence was solidifying but still emerging and somewhat indefinite. Moreover, these figures of speech are embedded in the period's specific historical conditions. As scholars have long articulated, the American economy's volatility and the vast disparities in the class structure at the turn of the twentieth century provoked violence on the sides of both labor and capital. But the contradictions of capitalism and the instantiation of a permanent working class during this period went beyond a simple cause and effect relationship that resulted in dramatic outbursts of violence, such as the 1886 Haymarket bomb, the bomb that killed Idaho's former governor in 1905, or the 1910 dynamiting of the *Los Angeles Times* building. More particularly, the economy's contradictions and disparities provided the grounds for an emergent way of imagining, understanding, and narrating certain forms of violence as "terrorism" across a wide representational range, including, among other places, the mass media, highbrow literature, the labor press, best-selling novels, and poetry aimed at mobilizing America's working class.

One primary objective of this book is to uncover a genealogy of modern terrorism that is visible in literary and other cultural artifacts produced in the decades on either side of 1900, a genealogy firmly rooted in the political and economic upheavals specific to those years. Yet while I am tracing the historical and literary contingencies, contradictions, and ambiguities that constitute the late-nineteenth-century aspects of a form of violence usually assumed to have originated much later, I do not wish to bracket aside the radical confusion that exists among both scholars and politicians concerning how to define terrorism in the first place. As Alex P. Schmid has noted, the terms "terror" and "terrorism" appear to have emerged in the revolutionary France of Maximilien Robespierre during the 1790s, while of course the application of coercive force to threaten society or its political leaders has existed and been theorized for centuries.[8] But as the meaning of terrorism shifted in the latter half of the nineteenth century from what we would now identify as the state terror of revolutionary France to ideas about terrorism that resonate strongly with our contemporary notion of it as insurgent and often conspiratorial violence performed by substate actors, questions about which forms of such violence should be considered terrorism have become notoriously variable, contradictory, and conflicted within both academic and political spheres.[9] Indeed, the definitional problem is perceived as so crippling that important scholars occasionally dismiss the issue out of hand. Paul Wilkinson, for instance, refuses to "become bogged down in days of definitional debate," choosing instead to focus on establishing "culpability for specific attacks or for sponsoring or directing them."[10] While viewing terrorism as simply a self-evident problem to be solved may be appealingly straightforward, such an approach nonetheless begs more questions than it can answer about understanding both political violence and the way we talk about it.

As my opening anecdotes suggest, I argue that emergent means of narrating industrial capitalism and classed identity were deeply intertwined with the way modern terrorism was imagined as a form of violence in turn-of-the-century America. For some writers, the "terrorist" materialized in these decades as a blameworthy, violent figure onto which the disruptions and chaos of a rapidly capitalizing economy could be projected and displaced. Alternatively, for other authors and commentators, the invisible, shocking, and unpredictable nature of terrorist violence offered a material, symbolic, and fitting response to both the seemingly veiled workings of corporate capitalism and the ideological contradictions of a capitalist economy. And certainly, on the other side of the coin, workers themselves were regularly the victims of capitalist-sponsored assaults committed by the likes of Pinkerton agents, private armies, and even state officers. The aftermath of the 1886 Haymarket bombing, violence during the 1892 strike at Andrew Carnegie's Homestead, Pennsylvania, steel mills and throughout the 1890s in Idaho's silver mines, and the machine-gun massacre of striking miners housed in a temporary tent encampment at Ludlow, Colorado, in 1914 provide only the most notorious examples. Working-class victims and important writers, such as Jack London, vigorously protested these violent encounters, even using the word "terrorism" to describe the authorities' brutality. For example, a Chicago anarchist sheet decried the "legalized terrorism" of the Red Scare that followed the Haymarket bombing, and workers also drew upon this language during the Texas and Louisiana lumber wars after the turn of the century.[11] Yet the historical episodes in this book repeatedly underscore the ability of mainstream commentators, spokesmen of capital, and state officers grounded in legitimating institutions to convey a dominant idea that government violence effectively protected law and order against the truly conspiratorial and nihilistic violence of working-class terrorists.

In addition to this late-nineteenth-century ideological struggle over what constituted terrorism, the 1866 invention of dynamite prompted Americans to worry about anonymously committed mass violence in ways that were qualitatively different from earlier fears of slave uprisings, urban mobs, riots, or even, in a labor context, the rural revenge killings of the Molly Maguires. Invented by Alfred Nobel, and so tremulously referred to by Gilder in his 1885 communication with Howells, dynamite in large part precipitated the emergence of the kind of terrorist activity (and the widespread disquietude it incites) that is recognizable as such by citizens of the early twenty-first century.[12] Rendering the dagger or the pistol obsolete weapons of, to use Howells's term, "personal violence," dynamite exponentially increased the scale and magnitude of violence while also offering anonymity to the bomb thrower. Suddenly, social fear, rather than being focused on a highly visible mob or a spontaneous uprising, could coalesce around the notion of a dangerous and often indistinguishable individual, perhaps even, as with Howells's Bromfield Corey, someone who looked nothing like the usual image of an anarchist or outlaw. Representing a key development in the cultural and imaginative history of terror, a dynamite bomb's potential for extensive and targeted damage far outstripped earlier forms of assassination, regicide, and the relative unpredictability of arson.

Recognizing this fact, General Philip Sheridan nervously reported to the president and Congress in the early 1880s that "it should be remembered *destructive explosives are easily made,* and that banks, United States sub-treasuries, public buildings and large mercantile houses can be readily demolished, and the commerce of entire cities destroyed by an infuriated people with means carried with perfect safety to themselves *in the pockets* of their clothing."[13] Sheridan realized that, unlike the individuated killing that is the ruling logic of gunfire (including even the recently invented Gatling gun), the paradoxically small size and substantial power of dynamite precipitated the transcendence of personal violence by giving a bomb thrower the ability to produce mass carnage. The anonymity offered by a catastrophic weapon that could be concealed in one's clothing meant that the opportunities for violence that was both public and seemingly random increased dramatically. Hustling along the crowded urban streets of a modern metropolis and indistinguishable from other citizens, the dynamiter could wreak his or her destruction and possibly escape in the ensuing havoc. Thus, while assassinations, kidnappings, and other singular events can operate as forms of terrorism, the invention of dynamite was one integral material condition that incited "terroristic" thinking in both would-be terrorists and those who feared them.[14] Dynamite, for instance, prompted European and American radicals after the 1860s to proclaim repeatedly that at last a weapon had been found that could, as if by magic, bring down capitalism in one fell swoop through carefully plotted applications of dramatic public violence. This new, cataclysmic power precipitated the intensely unnerving fear and perplexity, such as that expressed by Gilder and Sheridan, that we have come over the last century to associate with the paranoia-inducing dread of terrorism.

While the emergence of modern terrorism as a particular form of political violence was made more imaginable with the invention of dynamite, the growth of a mass press during this same era is another material development that made terrorism into a seemingly potent political weapon. Brought about to a great extent by the thickening density of telegraph wires crisscrossing the nation, the increased prominence and geographic reach of print media in the late nineteenth century helped to make events instantly available for a widely dispersed audience that did not directly witness them. In this expanded media environment, sudden acts of violence could potentially frighten or coerce the citizenry on a much larger scale, and the national public sphere, rather than highly localized settings, increasingly became the arena in which the meanings of spectacular events were discussed and their implications contested.[15]

Mass media radically increased the potential for publicity, especially since the late-nineteenth-century press in Europe and the United States gave ample coverage to terrorists. Johann Most, for instance, emigrated to the United

States in 1882 and quickly became vilified by the media as the most threatening person in America due to his "advice for terrorists" in his writing and incessant calls for mass violence on his lecture tours.[16] With his bushy beard and gesticulatory speaking style, the German Most also became the prototype for the ubiquitous caricatures of anarchists as unkempt and wildly buffoonish figures that appeared in mainstream newspapers. But while newspapers lampooned figures such as Most in an effort to undermine their social commentary, the media's worried parodies could nonetheless serve as rallying points for dispossessed Americans searching for ways to articulate and understand their alienation from America's dominant culture.

The mass press also paid continual attention to a barrage of terrorist incidents in this period, including the rash of bombings in France during the 1890s as well as attempts to blow up the Greenwich Observatory and the Tower of London. Although the relationship between the media and terrorism is too complex and historically variable to analyze sufficiently here, heavy press coverage surely contributed to the spread of terrorism as a modern style of political confrontation.[17] To take one example, Leon Czolgosz explained his 1901 assassination of President William McKinley by declaring that he had decided that McKinley "should not claim so much attention, while others receive none." To give a statistical measure to Czolgosz's effort to tap into the power of publicity, McKinley's own 1896 election had marked the first time that an American newspaper had published one million copies, disseminating information and publicity over an exponentially greater area than had been imaginable only a few decades earlier.[18]

Yet if Czolgosz sought to bring attention to the disempowered, his assassination of McKinley set off a renewed round of antiradical fervor in the United States that subjected Emma Goldman and other prominent activists to severe public abuse. Occurring shortly after several assassinations of European leaders, Czolgosz's act fired fears of an international anarchist plot to murder heads of state around the world. Czolgosz, however, maintained throughout his trial and execution that he had acted alone.[19] Whether he indeed acted alone or was part of a plot, and whether he believed that assassinating McKinley would be a revolutionary spark, we cannot say definitively. However, the question of intentionality in terrorism, as in communication generally, is problematic at best. Acts labeled terrorism are subject to the vicissitudes of interpretation. Whatever Czolgosz believed himself to be doing when he used a pistol concealed in his heavily bandaged hand to assassinate McKinley at the Buffalo Pan-American Exposition, citizens at the time of the killing smelled a terrorist conspiracy and instantly transformed the assassination into another chance to suppress radicalism in America. As in the earlier Haymarket era, the notion of a foreign-sounding villain importing anarchism and terrorism to America fired this country's nativist imagination.

Though Czolgosz claimed to have planned and orchestrated the assassination on his own, his terse explanation clearly imagines violence from a communicative, symbolic, and terroristic point of view. Czolgosz regarded the assassination of the president, the figural embodiment of the state itself, as a way to alleviate or at least bring attention to the muteness of the dispossessed. Yet the widespread condemnation of Czolgosz in American newspapers underscores the fact that political violence often produces a reaction in its audience whereby citizens cling to organized political structures rather than begin to question them. If terrorist violence attempts to send a coercive message, there is vast opportunity for that message to be either misconstrued or to produce undesired results.[20] Czolgosz's grasp of violence's power when leavened with publicity bears out that publicity is absolutely central to modern terrorism, while also showing that the relationship between the media and terrorism is neither simple nor straightforward.[21] At the least, newspapers and terrorists share an interest in generating public impact (and selling newspapers) by rendering the sudden eruptions of political violence as dramatic, perplexing, and horrific as possible.[22] Newspapers' dependence on the regularly occurring disruptions of the norm that count as "news" seems ready-made for terrorist incidents, which is of course one reason that modern terrorism and the mass press came to maturity together in the decades around the turn of the century.

Terrorism and Contemporary America

Developing notions of modern terrorism in the late nineteenth century grew out of a dense thicket of economic shifts, ideology, and technological change. During those years between the 1886 Chicago Haymarket and the 1920 Wall Street bombings, terrorism loomed large in the American cultural imagination. Present-day America, of course, finds its citizens more preoccupied with the dreadful reality of terrorism than they have ever been. The 11 September 2001 attacks on the World Trade Center and Pentagon, the appearance of anthrax spores in our nation's mail, and the new war on terrorism around the globe have galvanized and frightened Americans. But even before the utter devastation of 9/11 and the emergence of Al Qaeda as a familiar name, Americans were preoccupied with terrorism. The World Trade Center bombing of 1993, the 1995 destruction of the Alfred P. Murrah Federal Building in Oklahoma City, the Olympic and abortion clinic bombings in Georgia during 1996, and the government's discovery of certain militias' plots to blow up federal buildings and courthouses around the country during the 1990s made Americans rethink the possibility of terrorism happening in the United States well before September 2001.

When a Trans World Airlines (TWA) jumbo jet exploded just off the coast of Long Island in July 1996, this heightened sensitivity to terrorism fueled widespread press coverage suggesting that the explosion was a terrorist attack. And while conspiracy theorists added intricate explanations to the anxious mixture of fear, anger, and uncertainty that surrounded the jet's explosion, the crash ultimately appeared to have been caused by mechanical failure rather than terrorist violence. The TWA tragedy, however, is a good example of the infectious and overwhelming anxiety that fear of terrorism causes. Faced with the dreadful possibility of terrorist violence, Americans began to substitute the most far-flung and unlikely of scenarios in the place of much more plausible explanations. Living in fear of terrorism's radical unpredictability seems to create a psychological condition in which only the most debilitating and paranoia-laced explanations make sense, which is, in short, to be firmly in the grasp of terror.

But while the belief that terrorism is a real possibility produces, quite understandably, nothing so much as more fear, commentators on terrorism in America during the 1990s routinely repeated the refrain that this is a new psychological sensation in the United States. When the World Trade Center and Oklahoma City Federal Building were bombed, news reports repeatedly informed us that terrorism had finally happened here, where it supposedly could not happen. A putatively foreign form of violence had finally encroached on American soil, we were told.[23] And in the aftermath of the September 2001 attacks, the media again largely avoided relating the attacks to earlier episodes of terrorism in the United States. Perhaps this was because 9/11 seemed so beyond the pale of anything that had occurred in this country in the past that relating it to the 1993 World Trade Center bombing or to Oklahoma City appeared ludicrous; indeed, the tragedy's sheer magnitude led many commentators to look instead, though not without controversy, to Pearl Harbor as a precedent. Yet, if the massive violence of 11 September made many turn for precedents to other events not usually labeled terrorism, it also seems that it was politically important to deem the 9/11 attacks terrorism rather than, for example, a crime against humanity. This conception maintained an ideological continuity with Americans' conventional notions of the types of violence performed by Middle Easterners.[24]

Indeed, while the 2001 attacks were clearly organized and committed by men from the Middle East, the cultural link between Middle Easterners and terrorism was articulated just as forcefully, if incorrectly, after the Oklahoma

City bombing. The first accounts of the Murrah Federal Building's destruction indicated that a man of Middle Eastern descent was the primary suspect, while talk shows featured pundits and politicians such as former Oklahoma congressman Dave McCurdy whipping up anti-Arab and Islamic fervor.[25] Yet Americans Timothy McVeigh and Terry Nichols were eventually convicted for the bombing. While America was undoubtedly victimized by Osama bin Laden and Al Qaeda, this sense that terrorism is inevitably the work of foreigners, especially those from the Middle East, is reminiscent of the rhetoric produced immediately after the Haymarket bombing in 1886. If during the last decade the imagined figure of the terrorist in America was always, correctly or incorrectly, a religious zealot of Middle Eastern descent, in the 1880s the terrorist was, equally inevitably, identified as an anarchist from Germany, Russia, or Bohemia.

Among this book's aims is uncovering the rich historical and literary discourse of terrorism in America at the turn of the twentieth century that belies current notions of terrorism's newness within the United States at the end of the century. While continual invocations of terrorism's novelty in America are implicated in long-term ideas of American exceptionalism, they ignore the deep history of terroristic discourse in this country. But if terrorism is too often misrepresented as a new phenomenon in the United States, it has for the last several years nonetheless occupied the cultural stage with a vengeance. Serious and self-consciously literary writers, including Don DeLillo, Peter Kramer, Philip Roth, and Paul Auster, have all written books over the last decade or so that directly examine how concerns about terrorism and the particularities of capitalism's current form impact upon each other.[26] The corporate entertainment industry has transformed terroristic thrills and spills, as with other sensational subjects, into a marketable commodity. Blockbuster movies such as *Air Force One, The Sum of All Fears,* and *The Peacemaker,* best-selling novels by Tom Clancy and Robin Cook, television shows such as *La Femme Nikita,* and antiterrorist commando video games based on Clancy's novels all testify to what we might call the late-twentieth-century incorporation of terrorism.[27]

Before the events of 11 September 2001, the rash of terrorist bombings in America during the 1990s may have provided one reason for the popularity of terrorism as a form of entertainment in recent years. Al Qaeda's attacks complicated this dynamic. In the wake of 9/11, the release of major movies about terrorism, such as Arnold Schwarzenegger's *Collateral Damage,* was delayed out of sensitivity to Americans' traumatized condition. However, the early 2002 release of Schwarzenegger's movie suggested, perhaps not surprisingly, that monetary pressures within the movie industry can only allow Americans so long to recover, or even that a cinematic enactment of revenge against terrorists may have been part of that recovery process for many viewers. But as other scholars have noted, the reasons for the vogue of terrorism in popular culture prior to 11 September were also related to our post–Cold War existence.[28] Sudden eruptions of terrorism turn everyday citizens into martyrs, embodiments of a national character that is threatened by the terrorists' violence. Reinvigorating the nationalist logic of the Cold War era, if not quite the same cast of characters, the honoring of martyred victims in recent popular cultural products that build their plots around terror substitutes a simple "us vs. them" binary for the complex political, social, and economic problems that confront this country at the millennium and that provoke terrorism.[29]

For instance, Richard Preston's 1997 best-seller, *The Cobra Event,* demonstrates how concerns over terrorism can be used to orient readers' understandings of both the Cold War's fallout and American capitalism. In Preston's novel, a demented worker at a biotechnology firm specializing in drug research, but which also dabbles in weapons production on the side, steals a dangerous genetically engineered virus from the company and starts replicating and testing it on the New York public preparatory to a planned massive release of the deadly virus. Before September 2001, policy makers regularly feared that such a toxic attack would be the likely scenario for a cataclysmic terrorist event in the United States, and in the wake of the unclaimed and unsolved October 2001 anthrax scare, Preston appears unfortunately prescient.

In his novel, as the government's biosleuths work to track down the terrorist before he performs his massive attack, they realize that the technological brilliance of the genetically engineered virus "has to be American." But even if "looking at that virus is like looking at a starship," the deadly element of "smallpox in it—that's ancient and old and smells like Russia." As the novel painstakingly details, the Soviet Union had pushed ahead of the United States in the development of biological weapons during the Cold War, resulting in the detritus of languishing weapons and impoverished scientists looking for work in the post–Cold War world, possibly with "rogue" states. And so an undercapitalized American start-up company doing legitimate genetic research into a rare, and hence underfunded, disease goes into high-tech weapons manufacturing with the help of a Russian scientist. As a key member of the antiterrorist task force puts it, "Cobra has two makers. One is American and one is Russian. They've gotten together somehow, and there's money involved. There has to be. I think there's a company in this."[30]

In *The Cobra Event,* illicit weapons research and the exigencies of modern corporate capitalism combine to produce a dangerous breeding ground for terrorism. Yet the book is also interesting for the way it simultaneously avows and disavows this connection between modern capitalism and terrorism. A former employee convinced that the world's dense overpopulation needs to be thinned is ultimately found responsible for stealing the weapons-grade virus from the biotech firm and then unleashing it on the unsuspecting public. Displacing the contradictions and upheavals of both the former Soviet Union's lurching steps toward capitalism and the speculative market of advanced American corporate capitalism onto one individual's pathology, Preston's novel replays the manner in which social and governmental authorities regularly represented violence during the earlier era covered by this book. In this ideologically powerful scenario, economic contradictions are naturalized and violence becomes the product of maladjusted or sick individuals, rather than the logical outcome of the economy's inconsistencies.

Though Preston's novel offers the reassurance that its terroristic plot was produced by a lone madman, this narrative line differs from much contemporary discourse about terrorism, which routinely imagines terrorist cabals and multilayered conspiracies. *The Cobra Event*'s plotline does, however, exemplify one crucial cultural role of terrorism as an idea and a concept. Though terrorism appears to embody disorder and to convey the irrefutable fact that we live in a chaotic world, one reason terrorist events make for good movie and novel plots, as well as good copy for newspapers, is that they actually provide a sense of order. That is, the common preoccupation with terrorism's unexpectedness, its "spasmodic immediacy," makes it into something that can actually cause the rest of our lives to seem orderly. As James Der Derian puts it, "Conversely — sometimes perversely — we constitute and preserve our own 'normalcy' by the terrorist's deviance."[31] In this respect, the idea of terrorism is an important hegemonic prop in the maintenance of America's capitalist order, since life under late capitalism is notoriously disorderly, rife as it is with economic ups and downs, job losses, and racial divisiveness.

In its focus on the foreign connections of terrorism occurring on American soil, *The Cobra Event* represents an imaginary version of much contemporary nonfictional terrorist discourse. But this aspect of the novel also conjures up, equally strongly, the rhetoric about terrorists produced over a century ago. Since the very form of terrorist violence forces us to make sense of unexpected and cataclysmic disasters, we should not be surprised that the knee-jerk 1990s invocation of foreign terrorists and "us vs. them" binaries is continuous with 1880s explanations of mass and random violence. Even though the Oklahoma City tragedy forced Americans to realize that U.S. citizens are capable of targeting each other as victims of terrorism (or, more accurately, to realize that fact *again* for perhaps the first time since the now largely forgotten bombings of the Weather Underground in the early 1970s),[32] the trauma of mass violence prompts both leaders and citizens to cling to a shared patriotism and reaffirm notions of a collective identity vis-à-vis foreigners as a refuge against calamity. The upshot, frequently, is the loss of terrorism's context, specifically, in Preston's fictionalized version of this scenario, the market exigencies that underlay modern, corporate drug research and the collateral damage associated with the USSR's capitalist transformation.

Terrorist Theory: Words and Deeds

Though nationalist reactions to terrorist events at the turn of the millennium and in the late nineteenth century bear a striking resemblance to each other, the analogous similarity in the logic of terrorism's contemporary theorists and proponents of terrorism at the end of the 1800s is more unexpected. Terrorist violence, in its apparent emphasis on the cataclysmic deed, is often thought to be the province of those persons who have lost faith in language and the more mundane cycle of politics. For example, the influential late-nineteenth-century Russian theorist of terrorism, Sergey Nechayev, decried those nonviolent reformers whom he acerbically termed the "doctrinaire champions of paper revolution." Nechayev further claimed that "far from everything that is nowadays called a deed *is* a deed. . . . We term real manifestations only a series of actions which destroy something absolutely: a person, a thing, or an attitude which is an obstacle to the liberation of the people." Finally, in a harrowing (and paradoxical) rhetorical flourish, he succinctly stated, "We have lost all faith in the word."[33] The Frenchman Paul Brousse elaborated the position of the more inflammatory Nechayev in a series of articles published in 1877 and 1878. Intellectual theorizing and the dissemination of propaganda, Brousse maintained, were largely ineffective means of inciting a revolutionary uprising, partially because the mainstream press could and would misrepresent revolutionaries' political positions and aspirations. Moreover, exhausted workers, if they were fortunate enough to be literate, had little energy to devote to complex political literature after an enervating day of physical toil. Instead, apparently spontaneous and brazen actions were far more politically efficacious than mere words.[34]

Unfortunately, terrorism's contemporary analysts and commentators have too often tended to take figures such as Nechayev and Brousse at their word, regularly organizing studies of terrorism around the binary Nechayev so elegantly articulated over a century ago.[35] Richard E. Rubenstein's otherwise informative and interesting *Alchemists of Revolution* can synecdochically represent a large number of other studies here. Speaking broadly, Rubenstein argues that "the modern terrorist . . . divides his or her world in two. On one side, he or she ranges all of the talkers: the politicians, priests, labor leaders, armchair radicals, and publicists whose words and 'wordy' acts, no matter how seemingly radical, induce people to obey unjust authority. . . . But violent action — 'something that destroys something absolutely' — can rend the fabric of illusion, or so the guerrillas think."[36] Rubenstein's analysis is certainly correct insofar as it recapitulates how late-nineteenth-century as well as some contemporary terrorists theorize their own practice. Yet there is no solid reason why this guiding rationale has to mark both the beginning and the end points of our analysis of terrorism's cultural meanings and significance. As Pierre Bourdieu wryly observes in *Outline of a Theory of Practice,* "It is because subjects do not, strictly speaking, know what they are doing that what they do has more meaning than they know."[37] Bourdieu is suggesting here that our actions are enmeshed in larger social structures that inform our desires and our options for fulfilling them, which in turn freights our behavior with cultural significance outstripping an action's ostensible limits and consequences.

In the late nineteenth century, the phrase "propaganda by the deed" served as the summation of terrorists' dichotomous split between denigrated language and exalted action. Paul Brousse popularized this phrase, whose catchy, jingoistic quality belies the claims of terrorism's early theorists, including Nechayev and the Italian Carlo Pisacane, concerning language's irrelevancy.[38] Even as they claimed their disillusion with and disavowal of words, late-nineteenth-century theorists of terrorism nonetheless found themselves turning to a linguistic metaphor to describe their actions. "Propaganda" here also asserts the continuing importance of interpretation and communication to terrorist events, further underscoring that the logic of representation and language is integral to terrorist violence, even if both terrorists and their commentators often assume that their brand of violence embodies a frustration with language's power. Indeed, language is just one form of representation. Terrorists have changed registers; by turning violent, they still traffic in the symbolism evoked by who, what, when, and where they strike.[39] This is in no way meant to substitute narrative for reality, or to glibly dismiss the devastating effects of political violence, but is instead meant to underscore the centrality of interpretation that is presupposed by the lack of identity between physical victim and psychological target in terrorist actions. Since terrorist targets are generally chosen specifically for their symbolic value — a value that will be fought over in language — the notion that terrorist violence unproblematically hinges on a faith in the sheer materiality of violent action also ignores the variable interpretations available to material forms of action. By taking late-nineteenth-century terrorists at their word (so to speak), we prematurely foreclose too many valuable paths of literary and historical investigation.

As encapsulated in the catchphrase "propaganda by the deed," questions about the cultural work performed by a terrorist act cannot be so easily parceled off from larger issues of language. The very form and logic of terrorist actions proceed according to a linguistic model. Terrorist violence is generally metonymic, in that the victims stand in for the person or group whom the terrorists hope to coerce via their act. In terrorist acts, political and social conflict between groups is represented by violence against a separate, but symbolically rich, group. Alex P. Schmid and Janny de Graaf have fleshed out the implications that terrorism's metonymic logic presents. They write that "terrorism cannot be understood only in terms of violence," since "terrorism does not murder to kill somebody, but to obtain a certain effect upon others than the victim. Terrorism, by using violence against one victim, seeks to persuade others." Therefore, they argue, "terrorism can best be understood as a violent communication strategy. There is a sender, the terrorist, a message generator, the victim, and a receiver, the enemy and/or the public. The nature of the terrorist act, its atrocity, its location and the identity of its victim serve as generators for the power of the message."[40]

Schmid and de Graaf's analysis is particularly adept because it allows us to historicize and understand terrorist violence as a phenomenon that emerges from within particular political situations and contexts in which certain objects carry varying amounts of symbolic capital for different constituencies. As Martha Crenshaw further argues, terrorist activity needs to be understood within a framework that theorizes the "relationship between terrorism and its political, social, and economic environment; and the impact of terrorism on this setting."[41] Such an approach helps us to see terrorism as one political strategy, if an often repugnantly violent one, among other strategies. Terrorism in this view proceeds by generally identifiable, though not universal, tactics and logic, and the analysis of these material conditions lends insight into the circumstances that both make terrorism seem a viable political option and contribute to the inevitable cultural struggles that occur via language to deem some acts terrorism, other acts warfare, and yet other acts simply crimes.

In their analysis of terrorism as a "violent communication strategy," Schmid and de Graaf importantly push terrorism scholarship beyond abstract considerations of violence qua violence or arguments proposing the universal psychopathology of terrorists. Yet, whereas other scholars such as Rubenstein have emphasized the deed to the detriment of the propaganda component of terrorism, Schmid and de Graaf, in their desire to bring the communication element back into focus by regarding terrorism "primarily in terms of propaganda,"[42] overlook one of the more fascinating paradoxes of late-nineteenth-century terrorist discourse and theory. They cite the important theorist of anarcho-terrorism, the Russian prince Peter Kropotkin, to make their point about terrorism's efficacy as propaganda: "'By actions which compel general attention,' Kropotkin held, 'the new idea seeps into people's minds and wins converts. One such act may, in a few days, make more propaganda than a thousand pamphlets.'" Following Kropotkin's logic, Schmid and de Graaf then argue that "in the nineteenth century the deed had to be so specific that it would, as it were, *speak for itself*."[43] But what is so interesting about Kropotkin's theory is the very notion that Schmid and de Graaf unwittingly make explicit: that a terrorist deed, even a very specific act, can in some way "speak for itself." Thus, while late-nineteenth-century terrorists preferred "deeds" to "words," ironically still mobilizing a linguistic metaphor to undergird their belief in the deed's ability to communicate propagandistic meanings, they also, in yet another logical pirouette, held that the meaning of an action was transparent or self-evident. In short, a terrorist action escaped words and narration even as it clearly communicated a political meaning. But if terrorism is a form of violence that operates on a linguistic model, acts will always reach multiple audiences whose attitudes, sympathies, and political orientations will diverge significantly. And just as terrorists cannot totally preordain who will receive their violent political message, either (or both) their intended or unintended audiences, as I suggested earlier, may very well misinterpret a bombing's message.

These logical inconsistencies do not simply underscore the contradictions of nineteenth- and twentieth-century terrorist theory. Rather, terrorism is a fascinating cultural phenomenon precisely because it is often mediated by a paradoxical combination of a longed-for representational transparency and the inevitability that both historical actors and actions must be narrated to have cultural meaning. The Haymarket anarchists, for example, regularly preached the power of dynamite in their public speeches in 1880s Chicago, taking for granted that their bombs, should the threats ever be converted to dynamite, would quite literally be "read" by American citizens as the transparent sign of capitalism's downfall. Nonetheless, Chicago's anarchist radicals, from a position of political weakness, also routinely felt the need to place themselves within American history, posing, for instance, as both latter-day Founding Fathers and African American slaves. And from a radically different political position, members of the Ku Klux Klan (KKK) proceeded as if their gruesome lynchings of African Americans had a self-evident meaning as retribution for black men's purported rape of white women. Thomas Dixon, however, felt obliged to recast the KKK as the revolutionary vanguard of a colonized territory, while Ida B. Wells's journalism worked to undermine these ideas by narrating the brutal racism and economic conditions that underlay terrorist lynching. As these brief examples demonstrate, advocates of political violence regularly plot themselves within discourses of history in order to express, paradoxically, their embodiment of a nation's ideological principles vis-à-vis a dominant regime's alleged deviation from those beliefs, while their opponents attribute significance to their actions by drawing upon alternative cultural plots and scenarios.

When faced with the sudden eruption of apparently irrational terrorist violence, the cultural rhetoric spun out to control an act's signification reaches a crescendo. Recognizing this fact, some recent attempts to theorize terrorism have employed poststructuralist models of representation, specifically the realization that actions do not exist outside the language we use to describe them. This approach supplements traditional theories that, on the one hand, view terrorism as the abandonment of language or, on the other, tend to forestall all other possible avenues of investigation in a search for a universal and ahistorical explanation of terrorism's root causes.[44] Among those scholars using contemporary theory to conceptualize terrorism, Allen Feldman has argued that "narrativity is the condition for the identification of events, agents, and mediating sequence. Event, agency, and narration form a 'narrative bloc,'" which Feldman, following Jean François Lyotard, defines as "plastic organizations involving language, material artifacts and relations. The narrative bloc of violence puts into play a constellation of events, and discourses about events, as an *Event.*" Furthermore, "sequence and causality are both moral and metaphorical constructs," so that "the event is not what happens. The event is that which can be narrated. The event is action organized by culturally situated meanings."[45] Applying the concept of "narrative bloc" to terrorism, Feldman thus usefully theorizes how narratives of political violence weld together certain operative cultural discourses and social actions to create a meaningful, memorable, and singular "Event."

Similarly, Joseba Zulaika and William A. Douglass provocatively claim that "whatever else it might be, 'terrorism' is printed text," whether a prescriptive pamphlet, a story in the daily newspaper, a text outlining a government's policy of not reporting terrorist acts, a subject of fictional thrillers, or an academic monograph. Terrorism "is a genre of 'emplotted' action in which narrative sequence is a moral and discursive construct." For these theorists, terrorism is both constituted and understood within culture's symbolic world by way of various competing and always interested narrative plots and rhetorical strategies. The meanings of a bombing thus extend far beyond the deaths and damage that are its immediate results to find their "true impact" in "the halls of the collective imagination."[46] From the moment of labeling an event an act of terror, then, to the divergence of cultural meanings attributed to an act, terrorism hinges upon writing and narration.

Yet, if understanding violence almost strictly in terms of a narrative plot seems a problematic reduction, especially after the terrible acts of 9/11, David Apter's analysis of the cultural rhetoric that seeks to identify certain species of action as terrorism usefully integrates the narrative theory and forms of collective, social identity that are implicit in Feldman's and Zulaika and Douglass's work. Attempting to theorize the relation between actions and narrative in modern terrorism, Apter outlines what he terms a "discourse theory" of violence. Citing "linguistic alchemy," he suggests that a historical act only becomes resonant and meaningful when it is incorporated into an interpretive discourse that is itself anchored in "discourse communities." Explaining the give-and-take of events and narrative, Apter proposes that cultural norms of order and disorder "are recounted and rendered in events." In this view, an action not only prompts a surfeit of narrative explanations but also serves as a crucial site for legitimating other narratives that are emerging or already in circulation. The event thus "'thickens' symbolically," becoming "endowed with a surplus of signifiers. There is a troping of facts. Events become metaphors, as part of a narrative process and metonyms for a theory." For Apter, violent acts are remembered, understood, and even, in some ways, created as symbolically resonant mechanisms that underwrite political and moral boundaries and relations of power among competing groups. Violence, in this theory, becomes a powerful cultural site from which individuals draw meanings, social narratives, and political connections that simultaneously cement ties to some people while drawing lines of alienation and discontinuity from other groups.[47]

The material conditions of any particular historical action thus cannot be separated from the explicit and implicit logic underpinning the event's description and narration. However, it is also imperative that we do not simply imagine that spectacular and brutal acts of violence can be unproblematically captured by theories of narrativity. To reduce the cultural conditions of violence to a case of historical semiotics would in some ways make the work of theorizing terrorism proceed along the more familiar path paved by notions of textualization, but it also risks dangerously misconstruing the sheer intractability of massive and seemingly random political violence. It seems, instead, that both material conditions and cultural forms of narration or emplotment have their own aspects and contingencies that exert powerful reciprocating forces and influences upon each other. Without trivializing the dismaying loss of life political violence can produce, in order to understand the development of terrorism as a cultural idea, we need to determine how certain acts become implicated in various plots, scenarios, and narratives that are woven both before an incident and in its aftermath. As interested parties scramble to secure discursive control of a volatile situation, acts and narratives fuse into the politically resonant, potent, and frighteningly spectacular act of "terrorism."

Terrorism and the Late-Nineteenth-Century Economy

If cultural narratives and material conditions exist in a reciprocating relationship, dynamite and the late-nineteenth-century print media represent key cases in point. Together they formed a potent hybrid consisting of massive bloodshed and the possibility for widespread public dissemination of a terrorist act. Yet, while dynamite made certain new forms of violence imaginable and the mass press promised a voyeuristic audience for such atrocities, these material developments are nonetheless a historical scaffolding that obscures as well as supports other important questions and issues. To the extent that it is possible, we also need to examine the conditions of life at the turn of the twentieth century that made shocking and massive violence appear to be an effective tactic, identify those against whom it was directed, and ask for what purposes it was used. Further, when such seemingly random forms of violence did occur in the United States, or were simply feared to be imminent, why and how did certain modes of explanatory narratives emerge that understood and identified such violence as the result of conspiratorial terrorism? What, also, was the discursive relation between conspiratorial violence directed at workers and secretive violence presumed to be performed by radicals? Finally, as Howells's hesitant relationship to dynamite impels us to ask, how did America's authors and cultural figures represent and intervene in the cultural politics of terrorism during this period when the notion of terrorism itself was taking shape? In essence, then, the emergence of modern terrorism at the end of the nineteenth century presents a problem of double-entry bookkeeping. Understanding terrorism necessitates explaining both the form or structure of certain actions *and* how those acts were narrated and given meaning by and for American citizens, even as events and explanatory scenarios impinged on and influenced each other across time and space.

In the context of the late nineteenth century, as the following chapters trace out, the crucial mediating factor for understanding the complexity of modern terrorism's development is the concurrent and related development of industrial capitalism. During these years, the defining images and causes of terrorism were fought over and deployed by writers and historical actors with widely divergent political points of view. Rhetorical struggles over the range of cultural meanings associated with terrorism and terrorists operated as a crucial site where the economy merged with politics and material life. The cultural construction of terrorism thus became one place where classed identity emerged in relation to contingent power struggles played out within intertwined economic and political shifts in late-nineteenth-century American life.[48]

Within the realm of daily labor, the technological and managerial innovations of industrial and finance capitalism in the late nineteenth century calcified America's economic structure and spawned the conditions of economic and political desperation that underlay a turn to the dramatic violence called for by America's radicals and feared by its dominant factions. Along with the astonishing industrial progress measured in blast furnaces, steel tonnage, and railroad mileage came the segmentation and alienation of labor and the ever-widening gulf between the wealthy and the impoverished. According to the 1890 census, for instance, America's most affluent 1 percent earned more than the aggregate income of the poorest 50 percent and controlled more capital than the remaining 99 percent. Moreover, in a study based on the census statistics, Charles Spahr found that eleven of every twelve families lived on annual incomes below $1,200, while the average was only $380, well below the poverty line.[49]

The material conditions of industrial labor that loom behind these statistics also undermined the antebellum "free labor" ideology's emphasis on self-made men, class mobility, and the security and dignity of labor.[50] The routine cycle of depressions in America's boom-and-bust economy meant that between 23 and 30 percent of the workforce was out of work every year in the turn-of-the-century decades.[51] Both within the overall economy and within the developing factory workplace, the situation of laborers consistently deteriorated during the postbellum years. The story, similar across many industries, featured irregular pay at abysmal wages, unsteady work, dangerous and unsanitary working conditions, ten- or fourteen-hour days and six- or even seven-day weeks, small or no compensation for the devastatingly frequent on-the-job injuries, and the ever-expanding use of women and children as a means to drive wages even lower.[52]

Indeed, within the walls of factories workers faced the twin evils of frequent injury by the machines and the less immediate but no less dangerous physical decline produced by exhausting labor in, at best, uncomfortably hot and poorly ventilated, but also often toxic, environments. As the *American Machinist* put it in 1895, "Good work and great production at low cost can be secured without much consideration of fatigue, accommodations for meals . . . or cleanliness of workmen." Like Carrie Meeber in Theodore Dreiser's *Sister Carrie,* who becomes Charles Drouet's mistress rather than face the toils of factory labor, or the deformed characters who populate Jack London's and Rebecca Harding Davis's stories of factory life, America's working class found itself facing widespread and gross indifference to the conditions of its labor. In the United States, which had the highest industrial accident rate among all industrialized nations in the years leading up to World War I, the dismal corollary to the vast growth in the production of material and capital goods was the analogous production of vast numbers of diseased, damaged, and dead bodies of workers.[53]

As industrial capitalism evolved during this period, workers confronting the changing nature of labor seized particularly on machines and control over them as a primary source of their subjugation. As Harry Braverman has explained the implications of machinery's widespread introduction into the factory workplace, and as late-nineteenth-century workers intuitively realized, the ability to control the labor process via machinery was seen by management as the primary way in which production could be brought under the control of the owners and representatives of capital rather than the direct producers.[54] Indeed, one significant way that workers represented this struggle for workplace control was by viewing their own standing within the factory as merely another machine. John S. McClelland, when speaking before an 1883 Senate committee convened to investigate the deteriorating relations between workers and owners, testified that "the men are looked upon as nothing more than parts of the machinery that they work. They are labeled and tagged, as the parts of a machine would be, and are only taken into account as a part of the machinery used for the profit of the manufacturer or employer."[55]

While McClelland's statement suggests the extent to which workers were viewed by their employers as just so many cogs in a machine, the rhetoric of the era's factory workers—or "operatives," as they were becoming known in a very resonant phrase—is saturated with a perceived loss of agency and autonomy due to the mechanization of production. As factory owners turned to mechanization to increase production and decrease cost, labor agitators constructed the machine itself as an instrument of terror for the worker. Writing in 1887, the year after the Haymarket bombing, George McNeill argued that, for a factory laborer, "the machinery that renders his skill and time of less value to himself and more to his master, becomes the hated instrument of torture; its monotonous hum keeping time to his groans and curses."[56] McNeill's rhetoric here is inflected by the discourse of servitude that was common to postbellum descriptions of industrial wage-labor as a latter-day form of slavery. Moreover, his emphasis on the centrality to factory labor of time and time-keeping also registers the different notion of work brought about by factory labor. The "monotonous hum" of the machines "keeping time" with the workers' anguish suggests the new and destabilizing idea of work that was regimented by the time clock and factory whistle and that consisted of selling one's time rather than a product of one's labor.

This rhetoric also appeared at the trial of the anarchists who were convicted for the bombing at Chicago's Haymarket Square. Samuel Fielden, when given the opportunity after the verdict had been rendered to state why he should not be executed, instead used his time to explicate the relation between workers and machines in the modern factory. Citing recent technological innovations at Chicago's McCormick Reaper Works that had reduced the number of workers needed to do a particular job by 80 percent, Fielden suggested that machines robbed the workers of any power or autonomy. Machinery, Fielden told the packed courtroom, decreased the number of necessary workers, thereby increasing the number of unemployed, and, in turn, drove down wages for those still on the job. But the particular metaphors he invoked intriguingly suggest the extent to which machinery had even come to inform the very notion of subjectivity under industrial capitalism. Fielden argued that "wages are the means of existence of those who have no property, and who are compelled to live by the sale of their labor. It is their machinery."[57] Fielden here conceives of workers' labor as machinery; the body, or what in the twentieth century Antonin Artaud would call "an over-heated factory,"[58] represents the only form of capital-generating property available to workers. By equating industrial labor's endless repetition of the same dreary and undifferentiated task with the continually running machinery of the modern factory, Fielden, like McNeill, suggested that the most appropriate way to understand a factory worker's identity in the new economy was as a machine.

The metaphors of slavery evidenced in McNeill's lament and the discourse of machinery that is striking in his and Fielden's language provided two rhetorical forms for workers' anxiety about autonomy and agency in the industrial workplace. Oscar Neebe, in the autobiography that he wrote shortly after he had been sentenced to fifteen years in prison for his alleged role in the Haymarket bombing, made the implications of McNeill's and Fielden's rhetoric concrete. Decrying the effect of the "curse of piece work" on workers, Neebe writes that "now they are regular machines."[59] Even the notion of workers as organic machines was sometimes given a more grisly twist during this period. It was imagined, for instance, that the ever-increasing sophistication of machines and the corresponding devaluation of thinking skills in their operators would result in the machine tenders' dehumanization to the point that the mechanical inventions would actually exchange places with the operatives. Allen Clarke, in *The Effects of the Factory System,* spelled out what he saw as the terrifying outcome for workers that would result from technological advancement: "The machine, in its wonderful development, has become almost human," and, more alarming, "it may happen, if the factory system continues, that the operatives' heads will, in course of time, shrink to a rudimentary fraction of empty skull, just as man to-day has at the base of his spinal column the bit of bone which proves that he once sported a simian tail."[60] Machines, in Neebe's account and Clarke's macabre, vestigial nightmare, contained the potential to render the brain unnecessary and literally make mindless machines out of people who no longer need any analytical skills to perform their repetitive and simple jobs. The segmentation and alienation of labor that is at issue in this rhetoric suggest the extent to which nineteenth-century notions of autonomous, self-identical personhood were becoming attenuated in an emergent era of large-scale industrialism. Fears of being a slave or a machine or of no longer needing a brain are all variations of the fear of no longer being distinguishable from other workers who are performing exactly the same tasks. More precisely, it is the fear of no longer being able to imagine one's self as a discrete individual capable of autonomous action.

In response to this devaluation of laborers, some of America's most radical workers tried to narrate themselves into more powerful social positions through the philosophy of the bomb. Threats of violence, dynamite, and bombs sometimes served as a means by which America's disempowered tried to gain leverage or clear a space for negotiation on a more even footing. Much of the rhetoric of bravado produced by and for the more militant strains of the U.S. working class in this period was also either implicitly or explicitly trying to gauge the possibilities for—and limits on—social action and individual agency in the emerging mass culture produced by industrial and finance capitalism. For Americans who advocated terror in this period, violence was often filtered through concerns about autonomy and individuality in a culture seemingly beset by the automaton-like factory work that undermined traditional concepts of selfhood hinging on will and intention. The philosophy of the bomb, in this case, appeared to offer one prosthetic way of becoming an actor in mass culture.[61]

While workers were attempting to negotiate massive changes in the organization of labor, which in some cases led to an alienation that precipitated threats and violent acts, America's macroeconomy was also experiencing certain seismic shifts that directly affected how terrorism was imagined and understood. American capitalism at the turn of the century was transforming from a proprietary-competitive stage to a corporate-administered stage of development. At that time, as depicted in some of the era's most representative fiction, such as Frank Norris's *The Octopus,* America underwent an uneven and sometimes irregular, but ultimately ineluctable, march toward what Martin J. Sklar has termed "the corporate reconstruction of American capitalism."[62] The corporate form developed in these years as a mechanism for gaining some control over an economy that was clearly no longer understandable in terms of classical economics' theoretical equilibrium between production and demand. Heated competition between manufacturers and heavy investments in fixed machinery that lost money when idle — and lost even more money when incessantly producing too many goods at too low a profit margin — contributed to the frequently lamented and seemingly chronic problems of overproduction, market instability, and financial precariousness. Unable to easily transfer the capital that had been invested in specialized equipment without incurring substantial losses, manufacturers were forced to choose either continual production, even if it meant selling at a loss, or instigating labor unrest through wage reductions and layoffs.[63]

Consequently, as Sklar details in his book, "corporate capitalism . . . had to be constructed. It did not come on the American scene as a finished 'economic' product, or as a pure-ideal type; nor did it 'take over' society and simply vanquish or blot out everything else."[64] The incorporation of America, to use Alan Trachtenberg's famous phrase, involved frequently contentious and fraught shifts in modes of consciousness, altered patterns of authority in both corporate offices and factory workplaces, and changing ways of narrating or explaining the economy's impact on and involvement in the day-to-day lives and social relations among its citizens. The ideological interests and presuppositions of a corporate nation thus developed along with the often contested legal, historical, and material mechanisms of incorporation.

One particularly significant way in which the discursive terms and expressions of social life intersected with the material history of America's corporate reorganization occurred, as Walter Benn Michaels has argued, in the development of a legal conception of corporations as persons.[65] Ironically, as workers felt themselves becoming more like machines, the legal discourse of the day was making corporations — the machinery of capital — more like persons. As corporations' detractors never tired of pointing out, it was bad enough that incorporation relieved individual investors from liability should an enterprise fail, but granting corporations status as legal persons compounded their exemptions from responsibilities. In his 1894 denunciation of monopoly capital, *Wealth against Commonwealth,* Henry Demarest Lloyd lambasted the corporate form and its "personhood" status: "What chance have we against the persistent coming and the easy coalescence of the confederated cliques, which aspire to say of all business, 'This belongs to us,' and whose members, though moving among us as brothers, are using against us, through the corporate forms we have given them, powers of invisibility, of entail and accumulation, unprecedented because impersonal and immortal, and, most peculiar of all, power to act as persons, as in the commission of crimes, with exemption from punishment as persons?"[66] As Lloyd passionately demonstrates, three interrelated aspects of corporate personhood were particularly maddening to those who spoke out against the American economy's reorganization. Invisibility, immortality, and personhood especially riled critics such as Texas judge A. W. Terrell, who complained in 1885 that corporations enjoyed "an exalted position of supremacy over and above that occupied by natural persons."[67] In their seeming ability to operate throughout the nation and wield influence without providing their antagonists with a clear sense of who or what they were up against, in their ability to live on well beyond the death of a founder, and in their enjoyment of rights deriving from personhood, corporations, according to Lloyd, functioned perhaps as conspiratorial and certainly as malevolent organizations.

If corporations appeared to some as a suspicious and unnatural combination, their linking in the form of "trusts" only exacerbated the problem. Developed first by John D. Rockefeller's Standard Oil in 1882, the trust form empowered a board of trustees to manage the corporations that, either voluntarily or under coercion, joined the trust. During this era, the trust form paved the way to both horizontal combination, which conjoined firms operating at the same level in the productive process, and vertical organization, which involved the distribution and marketing of products as well. Even more than the corporate form, trusts incited worries about conspiratorial price-fixing, invisible dealings, and shadowy financial arrangements. Describing these "soulless and mercenary combinations" that "like vampires are sucking the life-blood of the people," a writer for the *North American Review* in 1888 argued that the purpose of "trust conspiracies" was "to effect an illegal purpose by legal means." Similarly, Albion Tourgée, soon to embark on his ill-fated defense of Homer Plessy in the landmark case of *Plessy v. Ferguson,* focused on the "secret agreement" that was sometimes used "to limit the supply, destroy competition, and so regulate price and monopolize profits." More graphically, Joseph Dana Miller lamented that "we have sent the Trust forward armed with special privileges created by law, and we behold a Frankenstein that is fast swallowing our liberties."[68]

The flights of rhetorical fancy exhibited in this antitrust fervor dramatically register just how massive the economy's reorganization was perceived to be. But the particular rhetorical form of these worries is also interesting because it resembles the forms denunciations of terrorist violence took in this period. For example, anarchists in the Haymarket era and afterward were described as vampires and monsters who threatened to destroy American civilization, and, as with trusts, it was always feared that terrorists plotted conspiratorially outside the view of respectable society. In some ways, this is not surprising, as writers instinctively grasped for the most sensational language to describe severe problems. Yet anxiety over trusts and fears of politico-economic violence took a similar shape in this period for other, more substantial reasons as well. As the corporate and industrial reconstruction of the economy proceeded apace, it produced, as Lloyd testified, a thickly obscurant layer of mystification over the way it worked. This economic reorganization also helped to create an alienated and permanent working class that was in many ways equally obscure and unknowable. A worry, then, about what was being plotted invisibly, either behind the closed doors of boardrooms or in the cramped quarters of the working classes, loomed over commentators' attempts to conceptualize how economic shifts would affect the everyday lives of Americans.

But while anxieties about megacorporations and violent radicals operated by a demonstrably similar logic, fear of politico-economic terrorist violence nonetheless functioned as a critical site of displacement for the corporate reconstruction of the American economy's own violent energy. One way to understand this process is to examine the vilification of unions and labor organizations during the century's closing decades, and that vilification's relation to life within corporate capitalism. Like corporations, unions were collective enterprises bound together for the collective advancement of shared economic interests, though, of course, the relation of members to the organization as a whole was wildly different in each. Within the emergent corporate form in particular, the new departments — such as planning, marketing, accounting, legal, and public relations sectors — intensified the separation of production and management, thus also helping to create a professional-managerial middle class. This class of middle managers developed alongside, and somewhat as a consequence of, the American economy's shift from small-scale competitive capitalism to a corporatized, finance capitalism that sent smaller firms in and out of business as the victims of market fluctuations, takeovers, and economic depressions. Instituting a middle class of white-collar workers who found themselves lodged in the era's new desk jobs and bureaucratic enterprises, the very form of corporations, like wage labor for factory workers, suddenly abrogated long-cherished shibboleths of agency, autonomy, and individualism in the workplace. The fierce and relatively rapid transformation to a corporate managerial culture, with its sweeping changes in both the make-up of business enterprises and the structure of jobs, wrenchingly destabilized traditional notions of work.

One way that the dominant capitalist ideology came to terms with these contradictions and upheavals was to imagine an even more dangerous threat of upheaval embodied in America's other emergent large-scale economic enterprise, labor organizations. As the *New York Tribune* editorialized in 1876, "At least the unjust employer has law upon his side, whatever may be his moral delinquency. But the union man who seeks to force all of his craft into his organization, not by argument or persuasion, but by shooting and beating and other varieties of terrorism . . . intensif[ies] the hostility between capital and labor." A writer in the *North American Review* similarly argued in 1889 that in those workplaces where owners "employ no new men who are members of any of the labor unions" and where "those who prefer the unions are required to quit the service . . . the day of terrorism from the unions and their salaried and titled leaders is over."[69] More generally, from the antipathy directed at the early Knights of Labor, which included all "producers" and originally deployed secret handshakes and arcane rituals, through the vitriol directed at Chicago's anarchist community and, with the new century, up to the great fury directed at the militant IWW, attempts to organize labor along lines differing from the march of capitalism were met with denunciations of the havoc, chaos, and bedlam that would ensue from such rearrangement.

The frequently repeated fears that terrorist cabals would take the form of violent working-class conspiracies, often assumed to be percolating in unions, thus functioned as a shadow narrative accompanying the corporate reconstruction of the American economy during this period. Indeed, as I have suggested, some forms of emergent corporate life and the ways they were written about and explained in public found surprising analogues in the cultural construction of class violence. These connections, finally, are best summed up in the period's resonant colloquialism, "infernal machine." While denoting bombs and their hellish consequences, this phrase also inadvertently connoted what many workers perceived to be the torture of the new economic order. The dramatically named "infernal machines"—those explosive bombs detonated and threatened to be detonated as both a material and metaphoric response to the ideological contradictions of industrial capitalism—cogently exemplify the tight weave between the development of American capitalism, terrorism, and the cultural imagination in this period.

In the chapters that follow I turn more directly to the interactions between America's writers and this country's history of terrorism at the turn of the century. Collectively, the chapters dwell on how terrorism was imagined by several overlapping constituencies in the decades around 1900, including those who advocated it, those who feared it, and those writers who brought these fantasies, projections, and displacements to paper. Writers imagined and deployed the figure of the subversive and dangerous terrorist in strikingly varied ways as they attempted to represent and intervene in the cultural politics of an era characterized by economic uncertainty and class antagonism. For some, terrorism became a magical fantasy of violence that could dissolve pernicious hierarchies in a sudden, dramatic outburst. For others, however, making accusations of terrorism offered a way to channel or deflect attention away from the real complexities of class antagonism and that antagonism's points of contact with other forms of social disruption, such as racial politics or xenophobia.

Chapter 1 analyzes contemporary understandings of the 1886 Haymarket bombing as the first outbreak of terrorist violence on American soil, despite the fact that neither the bomber nor his or her purpose was ever identified. After the bombing, America, via its quickly growing media infrastructure, was saturated with the notion that the blast was orchestrated by dangerous dynamite fiends. The bombing at Haymarket thus became an early moment that helped inaugurate a mass-mediated discourse of disaster, atrocity, and terrorist violence. As the dramatic and unexpected bombing was taken up by the mass media, it was rendered for contemporary audiences as a violent spectacle, an approach that meshed with the state's own desire to depict the tragedy as a terrorist assault against America itself. Early interpretations of the Haymarket bombing that regarded it as a terrorist attack on America also routinely exhibited a panic about privacy, anonymous acts, and unidentifiable conspirators. As Haymarket's commentators concocted ever more farfetched conspiracy theories to explain the blast, they also implicitly struggled to understand the effects generated by a dramatic bombing's transformation of private citizens into a public identity. In the contradictions and discontinuities between publicity, privacy, anonymity, and embodiment that seam these writings, we can begin to see how terrorism was imagined and deployed as a particular form of violence in late-nineteenth-century America.

Chapter 2 examines Henry James's novelistic contribution to American literature's discourse of terrorism, *The Princess Casamassima,* which James published in 1886, the year of the Haymarket bombing. Having lived in London for several years when he sat down to narrate the relationship between his would-be terrorists, the Italian American Princess Christina Casamassima and the hapless bookbinder, Hyacinth Robinson, James had already witnessed the rash of bombings that reverberated throughout that city during the 1880s. The knotty ties between classed identity and violence surface directly in both Hyacinth and the Princess, and I read the novel for its complex links between gender, class, and terrorism. James's depiction of the Princess is also especially significant for the way it can be situated within contemporary discussions of female terrorists, particularly Russian nihilists. But unlike the Russian female terrorists, whose specter seemed both to titillate and horrify contemporary audiences, and crucially also unlike Hyacinth Robinson, Christina Casamassima is never allowed the opportunity to follow through on her expressed desire to perform a terrorist act. Indeed, if the Princess frequently attempts to pressure the proscriptions that gender and class position place on her behavior in order to be taken seriously as a revolutionary, James ultimately makes her the force that brings terrorism to a screeching halt. Forcing the Princess back into her unhappy marriage with an Italian nobleman, James ties together and defuses the threats of gender subversion and radical class violence that are embodied by female terrorists.

Chapter 3 theorizes the meanings of terrorism in the turn-of-the-century American South, particularly emphasizing the reciprocal influences of ideologies associated with nationhood and economics as they emerge in Thomas Dixon's fictional romances of the Ku Klux Klan and African American journalist Ida B. Wells's pioneering antilynching articles. Wells's journalistic accounts of the KKK contextualize Dixon's trilogy of Reconstruction novels. She offers a trenchant analysis of the gendered and economic motivations for lynching and situates her ideas within a rhetoric of citizenship and statehood that makes the North complicit in "southern horrors" if it continues to ignore the national rights guaranteed by the bestowal of citizenship to African Americans. Alternatively, Dixon's novels describe black terrorist cells organized by a northern politician and startlingly recast the KKK as the last line of defense for the American Constitution. Dixon mobilizes the discourse of northern class politics that coalesced around terms such as "anarchy," "dynamite," and "terror" in the 1880s but melds it into a volatile mixture of racial and class politics in the twentieth century's first decade. In his trilogy not only are black Americans infamously and viciously excised from the body politic, but, of equal importance, the Klan's defense of the Constitution converts key northern investors to the southern viewpoint and leads to the introduction of northern manufacturing in the South. Imagining cotton mills that evoke the pastoral image of the antebellum South and locating them at the former meeting place of the KKK, Dixon rewrites racial terrorism against blacks as a benign and lily-white industry that reunites North and South. In Dixon's ideological revisions, this harmonious industry even provides a bulwark against the day when "foreign anarchy" may again threaten the nation, thus transforming the industrial workplace from the site of working-class agitation led by immigrant Americans to the place that thwarts immigrant class radicalism.

Chapter 4 shifts from racial terrorism to a study of Jack London's analysis of the surprising synergy between white-collar businessmen and terrorism. Integrating a discussion of London's writing about the 1905 assassination of Frank Steunenberg, which resulted in the first spectacular trial of the twentieth century—featuring "Big Bill" Haywood as a defendant and Clarence Darrow as his attorney—this chapter traces an overlooked vein of London's journalism and fiction that demonstrates his fascination with terrorism. The chapter focuses especially on London's famous dystopia, *The Iron Heel*, and his 1910 novel, *The Assassination Bureau, Ltd.* This latter novel narrates the story of an elite firm of killers that is arranged as a for-profit corporation and aims to right America's wrongs with systematic terrorist assaults against those "criminals" whom the law protects (e.g., unscrupulous capitalists and corrupt judges). London's conception of the terrorist organization as a corporate entity founded on the very structure it wants to overturn asked Progressive Era readers to question commonsense dualisms between the often-presumed irrationality or psychopathology of terrorism and the presumed rationality and order of the industrial capitalist state.

Chapter 5 maintains the focus on corporate America during the Progressive Era but torques the emphasis by dwelling on the struggle between capital and labor in this period as it was represented in discussions of sabotage. For conservatives and radicals alike in the 1910s, sabotage loomed large, both for what it embodied in itself and for what it seemed to represent. Whether it included violence against bodies or only against property, its relative effectiveness, who controlled its definitions, and the forms of fear it produced all emerged as key issues. The chapter focuses on three interconnected sets of artifacts, including the accounts and rhetoric that emerged after the 1910 *Los Angeles Times* bombing, the IWW's engagement with the politics of sabotage, and the poetry of Covington Hall, a labor agitator involved with the IWW. As the era's literary and extraliterary production makes clear, notions of sabotage encompassed many ideological contradictions that made the concept crackle with cultural energy. Sabotage became a preoccupying concern in the early twentieth century not only because it exemplified the violence that by then had long been associated with industrial capitalism, but also because it conjured up questions about what undergirds definitions of social and antisocial behavior, what actions constitute violence, how particular persons come to be imagined as dangerous, and how the relationship between private desires and public actions is mediated by mass culture.

In different ways, then, each of these chapters focuses on that strange brew of narrative, social violence, and class politics that Richard Watson Gilder so dramatically expressed when he blue-penciled Howells's words. This book follows through on the lines of inquiry implied but never enunciated by Gilder over a century ago. More particularly, it is the fascinating mix of representation and narration within the logic of terrorist violence that makes the phenomenon so amenable to a literary investigation. By examining this series of American writers' interactions with the intensely symbolic world of terror, I mean to elucidate the surprising ties between the emergence of terrorism as a cultural force and the development of capitalism in an America on the cusp of modernity.

CHAPTER ONE

Imagining Terrorism in America
The 1886 Chicago Haymarket Bombing

On 4 May 1886, about 2,000 Chicagoans gathered near Haymarket Square to protest against the city's police, who had shot and killed at least two striking workers outside the McCormick reaper factory on the previous afternoon. The principal speakers at Haymarket that evening lashed out with the inflammatory rhetoric that had been common to Chicago anarchist rallies throughout the 1880s, but the demonstration was generally peaceful. Chicago's mayor, Carter Harrison, was on hand to break up the mass meeting if it threatened to turn violent, but the mayor went home early, confident that the demonstrators posed no threat on that particular night. Later in the evening, a sudden rainstorm kicked up and drove most of the other listeners away, so that only a few hundred people remained when 170 Chicago policemen abruptly arrived and demanded that the protesters disperse. Nonplussed by the anticlimactic arrival of the police at the close of a peaceful, rain-shortened rally, Samuel Fielden, the night's last speaker, pointed out the meeting's nonviolent nature in response to the peremptory dispersal order. At this point in the exchange, someone tossed a dynamite bomb into the police ranks. The explosion immediately killed Officer Mathias Degan, wounded several others, and prompted a cacophony of gunfire, most of it from police pistols. In the chaos, the police shot several of their own officers as well as many of the fleeing civilians. While the number of dead among the police rose to seven over the next few days, the actual number of casualties among the protesters, like the bomb thrower's identity, was never determined.

In the weeks after the bombing, in a display of police power that brazenly disregarded its victims' constitutional rights, the police rounded up and arrested virtually all known radical sympathizers in the Chicago area. In late May, ten men caught in the police dragnet were indicted by a grand jury, though charges were dropped against one man, William Seliger, in return for his willingness to testify for the state. Another indicted man, Rudolph Schnaubelt, evaded trial by fleeing the country. Court proceedings against the remaining eight men, some of whom were demonstrably not at Haymarket Square at the time of the bombing, and none of whom were identified by credible witnesses, began in June 1886. Unable to prove conclusively who had thrown the bomb, State's Attorney Julius Grinnell proposed that the incendiary language used by the anarchists had brought about the death of the policemen as surely as if one of the accused men had himself hurled the bomb. At best, as Carl Smith has argued, this narrative denied the anarchists' constitutional right to free assembly, and at worst, it "turned sedition into murder and made no distinction between word and deed."[1] Yet on 20 August a jury comprised mostly of men who openly admitted antiradical prejudices handed down eight guilty verdicts as the outcome of a trial beset by paid prosecution witnesses and a judge clearly partial to the state.[2]

One defendant, Oscar Neebe, was sentenced to fifteen years hard labor, and the other seven men were condemned to hanging. The case then worked its way up through the courts. The decision was upheld by the Illinois Supreme Court, and in November 1887 the U.S. Supreme Court refused to hear the case. Within days of the scheduled execution, however, Governor Richard Oglesby commuted two of the condemned men's sentences to life imprisonment. A third man, Louis Lingg, committed suicide in his cell by biting a fulminating cap. Amidst high tension and tight security, especially around the Chicago Board of Trade, where a retaliatory anarchist dynamite attack was feared, the other four men—Albert Parsons, August Spies, George Engel, and Adolph Fischer—were hanged on the morning of 11 November 1887.

Prescience, Paranoia, Terrorism

The Haymarket bomb exploded in an ethnically divided and class-striated city. July 1885, for instance, saw the worst example of what was by then nearly routine police violence, as officers broke up a citywide streetcar strike by ferociously and indiscriminately clubbing bystanders, strikers, and even shopkeepers along the streetcar line. The city had also been a frequent witness to massive labor demonstrations, boisterous workingmen's rifle clubs with militias that regularly drilled and practiced, and large anarchist celebrations, picnics, and holiday revelry. Chicago's anarchist community additionally included a thriving radical press, fraternal halls, singing societies, and other sites of class- and ethnic-based communal gathering. And throughout the years leading up to the Haymarket bombing, the city's radicals had particularly and repeatedly antagonized middle-class Chicagoans with annual fetes that celebrated the 1871 Paris Commune and the 1881 dynamite assassination of Russia's Czar Alexander II as key moments in the working class's economic and political liberation.[3]

The Haymarket Square bombing thus occurred in an already highly confrontational environment. The blast appeared to culminate the frequent smaller skirmishes between Chicago's most radical workers and factory owners that had taken place since the spontaneous violence of the 1877 railroad strikes had rocked Chicago and many other cities. Indeed, the 1877 strikes had catalyzed Americans to prophesy future violence. Pennsylvania Railroad president Thomas Scott, writing in the staid *North American Review*, had nervously suggested that "the late troubles may be but the prelude to other manifestations of mob violence, with this added peril, that now, for the first time in American history, has an organized mob learned its power to terrorize the law-abiding citizens of great communities." In 1883 E. L. Molineux, a commander of a New York National Guard regiment, wrote in "Riots in Cities and Their Suppression" that "the mob of the future," the "restless and implacable associations of Socialists, Communist and Nihilists that have taken root in our midst, . . . sooner or later, must inevitably precipitate a conflict upon us." And in November 1885, only a few short months before the Haymarket bomb exploded, genteel clergyman Lyman Abbott also warned that "communism" and radical labor organizations not only had become "fatally prolific" in America but were both "armed by modern science with fatally efficient equipment for destruction, and officered by leaders often both unscrupulous and daring."[4]

Abbott's remarks concerning "modern science" refer to Alfred Nobel's 1866 invention of dynamite and express the fear, often exploited by Chicago's labor radicals in the 1880s and seemingly foretold in the glare of Haymarket, that dynamite could entirely rearrange the social order in one spectacular blast by "destroy[ing] in an hour the products of a century's industry."[5] Abbott's worry about the workers' "unscrupulous and daring" leaders also speaks to Scott's enigmatic and seemingly contradictory phrase "organized mob."[6] Scott's curious wording says volumes about mainstream America's nearly palpable fear that the nation's large and amorphous working classes could be channeled or directed into confrontation against its wealthier citizens by demagogues and malcontents. Indeed, John Hay explicitly addressed this concern in his virulently antilabor fictionalization of the 1877 strikes, *The Bread-Winners*. In Hay's 1883 novel, the forces of law and order ultimately suppress the strike led by socialist Andrew Offitt and his sidekick, Sam Sleeny, a "dark-skinned, unwholesome-looking Bread-winner."[7] With the invention of dynamite, which appeared to promise both anonymity and puissance since a bomb could easily be "carried in a carpet-bag,"[8] it seemed to radicals and conservatives alike that a mob's ability, as Scott put it, to "terrorize" others had shaded into a terrorist's more invisible, more powerful, and more dangerous ability to commit specific and deadly acts of mass violence with dynamite bombs.

When the oft-predicted blast finally happened on that 1886 evening in Chicago, dire warnings such as Scott's, Molineux's, and Abbott's took on the tint of prophetic truth for many and became the foundation of an interpretive framework that imagined the bombing as the inaugural blow in a campaign to overturn the American state.[9] Paranoia thus became prescience, despite the crucial fact that nobody knew who threw the bomb or for what purpose. Indeed, Michael Schaack, a Chicago police captain who led the postbombing roundup of radicals and also wrote the most comprehensive contemporary history of Haymarket, followed these earlier writers' lead in his interpretation of the bombing but offers an additional important gloss on the night's events. Schaack writes that the bombing was committed by a band of immigrant and radical "terrorists" and that it marked the moment when "the crash of dynamite was for the first time heard on the streets of an American city."[10] Technically, Schaack is incorrect here because dynamite had previously appeared on America's streets during moments of class conflict and had even been used in Chicago itself. In December 1885, for instance, the *Chicago Tribune* reported that an "infernal machine" had been found on a judge's doorstep.[11] But the labeling of Haymarket's unknown bomb thrower as a terrorist who is presumably part of a larger plot updates Scott and Abbott's fears of dynamite and organized mobs precisely by imagining an apparently covert terrorist network operating in America. As the *New York Times* put it in a front page story the day after the bombing, "Before daylight at least a dozen stalwart men will have laid down their lives as a tribute to the doctrine of Herr Johann Most." With this single sentence, the *Times* linked the bombing to the most notorious and reviled advocate of terrorism in America during the late nineteenth century.[12]

In this chapter, I focus on the contemporary understanding of the Haymarket bombing as a terrorist event.[13] It is important to note that Schaack's and other commentators' conception of the tragedy as terrorism did not appear ex nihilo; instead, it was an idea made up of identifiable essentials that fused in the crucible of Haymarket into an emergent notion of modern terrorism in America. For instance, when the bomb exploded, a cultural narrative connecting American labor violence with class uprising and terrorism in Europe, which was partially constructed, if not controlled, by Chicago's radicals themselves, already existed. Beyond this, dynamite's cataclysmic appearance at Haymarket was clearly the most dramatic example up to that time of this relatively new technology's potential for sudden, anonymous, and unanticipated destruction. Finally, a burgeoning mass media and a recurrence of a by-then longstanding American fascination with conspiracies were essential components that parleyed the dynamite blast into a vastly more resonant, widely discussed, and terrifying event. The sudden and cataclysmic violence of dynamite, that is, was made all the more immediate and horrific during the Haymarket events by an emerging mass media's ability to reproduce images, reports, and testimonials again and again for an audience that did not directly experience the bombing, and, through this repetition, to help shape common understandings of the bomb as terrorism.

Sudden violence such as occurred at Haymarket brings private bodies into a public identity as a spectacle. This is not necessarily different from other catastrophes that stimulated large-scale media coverage in the nineteenth century, such as the Chicago fire or the train wrecks that frequently captivated public attention. Yet violence that is labeled terrorism is different from such natural catastrophes or industrial accidents because its sudden eruption is presumed to be actively planned by some person or persons. As an event whose outcome is known, but whose orchestration remains obscure, terrorism summons forth narratives to reconstruct and explain it. At Haymarket, in a scenario repeatedly played out in events labeled terrorism throughout the twentieth century, a lack of concrete knowledge provoked a surplus of narratives dwelling on conspiracies, secret plans, and covert actions. The bombing's apparently sharp swerve from the norms of political behavior inspired individuals in several different social positions, including the media, the police, the accused, and the state's prosecutors, to imagine incredibly complex and Byzantine conspiracies organized by anonymous plotters. For example, in response to the conspiracy theories implicating them, the men falsely accused of organizing a terroristic cabal against the state even formulated their own conspiracy theory in which state-supported capitalists actively plotted to throw a bomb that could then be blamed on Chicago's radicals.[14] The ubiquity and variety of these purported schemes during the Haymarket events highlight how chimerical conspiracies inevitably seem to emerge after a sudden and unexpected outburst of political violence. Their sheer excess of machination offers compensation for the brute inexplicability of apparently arbitrary mass violence by providing both apocalyptic and airtight explanations.

Though the men on trial for the Haymarket blast articulated their own version of the tragedy, their voices were overwhelmed by the mainstream print media's raging antipathy.[15] Public discourse after the bombing everywhere encouraged Americans to think of themselves as collectively opposed to radical politics. Crucially, this shaping of events occurred at the same time that a developing print media had expanded the possible forms that mass public gathering around disasters and catastrophes could take. Haymarket, that is, was a formative event in the emergence of what Mark Seltzer has termed this nation's "wound culture"—our collective fascination with wounded, torn, or devastated private bodies and their representations across a wide range of print and visual media.[16] Michael Warner's theorization of a media audience's relationship to spectacles of mass catastrophe since the late nineteenth century can gloss Seltzer's provocative concept. According to Warner, the media makes a transitive form of identification available for its audience. Faced with a disaster occurring somewhere else but made available for consumption by the media's frequent repetitions that dissolve differences of time and space between an event and its belated audience, readers and viewers are convened as a "mass subject" or "noncorporeal mass witness" to a tragedy.[17] At Haymarket, mainstream newspapers, instant histories, and cheap pamphlets kept the gruesome tragedy of the bombing constantly before Americans and politicized the event even further by feeding fears that seemingly imminent terrorist violence could transform readers from the anonymity of print media's belated form of mass witnessing into the iconicity of public spectacle.

Haymarket thus provided one of the earliest sites where citizens were convened as a public body around mass-mediated repetitions of an intentional atrocity. Beyond this, rhetoric churned out to describe the Haymarket events in the months following the blast was also riddled with panics about privacy, anonymous acts, and unknown conspiracies. Haymarket, though certainly not the first American example of mass violence, conspiracy, or media frenzy, fused these elements into a terrifying episode that hinged on how the private bodies of victims, of accused terrorists, and of a tragedy's belated audience are brought into public identity by the cultural narratives spun out to represent and make sense of sudden violence. I examine this complex and often contradictory history of public iconicity and anonymity from several related angles, including contemporary representations of the blast, the seemingly irresistible pull toward theories of covert terrorist conspiracies as explanations for the bombing, the profiles of a "terrorist" generated to explain it, and the very nature and manipulation of fear itself. By analyzing these aspects of Haymarket's cultural and historical resonance, we can begin to understand the logic of how terrorism was imagined as a particular form of violence in the late nineteenth century. Specifically, the notion of modern terrorism that emerged in the aftermath of Haymarket provided a concept that Americans could use to psychically process and categorize apparently new forms of deadly violence.[18]

The Media and the Bombing's Absent Witnesses

An illustration that appeared in *Anarchy at an End,* one of the many instant and inexpensive histories of Haymarket that rolled off the presses immediately after the bombing and trial, succinctly brings together many of my concerns in this section (see figure 1.1).[19] The picture provides an aerial view of the Haymarket rally immediately after the bomb has been thrown, while the police and crowd are still firing at each other. There is an empty space in the middle, where the bomb has just landed, in which are strewn a few fallen and twisted bodies. A throng of largely indistinguishable persons crowds around, ringing the bomb site; indeed, in this artist's depiction, the entire square is jammed with a massive and completely uncountable mob of people standing elbow to elbow. And in the middle of that circle formed by the masses stands a telegraph pole with wires extending forward and backward out of the drawing's frame.

Like most of the instant histories produced in the wake of the bombing, the anonymously authored *Anarchy at an End* simply reproduced images and accounts lifted directly from newspapers and gets many details wrong. That pervasive cribbing of sources and overlap between newspapers and other forms of print media, usually without any acknowledgment, represents an early form of the ceaseless repetition of atrocity footage that makes up our own twenty-first century, mass-mediated discourse of terrorism. More centrally, if the crowd this artist imagined witnessing the Haymarket blast far exceeds the few hundred individuals who were still in the square when the bomb was thrown, that mistake, along with the telegraph pole that dramatically occupies the illustration's center, obliquely registers the sheer importance the mass press played in contemporary understandings of Haymarket.

In fact, the blast at Haymarket occurred before relatively few live witnesses. Unlike the Chicago fire of 1871, which was directly experienced by hundreds of thousands, the explosion at Haymarket was seen by only a few hundred workers and several dozen police officers.[20] Most Americans learned of the bombing through the press at a moment when the media itself was undergoing some rather remarkable changes in its technological infrastructure. The expansion of telegraph wires and newspapers' growing dependence upon them throughout the post–Civil War years had dramatically altered the dissemination, organization, and definition of news by the time of the Haymarket bombing. Equally important, rapid advances in printing press tech-

FIGURE 1.1. "Chicago: The Haymarket Massacre—The Charge
of the Police after the Explosion of the Bomb." *The Graphic News,*
15 May 1886. Chicago Historical Society ICHI-03685.

nology made it possible for a previously unimaginable number of newspaper copies to be printed.[21] Another early history of the bombing, this one written by Dyer Lum, and one of the few such accounts that took a prodefendant slant, begins specifically by acknowledging the telegraph's mediation of experience via the mass press: "A bomb! A dynamite bomb! Such was the startling intelligence which went over the wires from the city of Chicago on the night of May 4th, 1886."[22] In this dramatic opening sentence, Lum registers how the mass media itself became a constituent part of Haymarket as the press instantly shaped the largely unwitnessed bombing into a huge public event via telegraphic technology.

A slightly earlier article that appeared in *Harper's* magazine in 1873 can flesh out the importance Lum implicitly gives to the telegraph. Describing the social impact and particular form of mediation that the telegraph made possible, the anonymous author states that it exerts enormous "influence upon the mental development of the people" and "has penetrated almost every mind." Ultimately, the telegraph "lifts every man who reads its messages above his own little circle, gives him in a vivid flash, as it were, a view of vast distances, and tends by an irresistible influence to make him a citizen of his country and a fellow of the race as well as a member of his local community."[23] While this statement rehearses an early form of the common insight that technology has tended to obliterate space and time, it also, quite interestingly, imagines this compression specifically through the lens of a national culture. The telegraph, that is, helped to make people into "citizen[s] of [their] country," thereby making it possible to hail them as a collective national body.

In the aftermath of the Haymarket bombing, the mass mediation of disaster that the telegraph and new printing technology helped to make possible intersected in clear, material ways with the prosecuting attorney's desire to produce a national culture that had no space for radical anarchists, bomb throwers or not. One place to locate this intersection is in the political illustrations that regularly accompanied the news stories, especially those illustrations that implicitly commented on Haymarket as a media event as they told of it. One such illustration that was frequently reproduced in various accounts presents a highly intricate series of tableaux and focuses on the second of Haymarket's two scenes of multiple deaths, in this case the executions of the condemned men (see figure 1.2).[24] The illustration is divided into quadrants, with one additional dramatic scene featured prominently in the middle and three smaller insets depicting the Cook County Courthouse and Jail at the top. In the upper left scene, the death warrant is read to the condemned

FIGURE 1.2. "The Chicago Anarchists,—Scenes and Incidents of the Execution of Spies, Parsons, Engel, and Fischer." *The Pictorial West,* November 1887. Chicago Historical Society ICHI-31348.

men. The upper right panel depicts the ensuing "March to the Scaffold." The bottom left quadrant then offers us a view of one official watching as another state officer fits the noose around the last of the four shrouded figures on the gallows. In this frame, we also look out at a sea of people who form the audience. The next scene, "After the Drop," depicted in the middle of the illustration, reverses the previous vantage point and offers us a view of the hanged bodies and the backs of the audience's first two rows. The fifth and final tableau, in the bottom right, features a newsboy selling papers to a crowd of men who are already reading the "Latest News."

This style of pictorial representation was certainly not new in 1886; in fact, by the standards of immensely popular late-nineteenth-century illustrated journals such as the *National Police Gazette* or *Frank Leslie's Illustrated Newspaper,* it was not even particularly lurid.[25] Yet, in presenting viewers with multiple hangings, a public death spectacle figured forth as compensation for the mass deaths caused by the Haymarket bomb, this illustration suggests a number of the connections between mass-mediated terrorist discourse, the state, and how individual viewers could be hailed as a collective body. For instance, the upper left panel, "Reading the Death Warrant," exemplifies one way in which cultural narratives attempting to explain violence bring private bodies into a public identity. Here the usually inaccessible and confined interior of the jail is rendered visible for us, as, fittingly, we are presented with an image transforming the private, individual experience of death into a social symbol by way of a legal decree of execution. This vignette also exemplifies what Mark Seltzer has identified as the frequent conflation of national and natural bodies where extreme violence or a severe threat to the social order is seemingly at stake,[26] since the death warrant held by the sheriff emblematizes the expulsion of the anarchists from the American body politic that will occur with their deaths. Samuel McConnell, a Chicago lawyer at the time of the hangings, made this conflation particularly clear in his reminiscences about the case published some years later. He writes that "the hanging of these men did do away with the hysteria which had pervaded the body of the people."[27] McConnell's retrospective statement literalizes what is implicit in this first tableau, as he suggests the way individual members of a society were conjoined into one mass body, the body politic, which had been beset by "hysteria" that seemingly could only be cured by the deaths of the condemned men.

While the first panel invites viewers to witness the death pronouncement, the center and bottom left panels are interesting for the very way in which they include acts of witnessing in the illustration itself. One scholar has suggested that the illustration's audience members are "surrogates for the rest of the 'nation of spectators.'"[28] I agree that the illustration offers such a fantasy of collectivity and proposes an identification between its material audience and the audience it depicts. But since several dozen of the execution's audience were, in fact, reporters, the two panels also more directly emphasize the media's ability to shape stories for that "nation of spectators." The illustration dramatically presents this idea in the bottom right frame, where the public is represented and addressed specifically as a community of newspaper readers drawn together by the calamity of Haymarket. Hal Foster has termed this cultural situation in which a mass-mediated public is convoked and addressed specifically as a collective subject around catastrophic events the burgeoning of a "psychic nation."[29] Distancing the public from the actual event even as it depicts the community of readers internalizing a particular, legitimated, and dominant representation of the Haymarket executions produced by those reporters, this vignette graphically illustrates how private acts such as reading can also be understood as public, collective mental acts.

The last frame of this illustration in particular suggests how the public can be invoked as a body around the display of "atrocity exhibitions" (for what else can one call the representation of four hanged men?).[30] This scene may be taking place in Chicago, but it could just as well be occurring almost anywhere else. Indeed, the caption's notion of "Latest News" suggests the frequent updates across wide geographic distances made possible by the telegraph, which, ironically, by 1886 had thoroughly changed the meanings and social significance of time and distance that are emblematized in the clock and painted ship hanging in the background. This drawing thus portrays a notion of the press's expanding reach and at the same time, by employing an equivalent stylistic representation for the solemn, formal procession to execution and its media coverage, metaphorically instantiates for its viewers the idea that the press can be relied upon to present citizens with a public and legitimate model of social order.

Furthermore, the illustration's distinct center panel, with its four legally strangled bodies and its small glimpse of an audience, most likely themselves reporters, underscores how the framing of the news for that absent body of witnesses also directly participated in the ideological invocation of the Haymarket anarchists as justly punished fiends. As Murray Edelman has argued, the creation of a public crisis that seems to need strong redress is itself a political act, not merely a recognition of a rare, dangerous, or unexpected event that has a self-evident meaning already built into it.[31] The bomb throwing at Haymarket was obviously a dangerous and exceptional act, but it came after years of heated rhetoric and smaller conflicts between Chicago's anarchists and the city's power structure. One reason that the mainstream print media presented it for contemporary viewers in such stark terms and helped make it such a landmark event, even in the absence of incriminating evidence, was that the explosion dramatically highlighted the American class antagonism then threatening the very types of middle-class citizens depicted as newspaper readers in the illustration's final frame. To employ Edelman's useful terms once again, extreme social "problems" or threats emerge within an ideological framework and thus provide object lessons on, for example, who is virtuous or dangerous, or who can conjure authority and who must accept it.[32] Both providing a model of social order and offering its viewers certain legitimated positions to take in relation to the executions of the condemned men, this illustration, and the Haymarket press coverage more generally, suggested the increasing ability of major newspapers and other print media, which often reproduced newspaper accounts, to inform readers' subjectivities in a political world in which the press itself would play a major role.

One way of understanding this process is through the notion of an "absent witness." There is an odd moment in George McLean's popular 1890 history of Haymarket that further exemplifies this seemingly paradoxical concept. McLean describes the execution in the melodramatic tones that characterize both his entire book and much of the nineteenth century's sensational and prurient literature of crime and punishment.[33] He writes, "There they stood upon the scaffold, four white robed figures, with set, stoical faces, to which it would seem no influence could bring a tremor of fear. And now a bailiff approaches, and, seizing Parsons' robe, passed a leather strap around his ankles. In a moment they were closely pinioned together. . . . Spies was the last, but he was the first around whose neck the fatal cord was placed. One of the attendant bailiffs seized the noose . . . and then the bailiff tightened it till it touched the warm flesh, and carefully placed the noose beneath the left ear."[34] What is odd about this otherwise conventional account is the sudden shift to the present tense when McLean describes the bailiff's treatment of Parsons. It is as if we are suddenly there, witnessing the execution live as it happens. But McLean's account, it is also worth noting, is not exactly his. As he prefaces his chapter on the executions, "The following description of the execution is copied from the *Daily News*."[35] One function of such reiteration of traumatic events in words and images is to incorporate them into a dominant social, political, and symbolic order for readers.[36] In the mass-mediated public sphere that was emerging during the Haymarket era, this repetition of the same stories and images also served as a way in which notions of the public and public attention could be consistently evoked, but, crucially, in the absence of actual public participation. At Haymarket, that is, the media regularly dramatized and replayed the state's redemptive executions as a benefit for the public, and, I would argue, thereby positioned readers in the role of belated and mediated witnesses, a role in which their only responsibility was to observe the state's highly ritualized response to the tragic bombing at Haymarket.

While representations of the Haymarket anarchists' bodies helped to construct the bombing and its aftermath as a political spectacle, the bodies of the slain policemen and their representation also played important roles in the contemporary discourse of Haymarket. This was perhaps most spectacularly apparent at the trial and in discussions of the court proceedings. Surprisingly, Judge Gary allowed into evidence several highly prejudicial, tattered, and blood-stained uniforms that were said to have been worn by the slain policemen at Haymarket. Dyer Lum, however, noted that "it was not [Officer Mathias] Degan's clothing thus paraded, showing holes made by fragments of the shell, and it was not shown in evidence that the clothing belonged to officers who died."[37] Whether those gory remnants of police uniforms were legitimate or not, these "silent witnesses," news reporter Frederick Trevor Hill surmised, "spoke louder than any words" and were therefore most instrumental in gaining the anarchists' convictions.[38]

The almost unimaginable and eerie power that contemporary observers attributed to the courtroom display of the (possibly fraudulent) bloody police uniforms dramatically exemplifies the range of purposes to which bodies and their representations were put during Haymarket. By way of the bloodied uniforms, a putatively direct link to the night of the bombing, Americans were again hailed as witnesses, called into collective being around representations of devastating wounds. Yet such images of the shocking effects to which the technology of dynamite could be put may very well have evoked a contradictory series of reactions in Haymarket contemporaries. Even as the initial witnesses of those soiled uniforms may have grieved for the victims and been offered the psychic relief that the suffering bodies were not theirs because they were elsewhere, they were also presented with the raw possibility that sheer chance could bring them into a public identity as a representative victim.

Such images of violence and disaster thus operated at Haymarket as important moments of public identity, moments that specifically made clear the way the discourse of terrorism dissolves distinctions between anonymity or privacy and publicity. Jeremy Green, in a provocative study of more contemporary depictions of mass violence, has argued that morbid images "forge a palpable link between the faceless loner's violent action and the faceless crowd's spectacular consumption of such actions, such violence."[39] One problem that Haymarket presents is trying to theorize how rhetoric attempting to explain and situate outbreaks of mass violence might have worked in different times and through different media, but it is at least important to note the ways in which anonymity and publicity intersected in the often gruesome accounts produced for Haymarket's contemporary audience.

This translation of anonymous readers into a mass but absent public was most evident in conceptions of Haymarket specifically as a terrorist event. Michael Schaack's contemporary history of Haymarket is exemplary in this regard. Schaack begins his book with a section on the European "Red Terror" of the 1870s and 1880s, paying special attention to the 1881 dynamiting of the czar by Russian terrorists.[40] The point, of course, is to show how the Haymarket bombing is a terroristic outrage of a piece with this European violence. But it is Schaack's report of the Haymarket bombing's immediate aftermath that clarifies the cultural work performed by a conception of Haymarket as a terrorist attack. He notes that when "the news had spread throughout the city of the terrible slaughter . . . the one inquiry, the one great sympathy, was with reference to the wounded officers and their condition" (149). An act of mass violence, as Schaack conveys, brings a community together in a show of solidarity as little else can. More important, though, Schaack's wrenching description of the bombing ("The [police station's] floors literally ran with blood dripping and flowing from the lacerated bodies of the victims" [149]), and his account of the city's individual residents exuding an identical and anxious concern after learning the "news" of the mangled officers, reveal how the rhetorical construction of Haymarket as a terrorist event exemplifies both the voyeurism inherent in mass absent witnessing and the dissolution of boundaries between public and private identities. Specifically imagining an audience that was somewhere else at the time of the bombing, Schaack depicts a social collectivity around those "lacerated bodies" that forms by way of an absent witnessing mediated by the "news" that provided Haymarket's audience with an experience of the event. By imagining Haymarket as a terrorist bombing and finding its witnesses in the abstract public (those citizens with "the one inquiry, the one great sympathy"), Schaack's rhetoric underscores the cross-fertilization between accounts of an emerging form of violence labeled terrorism and the early mass-mediated public sphere. His account makes visible how notions of terrorism also routinely imagine that body of absent witnesses as a single body that views the tragedy with one undivided mind-set. Along these same lines, contemporary political theorist David Apter has argued that the recitation of violent acts in print creates a form of "symbolic capital," a "conveyance, [by which] people giv[e] over a piece of their minds to the collective, enabling them to draw down more power than they give up."[41] That "symbolic capital" available in legiti-

[47]

mated accounts of political violence, as Schaack's description demonstrates, thus works to knit individual readers into a like-minded community.

While the dissolution of boundaries between private subjectivity and a mass public identity was at stake in the media-driven and belated gathering around fallen bodies in the contemporary discourse about Haymarket, this early exhibition of our wound culture obviously took place in a very politicized context. At this moment of crisis when the state wished to convene its citizens as a collective body against a designated threat, the media was becoming more able to depict atrocities for a mass audience. We can now begin to see that spontaneous violence labeled terrorism might be considered the prototypical, highly politicized violence of the mass culture that emerged with the late nineteenth century's revolutionary transformations in communication technologies. But this crisscrossing of anonymity and publicity that I have been tracing through representations of the bombing and its aftermath is also evident in another of Haymarket's most salient aspects, the overwhelming drive toward conspiracy theories on the part of all participants.

Conspiring to Thwart Conspiracies

On the one hand, as Richard Hofstadter demonstrated decades ago, anxiety about conspiracies is at least as old as the American republic itself and appeared, among other places, in the widespread postrevolutionary panic over secret plots to overthrow the government and the antebellum southern fear of slave uprisings.[42] Yet the strikingly ubiquitous appeal of conspiratorial explanations at Haymarket suggests that we need to understand them not only in a historical relation to earlier paranoia about conspiracies, but also in conjunction with their immediate historical conditions. The widespread turn to theories of hidden conspirators and the desire to make them visible grew out of the new danger posed by easily transportable and concealable dynamite. In a roiling urban culture, in which anarchists regularly threatened dynamite attacks and almost anyone could conceivably be a terrorist, the pressure created by anonymity was surely intense. Additionally, these conspiracy theories, which are suffused with notions of mass, even seemingly disembodied, conspirators, speak to the contradictory possibilities of publicity and anonymity that the technologically driven mass press was itself helping to redefine during the late nineteenth century.

In the press, at the trial, in the contemporary histories written of Haymarket, and even at the execution of the condemned men, a notion that the Haymarket bomb was not an isolated tragedy but was actually just the first blow of a widespread terrorist conspiracy designed to wipe out all law and order in Chicago—if not America itself—was constantly in circulation. For instance, Charles Edward Russell, a reporter who covered Haymarket for the *New York World,* wrote that in the months after the bombing police captain Michael Schaack was a man who "saw more anarchists than vast hell could hold. Bombs, dynamite, daggers, and pistols seemed ever before him."[43] And indeed, a lengthy part of Schaack's own history of Haymarket details and glorifies his role in identifying and breaking up a massive network of conspirators of which the Haymarket anarchists were only one small part. According to the police captain, the purported conspirators were "a set of wily, secret and able men, who had made a special study of the art and mystery of baffling the law and avoiding the police" (183).

Yet the fascinating and bizarre manner in which Schaack's paranoia about conspiracies incited him to form his own Byzantine and conspiratorial "secret service" is perhaps even more striking. In order to infiltrate the terrorist cells that he believed were honeycombing the city, Schaack "did not depend wholly upon police effort, but at once employed a number of outside men." With his spies posing as radicals, he writes, "at each anarchist meeting I had at least one man present to . . . learn what plots they were maturing" (206). Schaack's narrative is punctuated throughout by escapades including midnight meetings with masked informants in creepy alleys, stories of his spies' eavesdropping on unsuspecting anarchists through holes drilled in the floorboards of their meeting houses, and murders of his detectives by double-crossing female anarchists. Ironically, outfitted in their anarchist disguises, which meant carrying reputed terrorist Johann Most's books and "wear[ing] a red necktie" (210), his secret agents were also occasionally seized by the regular and unknowing Chicago police and forced to spend a night in jail. In these moments, Schaack would let his men stay in jail overnight rather than divulge their true identities to his colleagues in the police department (218).

But while the months after the bombing found the police captain and his secret service scheming against the anarchists in order to infiltrate their supposedly ubiquitous meetings and break up a nefarious conspiratorial ring, Schaack himself was also actively conspiring with Chicago's wealthier citizens and businessmen. Detailing his covert operations nearly three years after the end of his roundup (which the economist Richard T. Ely termed Chicago's "period of police terrorism"),[44] Schaack claims that "the funds for this purpose were supplied to me by public-spirited citizens who wished the law vindicated and order preserved in Chicago" (206). Ironically, while Schaack, through a combination of paranoia and an insatiable desire to gain fame as the one man capable of protecting the distressed metropolis, envisioned terrorist conspiracies where they did not exist, the only verifiable conspiracy in the bombing's aftermath was the one involving the rogue Chicago policeman and many of the city's financial leaders.[45] As Paul Avrich describes this paradoxical scenario in his history of Haymarket, "Some three hundred citizens, including Marshall Field, Philip D. Armour, and George M. Pullman, met in secret and subscribed more than $100,000 to help stamp out anarchy and sedition."[46]

Intense paranoia in the bombing's aftermath thus produced an imbroglio that found businessmen secretly plotting against an imagined anarchist cabal and a police captain running a complex espionage ring without the knowledge of his fellow officers. If the Haymarket blast turned prebombing paranoia into prescience, paranoia after the bombing seemed to overwhelm alternative methods for interpreting the bombing. In other words, terrified that anarchist conspiracies were brewing in all directions, Chicago's leaders appeared capable of understanding and combating secret plots only by imitating and practicing conspiratorial behaviors themselves: "Had it not been for the caution and secrecy which we made our rule all through the investigation," Schaack writes, "the plot would not have been successfully unraveled" (193). Meeting surreptitiously, donning disguises, concealing knowledge from their colleagues—such behaviors on the part of Schaack and his cohorts are separated from the anarchists' imagined actions only by the police captain's discursive power to define Chicago's radicals as the "Red Terror" (184) while envisioning the city's economically powerful citizens as the protectors of law and order. When juxtaposed with the illusory but repeatedly described anarchist cabal, the very real coercive and conspiratorial methods used by Schaack's men, including illegal arrests compounded by physical, verbal, and mental abuse of prisoners,[47] demonstrate the interpenetration and instability of fact and fiction in discourse about terrorism. That is, the Haymarket bombing was undeniably terrible, but in Schaack and his allies' attempts to narrate the bombing as an act of terrorism, the recitation of a stark atrocity goes hand in glove with tremendous excursions into rhetorical phantasmagoria.[48]

Schaack's narrative suggests that a conspiracy theory is a form of knowledge that breeds nothing so profusely as more conspiracies. Indeed, as if on cue, Albert Parsons, the prominent Chicago anarchist who avoided capture during the postbombing police dragnet, only to march freely and dramatically into the courtroom on the trial's opening day to stand with the other accused men, imagined a rather different conspiracy behind the bombing. At the trial, when his turn came to offer reasons why the death sentence passed against him should not be fulfilled, Parsons, in the course of speaking—to the judge's great consternation—for an extraordinary stretch of eight hours, explained who he thought threw the Haymarket bomb. After reading aloud a Pinkerton circular in which the famous detective agency advertised its agents' abilities to don disguises and infiltrate labor organizations in order to "discover the ring-leaders, and deal promptly with them," Parsons told the courtroom: "I want to call your attention to what I regard as the origin of this bomb at the Haymarket. I believe it was instigated by eastern monopolists to produce public sentiment against popular movements, especially the eight-hour movement then pending, and that some of the Pinkertons were their tools to execute this plan. . . . Often before have they done such things; it has been proven on them in numerous parallel cases of conspiracy to bring odium upon popular movements in all parts of the country."[49]

Parsons's statement crystallizes nineteenth-century radicals' long-standing frustration with capitalist-sponsored and sometimes state-supported violence directed at workers. Moreover, his evocation of a world populated by double agents and spies is crucial for our understanding of Haymarket's particular cultural and historical significance. He depicts a scenario, much like the "secret service" actually headed by Schaack, in which a private police force hired to protect order within society is in reality the fomenter of disorder and havoc. Imagining a Pinkerton agent who posed as a working stiff at the Haymarket rally only to get close enough to throw the bomb that would discredit the labor movement, Parsons is also rehearsing the contingency and instability of identity in modern mass culture. He suggests that an unpredictable force that wants to subdue the social order cannot be securely located or definitively identified. Using logic similar to those Chicagoans who imagined terrorists to be everywhere but always unseen, Parsons is here drawing out the consequences of Pinkerton's own slogan, "The eye that never sleeps." In his countercharge, it is the privatized police force of modern capitalism that is unidentifiable, ubiquitous, and exists solely to terrorize workers.

Yet, while Parsons imagined a capitalist conspiracy carried out by Pinkertons, his conspiratorial imagination was dwarfed at the trial by State's Attorney Julius Grinnell, who delineated an ambiguous but seething prebombing conspiracy masterminded by the anarchists and intended, as Judge Gary put it, to "coerce by terror" Chicago's citizens. Elucidating this conspiracy to "strike terror to the hearts of the capitalists," Grinnell informed the jury that on the night of 4 May 1886, "bombs were to be thrown in all parts of the city of Chicago. Everything was to be done that could be done to ruin law and order." And worse, continued Assistant State's Attorney George C. Ingham, "when the bomb was thrown it was the opening shot of a war which should destroy all government and destroy all law." The notion of inevitable terrorist attacks in the near future was also fueled by trial testimony, such as that of police officer Thomas McNamara, who swore that in the bombing's aftermath he "found thirty loaded and one empty gas-pipe bombs under the sidewalk . . . about four blocks from Wicker Park." Detective Michael Hoffman also testified to finding explosives hidden dangerously under sidewalks.[50] Such apocalyptic rhetoric was further bolstered by the *Chicago Tribune*'s terrifying post-Haymarket reports of citizens stumbling across bombs hidden under sidewalks in their daily activities, where they could, it appeared to the trial watchers, be ready at a moment's notice for revolutionaries who wished to ignite an urban apocalypse.[51]

This perception that a nest of wild anarcho-terrorists was invisibly conspiring within Chicago reached its apogee of dramatic intensity in the widespread paranoia expressed at the time of the execution that an anarchist plot was afoot to strike a deadly blow against prominent capitalists, government buildings, and state officers. The *Chicago Tribune* ran stories in the days leading up to the 11 November 1887 hanging detailing the possible forms an anarchist retaliation might take.[52] Charles Edward Russell wrote in his memoirs that in the days immediately before the execution, "the nervous strain upon the public had become almost intolerable. The stories circulated, printed, and believed in those days seem now to belong to the literature of bedlam. There were 20,000 armed and desperate anarchists in Chicago, an assault upon the jail had been planned, all the principal buildings were to be blown up, the streets were filled with anarchist spies, the city was in imminent danger."[53] Similarly, Mary Harris "Mother" Jones in her autobiography remembered 11 November 1887 as a day on which "Chicago's rich had chills and fever" and "ropes stretched in all directions from the jail" to prevent anyone from lobbing a grenade at the building. Russell, in his account, goes on to remark that it is hard from any historical distance to comprehend the "tremendous power of the infectional panic that had seized upon the city," and that "for months" after the bombing, "we were disturbed with stories of anarchist plots" appearing in the "paranoiac" press. Yet, Russell reports in retrospect, "the idea of an anarchist conspiracy was purely a dream."[54]

Whether the imagined scheme was "purely a dream" or not, the widespread and refueled preoccupation with conspiracy months after the immediate postbombing plot had supposedly been infiltrated and quashed resulted from several different causes. One important impetus was the newspaper industry's need to sell its product and the fact that reports of spectacular violence or impending tragedy make good copy. Russell even recalls that one Chicago newspaper released an "Extra" mere minutes before the scheduled execution, "seriously announcing that . . . at the moment of the hanging the whole structure and all in it were to be destroyed."[55] Another, more material reason for the widespread fear occurred when bombs actually were found in one condemned man's cell only five days before the scheduled execution.[56]

But there is more at stake in what Russell calls this "paranoiac" atmosphere. Paranoia is an obsession with the elimination of surprises, and, as D. A. Miller has argued, should surprise occur, the paranoid "survives by reading [it] as a frightening incentive: he can never be paranoid enough."[57] Paranoid knowledge thus thins out to sabotage the possibility for bad surprises in any and all phenomena by relentlessly imagining all persons and events as always and already dangerous. In the closing days of the Haymarket affair, the particular form taken by paranoid knowledge was that "infectional panic" generated by the widespread idea that everyone milling in the streets could be an anarchist spy and that conspirators were plotting terrorist destruction behind every door in working-class neighborhoods. This intense preoccupation with a massive but illusory bomb plot is especially intriguing — and logically identical but effectively opposite to Parsons's trial claim — because it imagined urban terrorists to be generally everywhere but specifically nowhere. By imagining everything and everybody as already a sign of imminent destruction, Chicago's middle-class citizens conjured up and feared a mass anonymous collectivity that could not be localized in any particular person. But while this anticipatory fear is the very essence of the unpredictable, unnerving, and undesirable condition of terror itself, the appeal of envisioning a conspiracy of imperceptible plotters as the mechanism behind possible violence was also beautifully simple. The theory that an invisible anarchist conspiracy was at hand offered discursive coherency, a simple and absolute "us vs. them" binary. Imagining a massive conspiracy avoided the messy contingencies of politics by reducing the complex economic and social problems embodied by the condemned anarchists to the simple, if terrifying, workings of a narrative plot.

Profiles of a Terrorist

Theories of carefully orchestrated but shadowy conspiracies operated as a centrifugal force that drove out other possible forms of knowledge in the months following the Haymarket bombing. Yet, in order ritualistically and symbolically to exorcise the specter of terrorism from America, it had to be firmly located in a particular body or bodies. This figuration of the body as the ultimate site where political will could be enforced led to a desire for a purification through violence.[58] While not historically unique to Haymarket, the postbombing vitriol was extreme, and the articulation of this vengeful desire took one of its most rabid forms in the media's repeated calls for sum-mary and repressive violence against socialists after the bombing. The *Boston Herald,* for example, called for a swift fitting of "hemp cravats," the *Mobile Register* argued that the "best thing for the country would be to drive these reptiles out of it," and the *Philadelphia Inquirer* demanded "a mailed hand" to "put down" Chicago's anarchists.[59]

Though this media outcry for retributive vengeance was almost overwhelming, the state's inability to produce the bomb thrower also meant that there was no identifiable and singular person on whom to pin the crime. Of course, this ultimately mattered devastatingly little to a jury willing to convict eight accused anarchists even though the prosecution, without knowledge of the bomb thrower's identity and purpose, could not say definitively whether the assailant was carrying out a nefarious conspiracy or had even been influenced by the defendants' public pronouncements. While the lack of a known assailant did not slow the inexorable movement toward a speedy conviction, this glaring absence in the prosecution's case did serve as an incitement to discourse about the profile or dimensions of a terrorist in late-nineteenth-century America. In a situation defined by a scarcity of knowledge, an excess of public rhetoric about what a terrorist identity implied and entailed emerged in the months after the bombing. The figure of the terrorist took shape in these narratives as a site where the roiling problems of nationalism, immigration, class strife, and the legitimacy of violence were reified, narrated, and fought over. Entangled with and ultimately at stake in these literally life-or-death disputes about how the men on trial for the bombing should be characterized were crucial struggles regarding both the rhetorical terms upon which a person could act as an agent of change in America and the narratives that could be mobilized to enforce a dominant order and suppress radical dissent.

Seven of the eight men put on trial for the Haymarket bombing had come from Europe, though Albert Parsons was born in Alabama and could trace his roots in America to 1632. The foreign birth of the defendants acted as a magnet for late-nineteenth-century anxieties about immigrants in America, resulting in a particularly combustible trope that many antianarchist commentators seized upon in the months after the bombing to demonstrate that the anarchists and their philosophies were dreadfully inappropriate for American soil. Michael Schaack, though born in Luxembourg himself, condemned the anarchists as "exotics," claiming further that "discontent here is a German plant" that "in our garden . . . is a weed to be plucked out by the roots and destroyed" (25–26). Similarly, the xenophobic *Chicago Tribune* charged a few short days after the bombing that "Chicago has become the rendezvous for the worst elements of the Socialistic, atheistic, alcoholic European classes. . . . It is this alien and un-Americanized element . . . which has been flaunting the red flag of blood and the black flag of murder in our midst." Assistant State's Attorney George Ingham brought the charge home at the trial, claiming, albeit incorrectly, that aside from Parsons, "not one of the others is a citizen here."[60]

Dwelling on the anarchists' foreignness served to terrify American citizens by conjuring up the specter of European class warfare, particularly the still memorable Paris Commune of 1871 and the Russian terrorist bombing of the czar in 1881. George McLean's ardently pro-police 1890 history of Haymarket directly supplied this connection. Rehearsing the conspiracy theory to explain the bombing, McLean informed his readers that Chicago's foreign element "held secret meetings in organized groups armed and equipped like the nihilists of Russia, and the communists of France." Furthermore, during the trial Ingham attempted to link the Haymarket bomb with several bombs found in Louis Lingg's possession as well as the bomb used to assassinate the czar by noting that the "Czar bomb was composed of nearly the same material that the Lingg bombs were."[61]

The point of Ingham's accusation was not simply to demonstrate Lingg's possession of dynamite and his history of bomb-making, as Lingg himself openly acknowledged that he made and possessed bombs. Rather, the point of rhetoric such as McLean's and Ingham's was to depict an image of the labor radical as a complete aberration in America. This strategy of vilifying the anarchists was intended to drive a nativist wedge between the much mythologized American workman and foreign "scoundrelly demagogs [such] as Spies, Schwab, [and] Fielden." As the *Buffalo Courier* righteously put it, "The souls of the toiling millions burn with indignation over the devilish deeds done by Anarchists in the noble name of Labor."[62] American labor, according to this viewpoint, needed to trust in capitalism and endorse the expulsion of radicalism from the United States that would symbolically occur with the execution of the anarchists. Imagining a terrorist as the denouement of immigration gone awry, the newspapers and trial prosecution projected their anxieties about the condition of American class relations onto this demonic figure who could be publicly labeled as a pernicious outsider and ritualistically extinguished.

The mainstream media and trial attorneys invoked a narrative of American nationalism in order to imagine the Haymarket anarchists as the dynamite-wielding leaders of "an incendiary and alien rabble."[63] The stridency of this rhetoric is implicated in long-term patterns of American xenophobia over the course of the nineteenth century. But the frequently applied labels of "nihilist" and "terrorist" also expressed such urgency because they were salvos in a rhetorical duel with the anarchist defendants for interpretive control of America's past. The anarchists, cloaking themselves in the garb of 1776, mobilized the same rhetoric of nationalism to explain their position in American culture. This can be understood as their attempt to write themselves into American ideology, to become "public" by way of already iconic figures. For instance, their trial testimonies, newspaper articles, and autobiographies are saturated with the belief that they embodied the principles of the Founding Fathers, especially with regard to Thomas Jefferson and the Declaration of Independence's justifications for casting off tyrannical governments. Parsons's newspaper, *The Alarm,* told its readers that "our forefathers have not only told us that against despots force is justifiable . . . but they themselves have set the immemorial example." Parsons also quoted the Declaration's clauses outlining "the right of the people to alter or abolish" an oppressive government in his autobiography. In an even more direct comparison, Spies argued in court that the leaders of America's revolution, "if they lived today, would clean the Augean stables with iron brooms, and that they, too, would undoubtedly be characterized as 'wild Socialists.'"[64]

The narratives the anarchists offered at their trial and in their writing represent an exemplary early attempt by radical Americans to subvert an emerging discourse that used the idea and fear of terrorist activity to pathologize industrial capitalism's dissenters as a menacing threat to American democracy. The *Chicago Tribune* demonstrated its own understanding of this discursive struggle when it maligned the "followers of Parsons, Spies, and other blatant demagogs" who "have the effrontery to claim that . . . they are defending the liberty for which their sires fought. Not one of them," argued the *Tribune* editorialist, "is a true American citizen."[65] Yet branding the indicted men as terrorists and nihilists while denying them symbolic participation in the nation's mythologized history was, ironically, a particularly effective way for the antianarchist Haymarket commentators to evade history. That is, if the populace could be frightened enough by the image of a maddened terrorist, then—as the postbombing hysteria bore out—they would be much less likely either to look seriously at the social, political, and economic issues raised so passionately by the anarchists or to question the farcical trial accorded them.[66]

While the peculiar alchemy of nationality and history provided one method for understanding the politically violent person in the public rhetoric generated to explain Haymarket, race provided an equally important discursive trope. The anarchists called on America's slave-owning past to represent their current condition, transgressing racial boundaries to term themselves black slaves of the industrial regime with a right to revolt by any means available. In a fiery broadside distributed to advertise the Haymarket rally, August Spies galvanized the workers with the images of slaves, slave catchers, and slave revolt: "You have been miserable and obedient slaves all these years. Why? To satisfy the insatiable greed, to fill the coffers of your lazy thieving master? When you ask them now to lessen your burden, he sends his blood-hounds out to shoot you, kill you! . . . To arms we call you, to arms!"[67] In this double-edged language, the anarchists become not only the descendants of American radicalism as it was encoded in the Declaration, but a racialized reminder of America's past failure to live up to the Founders' ideals. Further-more, by mantling themselves in the cloak of slave rebellion, the anarchists laid claim across temporal boundaries to the antebellum rhetoric of figures such as Frederick Douglass, who, in stories such as *The Heroic Slave,* imag-ined slave revolt as the quintessential latter-day expression of America's revo-lutionary heritage.[68] By moving back and forth across time and correlating the racial images and symbolic forms of the antebellum period with the class strife of later industrialism, the anarchists wrote themselves into the Ameri-can body politic as the Jefferson or Douglass for an industrial generation.

The anarchists' specific appeal to America's racial past in order to offer their withering critique of the industrial state is both extraordinary and symp-tomatic within the culture of late-nineteenth-century America. It is extraordi-nary in its mobilization of racial metaphors to demonstrate a continuity with a Constitution that, though it justified revolution, did not recognize black slaves as whole persons and also favored the interests of America's moneyed class. It is symptomatic because the category of race was a particularly elas-tic trope in the postwar years that could be hitched to widely heterogeneous ideological aims. For instance, though the metaphor of race was correlated in the anarchists' rhetoric with a mythical link between themselves and the revo-lutionary Ur-citizens of the United States, a different and particularly viru-lent form of nineteenth-century racial distinction also provided a way for the anarchists' opponents to exorcise them from the body politic. Carl Smith, following the paradigm set by Richard Slotkin's incisive study of the rhetoric used to depict insurgents during the 1877 strikes, has argued that the anar-chists were routinely identified as bloodthirsty Indians.[69] Indeed, Schaack's history refers to the anarchists' illusory secret meetings as "war dances" and anarchist women, for whom he has particular contempt, as "squaws" (207). The *Tribune* similarly dubbed those present at the time of the Haymarket bombing the "'raw reds' of Chicago" and also "a Communistic mob" of "red devils."[70]

Of course, there is plenty of straightforward anticommunism evident in the *Tribune*'s invocation of "red" as a constituent element of radicals' identity without necessarily interpreting it in a racialized context. Yet an implicit connection between eliminating the racial difference of Indians from the American continent and purging the foreign threat of anarchy from the American body politic ran like a thread throughout the Haymarket events as they unfolded and was carried all the way through to the execution, a full eighteen months after the bombing. On 7 November 1887, only four days before the hangings, the *Tribune* reported the final stages of the Crow Indian War on the front page alongside details of the clemency campaign on behalf of the condemned men.[71] Here the race war against "red men" in the West metaphorically paralleled the class war against the "red devils" in Chicago. In this Indian metaphor, two threats to American civilization are conflated. While the Indians represent a form of preindustrial terrorism on the frontier, the anarchists embody the much more devastating terror made available by dynamite in the anonymous and frightening modern city. Like the furtive Indians who issue surprise attacks on unsuspecting white settlers, the equally dangerous and skulking anarchists launch deadly bombs from the alleyways and crevices of America's cities.[72]

Though the Indian metaphor was particularly electric during the Haymarket years, it is also important to note that it did not take an equation with Indians for contemporaries to regard immigrant radicals as racially nonwhite. As Matthew Frye Jacobson has argued, such racialization was not merely a politically powerful metaphor. Notions of barbarism and savagery were deployed in newspapers and popular journals such as the *Nation, Harper's Weekly,* and the *Daily Graphic* to argue that "immigrants . . . embod[ied] a kind of 'savagery' that was neither rhetorical nor metaphorical" but was, in fact, racial in nature.[73] This racialist logic is perhaps clearest in one of the several antiradical cartoons drawn by Thomas Nast in the aftermath of the Haymarket bombing. Appearing during the trial in the 24 July 1886 issue of *Harper's Weekly,* the cartoon depicts several grimy, long-haired radicals who wave a flag of anarchy and shoot at the American flag above a caption that reads "Those Foreign Savages" (see figure 1.3). The rhetoric of "savagery" that regularly implied a racial difference in the nineteenth century is here mapped onto a denigrated image of anarchists taking pot shots at the primary symbol of American nationhood. In using this language, Nast suggests that the differences between the anarchists and Americans are not simply based on country of origin but are fundamentally in the blood. Race thus merges with class, shoring up American national identity by giving the antiproperty, foreign ideas held by anarchists the supposed permanence of a biological difference that is inassimilable to America.

These metaphors of race and nationality used by both radicals and their

FIGURE 1.3. Thomas Nast, "Those Foreign Savages."
Harper's Weekly, 24 July 1886.

antagonists in the bombing's aftermath represent particular emplotments
of terrorist violence in late-nineteenth-century America. To make political
violence either defensible or repugnant, both the anarchists and the state's
legal representatives believed it necessary to metaphorically occupy someone
else's skin, to become publicly visible and embodied sites of knowledge via
ready-at-hand, if contestable, discursive tropes. In the discourse of terrorism
at Haymarket, then, social fear followed from the possibility that a mass of
invisible conspirators was plotting unpredictable acts. Conversely, for both
the accused and their accusers, the move to public discourse represented an
attempt to gain control of Haymarket's volatile range of possible interpretations by locating signification within individual bodies.

Imagined during the Haymarket crisis as ways to categorize and comprehend the bombing's resonance, these plots all share a logic in which the private body becomes relevant as public knowledge, as public spectacle. Like the contemporary accounts that focused on Haymarket's various forms of grisly murder, and the conspiracy theories that imagined terrorists to be everywhere and nowhere at once, these profiles were also implicit attempts to understand how private bodies could be related to mass-mediated public spaces. This struggle developed with such intensity at Haymarket because it occurred at a moment when it seemed increasingly possible for anonymous bomb throwers to reshape society in one catastrophic second by transforming other private individuals into very public, and very horrifying, victims. Moreover, if catastrophe, as Mary Ann Doane writes, always refers back to the body in some way,[74] the discourse of terrorism that emerged at Haymarket hinged on this rhetorical battle for how the body as public spectacle would be understood during a period when the press was developing the ability both to center our attention as absent witnesses around atrocities and to influence public understanding of them.

Threats

As we have seen, imagined conspiracies and assumed identities provided Haymarket's early commentators with discursively coherent if fantastic narratives of the bombing that could be filtered through various political perspectives. By holding competing interpretations at bay, the sheer intrigue and complexity of conspiracy theories grant narrative closure and transform apparent mayhem into a situation that points to one particular absolutist interpretation. Yet the absence of an identifiable bomb thrower at Haymarket, which at least partially made possible the extreme leaps into rhetorical phantasmagoria that we have witnessed, is also the snag that unravels these various attempts at narrative closure. Floyd Dell, a reporter and editor of *The Masses,* pointed out in 1912 that "if one remembers that it has never been proved who threw the Haymarket bomb, and that it was certainly never traced to the Anarchists, the surprising fact appears that there is no bomb-throwing to discuss in the history of Chicago Anarchism. There is merely bomb-talking."[75] This "bomb-talking," the culture of public threats and calls for dynamite bombings that ricocheted throughout Chicago well before and after the bombing, ultimately defies the often fantastic attempts to pin down Haymarket's signification via narratives of terrorist violence. Specifically, if a discourse of terrorism draws some of its explanatory power and cultural resonance from hermetically sealed and politically interested binaries, the rhetorical threat, a genre that resists efforts to narrate it into a univocal meaning, alternatively suggests the instability of all such totalizing discourses of terror.

According to Jacques Derrida, language can be infinitely reproduced in contexts that differ from its original simply by being cited or put between quotation marks: "And this is the possibility on which I want to insist: the possibility of disengagement and citational graft which belongs to the structure of every mark, . . . which is to say in the possibility of its functioning being cut off, at a certain point, from its 'original' desire-to-say-what-one-means [*vouloir-dire*] and from its participation in a saturable and constraining context. Every sign, linguistic or nonlinguistic, spoken or written (in the current sense of this opposition), in a small or large unit, can be *cited,* put between quotation marks; in so doing it can break with every given context, engendering an infinity of new contexts in a manner which is absolutely illimitable."[76] Through citation, a sign accesses an array of new meanings that may reach a temporary signifying stability, but signification can never be permanently fixed or halted. Consequently, the writer's or speaker's intention cannot control the text's reception and interpretations. Derrida suggests that this is true for all language, but the threat is a genre of communication that makes this sliding movement particularly apparent and politically interesting. The bluffing, feigning, ritualistic nature of the "bomb-talking" threat, which exists somewhere between immediate intention and utter lack of actual intention, is unhinged from any even seemingly transparent meaning and, therefore, particularly available for reiteration in new contexts that defy narrative closure.

The Chicago public, as Dell's statement implies, had been well prepared for the Haymarket bomb's explosion by years of public and dramatic threats of both individual and mass terror issued by Parsons, Spies, Fielden, and other anarchists. Americans, as Thomas Scott, E. L. Molineux, and Lyman Abbott exemplified, were suspended in a nervous game of waiting for terror, the ultimate anticipatory and paranoia-inducing "always already" emotion. A year before the Haymarket bombing, for instance, the headline of the *Chicago Tribune*'s coverage of a massive anarchist-led demonstration protesting the gala held on 28 April 1885 to commemorate the opening of Chicago's new Board of Trade building simply but ominously read "THEY WANT BLOOD."[77] Yet nothing aside from marching, singing, and verbal threats took place on that night in 1885, despite the *Tribune* reporter's sensational claim that an anarchist informant pointed to several small containers of nitroglycerine and told him that "every man in that parade had some of these."[78] Undergirding the *Tribune*'s panicked headline and morning-after assertions that bombs were definitely present at the demonstration, even if none went off *this* time, is the adrenaline-charged and even anticipatory justification that the threat against the moneyed classes is indeed real. "They want blood," literally argued the *Tribune*'s article, thus participating in a culture of terror and promising, only slightly less literally, that the bomb would eventually go off somewhere.

When a blast finally did arrive, but without an attendant claim of responsibility, the oft-repeated threats of the 1880s such as those at the Board of Trade rally became, for most observers, the objective mark of the anarchists' complicity in the bombing, despite their fervent and steadfast disavowal of any involvement. Indeed, Carl Smith has noted that the majority of the 136 exhibits entered into evidence by the state at the anarchists' trial were words the indicted men had spoken or published in the years leading up to the Haymarket bombing.[79] In the tumult of the bombing's aftermath, the Chicago anarchists' dramatic language and frequently articulated visions of spectacular violence were enough for a judge and jury unconcerned with the niceties of the First Amendment to hang them. The lack of a claim of responsibility accompanying the Haymarket bomb helped make the Chicago anarchists' earlier menacing warnings available for interpretation as "objective" legal fact at the trial. But those constantly reiterated promises of dynamite blasts in the 1880s cannot be taken at face value any more than the brute fact of the bomb exists outside various and often competing networks of interpretation. The workers' culture of threats and predicted violence were a rhetorically complex, high-stakes gambit for public power that, as the *Tribune* story indicates, were made even more foreboding by the publicity machinery of the emerging mass media.

In the threatening rhetoric of Chicago's anarchists during the 1880s, dynamite took on an almost supernatural power. *The Alarm,* the anarchist newspaper edited by Albert Parsons, exuberantly proclaimed in 1884: "Dynamite is the emancipator! In the hand of the enslaved it cries aloud: 'Justice or— annihilation!' But best of all, the workingmen are not only learning its use, they are going to use it. They will use it, and effectually, until personal ownership—property rights—are destroyed. . . . Hail to the social revolution! Hail to the deliverer '*Dynamite.*'"[80] In February 1885, *The Alarm* similarly exclaimed: "Dynamite! of all the good stuff, this is the stuff. Stuff several pounds of this sublime stuff into an inch pipe, gas or water pipe, plug up both ends, insert a cap with fuse attached, place this in the immediate neighborhood of a lot of rich loafers, who live by the sweat of other people's brows, and light the fuse. A most cheerful and gratifying result will follow. . . . The dear stuff can be carried around in the pocket without danger. . . . It can be used against persons and things, it is better to use it against the former than against bricks and masonry. It is a genuine boon for the disinherited, while it brings terror and fear to the robbers."[81]

Such near-mystical paeans to the sheer power of terrorist acts involving dynamite also appeared frequently in August Spies's German-language *Arbeiter-Zeitung* and other anarchist sheets in the 1880s. Dynamite elicited apocalyptic rhetoric of destruction from the anarchists because it appeared to promise its adherents agency and an ability to instantly transform the course of events, to level class differences by simply destroying a "lot of rich loafers." Dynamite offered workers the opportunity to take direct action against their antagonists, ironically replacing the agency and autonomy that industrial laborers saw slipping away from them in the mechanized factory with the apparently controllable power of science. Parsons's *Alarm* constantly encouraged its readers "to study their school-books on chemistry and read the dictionaries and cyclopedias on the composition and construction of all kinds of explosives." If factory owners were transforming the economy by replacing workers with machines, as the Haymarket anarchists frequently argued, then science held out the chance to strike a blow not only "against men, but against systems," against the "economic bondage" of industrial labor.[82]

Dynamite also took on an almost prosthetic relation to the human body in the discourse of anarchist threats. Parsons's and Spies's newspapers routinely reminded the public that it could be "carried with perfect safety in the pockets of one's clothing."[83] Lucy Parsons gave the most dramatic twist to this particular logic of prosthesis in a notorious editorial entitled "A Word to Tramps" that she wrote for the inaugural edition of *The Alarm*. If the inability to find work makes you suicidal, she advised, then your death should not be wasted by drowning. Instead, one should learn the use of dynamite and "stroll you down the avenues of the rich," getting close enough to see the capitalist "robbers" clearly through the windows of their luxurious mansions. From this spot, Lucy Parsons suggested, the "red glare of destruction" should announce one's terroristic exit from the world as a human bomb who destroys the life and property of the rich.[84] Such self-sacrifices had forceful appeal because, as it was frequently threatened and longingly asserted, one such suicide bombing or other act of terror could wake the slumbering masses from their lethargy and ignite a revolution. "Accomplished deeds," editorialized Spies's *Arbeiter-Zeitung*, "wake the spirit of rebellion. . . . This right spirit is to be inflamed, the revolutionary instinct is to be roused, which still sleeps in the breast of man."[85] Moreover, this rhetoric about a terrorist act's capacity to incite broader rebellion put Chicago's anarchists squarely in agreement with Johann Most. As Most's radical newspaper, *Freiheit,* claimed in 1884, terrorists "stoke the fire of revolution and incite people to revolt in any way we can."[86]

This obsessive return to the drama of dynamite accorded it a rhetorical power that undoubtedly exceeded any effect that an actual blast could have produced. As Parsons claimed with mystical intensity at his trial, "Dynamite is the diffusion of power. It is democratic; it makes everybody equal. . . . It is the equilibrium. It is the annihilator. It is the disseminator of power. It is the downfall of oppression."[87] An orchestrated bombing catastrophe promised to entirely and miraculously remake American society, to simultaneously give power back to the oppressed individual, overturn capitalism, and usher in an era of general equality. Skipping political debate and argument, the dramatically violent terrorist act posits the resolution of social dilemmas in a single arbitrary and symbolic flash that immediately transforms the very basis of a society.[88]

As other scholars have noted, these appeals to dynamite in the anarchists' rhetorical performances had such a manic intensity because modern explosives made imaginable, at least in threats, a desperately seductive and cataclysmic break from the present that could offset the recalcitrance and police-supported power of Chicago's manufacturers and propertied classes.[89] Yet previous Haymarket scholars have not paused to fully consider the uneasy relationship between public threats and physical violence that is at stake in these manic appeals. Indeed, a central irony within the anarchists' frequent, almost obsessively reiterated threats to dynamite capitalists was that they were exactly that: threats. Again and again the anarchists insisted upon the power of the *deed* itself to remake American society, but these claims were put forth in speech and writing, currencies frequently devalued vis-à-vis direct violence in nineteenth-century anarchist and terrorist rhetoric. "We have lost all faith in the word," wrote Sergey Nechayev, a principle theorist of Russian terrorism whose "Catechism of the Revolutionist" was reprinted and endorsed in Chicago's anarchist papers during the 1880s.[90] Similarly, and despite the fact that he earned his living as a newspaper editor, Parsons declared in an 1885 speech, "We will never gain anything by argument and words. The only way to convince these capitalists and robbers is to use the gun and dynamite."[91] Smashing through the prison-house of language, the bomb is seen here as that which defies representation and obliterates dominant, but fallacious, constructions of law and civilization. "The statute book is a book of laws by which one class of people can safely trespass upon another. . . . Every statute law is always used to oppose some natural law. . . . Man's legal rights are everywhere in collision with man's natural rights,"[92] argued Parsons in the absolutist rhetoric typical of anarchist discourse. In a politically desperate situation where hope and strength could only be articulated in the terms of a clean and complete break with existing power relations, the anarchists, even as they effectively manipulated language, devalued it as the negative term in a speech/action binary. Accordingly, the bomb is magnified into an all-or-nothing mechanism that both escapes and obliterates current discursive constructions of citizens' "legal rights" and dominant notions of order.

With arguments such as Nechayev's and Parsons's, the logic of late-nineteenth-century terrorism appears committed to a rigid distinction between word and deed. However, the terrorist threat itself represents both the speciousness of this binary and the porous nature of the boundaries between speech and action. Dynamite existed as a material fact after 1866, but it was only within the particular rhetorical and semantic strategies of Chicago's anarchists and the publicity- and fear-generating machinery of the mass press that dynamite became a magical agent capable, depending on one's point of view, of either destroying civilization or remaking American society on an entirely transformed organizational plane. Moreover, the common nineteenth-century phrase used by terrorists to describe their threatened actions, "propaganda by the deed," bespeaks the slippage between word and deed in terrorism discourse. Perhaps Johann Most most saliently grasped the fact that terrorism does not exist outside the struggle to control narration. He urged terrorists and their followers to place broadsides in the area of a terrorist act immediately after its occurrence in an attempt to make the bombing "speak" in the ways desired by its perpetrators. Most also was one of the first to appreciate that mass media and modern communication systems meant that terrorist actions would immediately be known, discussed, and therefore discursively repeated all over the world.[93] The Chicago newspapers edited by Parsons and Spies also played a large role in generating this publicity. Lavishing praise on the rash of terrorist incidents that occurred in Europe during the early 1880s, they repeatedly extolled the perpetrators as revolutionary heroes,[94] thereby threatening that terrorism could and would happen in America as well. As Fielden, speaking in 1885 about a recent terrorist act in Germany, concretely put it, "I hope soon to see a few Liskas [*sic*] . . . in the United States, to put out of the way a few of the tools of capital."[95]

From a position of political desperation, terrorism's proponents in 1880s Chicago derided words as feeble agents of change while somewhat naively propounding dynamite's perceived substitution of force for discourse. Yet at other moments they grasped the often symbiotic relationships between words and power, publicity and dominance. Indeed, the terrorist threat itself —so often uttered and so often derided as mere words by Chicago's anarchists—most clearly embodies the precipitous power of language. I have already suggested why a perceived need to entirely overturn the material and discursive organization of American capitalism led to a devaluation of words and a reification of "force," but the sheer repetition of apocalyptic warnings in 1880s Chicago suggests the threat's capacity to be an act of public terrorism in and of itself.

In retrospect, we, like Americans of 1886, still do not know whether the threats and promises regularly issued by Chicago's radicals were meant to have genuine predictive force or were strategic bluffs and rhetorical feints, verbal analogues of an advance-and-retreat strategy. Samuel Fielden, for instance, proposed the latter interpretation at his trial. He claimed that his exhortations to his Haymarket listeners to "throttle the law" were only meant metaphorically: "If you take the metaphors from the English language, you have no language at all. It is not necessary, your honor, that because a man says 'throttle the law' he means 'kill the policemen.' "[96] As Fielden's testimony demonstrates, the threat, as a statement of purpose, is a linguistic genre particularly open to fear-generating rhetorical manipulation because it can never be determined in advance whether it was intended literally. And herein lies its power as a signifying act. As long as the predicted outcome appears within the broad range of the possible, the very absence of a bombing produces the destabilizing terror of uncertainty and unpredictability. Suggesting that at any moment terror could slip from the anticipatory and imagined variety to the random "administ[ration of] instant death, by any and all means, to any and every person,"[97] the threat exploits our fears of chance and contingency to generate widespread public intimidation.

In the era of mass communication emerging at the time of the Haymarket bombing, the efficacy of the terrorist threat was multiplied exponentially. As we saw in the *Tribune* coverage of the 1885 anarchist demonstration, the Chicago media magnified and sensationalized the danger and the exposure of the bomb threats. Likewise, in a dynamic choreography of bravado and press coverage, Chicago's anarchists took advantage of the media opportunities provided by the large daily newspapers. Spies, for instance, offered an empty bomb casing to a *Chicago Daily News* reporter in January 1886 and instructed him to tell his editor that Chicago's anarchists possessed almost 10,000 bombs identical to the proffered one—only the others were loaded with dynamite. Moreover, in a widely reported incident that would resurface as evidence against him at the trial, Spies, after the Board of Trade rally in 1885, brandished a large stick of dynamite and a lengthy fuse for several press men assembled in his office, suggesting all the while, at least according to the *Tribune*'s reporter, that he had intended to place the dynamite under the Board of Trade if he could have gotten close enough.[98]

Whether Spies was bluffing or speaking seriously is impossible to determine definitively. What we do know is that the culture of threats and menacing promises generated such a state of tension and paranoia in Chicago that a bomb exploding without any claim of responsibility was quickly and overwhelmingly interpreted as a terrorist attack against law and order. In the midst of the virulent postbombing Red Scare, the anarchists' oft-repeated narratives of destruction spun irretrievably out of their control. The mainstream media became a site where citizens were hailed as absent witnesses of a tragedy and as loyal state subjects, rather than a place anarchists could exploit to make themselves appear more powerful than they actually were. And at the trial, the threats became the tool used by the state's attorney to deem the indicted men, in a legal sleight of hand, accessories before the actual fact of the bombing even though neither the bomb thrower's identity nor purpose was known. Though the ambiguity embodied in threats offered a sense of agency and public power to Chicago's relatively disempowered labor radicals by forcing the city's citizens to wait nervously for a seemingly inevitable bomb blast, the trial also made distressingly clear the lengths to which a threatened state would go to seize control of those narratives. Draining the prebombing threats of ambiguity, the show trial accorded the anarchists put the state's full force behind the effort to reduce the anarchists' words to one simple and straightforward narrative, that of anti-American terrorism.

The story of the American state's justifying the execution of four innocent men in a brutal attempt to suppress all other interpretations of the bombing is undoubtedly the most chilling historical narrative that can be gleaned from the Haymarket tragedy. Yet the sheer fact that so many threats, both imagined and real, haunted the scene of execution suggests the impossibility of narrating a watershed event like the Haymarket bombing into a univocal meaning. In other words, the state needed to connect earlier promises of impending violence to particular bodies that could be executed, but the terroristic threats of reprisal at the execution demonstrate that the predictive and anticipatory quality of the threat makes it a genre particularly available for reiteration, even if the promised action has been temporarily forestalled. "Bomb-talking," a rhetorical act that is intimately linked both to how private bodies will be understood in public and to the publicity-generating powers of the mass media, thus suggests why Haymarket's early commentators went to such lengths to manage the bombing's signification in their overwrought conspiratorial narratives. Moreover, this menacing and unstable genre that is so important to Haymarket also encapsulates the reason that such narratives could not exhaust the event's meanings. As we will see in the following chapters, which focus on authors who plot terrorism in their fiction, it is just this rich mix of language's power combined with the pivotal if unstable role of narrative in producing meanings for acts of terrorism that writers of fiction also found to be a fascinating incitement to their own narratives of terror.

CHAPTER TWO

Gendering the Terrorist

Writing, Class Violence, and Gender in Henry James

Much as Chicago and the rest of the United States were staggered by the 1886 Haymarket bombing and the incipient fear of terrorism that emerged from it, London in the 1880s was rocked by a series of frightful bombings and seemingly ubiquitous bomb plots. In October 1883, dynamite was detonated in the Underground, tragically timed to correspond with periods of high traffic volume, and another subway tunnel was bombed in January 1885. February 1884 saw the bombing of Victoria Station, and on 30 May of that year, three nearly simultaneous blasts occurred. Two bombs exploded in St. James's Square, while a third struck at London's most famed symbol of law and order, Scotland Yard. Yet another bomb was discovered in a bag at the base of Trafalgar Square's Nelson monument that same night.[1] Aside from the emotional and psychic burdens to Londoners, the string of dynamite blasts in these years cost England £12,000 in 1884 and £50,000 in 1885 as the country struggled to develop more effective preventative measures and to repair damage.[2]

In the political climate of the period, discussions of terrorism in London routinely attributed an international dimension to the bombings, especially since many Englanders blamed Irish Americans for the blasts.[3] Debates over terrorism thus raged on both sides of the Atlantic in the early 1880s, often dwelling specifically on the supposed connections between European terrorists and their putative American sponsors. The English regularly argued that Americans not only harbored suspected terrorists but also funneled money to Irish terrorists. According to Kenneth Short, terrorist attacks in England were indeed committed by the Fenians, an Irish group agitating for independence from Britain, and were largely organized and financed by Irish immigrants in the United States operating through two militant organizations, Jeremiah O'Donovan Rossa's Skirmishers and the Clan na Gael.[4]

The *London Times* had no doubt that the Irish American Fenians were behind the rash of bombings in 1880s London, including one that *Harper's* labeled a "Dastardly Attempt to Destroy London Bridge."[5] The incident took place on a Saturday evening when the bridge was thick with pedestrian traffic and vehicles. After the explosion, the *Times* railed against the bombers:

> The miscreants who perpetrated this outrage are still at large; but from various circumstances one may presume that they belong to the same Fenian gang who have planned many similar crimes, with a diabolical cunning which seemed always to ensure success, but also with a skulking cowardice which has invariably caused their murderous work to be ill-done. . . . The fact that the destruction of the bridge would have occasioned the slaughter of a great many working men and poor women must be noted in evidence of the purely mischievous and senseless nature of the outrage. . . . There is little doubt that if the explosives used be now of English make the orders for their employment still come from America, where alone money for such a nefarious purpose can be raised.[6]

While the Fenians were blamed for the terrorist assault on London Bridge, their most horrific attack came on 24 January 1885. On that day, the Fenians struck at both the government and the full national symbology of the British empire with three successful and nearly simultaneous dynamite blasts at Westminster Hall, the houses of Parliament, and the Tower of London. Many persons were injured by the blasts, especially in Westminster Hall and the Tower of London, since the bombings occurred on a weekend during peak visiting hours, and the buildings themselves sustained major damage as well.[7] These carefully orchestrated simultaneous explosions sent Londoners into paroxysms of anxiety, fear, and anger directed at the United States. As the aghast *Times* editorialized, "To inspire terror is with the Irish-American enemies of England, as with the Jacobins of the French Revolution, both an end in itself and a means to other ends." While this writer groped for sufficient descriptive terms in the history of the French Terror, the editorialist found the shocking arbitrariness of the blast particularly astounding. Weighing forms of political violence, the *Times* noted that at least the methods of the "Nihilists and Anarchists of the Continent" are "intelligible" because "they go straight to their mark" by targeting rulers and legislators. In contrast, the paper continued (anticipating the *New York Times*'s future condemnation of the 1920 Wall Street bombing), "the Irish-American 'dynamite fiend' chooses, by preference, for the scene of his operations crowds of the labouring classes, of holiday-makers, of ordinary travellers, and sweeps them at random into the meshes of his murderous plot."[8]

As the *Times* was able to conceptualize—but unable to comprehend in this awful moment when public, random bombings were for the first time shocking London—the "dynamite fiend" exploited what is most ghastly about modern terrorism, the fateful dance of chance and innocence that indiscriminately turns everyday citizens into public victims. From our vantage point in the early twenty-first century, where we have lived with the threat of terrorist violence for a century, it is difficult even to get a concrete sense of how deeply dismaying this onslaught of bombings must have been to Londoners in the mid-1880s. Even though Russia's czar had fallen victim to terrorism in 1881, the rapid succession of "dynamite outrages" made it clear that everyday citizens could now also become the random targets of terrorists. Moreover, this conviction on the part of the London press that the bombings were choreographed by Irish Americans represents a specific twist on a common trepidation during the period, one that also played a role in the contemporary analyses of the Chicago Haymarket bombing: the idea of a shadowy and elusive international terrorist network, whether it is presumed to be Irish American, as in this case, Germanic, as in Haymarket, or, as was often the case in 1880s discussions of terrorism, French or Russian.

Henry James, America's most famous expatriate author of the late nineteenth century, who had by the mid-1880s made his home in London for several years, witnessed these bombings and the uproar they created with his signature ability to see many points of view simultaneously. In September 1884, a few months after he had inked a contract to produce *The Princess Casamassima* for the *Atlantic Monthly*, James wrote to his good friend Thomas Sergeant Perry and elaborated on the revolutionary rumblings and cries of social unrest that were then reverberating throughout London: "Nothing *lives* in England to-day but politics. They are all-devouring, & their mental uproar crowds everything out. This is more & more the case; we are evidently on the edge of an enormous political cycle, which will last heaven knows how long. I should hate it more if I didn't also find it interesting. The present political drama can't help being so, in spite of the imbecility of so many of the actors. The air is full of events, of changes, of movement."[9] James articulates a mixture of fascination and wariness that would drive his venture into political fiction when he turned to *The Princess Casamassima* shortly after writing to Perry. *Princess*, serialized in 1885 and released in book form the following year, represents, along with his fictional analysis of feminism and social reform in *The Bostonians,* James's only major literary engagement with contemporary social and political issues.[10]

When James wrote to Perry describing the almost palpable sense of unease and political change that was in the air in 1880s London, much of it created by the wave of bombings occurring in that decade, he was no doubt giving his friend an accurate account of the nervous tension brought on by the recent rash of political violence. Yet, in some ways, James's terrorist fiction is particularly fascinating because it enacts a remarkable series of displacements. Despite the fact that working-class deprivation and anger loom everywhere in the shadows of the plotline, James's model of terrorist violence and revolution is against aristocratic rather than capitalist foes. Moreover, his terrorists are Russian, German, and French rather than the Irish and Irish Americans who were performing terrorist acts throughout London in the 1880s. And most notoriously, he arms his ill-fated terrorist, Hyacinth, with a small pistol rather than with dynamite, the bête noire of the 1880s.

But if James's famous venture into the fiction of terror habitually invokes and distances itself from the late-nineteenth-century politics of violence, a fair amount of the critical attention that *The Princess Casamassima* has received over the last fifty years has been geared in one way or another toward assessing the impact that London's tense atmosphere had on James's plot. For instance, Lionel Trilling, who deserves much credit for resuscitating *Princess* in the middle decades of the twentieth century, argues for "the solid accuracy of James's political detail at every point" and posits that the novel "is a brilliantly precise representation of social actuality." Oscar Cargill similarly writes that James learned much about anarchism and radical politics through his association with Ivan Turgenev and also claims, more or less dubiously, that James read widely on these subjects.[11]

More recent criticism of the novel has shifted its focus away from attempting to gauge the verisimilitude of James's depiction of London's anarchist subculture. Taylor Stoehr and Deborah Esch, for example, focus on Hyacinth's vow to commit a terrorist act in the novel, with Stoehr suggesting that Hyacinth's pledge is more aesthetic than political and Esch, from an Austinian point of view, arguing that the novel may be read "as a mise-en-scène of the 'case' of promising."[12] Mark Seltzer has also famously offered a powerful Foucauldian reading of the book that redefines the form of its politics. Seltzer argues that *Princess* "is a distinctly political novel but that James's analysis of anarchist politics is less significant than the power play that the narrative technique itself enacts" because, aside from the novel's "explicit and local representations of policing power, there is a more discreet kind of policing that the novel engages, a police work articulated precisely along the novel's line of sight" in a "fantasy of surveillance."[13] Additionally, John Carlos Rowe perceptively reads the novel for the "secret complicity" it establishes "between the social utopia imagined by the anarchists and the aristocratic social order of contemporary London."[14] And in powerful revisionary readings of *The Princess Casamassima*'s social and cultural politics, Sara Blair interprets the novel in terms of late-nineteenth-century discourses of race and nation-building, while Wendy Graham has imaginatively and significantly read the novel as a prototypical queer text whose "anarchist melodrama [functions] as a screen for the underlying theme of sexual subversion."[15]

Furthermore, unlike an author such as Joseph Conrad, whose 1907 novel *The Secret Agent* reads like a parody of the theater of the absurd in its broadly drawn caricature of anarchists and would-be terrorists derived from the nineteenth-century criminal phrenology of Cesare Lombroso, James's *Princess Casamassima,* according to Eileen Sypher, more subtly "probes the questions: who becomes an anarchist and why, and what is the cost of such a political commitment both to the individual and to the larger society?"[16] Sypher's notion that James's novel explores both the individual and social stakes of anarchism and political violence is certainly correct. Moreover, to understand *Princess*'s central issues in this way also makes apparent the deep affinities between this novel's project and the cultural discourse about the meanings and possibility for personal agency in an emerging mass culture that were also a significant component of the Haymarket bombing on the other side of the Atlantic in the same year that James published *Princess.* Yet, where Sypher's provocative reading of James's text argues that the novel tries, though ultimately fails, "to contain the threat of individual male anarchists" by making politics hinge on domestic and gender relations with "the woman as a metonym for affection, social stability, and culture,"[17] I suggest instead that *The Princess Casamassima* even more resolutely maps and explores the reasons behind a privileged, upper-class woman's turn to terrorism as a strategy of political action. In other words, while Sypher is right to argue that James cannot think anarcho-terrorism without also thinking gender upheaval, *Princess* more directly and specifically analyzes the possible roles for women in late-nineteenth-century political movements than has been previously recognized.[18]

But while *The Princess Casamassima* tallies the relationship between issues of gender and subterranean political movements, it also, famously, makes this investigation in a literary form that is strikingly uncommon within the Jamesian canon. *Princess,* written in a Zolaesque naturalist literary style to which James would not return, represents the apogee of what Richard Brodhead has termed James's "realist episode."[19] James's exploration of and attempts to master the techniques of the French naturalists, as well as his commentary on his effort written some twenty years later when he appended a preface to the New York edition of *Princess,* are intimately related to his fictional analysis of the roles gender and class play in violent political movements. For James, the socio-political novel portraying that "mental uproar" produced by revolutionary violence hinges on an interwoven interrogation of writing's social consequences and the construction of gender roles within classed identity.

On the one hand, James's deployment of naturalism's programmatic generic emphases—its thick description, density of detail, and Balzacian particularity—operates as a mechanism for containing or holding at bay the possibility for radically divergent and competing interpretations of social and political events. As we saw at Haymarket, during a period when the rapid expansion of the print media meant that events and news were almost instantly available and given increasingly variable interpretations in the media's different forms, including the labor press, the mainstream papers, or staid middle-class serials such as the *Atlantic,* writing novels that were (in the language of James's 1883 notebook) "very characteristic of our social conditions"[20] seemingly offered a way to stabilize social meaning. James, that is, insists on a faith in naturalism's ability to capture reality in words, both at the time of *Princess*'s production and in the later preface. Yet that faith is everywhere belied within *The Princess Casamassima* itself by James's deployment of episodes of writing and interpretation. The novel is saturated with scenes that question the reliability of writing and narration. This occurs most spectacularly in the characterization of Princess Christina Casamassima herself, who surprisingly emerges in this novel as a figure of the naturalist writer[21] and also becomes an object of suspicion and distrust as the narrative progresses.

In *The Princess Casamassima,* a faith in the power of naturalism's ability to render accurately the contemporary social scene, and, more important, to control the interpretive possibilities at stake in the scenes of spectacular violence that were then thundering throughout London, is compromised by James's construction of gender roles. If James cannot think politics without thinking gender in his naturalist-inspired novel, his depiction of (and participation in) patriarchy's limiting of women's roles, even in subterranean and otherwise politically radical groups, destabilizes his politically conservative effort to contain the cultural meanings attributed in the 1880s to an emerging form of political action—dramatic, invisible, and conspiratorially plotted acts of terrorist violence. *Princess Casamassima* is so compelling, then, precisely because its depictions of writing, gender, and classed identity are perpetually at odds with themselves. Political violence fascinates and haunts James in the novel, as does the prospect of revolutionary women. But combining them results in an ultimately incoherent narrative that explores the possible gendered and classed motivations of terrorism only to pull away from the book's politically violent trajectory. Instead, the narrative finally and dramatically punishes the Princess—the book's own figurative naturalist author and would-be revolutionary.

Scripted Identities

James's novels of the mid-1880s mark a decisive departure from the form and technique of his earlier fiction. His painstaking adherence to the thickly textured descriptions of realist prose in *The Princess Casamassima,* the interest in heredity, and the resolutely un-Jamesian move to stitch his work to the contemporary social scene all suggest James's attempt to remake his authorial self, to will himself into being a different sort of writer. Richard Brodhead has put forth a convincing argument that James's move to realism was largely motivated by the determination to make his own indelible mark as a literary giant by emulating the form of Balzac, Zola, and Turgenev. "Its status as the masters' form of work," Brodhead writes, "is what makes realism a privileged style for James."[22] While Brodhead's argument is deft and persuasive, *Princess*'s recurring discussions of writing, the connections it insistently draws between terrorism, writing, and gender, and James's return to an edgy, self-legitimating defense of naturalism in his New York edition preface all indicate that the novel also develops a suggestive relationship between gender, naturalism, and political violence that exceeds a psychodrama of longed-for literary grandeur.

In 1884, the year before *The Princess Casamassima* began to appear in the *Atlantic,* James made a much-noted visit to the European realists working in Paris. Writing to his longtime friend, William Dean Howells, James informed the famous editor and novelist that "I have been seeing something of Daudet, Goncourt, and Zola; and there is nothing more interesting to me now than the effort and experiment of this little group. . . . They do the only kind of work, today, that I respect; and in spite of their ferocious pessimism and their handling of unclean things, they are at least serious and honest."[23] When writing *Princess,* James also sent another famous missive to Thomas Sergeant Perry extolling a Zolaesque excursion he had recently taken to gather firsthand information for his new novel. "I have been all the morning at Millbank prison (horrible place) collecting notes for a fiction scene. You see I am quite the Naturalist. Look out for the same—a year hence," James cheekily wrote.[24]

James's emphasis on his field research is worth pressing here. When he came to write the preface to *The Princess Casamassima* for the monumental New York edition some twenty years after the book's initial publication, James would again invoke his note taking as a way of assuring representational accuracy:

> My notes then . . . were exactly my gathered impressions and stirred perceptions, the deposit in my working imagination of all my visual and all my constructive sense of London. The very plan of my book had in fact directly confronted me with the rich principle of the Note, and was to do much to clear up, once for all, my practical view of it. If one was to undertake to tell tales and to report with truth on the human scene, it could be but because "notes" had been from the cradle the ineluctable consequence of one's greatest inward energy: to take them was as natural as to look, to think, to feel, to recognize, to remember, as to perform any act of understanding.[25]

Millicent Bell has argued that James is largely being ironic here, that his method is both redolent of the French naturalists' methods and a denial of them in what is actually a more impressionistic technique.[26] Yet James's formulation is especially intriguing insofar as it creates an unbroken and "natural" circuit between the physical sensation of looking, the mental acts of thinking, recognizing, and understanding, and the literary work of depicting "the human scene" with "truth." The upshot of his ideas is a flattening out of any mediation by the act of writing on the depiction of the social scene, so that looking, interpreting, and writing are all versions of the same action. By suggesting that written representation possesses this unmediated relation to the social, James eerily reproduces the discourse of the period's terrorists as well. They, too, claimed that the political message of their bombs was readily apparent without the mediation of language and rhetoric.[27]

James's preface, however, provides another gloss on his naturalist-inspired literary research, since he goes on to claim that "notes had been in other words the things one couldn't *not* take."[28] This negative definition of note taking bears a striking similarity to James's definition of the "real" (as opposed to "romance") in the preface to the New York edition of *The American,* where he writes that "the real represents to my perception the things we cannot possibly *not* know, sooner or later, in one way or another."[29] In the prefaces to these two novels, then, "notes" and "realism" become two forms of the same knowledge, as each represents the cultural and social information that we cannot avoid encountering. Indeed, access to the real appears here almost like a form of the "electric" or automatic writing that infatuated many of James's literary contemporaries. According to the prefaces, the social world flows neatly and unproblematically into notes and realism without a sense of boundaries or mediation.

Such a configuration may initially seem odd for an author who spent so much time exploring the nuances of perspective and representation, but the stakes of James's prefaces can be made clearer by juxtaposing them with the analysis of writing and gender that he offers in *The Princess Casamassima* itself. Although the link James makes between the real, his note taking, and his literary art appears remarkably untroubled in his prefaces, *The Princess Casamassima* offers a more complex and contradictory depiction of language and representation. In *Princess,* scenes proliferate where writing is considered a dangerous and unreliable genre. What makes this particular narrative paradox so interesting is not simply its contradictory relation to the preface James appended some twenty years later, but rather the way that he ties these questions about writing and representation directly to his conceptions of gender and gender roles in *The Princess Casamassima.*

This issue can initially be approached via Hyacinth Robinson, James's androgynously named protagonist. As critics have frequently noted, Hyacinth is a character who can be usefully understood by way of his relation to writing. On the one hand, he is a bookbinder, which gives him a metonymic relationship to writing and at least a tangential relationship to the production of art. Hyacinth, for instance, considers bookbinding to be "one of the fine arts."[30] And if not exactly high art, bookbinding in the 1880s was a vocation that had to that point largely managed to avoid the industrializing pressures of capitalism's turn to the techniques of mass production, leaving the bookbinding trade for the most part a zone of at least artisanal production.[31] But James's character also desires to leave his craftsman's tools behind. He repeatedly declares his own personal and surprising "dream of literary distinction" (112) and wishes to make a "transition — into literature" because "to bind the book, charming as the process might be, was after all much less fundamental than to write it" (403–4). Hyacinth's dream of attaining the proprietary laurels capitalist society offers to those it identifies as solitary geniuses is clearly at odds with his professed communitarian politics. Beyond this, his sensitivity and aspiration for literary fame have also prompted critics to point out the similarities between the bookbinder and James himself, and to suggest further that Hyacinth is in many respects an autobiographical character.[32]

That the artist manqué Hyacinth is in some respects a figure for James seems both likely and important. Nevertheless, the generally unremitting focus on Hyacinth in character studies of James's novel misses an equally important aspect of the novel. The Princess Casamassima can herself be seen as a female version of the naturalist novelist in the text who wants to be guided by the lower-class Hyacinth "into the slums—into very bad places" (253). Embodying the blend of sensationally prurient curiosity and desire for knowledge that is conjured up by naturalist authors' documentary practices, the Princess "wanted to know the *people*, and know them intimately—the toilers and strugglers and sufferers—because she was convinced they were the most interesting portion of society" (248, emphasis original). In her dizzying addiction to foreign sights and smells, she "can't leave them alone" because, as she tells Hyacinth, "they press upon me, they haunt me, they fascinate me" (248). The Princess here seems suspended between a claustrophobic aversion to the poor befitting her title and a need, as she puts it at one point, "to get out of [her]self" (256) by vicariously experiencing—or colonizing—the lives of London's poor.

The Princess goes so far in her attempts to experience the existence of London's poorer citizens that she ultimately abandons her wealthy home and moves to the devastatingly poor neighborhood of Madeira Crescent. Somewhat disingenuously, she sets up a home among a constituency of the poor and unemployed, taking delight in her new street's "soiled, dusty expression" that "possessed in combination every quality which should have made it detestable to [her]" (417). And while Princess Casamassima takes a certain gratification from her apparently reduced situation in life, she obtains the most pleasure from the abandonment of carriages in favor of "walk[ing] everywhere now" (415). "Deriving extreme diversion" from the notion that she now belongs to London's aggrieved poor, the Princess develops a taste for strolling about the seedier districts "look[ing] into the windows of vulgar establishments, and amus[ing] herself with picking out abominable objects that she should like to possess" (418). She also "profess[es] a curiosity to see the inside of a public-house" and other working-class haunts (419), as well as "queer types and . . . out-of-the-way social corners" generally (458).

The Princess's desire to move among and get to know the city's lower classes intriguingly anticipates a whole genre of what Eric Schocket has termed "class-transvestite narratives" that appeared in American and British publications during the 1890s. Jack London famously dressed the part of a London tramp for his book *The People of the Abyss,* Josiah Flynt's *Tramping with Tramps* was enormously successful, and Walter Wyckoff's two-year incognito wanderings from New Jersey to the Pacific resulted in *The Workers: An Experiment in Reality.* Similarly, Nellie Bly and Annie Laurie popularized this undercover form of class exploration for readers of the *San Francisco Examiner* and *New York World,* as they investigated factories and urban hospitals while in disguise.[33] As Schocket has noted about these episodes of class passing that depend on sartorial and behavioral mimicry of working-class identities, they unhinge shared class identity from a common economic exploitation. Economic relations are replaced by the cultural signifiers of classed identity, including clothing, housing, and speech.[34] This early example of class passing is possible in James's novel and in these later nonfictional episodes because class difference is perceived as both dichotomous and appropriable, that is, as a system of learnable signs rather than a material reality.[35]

Class passing's dependence on highly demarcated signs of class difference reaffirms class distinctions, even as it also suggests the permeability of the border between the classes. In James's novel, the Princess's class passing forms one part of a larger concern over class identity. It is fair to say that *Princess Casamassima* is obsessed with a person's ability to become someone he or she is not and with calibrating the effects of this transformation. Indeed, James is very concerned with nailing down notions of class identity and separating the authentic from the forged, yet the book at every turn nonetheless suggests a worry that such "truths" are slipping irretrievably out of grasp. This is most apparent, of course, in Hyacinth's character, and much of the novel revolves around whether the aristocratic or revolutionary side of his personality will ultimately win out. Hyacinth imagines "a hundred different theories of his identity" (166), but Paul Muniment, his radical friend who nonetheless acts more like a petit bourgeois, believes that he has a firmer grasp on the young bookbinder's identity. He tells Hyacinth at one point that the young man is nothing but "a duke in disguise" (445). Hyacinth himself believes that "he was to go through life in a mask, in a borrowed mantle; he was to be, every day and every hour, an actor" (109), though his mind changes frequently about which part of his self is real and which is mere masquerade.

Hyacinth, however, is hardly alone in this ambiguity over identity. Awe-stricken, he demands to know whether or not Paul is "the genuine article" (296) after an encounter with the "blast of imbecility" and "inane phrase[s]" (280) that other would-be radicals frequently spit out in the revolutionaries' meetings. Meanwhile, Captain Sholto, whom Hyacinth meets at these same underground meetings, turns out to be a gentlemanly aristocrat who dabbles in radical politics only to please Princess Casamassima. And beyond radical politics, the ambiguity of classed identity surfaces as an element of almost every character in the novel. For instance, Millicent Henning, Hyacinth's childhood friend who returns as a well-dressed young woman, is only a shop girl. Her work as a live dress model in a department store, in which her very job is to perform fantasies of enticingly different identities for wealthy customers, helps her develop an infectious, if implicitly unreal, "show-room laugh" (99) and a demeanor that make her appear more cosmopolitan than her economic station would seem to warrant. Like Theodore Dreiser's Carrie Meeber—but better educated in the period's emerging consumer culture—Millicent, with her "bracelets of imitation silver" (388), also wears cheap replicas of more expensive apparel that simulate a higher class status. On the opposite end of the class scale, Lady Aurora, the novel's most legitimate aristocrat, has "few of the qualities of her caste" (136) and could not care less about the trappings of aristocracy. Notwithstanding her class position, she exists to serve the poor and spends much time looking after Muniment's invalid sister, Rosy. And Rosy, despite being unable to leave her flat, paradoxically "know[s] more about London" (217) than anyone else. Furthermore, Hyacinth's shabbily genteel neighbor, Mr. Vetch, a fiddler, has "the nerves, the sensibilities of a gentleman" but works in a dilapidated theater and has "blasphemous republican, radical views" (67). Yet Hyacinth is also warned by a coworker about the "middle-class spy" because "there were a great many who looked a good deal like" the fiddler, though Vetch himself is apparently not a member of that "infamous brotherhood" of class spies (124).

Over and over in *Princess Casamassima,* James's characters threaten to turn out to be something other than what they initially appear to be. These contradictory and dissonant class identities metaphorically represent the contradictions of the late nineteenth century's capitalizing economy. And in addition to the discontinuities of capitalism, the characters' unstable and mysterious identities also generalize in the novel an important aspect of terrorism, that is, the anxiety and fear generated by the fact that anyone could be a terrorist in disguise. In James's terms, a princess or a bookbinder may also be a terrorist, a fiddler may be a radical, a "lady" may be a shop girl, a chemist could be an anarchist, or a scruffy radical may be only a poseur. Perhaps this is James's brilliant understanding of the chameleon-like qualities of terrorists. Generalizing this logic throughout the novel highlights the suspicion and culture of distrust that living in fear of sudden violence, as Londoners were in the 1880s, can create. Yet this uneasiness over the ambiguities of identity also produces a panic that results in the novel's harsh climax. Hyacinth's inability to reconcile his bifurcated class position emerges as the direct cause of his suicide. Unable to make a choice between radical and conservative ideologies, Hyacinth can only turn his gun on himself. Similarly, the narrative relentlessly forces the Princess back into her univocal role as a politically inactive wife at the novel's end, thus dramatically lopping off all but the most traditional social role for her as an aristocratic woman. For James, narratives of class passing and the possibility of mistaken identity ultimately become places where classed and gendered subjectivity can be reaffirmed rather than questioned. As the novel reaches its climax, James sacrifices his ambiguous characters to a narrative desire for more unitary and self-evident selfhood that is not mistakable for something else.

But intriguingly, the ambiguities of the Princess's particular trip down the sartorial and geographic scale of classed identity in the novel also start to make it apparent that James himself may have been involved in a case of something like mistaken identity as he wrote this novel. James, the personally well-liked author who was well settled in a comfortable apartment with a twenty-one-year lease by 1885,[36] was also, at other moments, venturing forth into London's seedier districts as the would-be naturalist writer in search of working-class experiences. Of course, James's novelistic descriptions of the Princess's downward mobility nevertheless point readers toward a critique of her bohemian slumming and radical chic, dramatically differentiating her working-class adventures from those of more proper, investigative novelists. The scenes we looked at earlier encourage us to laugh at her foibles along with Hyacinth, who wryly notes that even in her supposedly reduced conditions the Princess is unable to dispense with a particularly fetching "pair of immaculate gloves" (413).

However, Princess Casamassima's sudden penchant for walking is especially fascinating insofar as it bears a surprisingly close affinity to James's own self-described nighttime strolls through London's working-class districts as he looked for the raw material of urban night life and examples of Londoners' speeches that he would churn into fictional form. As James writes in his preface,

> The simplest account of the origin of "The Princess Casamassima" is, I think, that this fiction proceeded quite directly, during the first year of a long residence in London, from the habit and the interest of walking the streets. . . . The prime idea was unmistakably the ripe round fruit of perambulation. . . . "Subjects" and situations, character and history, the tragedy and comedy of life, are things of which the common air, in such conditions, seems pungently to taste; and to a mind curious, before the human scene, of meanings and revelations the great grey Babylon easily becomes, on its face, a garden bristling with an immense illustrative flora.[37]

Reproducing the exoticizing rhetoric of popular nineteenth-century urban exploration narratives, James here imagines himself as a neophyte in the mysterious and fascinating urban jungle. Yet this account of *Princess*'s genesis, which again makes it appear that the translation from observation to writing is both simple and straightforward, seems to be a beguiling bit of revisionary history or, at best, a false memory on James's part. When James was in the thick of writing the novel in the mid-1880s, he agonized that this "long-winded" and "beastly" book was doggedly "panting at [his] heels." Even well into the novel's lengthy serialization in the *Atlantic*, James worried privately that the story's "future evolution" was far from "clear to myself" and, more ominously, lamented, "I have never yet become engaged in a novel in which, after I had begun to write and send off my MS., the details had remained so vague."[38] The discrepancy between James's anguished remarks in the 1880s and the exploration narrative that he conjures up in the preface signals his attempt—even twenty years later—to write himself, as Brodhead argues, into the group of master European naturalists who claimed to proceed by careful documentation of the social scene.

However, if James's perambulations and investigations into the "great grey Babylon" of London are meant to signify his kinship with the masters of European naturalism, the Princess Casamassima's very similar behavior indicates something far different in his novel. As we have seen in the scenes where Hyacinth smirks at her affectations, the Princess's naturalist slumming is a mark of her disingenuousness. Further, her inability to convince others that her assumption of a poor lifestyle is sincere bears a close relationship to her inability to generate any faith in her revolutionary zeal among her anarcho-terrorist associates. Indeed, it is even suggested at several points that she may be a spy in the pay of the police (327, 497, 579). Since the Princess's actions make her into a metaphorical figure of the naturalist author, yet she is also represented as dangerously untrustworthy, we might also say that by extension, and contrary to what James sets out in his preface, writing itself is not to be trusted either in this novel. The key difference between James's preface and the novel itself is the difference of gender.

Of course, linking a distrust in writing with terrorist conspiracies was a standard plot trope in turn-of-the-century books featuring conspiratorial agitators, such as G. K. Chesterton's 1908 novel *The Man Who Was Thursday* and Jack London's 1910 work, *The Assassination Bureau*. In these texts, writing regularly functions as the mechanism by which private conspiracies are violated and made public before the plotted action has occurred. In other words, while terrorism does not exist without a concomitant discourse of publicity, as we saw in the last chapter, it is precisely the terrorist's ability to control when the gap between private plotting and public action is bridged that creates the tense anxiety and apparently unpredictable randomness that the terrorist violently exploits.

In James's *The Princess Casamassima*, this fear of publicity at the wrong moment and concomitant distrust of writing's potential to publicize private plots routinely redounds upon the Princess herself. For instance, in a pivotal scene in which she means to indicate the depth of her conspiratorial knowledge to the novel's most credible revolutionary, Paul Muniment,

> the Princess drew a small folded letter from her pocket, and, without saying anything, held it out to him. He got up to take it from her, opened it, and, as he read it, remained standing in front of her. Then he went straight to the fire and thrust the paper into it. At this movement she rose quickly, as if to save the document, but the expression of his face, as he turned round to her, made her stop. . . . "What are you afraid of?" she asked. "I take it the house is known. If we go, I suppose we may admit that we go." Muniment's face showed that he had been annoyed, but he answered, quietly enough, "No writing—no writing." (497)

In her effort—yet again—to convince a revolutionary of her sincerity, the Princess is here linked to the written word and made the unfortunate agent of publicity in such a way that writing, gender difference, and the uncovering of conspiratorial plots all converge in a tangle of suspicious activity. Writing and vicariously experiencing working-class life thus become markers of gender and a sign of female duplicity in the text. Conversely, James, who also carefully observed and noted the sartorial and speech habits of London's working-class citizens while strolling through the town in a conscious attempt to mimic Zola's techniques of literary production, makes clear in his preface that for him writing functions as a way to chart and "master contemporary life in all its social variety and physical particularity."[39] Or, as Zola put it, "The goal of the experimental [Naturalist] method . . . is to study phenomena in order to control them."[40]

James's self-professed penchant for naturalism during this period cannot be divorced from his reactions to the contemporary British social scene, which found him baffled but intrigued by the startling array of interpretations that could be applied to the tumultuous political climate engendered by the dynamite campaign of the early 1880s. And if James's interest in naturalism is at least partially motivated by his Zolaesque desire to conjure narrative's power to structure interpretations of the social scene via the thick detail of literary representation, then I would suggest that the Princess's metaphorical position as a figure of a (female) naturalist writer destabilizes those attempts to control social meanings through naturalism. In other words, while the surprising title of this novel suggests that James cannot imagine revolutionary politics without also thinking gender difference, his discrediting of the Princess as a revolutionary follows directly from his making her, in many important respects, a female version of his own authorial self.

The Terrorist Princess

In the novel, then, the Princess Casamassima finds herself in a double bind wherein she is unable to convince anyone of her revolutionary sincerity but is dissuaded by her coconspirators from taking any public action to demonstrate her good faith. For instance, Muniment, as we have seen, lashes out at her desire to proclaim openly her participation in anarcho-terrorist meetings (497). Yet the Princess also wishes to do more than simply attend fiery clandestine gatherings. As she somewhat melodramatically avows to Muniment, "'I want to help you,' . . . and as she made this earnest appeal her face became transfigured; it wore an expression of the most passionate yet the purest longing. 'I want to do something for the cause you represent; for the millions that are rotting under our feet—the millions whose whole life is passed on the brink of starvation, so that the smallest accident pushes them over. Try me, test me; ask me to put my hand to something, to prove that I am as deeply in earnest as those who have already given proof. . . . I am not playing. No, I am not playing'" (453). The Princess goes on to express her desire to commit, in Hyacinth's place, the terrorist deed to which he pledged himself before undergoing a change of heart regarding his rashly spoken vow. As she breathlessly claims, "I should like to do it in his place—that's what I should like" (454). Princess Casamassima's wish or choice to commit a terrorist act dramatically expresses her desire to be taken seriously as a revolutionary. John Carlos Rowe finds this request too individualistic on the Princess's part and suggests that she confuses "sympathy and domination, philanthropy and narcissism, charity and will to power."[41] Rowe may be correct that the Princess has not yet grasped the communal politics of revolt that could shake industrial capitalism. But because she is the only woman depicted among the novel's many male revolutionaries, this scene again focuses our attention on the fact that James is interested not only in why someone might turn to terrorism but also, in particular, in why a woman might wish to become a terrorist in the late nineteenth century.

James's construction of this melodramatic scene in which Christina claims a desire to perform terrorist violence is especially intriguing for the way it both clings to and subverts traditional patriarchal notions of femininity and "women's work." The scene is typically conservative in the motivations it gives to the Princess, since her desire to act in Hyacinth's stead is also the stereotypically feminine desire to protect and nurture. Sensing that the delicate Hyacinth is unable to protect himself from the consequences of his impulsive vow, Christina wants simply to protect the immature and much less worldly bookbinder. Yet her desire to shelter him by proposing such a dangerous and criminal action also disrupts the almost maternal image the scene initially sets out. To say the least, her proposal that she accept his assignment to perform cold-blooded murder undermines the nineteenth-century cult of true womanhood's emphasis on women's domestic role as providers of succor and comfort within the safe and private confines of the Victorian home.[42]

Indeed, James's depiction of the Princess as stronger and more willing than Hyacinth to commit violence puts his characterization of her into dialogue with a facet of late-nineteenth-century culture that fascinated, horrified, and titillated the era's readers: the specter of terrorism orchestrated and performed by women. Much of the period's journalism about female terrorists is patronizing, and the newspaper reports often make space for details about a female terrorist's attractiveness or lack thereof (the corollary in reports about men was a focus on their seemingly visible rabidity).[43] Yet the role of women in the era's political upheavals also carried a large amount of political freight because it put an especially nefarious spin on contemporary conflicts about the period's so-called woman question and the attendant debates regarding women's roles in public, in politics, and in the professional workplace that were summarized in the popular phrase of the period, "New Woman."[44]

During the time that James was living in London, preparing to write and then drafting his novel of political terrorism, the interpenetration of gender roles and violence became an especially combustible concern in the New World as well. This was especially true within Chicago's fraught social scene during the years leading up to the Haymarket bombing of 1886. Although I left this element of Haymarket largely unexplored in the preceding chapter's analysis of the rhetoric produced to explain the bombing, I want to pick up this thread now as a way to gloss the cultural work performed by James's own simultaneous concerns with gender and terrorism.

In Haymarket, notions of "manliness" became a crucial trope used in the rhetoric of both the men accused of throwing the Haymarket bomb and their accusers. The anarchists attacked their antagonists' masculine honor by charging that the police acted as sexual predators toward disempowered and frightened working-class women.[45] On the other hand, those commentators who sympathized with the prosecution, such as police captain Michael Schaack, argued that the anarchists angrily denounced American society but then cowardly looked to their female coconspirators for protection. As a corollary to what his book portrays as this disgraceful gender reversal in which women protect men, Schaack also labeled female anarchists, whom he regarded as more bloodthirsty than their male counterparts, the "'red' sisterhood" of "squaws."[46] For Schaack, unruly women were the most baleful force behind male anarchists. Schaack stands in here for a whole host of commentators who apparently could not envision what they deemed an inappropriate political stance in the late nineteenth century without also tying it to the breakdown of other cultural codes and paradigms.

Indeed, while the rhetoric of gender roles served as a shorthand for both anarchists and police to understand each other's actions, behind this rhetoric, as Schaack's concern with anarchist "squaws" intimates, exists the prominent involvement of many women in the anarchist movement, despite the fact that only men were hanged for the Chicago Haymarket bombing. Lucy Parsons, wife of the condemned anarchist Albert Parsons, is exemplary in this regard.[47] An extremely visible presence in Chicago's anarchist circles, Lucy Parsons was the author of the notorious essay, "A Word to Tramps," which was read into evidence at the Chicago Haymarket trial. In that article, which I briefly outlined in the preceding chapter, she counseled would-be suicide victims not to waste their deaths in a solitary act but instead to commit a suicide bombing in Chicago's wealthiest neighborhoods. And using a favorite rhetorical trick of anarchists that simply reversed the standard or received meaning of dominant cultural icons, Parsons both invoked and revised the meaning of "The Star-Spangled Banner" when she encouraged tramps to let "the red glare of destruction" be their lasting mark. Altering the eventual anthem's image of rockets' "red glare" that had inspired Francis Scott Key, Parsons's language violently condemns the United States for leaving available only an ironic or outright antagonistic relationship to the ideological shibboleths celebrated in official cultural forms such as the national anthem and the flag.

Michael Schaack's textual history of Haymarket thus demonstrates one way a discourse of gender was used to stigmatize both radical politics and women in the bombing's aftermath. Equally important, Lucy Parsons's aggressive calls for dynamite bombings in the period immediately before the Haymarket affair disrupt a patriarchal notion that the sphere of public political violence is necessarily gendered male. But while Lucy Parsons encouraged her down-and-out readers to commit spectacular acts of violence, the specific issue of a woman performing those terrorist deeds was also raised repeatedly by acts committed in Europe during the early 1880s, the years in which James was gathering information for *The Princess Casamassima*.

London's newspaper and magazine readers during the 1870s and 1880s were made well aware of many women directly involved with terrorism and assassination. The British press was especially intrigued by women terrorists in Russia. The dual fascinations of gender and national difference provided a means for the press to exoticize and distance political troubles that nevertheless had their analogues in Britain's own political milieu. In 1878 the press widely reported and sensationalized the assassination of a powerful Russian general by a woman named Vera Zasulich. In 1879 another woman, Sofia Perovskaya, "scion of a noble family," played an instrumental role in an unsuccessful attempt to blow up the Russian czar's train. While she and her fellow terrorists tunneled under the railroad track where the czar's train was scheduled to pass, Perovskaya encouraged her coconspirators to dig faster by brandishing a revolver in the direction of a vial of nitroglycerine that she threatened to ignite by gunfire, killing them all if necessary. And in 1884, the "not very good-looking" Mary Kaloojny drew a gun from the recesses of her petticoat and fired straight into the face of a Russian officer.[48] Also in 1884, the *Cornhill* magazine printed a lengthy essay titled "A Female Nihilist." This piece, written under the pseudonym "Stepniak" by a Russian terrorist-author named S. M. Kravchinskii, who was also responsible for several violent potboilers, detailed the life and eventual arrest of another Russian terrorist named Olga Liubatovitch. The essay is intriguing for the way it both resists and simultaneously upholds women's traditional social roles. Stepniak devotes much of the article to detailing Liubatovitch's hair-raising escapades and evasions of the Russian police. Yet he ultimately transforms his account into just another female romance plot as Liubatovitch, who had vowed that "love was a clog upon revolutionary activity," is nevertheless "vanquished by the invincible" and falls in love with another young Nihilist.[49] Liubatovitch's revolutionary career is foreclosed when she is captured while trying to rescue her husband from the police after he also has been apprehended. This outcome bears a culturally significant resemblance to James's own fictional plot in *Princess,* since, as we will see, James also ultimately reduces his storyline to a tangled love plot.

But while Stepniak finally transforms his article about a female terrorist into a love story, he also intriguingly ends by suggesting to his readers that this particular representation of "a female Nihilist" is in no way singular: "Such is the story, the true story, of Olga Liubatovitch. Of Olga Liubatovitch, do I say? No—of hundreds and hundreds of others. I should not have related it had it not been so."[50] In the uneasy political climate of 1880s England, this final line carries forth the suggestion to the *Cornhill*'s middle-class readers that many more terrorists in general, and female terrorists in particular, are at large than they might wish to believe. And in this, Stepniak's remarks again offer a parallel to James's novel. In a scene that has long vexed the *Princess*'s critics, Paul Muniment carefully explains to Hyacinth Robinson that the revolutionists' "game must be now to frighten society, and frighten it effectually; to make it believe that the swindled classes were at last fairly in league—had really grasped the idea that, closely combined, they would be irresistible. They were not in league, and they hadn't in their totality grasped any idea at all—Muniment was not slow to make that equally plain. All the same, society was scareable, and every great scare was a gain for the people" (292).

Powerful readers of James such as John Carlos Rowe have indicted Muniment here, and the picture of the terrorist plot in general that the novel presents, for its aestheticization of politics. Rowe reads Muniment's speech as a disingenuous act of bad faith that neither presents terrorism as a cataclysmic and "objectified form of violence that is the equivalent of the culture's buried contradictions" nor "offer[s] a utopian ideal as the revolutionary will toward transvaluation."[51] According to this logic, Muniment presents a simple picture of a public deluded by an illusory but seemingly massive and invisible conspiracy. What Rowe's critique misses, and what is pivotal to both Stepniak's article and this scene from *Princess*—and we saw this at Haymarket too—is that the feigning, bluffing, dissembling threat that Muniment proposes here is not political bad faith but a central operating tenet of terrorism itself. Crisscrossing the border between public and private, or visible and invisible, terrorists create fear—and thus power in the public realm—precisely by making it appear that they have the wherewithal to explode a bomb at any time and any place. Where Rowe suggests that James "indicts" the terrorist plot in *Princess*,[52] apparently because that plot is a forgery of what Rowe would consider a real revolutionary politics, I would argue instead that James, at least at this key moment, reveals a keen understanding of how relatively disempowered groups try to gain power through the bluffing threat of violence and the manipulation of public versus private spaces.

While James's novel offers a sophisticated rendering of how visibility and invisibility can function politically, Stepniak's "A Female Nihilist" glosses this division in terms of work. Stepniak writes that "a Nihilist who thoroughly determines to conceal himself can never be found. He falls into the hands of the police only when he returns to active life."[53] Stepniak's usage of the masculine pronoun is of course conventional, yet it is still fascinating since he is discussing Olga Liubatovitch. But more important, his usage of "active life," by which he means terrorist acts, to broker the border between public and private is particularly fraught in an 1884 discussion of female terrorists. On the one hand, women such as Olga Liubatovitch or Lucy Parsons who were committed to political violence not only pressured traditional ideas concerning women's involvement in political discourse and the types of work they could perform, they also, at a more theoretical level, reconfigured the boundary between public and private that imagined women as private caregivers and men as workers in the public marketplace.

Contemporary discussions of female terrorists thus often drew many anxiety-causing elements of fin de siècle Western culture into an explosive mixture of revolutionary violence and politically minded public women. This discussion of women who actively chose to participate in terrorist violence also throws more light on James's characterization of the Princess Casamassima. Unlike the historical actors Parsons or Liubatovitch, and crucially also unlike Hyacinth Robinson in James's novel, Christina Casamassima is never allowed the opportunity to follow through on her expressed desire to perform a terrorist act. Indeed, the novel's pivotal moment comes at the end of Book Two when Hyacinth, disgusted at the disingenuous revolutionary palaver spewed out by his pseudoradical colleagues, bursts forth with his vow to commit a terrorist act: "I'm not afraid; I'm very sure I'm not. I'm ready to do anything that will do any good; anything, anything—I don't care a rap. In such a cause I should like the idea of danger. I don't consider my bones precious in the least, compared with some other things" (294).[54] The remainder of the novel, then, works out the consequences that follow from Hyacinth's willful abandonment of society's laws in favor of his avowed terrorist destruction. But the scene of his pledge is crucial for more than just its depiction of a quintessential terrorist moment or its implications for the rest of the book, after Hyacinth has decided that he would much prefer to back away from his vow. Significantly, Hyacinth partakes here of a privilege traditionally allotted to men under patriarchy, that is, being able to make a positive choice from among several options. Women under patriarchy—and James's novel follows form in his characterization of the Princess—are accorded only a negative choice, the ability to say no to an offered proposal rather than the option to follow through on an active desire.

This is, of course, most clear in the logic and language of a marriage proposal, in which, at a theoretical level, men have the option of surveying the field of possible mates, while women are only presented with the option of saying yes or no to an individually offered proposal from a man who has already made a positive choice. And perhaps not surprisingly, the negative logic of a marriage proposal plays a decisive role in the Princess's development. The roots of the constricted options available to her in *The Princess Casamassima* can be traced directly back to her first appearance in James's fiction. Christina, who is the only major character to appear in more than one of James's books, played an important part in his early novel, *Roderick Hudson*. In that novel, among other things, James narrates her transformation from a young American woman, Christina Light, to the unhappy wife of the Prince Casamassima. In *Roderick Hudson* the proud but, as we eventually find out, illegitimate Christina Light is forced by her mother's "cruel" pressure to submit to a marriage with the "ugly," "sallow," and "extremely bored" but fabulously wealthy Prince Casamassima.[55] Though Christina flirts boldly with Roderick Hudson throughout the novel, may also be attracted to Hudson's patron, Rowland Mallet (374), and at one point dramatically commits the "great crime" of breaking off her engagement to the Prince (298), she nevertheless is ultimately allowed only the negative choice of rejecting or "accept[ing] the more brilliant *parti*" (204) with the Italian nobleman. As Christina's aged chaperone, Madame Grandoni, informs the Prince when he ventures to London to take back his wife in *The Princess Casamassima,* "The Princess considers that in the darkest hour of her life she sold herself for a title and a fortune" (259). The commodifying language is telling here. While the Princess's action is presented as a choice she has made, James is careful to make clear the repugnance of a choice between the poverty of illegitimacy and an awful marriage match. For the Princess, accepting the Prince is tantamount to selling her very selfhood, as she is made to bend her desires to accommodate those of her husband.

That Christina Light is initially reluctant but ultimately coerced into marrying the rather insufferable Prince is pivotal to understanding her role in James's later novel that bears her titular name. In *Roderick Hudson,* her illegitimacy is the trump card that compels her to marry the Prince against her will rather than "knock under to a revelation — to humiliation" (319). The stakes of her dilemma in *Roderick Hudson* are succinctly described in the appropriately ungrammatical phrasing of Madame Grandoni. When told by Rowland Mallet that Christina has accepted the Prince, she queries in return: "Christina was forced to decide then that she could not afford not to be a princess?" (318). The double negative construction of Madame Grandoni's question and her mercantile language again underscore the textual fact that Christina is allowed no choice at all, not even the small compensation that might be granted by a right of refusal.

Of course, Christina Light nonetheless finds herself in a relatively enviable position. The confines of traditional gender roles that Madame Grandoni identifies as the reasons standing behind Christina's ultimate willingness to accept the Prince are accompanied by the significant freedom seemingly to be gained with the class status offered by the Prince's fortune. Yet, when read against her role in *Roderick Hudson,* we can begin to see that Christina's desire in *The Princess Casamassima* to escape the conventions of gendered behavior that would regulate her entry into the political world of anarcho-terrorism stem from the forced bad match with the Prince Casamassima. Moreover, this desire to break with her socially prescribed role is figured in both *Roderick* and *Princess* by the Princess's repetition of a curious desire. As she tells Rowland in *Roderick,* "I would give all I possess to get out of myself" (182). And in *Princess,* she responds to her husband's attempts to force her back to him by bemoaning her fate: "I try to occupy my life, my mind, to create interests, in the odious position in which I find myself; I endeavour to get out of myself, my small personal disappointments and troubles, by the aid of such poor faculties as I possess" (256). In these closely repeated scenes, the Princess registers the power of cultural institutions and ideology to construct subjectivity, as well as the equally powerful yearning to believe that one can make one's own identity. The repetition of the word "possess" is also integral here. Even as the Princess realizes that the interlocking discourses of patriarchy and classed identity provide her with certain freedoms not available to other women who do not share her class privilege, that same patriarchal economy firmly delimits the experiences and social roles available to her. Ultimately, the Princess's desire "to get out of" herself is both the longing to see clearly the social discourses—family, laws, religion, gender—that make us and the wish to be able to break away from them to independently authorize her own identity. And if this latter wish is perhaps always necessary, it is also always futile, as borne out in *Princess* by Christina's final inability to authorize her own subjectivity, to transform herself, that is, from a princess into a terrorist.

Domesticating the Terrorist

If the desire to transcend the cultural discourses that constitute us is ultimately futile, one of the Princess's key insights in the novel, nevertheless, is her appreciation of the interpenetration of class and gender discourses in the construction of subjectivity. Despite the Princess's recalcitrant and risible attachment to her class status, her attempt to escape her class by selling her possessions and moving into the dilapidated house in Madeira Crescent suggests the extent to which the subject position as a nobleman's wife delimits her socially possible identities. And by violating those class boundaries, the move into a working-class neighborhood also specifically strains the gendered constraints on her behavior as a woman. Yet, if Christina's actions in *Princess* make her into a liminal figure in terms of class and gender roles, it is a liminality that is prefigured by the crucial element of her parentage in *Roderick Hudson.* In the earlier novel, we learn that the Italian Cavaliere who attends Christina and her mother is in fact Christina's father (318). The Princess's traversing of cultural boundaries in the latter novel flows directly from her mixed genealogy. Specifically, her mother's implied threat in *Roderick* to "let the skeleton out of the closet and create a panic" (318) by publicizing Christina's mixed blood forces her into accepting the Prince, which leads, in turn, to her rebellion against the gender and class codes that define her subjectivity.

For the Princess, then, her refusal to respect the normative boundaries prescribed by cultural discourses of class and gender is bound up with her liminal position with regard to nationality. And this is particularly interesting insofar as it rather neatly, if somewhat surprisingly, reproduces the social situation of Hyacinth Robinson in *The Princess Casamassima*. Just as the Princess's mixed genealogy is the catalyst that stands behind her gender and class subversions, so too does Hyacinth's notorious class indecisiveness follow directly from his mixed parentage, as James is at pains throughout *Princess* to make clear. The illegitimate son of an English Lord and a French woman of lower origins who murders Hyacinth's father for refusing to acknowledge his paternity, Hyacinth believes "he must either suffer with the people" or "apologize to others . . . for the rich." Moreover, "there were times when he said to himself that it might very well be his fate to be divided, to the point of torture, to be split open by sympathies that pulled him in different ways; for hadn't he an extraordinarily mingled current in his blood[?]" (165). This mixture of French revolutionary fervor and English aristocratic privilege in his veins results both in Hyacinth's pledge to commit a terrorist act and in his ultimate suicide when he cannot bring himself to do the deed.

On the one hand, James's interest in blood and a hereditary taint (Hyacinth refuses to marry because he does not want to pass on "the inheritance which had darkened the whole threshold of his manhood" [105]) again reveals his debt to Zola in the construction of Hyacinth. The plot relentlessly figures this schism in Hyacinth's blood in terms of class, as it works through the double bind created by his allegiance to his working-class heritage and his simultaneous desire to come into what he believes is his rightful aristocratic legacy. And although James may seem much less overtly interested in gender than class in his delineation of Hyacinth's character, the plot nonetheless makes clear that Hyacinth's relation to gender and sexuality is as riven and conflicted as his class identity.

Hyacinth's ambiguous sexual identity is signaled initially by his name, which evokes Hyacinthus of classical Greek mythology. An extremely beautiful youth, Hyacinthus was loved by Thamyris, the first man in Greek mythology to love another man. The god Apollo passionately loved Hyacinthus as well, until he accidentally slew the beautiful boy in a game of quoits. It was, however, also believed that Zephyrus, the West Wind, who was also in love with Hyacinthus but jealous of the lad's preference for Apollo, blew the discus off course and made it strike Hyacinthus. Unable to restore Hyacinthus to life, Apollo transformed the young boy's flowing blood into a beautiful flower and inscribed the petals with phrases of lament. And at the turn of the nineteenth century, as Wendy Graham has noted, "Hyacinths" connoted attractive, sexually available young males for Georgian homosexuals, while the hyacinth flower was itself a common symbol of boy love throughout the nineteenth century.[56]

The sexual complexity of James's Hyacinth, who is at times something of a halfhearted suitor of the Princess and at other moments is clearly much more emotionally involved with Paul Muniment, is thus prefigured in the tragic story of the Greek character for whom he is named and in the nineteenth-century history of male same-sex love.[57] Like his namesake, Hyacinth plays the beautiful boy companion to an older, more masculine figure, Paul Muniment, who is "tall and fair and good-natured looking . . . with his large head and square forehead, his thick, straight hair, his heavy mouth and rather vulgar nose, his admirably clear, bright eye" and "glance of a commander-in-chief" (127–28). Hyacinth, by contrast, is a sensitive youth with "abundant curly hair, which grew thick and long," "features [that] were smooth and pretty," and a "slim little neck" (62–63). Sexually ambivalent and gendered effeminate, Hyacinth's character, like the Princess Casamassima, transgresses cultural paradigms on several levels. Yet Hyacinth's gender ambiguity is also crucial because it complicates the luxury of choice that, as we have seen, the novel parcels out to Hyacinth and denies the Princess seemingly on the basis of gender. That is, while Hyacinth is allowed the opportunity to follow through on his terroristic vow and the Princess is systematically denied such a possibility, Hyacinth is ultimately unable to deliver on his pledge. And this redounds, once again, upon the imaginative dimensions of James's construction of gender in the novel.

Hyacinth is, of course, famously unable to go through with his pledge after the Princess reveals to the young bookbinder the sphere of art and beauty at her country home, a world that Hyacinth comes to believe would necessarily be destroyed by revolutionary politics. "What has struck me," Hyacinth informs the Princess, "is the great achievements of which man has been capable. . . . They seem to me inestimably precious and beautiful, and I have become conscious, more than ever before, of how little I understand what, in the great rectification, you and Poupin propose to do with them" (396). Yet, despite his mounting disillusion with the radical politics in which he has enmeshed himself and his growing differences of opinion with the Princess,

Hyacinth increasingly makes her the center of his existence as the narrative progresses. After the Princess moves into the working-class neighborhood, Hyacinth continues to pay regular visits at her new domicile: "The little parlour in Madeira Crescent was a spot round which his thoughts could revolve, and toward which his steps could direct themselves, with an unalloyed sense of security and privilege" (481–82). Hyacinth regards the situation with a certain self-satisfaction, as "his relations with the Princess had long since ceased to appear to him to belong to the world of fable." Indeed, Hyacinth, regularly occupying his usual chair "on the opposite side of the fire, felt at times almost as if he were married to his hostess, so many things were taken for granted between them" (482). The proliferation of these domestic scenes has led Eileen Sypher to argue that gender relations are the surprising engine driving James's tale of subterranean anarchist politics. As Sypher reads *Princess*, James ultimately mobilizes "the conventions of the domestic novel, where gender relations are offered as the cause of all social behavior . . . to contain the threat of individual male anarchists, and so, [he] hope[s], of anarchism itself, by blaming inappropriate domestic arrangements." A politically aggressive woman such as the Princess who leaves her husband is, according to Sypher's reading, held culpable for the anarchist politics of men who come in contact with her: "According to the project of *The Princess* . . . women who are out of line . . . violate the rules and should be blamed for public political disruption."[58]

Sypher's analysis has much to recommend it. Nevertheless, I believe that in her rush to pin a more-or-less accurate charge of misogyny on James's text, Sypher ignores much of the complex gender work that is actually at stake in those scenes where Hyacinth plays the lackluster suitor to the Princess. While James does deploy a highly conventional depiction of domesticity in which a woman—even (especially?) a highly unconventional woman such as the Princess—takes it as her charge to provide comfort and succor for a man, the most interesting thing about these scenes is not that she in some way "fails" to play her role properly. Sypher interprets this failure, by way of Pierre Macherey's theories, as the inadequacy of an outdated "mid-Victorian ideologeme of 'home.'"[59] But what is most pressing about the gender politics of *Princess*'s domestic scenes is the manner in which, according to the logic of this novel, these textual moments gender *both* Hyacinth and the Princess feminine.

Specifically, the extreme visibility of the would-be terrorists Hyacinth and Princess gender them feminine in relation to the hypermasculine archterrorist of the novel, Diedrich Hoffendahl. Hoffendahl, crucially, never appears on stage in this novel; we only receive other characters' reports of his cunning and bravery. Mastermind of an attempted simultaneous terrorist assault in four European cities in the 1860s, the "great Hoffendahl" had withstood severe torture at the hands of the police without giving up the names of any of his comrades after the incident failed and he was captured (288). Moreover, Hoffendahl's attempted terrorism in the 1860s had been significant despite its failure, one of the text's anarchists explains, precisely because the "invisibility of the persons concerned in it had given the predatory classes, had given all Europe, a shudder that had not yet subsided" (288). This invisibility, as well as the complete invisibility of Hoffendahl throughout the text, is key. As theorists such as Michael Warner have argued, the "bourgeois public sphere has been structured from the outset by a logic of abstraction that provides a privilege for unmarked identities: the male, the white, the middle-class, the normal." Further, "to acknowledge their positivity would be to surrender their privilege, as for example to acknowledge the objectivity of the male body would be feminizing."[60] In other words, the public sphere operates by a logic that abstracts certain privileged bodies into invisibility while the cultural markers of race and gender identify other bodies as visibly different.

The construction of a terrorist subjectivity in James's novel through Hoffendahl is remarkable for the way it both enacts and complicates this cultural dynamic. James's text poses a theoretical link between, on the one hand, the well-hidden and seemingly unlocatable terrorist who relies precisely on anonymity and invisibility for his cultural power and, on the other hand, the disembodied abstraction of the public sphere's privileged citizen, whose race and gender is everywhere suppressed so that other bodies bear the mark of visible and problematic difference. From this point of view, the narrative possibilities laid out in the domestic scenes that structure Hyacinth and the Princess's interactions, as opposed to the sheer imperceptibility of Hoffendahl, suggest that these scenes are pivotal not only for James's failed attempt to mobilize the home front to domesticate radical politics. They make it clear that Hyacinth, according to the narrative's logic, cannot be allowed to be a terrorist because he is also gendered feminine. Embodiment and visibility in this text bear the mark of gender difference and equate with the inability to perform terrorist acts, whether because of indecisiveness, as in Hyacinth's case, or because of insurmountable obstacles, as is the Princess's dilemma.[61]

James's politics here are unsurprisingly conservative. Yet the logic of his novel also suggests how a terrorist subjectivity complicates the very cultural logic in which it seems to participate so vigorously. While a terrorist gains cultural power through invisibility and the seemingly random quality of an attack that results from that imperceptibility, the dynamics of power change after a terrorist incident (or, more precisely, an event that is labeled terrorism) actually occurs. As we saw in the last chapter's discussion of Haymarket, at the postincident moment when various parties are scrambling to achieve discursive control over the event's possible interpretations, the crucial questions become according to what terms and what cultural logic (such as criminal, freedom fighter, or lunatic) a terrorist will be made public, and whether the terrorists or some other faction of the public will gain power over the interpretative possibilities. This dynamic is played out in *The Princess Casamassima* when interpretive control of the attempted terrorist assault orchestrated by Hoffendahl is taken over by the governments involved as they conspired to make "every effort to smother it up—there had been editors and journalists transported even for hinting at it" (288). The effect of this, as *Princess*'s representative survivor of the French Commune, Eustache Poupin, realizes when he narrates Hoffendahl's extraordinary revolutionary credentials, is that his auditors "didn't remember that great combined attempt, early in the sixties" (288). This scene in James's text thus illuminates how terrorism shifts Michael Warner's brilliant discussion of the ways in which abstraction and disembodiment in the public sphere are the guarantors of cultural hegemony. The interpenetration of publicity, terrorism, and invisibility in Hoffendahl's nonappearance suggest that the site of real cultural power is found not only in the dynamic between abstraction and embodiment but also, more precisely, in the ability to mediate that line between visibility and invisibility.[62]

With the nonappearance of Hoffendahl, James's novel can begin to suggest the ways in which terrorism, with its delicate choreography wavering between publicity and invisibility, complicates theoretical and cultural analyses of abstraction and gender in the public sphere. And beyond Hoffendahl, James's text reenacts but slightly alters the terms of this distinction between embodiment and abstraction via another of the novel's central concerns—its construction of a gendered relationship to art. As many critics have noted, Hyacinth decides he cannot enact his terroristic pledge after he discovers the beauty of art in the Princess's country home and, more important, in his tour of Italy and France. To destroy the current fabric of society, Hyacinth reasons, would be to destroy the very conditions that made the creation of such beauty possible. Yet the intersection of art and terrorism in the novel involves more than just its antiterrorism capacity. Art functions as a crucial way that gender difference is imagined in the novel, and it is within this triptych of art, terrorism, and gender that we can gain yet another perspective on James's gendered politics of terror.

The Princess has a place alongside Gilbert Osmond, Rowland Mallet, and other art collectors who occupy significant roles in James's fiction. She possesses "innumerable *bibelots*" of marked "beauty and oddity" (244). But what makes the Princess different is that she is also something of an objet d'art herself. When Hyacinth first meets her, she is "dazzling" and possesses "a light about her which he seemed to see even while his head was averted." Her own "head, where two or three diamond stars glittered in the thick, delicate hair which defined its shape, suggested to Hyacinth something antique and celebrated, which he had admired of old—the memory was vague—in a statue, in a picture, in a museum" (190–91). Put simply, the Princess is "the most remarkable woman in Europe" (186). But if she is such an exceptional person, it is telling that the language Hyacinth finds most appropriate to describe her renders her as an immobile, if exquisite, art object, a desireless and silent creation. The Princess's gender, class position, and particular tastes thus combine to make her an anomaly in the Jamesian canon, both a collector of precious and unusual works of art and herself a dazzling prize to be collected. Yet the Princess longs to undermine this highly classed relation to art with her repeated desire for collecting what she regards as genuine experiences, "everything that was characteristic" (184) and that smacks of the "real London, the people and all their sufferings and passions" (201). For Princess Casamassima, as we saw earlier, "get[ting] out of [her]self" (256) involves a self-melting immersion into a romanticized everyday ordinariness.

It is precisely this tension between being "remarkable" and being "characteristic" that both extends and slightly shifts the terms of visibility and invisibility that structured Hoffendahl's absence in the text. On the one hand, the tension between being unique and being ordinary that drives the Princess's desire to appropriate and collect what she believes Hyacinth represents in order to have her own "genuine" experiences is a class tension symptomatic of her wish to escape the rarefied life charted out for her as the wife of an Italian nobleman. But more important, the descriptions of the Princess and Hyacinth suggest the way art works in this novel to mark out gender difference, even if, as we have seen, it is a gender difference that is repeatedly destabilized throughout the text. This novel makes it clear that the discrepancy between being "remarkable" and being "characteristic" is also a gendered distinction that hinges on the ways in which Western culture encourages women to make themselves into objects of desire for the viewing pleasure of men. Indeed, as the Princess bitingly and abruptly suggests during a moment when she is chafing at the artifice and strictures of societal obligations in *Roderick Hudson,* "I think I have posed enough" (150).

In *The Princess Casamassima,* the principal way that she stops posing for the viewing pleasure of men is, as her detractors within the novel note, by posing instead as a lower-class woman in the tawdry neighborhood of

Madeira Crescent. For the Princess, shifting the form of her pose away from a patriarchal logic objectifying women also involves a class-based disposal of her rich treasure of artworks. The Princess's sense here that she needs to escape a "self" comprised of a series of poses rather than some interior essence is in itself interesting since James at many places seems determined to lock her into a more essentialist identity, while the novel also relentlessly and painstakingly traces Hyacinth's own selfhood to the paradox contained within his very blood. Yet, before the Princess abandons her art collection and makes the move to Madeira Crescent in the hope that her doubtful associates will take her seriously as a revolutionary, she introduces Hyacinth to the world of art and beauty. She invites him to her country estate, solely to "observe the impression made by such a place . . . on such a nature as [Hyacinth's], introduced to it for the first time" (321). Since Hyacinth's deep appreciation of beauty creates an impasse that he can only resolve by taking his own life, the Princess thus in a very real way acts as the catalyst of Hyacinth's demise.

The point, then, is that in *The Princess Casamassima* the sheer force of art's beauty prevents social revolution, but it is women who are made the unwitting agents of this conservative movement. The cultural politics of James's novel, I would argue, are therefore not found in the production of male anarchists that stems from what Eileen Sypher reads as the book's troubled domestic arrangements and the Princess's failure to accommodate herself to the cultural codes of late Victorian womanhood. It is not so much that unruly women bear responsibility for the conditions that promote anarchy but rather that, while the implications of James's politics are inarguably conservative, the conservatism lies in his making the Princess Casamassima into the force that brings revolution to a screeching halt even as she longs to be taken seriously as a revolutionary. Introducing Hyacinth to the world of high culture simply to see how he will respond, the woman who would be a revolutionary also creates the ideological confusion in him that thwarts political violence.

The politics of James's text find their denouement when the Princess is forced back to her husband near the novel's close. As Paul Muniment coldly informs her, "I should let you know that I *do* consider that in giving your money — or, rather, your husband's — to our business you gave the most valuable thing you had to contribute. . . . You will go back to your husband!" (579–80, emphasis original). After predicting, or even demanding, her unfortunate return to her husband in this penultimate scene, the book ends with the Princess distraught and "upon her knees" over Hyacinth's dead body, uttering "a strange low cry" while her own body is wracked by "a convulsive movement" (590). Sending the Princess back to her husband and placing her for the first time in the stereotypically feminine position of highly emotional grief, James's novel ends by stepping back from the cultural terrain that it had initially appeared to map: the genesis of a female terrorist. In *Princess Casamassima,* one cannot escape one's destiny, as it were. The would-be anarchist, Hyacinth Robinson, torn between aristocratic and proletarian longings, can only commit suicide, while the independent-minded Princess remains mired in the late nineteenth century's patriarchal economy and is violently sent back to her status as the prize possession of a jealous husband.

James thus ultimately pulls away from tracing the full implications that the Princess would have for notions of late-nineteenth-century gender roles were she to become a successful terrorist. But the plot of his novel does nonetheless move toward an exploration of the psychological imperatives that could lead an economically privileged woman to take up the cause of revolutionary movements in a much more thorough way than is usually acknowledged by James's critics. However, if the Princess everywhere attempts to undermine the proscriptions that gender and class position place on her behavior in order to be taken seriously as a revolutionary, James still makes her into an unwittingly reactionary force within the book. Forcing the Princess back into her unhappy marriage with Prince Casamassima, James ties together and defuses the threats of gender subversion and radical class violence that are embodied by female terrorists who want political violence, in the Princess's words, "to burst forth some fine morning and set the world on fire" (200). And while the Princess claims throughout the novel that she is "only trying to be natural" (466) when she attempts to be taken seriously as a revolutionary, the thrust of James's venture into naturalist-inspired fiction finally produces a very different notion of a woman acting "naturally." *Princess Casamassima* makes questions of reality versus appearance central to the narrative in such a way that being "natural" or authentic comes, against the Princess's longings, to mean that she is only allowed the cultural position of an unfaithful wife, distrusted and silenced both by male revolutionaries whose cause she wishes to join and by a husband who desires an apolitical, beautiful, and tractable wife.

CHAPTER THREE

The United States of Terrorism

The Political Economy of Lynching and Citizenship in Thomas Dixon and Ida B. Wells

When writing *The Princess Casamassima,* Henry James made an anomalous choice in his depiction of late-nineteenth-century anarchists. His novel takes place during a decade known for dramatic terrorist incidents caused by dynamite, and on the eve of another rash of bombings that would occupy continental authorities throughout the 1890s.[1] Yet, other than a minor moment when Madame Grandoni very mistakenly tells Hyacinth Robinson that he looks like one of those young men likely "to throw bombs into innocent crowds,"[2] James's text makes no serious mention of dynamite. And while Joseph Conrad built the entire plot of *The Secret Agent* around the unintentional and calamitous explosion of a bomb that went off too early, James's hapless and anachronistic terrorist, Hyacinth Robinson, wields only a small pistol. James's choice of weapons in this novel most likely results from the alchemy of conservative politics and curious fascination that fueled his intervention into terrorist fiction. Captivated by the invisible world of underground politics, but understandably dismayed by the potential for appalling destruction contained within Alfred Nobel's invention, James shied away from a brush with the traumatic psychological effects that terrorism's technological modernity would have necessitated in his fiction.

But while James's omission of dynamite in an 1886 novel whose plot delineates a secret anarcho-terrorist plan to assassinate a powerful political figure seems odd, that same year found the influential black newspaper editor, T. Thomas Fortune, musing on the strangeness of American blacks *not* turning to dynamite as a way to defend themselves against the terror southern whites were unleashing on them. Fortune was editor of the *New York Freeman* in the 1880s and the *New York Age* in the early 1890s, where he would become Ida B. Wells's boss after she was exiled from Memphis under threat of lynching. Anticipating the Haymarket bomb by only a few months, the militant newspaperman wrote in the *A.M.E. Church Review* in January 1886 that the "essential element in which the Afro-American character was most deficient [was] the *dynamite element,*" a character trait that "resists an injury promptly."[3] Why southern blacks did not turn to dynamite is an interesting historical question, and the answer surely involves fear of even more aggressive retaliation by whites.[4] Additionally, an oppressed minority's difficulty in obtaining dynamite in an apartheid state fearful of uprisings certainly contributed to what Fortune regarded as dynamite's curious absence as a weapon in the black South.[5]

Nevertheless, some six years later, in 1892, Frederick Douglass warned that "if the Southern outrages on the Colored race continue the Negro will become a chemist."[6] In the early 1890s, this galvanizing declaration was tantamount to warning white Americans that blacks were willing and able to take over the legacy of the Haymarket anarchists, who had counseled their followers to learn "chemistry," or bomb-making, for years before the 1886 Haymarket explosion.[7] Douglass even went on to alert his readers that "anarchists have not a monopoly of bomb-making, and the Negro will learn to handle the terrible engine of destruction unless the wrongs against him cease."[8] This last statement is particularly important because it hints at the seemingly insuperable obstacles separating African Americans and anarchists, even as Douglass's rhetoric also symbolically, if unwittingly, makes black Americans the inheritors of the Haymarket anarchists' radical tradition. But if Douglass's remarks thus appear somewhat contradictory, a *Boston Republican* editorial of the same era that was widely reprinted in the nation's newspapers can clarify his rhetoric. While warning Americans that "there are colored men in Boston and Cambridge who have banded themselves together with an oath to make dynamite and bombs to be used in the South to protect themselves against tyranny and despotism," the *Republican*'s editorialist tellingly added that "we do not encourage dynamiters and bomb-throwers where no cause exists for indulging in such a warfare, *as in the case of the Chicago anarchists of a few years ago.*"[9] Distressingly absent from such an editorial is a recognition of the very real economic issues raised by Chicago's anarchist community, especially the agitation for the eight-hour work day. And more important, by completely parceling northern economic upheaval off from southern racial distress, the *Republican*'s editorial misses the key economic component of southern racial violence, a recognition that might have led to identifying the possibility of shared dilemmas between northern workers and southern blacks. But the *Boston Republican* was not alone. T. Thomas Fortune had himself written concerning Haymarket that, for their crimes, "the Anarchists are hunted down and punished by the officers of the State," while that same government ignored white crimes against blacks. As David Roediger has suggested, Fortune thus unfortunately made the parallel between the anarchists and southern lynchers rather than between the Haymarket anarchists who were subjected to a "legal lynching" and blacks who lived under the constant threat of illegal lynchings.[10]

This brief history of race, class politics, and dynamite in the late nineteenth century demonstrates a weblike relationship between these seemingly discrete cultural forms that belies what may initially appear to be their lack of connection. If African Americans and white anarchists were largely prevented by the chasm of racial difference from joining forces to fight their different oppressors, certain key terms were nevertheless shared in significant ways by the discourse of racial violence in the South and economic conflict in the North. The rhetorics of anarchy, nationhood, and politico-economic upheaval were three important common, if differently accented, languages that underwrote the often bloody quest for social dominance in turn-of-the-century America. I borrow the term "accent" here from the Soviet theorist of language, V. N. Vološinov, who argues in *Marxism and the Philosophy of Language* that

> existence reflected in sign is not merely reflected but *refracted*. How is this refraction of existence in the ideological sign determined? By an intersecting of differently oriented social interests within one and the same sign community. . . .
>
> . . . Various different classes will use one and the same language. As a result, differently oriented accents intersect in every ideological sign. . . .
>
> This social *multiaccentuality* of the ideological sign is a very crucial aspect. By and large, it is thanks to this intersecting of accents that a sign maintains its vitality and dynamism and the capacity for further development. . . .
>
> In actual fact, each living ideological sign has two faces, like Janus. Any current curse word can become a word of praise, any current truth must inevitably sound to many other people as the greatest lie. This *inner dialectic quality* of the sign comes out fully in the open only in times of social crises or revolutionary changes.[11]

Though Vološinov is writing here specifically of the class struggle, his ideas are also applicable to the tangled mesh of class and racial politics in the late-nineteenth-century United States. While, as we saw in Chapter 1, the Haymarket anarchists turned to the metaphors of racial slavery to describe their existence in an industrial economy, black leaders in the postbellum era often worked equally hard to avoid any implied resemblances between the purportedly anti-American activities of the anarchists and blacks' own attempts to gain their newly guaranteed rights as American citizens under the postwar constitutional amendments. In this fraught cultural context, anarchy too often had the residue of a perceived anti-Americanism, which would have made it politically unaffordable for black activists to find a common cause with the nation's economic radicals, even if the difficult chasm of racial difference could have been bridged.

Yet it was not only for America's most radical labor militants and black activists that the language of race, class, and anarchy both coalesced and diverged in complex ways. These signs also functioned as key terms of address that were accorded sometimes surprisingly similar and sometimes widely different political inflections in the writings of Thomas Dixon and Ida B. Wells. Dixon and Wells may, however, initially appear as the most unlikely of pairings. Wells, an important African American feminist and journalist, laid bare the economic and patriarchal reasons that stood behind the usual justification of lynching as punishment for black rapists. Dixon, on the other hand, is perhaps best known for writing the novel that inspired D. W. Griffith's *The Birth of a Nation,* as well as the screenplay of Griffith's landmark film. At the turn of the century, however, Dixon was also a best-selling if highly controversial author famous for combining repulsively racist and nearly unreadable depictions of African Americans with a glorification of the Ku Klux Klan's sickening violence. In his Reconstruction trilogy, made up of *The Leopard's Spots, The Clansman,* and *The Traitor,* which was rapidly written between 1902 and 1907 but mostly set during or in the immediate aftermath of Reconstruction, Dixon published a steady stream of racial vitriol.

I study Dixon's and Wells's work together in this chapter for two reasons. On the one hand, I briefly analyze their startlingly opposed methods for documenting and portraying what each regards as the conditions of southern life in the last quarter of the nineteenth century. As Wells puts it in her preface to *Southern Horrors,* her work "is a contribution to truth, an array of facts, the perusal of which it is hoped will stimulate this great American Republic to demand that justice be done though the heavens fall."[12] Similarly, Dixon writes in the "Historical Note" appended to the beginning of *The Leopard's Spots* that the "incidents" of his text "were selected from authentic records."[13] Dixon echoed this sentiment in his preface to *The Clansman,* writing that "'The Clansman' develops the true story of the 'Ku Klux Klan conspiracy,' which overturned the Reconstruction régime."[14]

The disparity between these authors' chosen representational forms (Wells's reportage and Dixon's romance) involves more than the difference in their professions (journalist and novelist). It is a politicized question of the relationship between representational form, history, and the role of race and gender in the construction of authorship that speaks to how turn-of-the-century Americans were prepared to understand the racial climate in which they existed. From a position of relative political weakness defined by her race and gender, Wells's work is overrun with statistics documenting and proving the hypocrisy of explanations for lynching that regard it as justifiable punishment for rape. More important, Wells draws the majority of her statistics and reports from white-owned newspapers, especially the *Chicago Tribune,* in an effort to prove her objectivity. Dixon's works, however, depicting what Wells herself admits is the dominant version of events, are historical romances and racist fables. Written for a white audience ready to accept his version of events, Dixon's best-sellers are excellent examples of propaganda that did not need to marshal evidence that could in any way be thought of as objective, because his narratives already meshed with the naturalized and ideologically dominant conception of lynching. As Joel Williamson has argued, Dixon's "work said in a total way what his audience had been thinking in fragments. His grand themes educed precisely what a vast number of people were instinctively and passionately certain was true."[15]

The literary forms available to and chosen by Wells and Dixon provide valuable information about their relative authorial positions. Nevertheless, in this chapter I am more interested in exploring how each of these writers, in their own particular ways, fashions a notion of citizenship and nationhood to undergird their larger projects of, in Wells's case, unflinchingly documenting the horrors of racial terrorism in the postwar South and, in Dixon's case, unapologetically calling for acts of racial violence against African Americans. In Wells, the violence directed largely against black men threatens the very foundation of America, while Dixon finds the violence of the Klan to be the spring that launches the South into the nation's new industrial economy. Therefore I attend closely to Wells's strategic manipulation of a rhetoric of nationhood and citizenship in her antilynching pamphlets of 1892 and 1895, *Southern Horrors* and *A Red Record,* respectively. Explaining lynching as a form of patriarchal and economic terrorism, Wells sought to cajole Americans into recognizing what she calls "the blot of a national crime"[16] by grounding her arguments in a rhetoric of civilization and patriotic nationhood in which the North and South are made equally accountable for the era's racial terrorism. Thus Wells not only deploys a trenchant analysis of the gendered and economic motivations for lynching but does so within a paradigm of citizenship and nationhood that makes the North complicit in "Southern horrors" if it continues to ignore the national rights guaranteed by the bestowal of citizenship to African Americans.

In relation to Dixon, however, Wells represents something like the return of the repressed. With one key exception in *The Clansman* that I discuss below, Dixon's works excise and silence black women. Before turning to Wells, therefore, I will explore the racialized and economic nation-work of Dixon's "Trilogy of Reconstruction." In a very real sense, of course, the message of Dixon's texts is painfully obvious—without the civilizing effects of slavery, post–Civil War blacks were regressing toward barbarism and aggression toward whites that must itself be checked by massive and awe-inspiring retributive violence. The books, suffused with excessive melodrama, unbelievable coincidences, tangled love plots (and, of course, a surfeit of racist tripe), have little literary merit and perhaps even less literary aspiration.[17] Even so, they are worth examining because Dixon formulates his racial hatred within the confines of a rhetoric of nationhood precisely at a time when American imperialism abroad and Jim Crow disfranchisement of African Americans at home were making notions of statehood, political economy, and anarchy volatile terms of political address. Moreover, if one of Dixon's clear aims seems to be a justification of violence against blacks at the turn of the century,[18] the question still remains of why he returns in two of the trilogy's three novels to the rise and fall of the Ku Klux Klan thirty years in the past to deliver this message. The trilogy's first novel, *The Leopard's Spots*, narrates southern history of the entire postwar period up to the time Dixon was writing in 1902 and telescopes the rise and dissolution of the KKK into a small number of pages at the end of Book 1. *The Clansman* and *The Traitor*, however, focus more narrowly on the immediate postwar years of Reconstruction, narrating, respectively, the rise and fall of the Klan. This narrowing of focus is important. While *The Leopard's Spots* lays out the broad sweep of postwar southern race relations from Dixon's point of view, the return to Reconstruction, and consequently to the history of the Klan, allows him to disown the more random violence of lynching that occupies a pivotal scene in the post-Klan era of *The Leopard's Spots*. Indeed, random violence in Dixon's fiction starts to look like anarchy and terrorism; returning to the height of the Klan's power in the late 1860s, Dixon is able to make the KKK into the surprising upholder of law and order, a virtual agent of the state. In this role, Dixon's paramilitary and white-sheeted KKK can supersede the official military uniforms of the Union and Confederate soldiers. It is thus no coincidence that *The Leopard's Spots* begins on a southern battlefield with General Lee preparing to surrender, for the collective project of Dixon's three novels is to replace the national uniforms of Yankees and Confederates—uniforms that can be removed or worn by the wrong race—with the putatively "black" or "white" uniform of skin that can be neither removed nor forged.

Thomas Dixon's Novels: In Fear of a Mulatto Nation

Though the three books of Dixon's trilogy do not share a single plotline, there is significant overlap among them. *The Leopard's Spots* is the lengthiest and most complex of the three; it is set in a village in the North Carolina foothills and opens with a faithful slave returning from the Civil War, bringing the sword of his dead master to the man's son, young Charles Gaston, the novel's eventual protagonist. Book 1 of the novel details the corruption of the Reconstruction regime, with none other than Harriet Beecher Stowe's Simon Legree making a return appearance as a powerful North Carolina politician. In Reconstruction's "experiment" with "social dynamite" (*LS* 98), southern blacks are made the rulers of whites and marauding blacks begin to terrorize, threaten, and attempt to rape the local white women. Eventually, however, the Klan emerges to save the day by lynching the black school superintendent in retaliation for his attempt to kiss a young southern belle. In the wake of the murder, the government is "redeemed" by southern whites and Legree flees to New York.

Book 2 of *Spots,* dedicated to the novel's love plot, opens some two decades later with Charlie Gaston grown to young adulthood and already an influential politician. The races have become almost entirely alienated, with whites "seeking refuge from a new terror . . . the roving criminal Negro" (*LS* 202). Nevertheless, white Republicans have combined the black vote with the poor white vote into a "fusion" ticket that has seized control of the state government. Suddenly Dick, a black vagrant who had been a playmate of young Charlie before he inexplicably disappeared twenty years earlier, returns and brutally rapes a white child. Dick is lynched, and Gaston comes to realize that the black and white races cannot live together. Finally, the Spanish-American War arrives to unite the white race across lines of class and ethnicity, and black insolence is again smothered as a small race war breaks out in the never-subtle Dixon's aptly named Independence, North Carolina. Gaston ultimately manages to rejuvenate the Democratic Party on a platform with one plank, white supremacy, wins the governorship of the state, and, at the end of the novel, moves into the governor's mansion in Raleigh with his new bride.

Like *The Leopard's Spots, The Clansman* opens with a wartime scene, but with a twist. At the beginning of the latter novel, a beautiful young white woman from the North is singing folk songs in imitation slave dialect to a wounded Confederate soldier, Ben Cameron, the novel's hero. The woman, however, happens to be the daughter of Austin Stoneman (a thinly disguised Thaddeus Stevens), leader of the Radical Republicans, who organizes and directs the Reconstruction government's "reign of terror" over the South (*C* 110). Again the Klan is organized to halt the blacks' abuse of freedom and their newly acquired governmental power. Therefore, when Gus, a former slave, rapes a young white woman, Ben Cameron presides over the KKK's retaliatory murder of him. The Klan serves as a focal point for the white community, which is knitted together against its black oppressors. The novel ends with Cameron crowned "a successful revolutionist" against the illegitimate Reconstruction government since "Civilisation has been saved" (*C* 374).

The Traitor, the last novel in Dixon's trilogy, is sometimes regarded as the most moderate of the three, largely because it omits narrating a scene of lynching.[19] Set between 1870 and 1872, the novel depicts the dramatic dissolution of the North Carolina Klan in an early scene.[20] The action then interweaves an interesting cross-class love story with the attempts of the authentic Klan's former leader, John Graham, to subdue the roguish and irresponsible new Klan that has sprung up to fill the power vacuum created by the original KKK's disbanding. Eventually, the new Klan's leader severely breaches the order's code of conduct by naming the Klan's original members for the authorities. This leads to the arrest of Graham, though he is ultimately pardoned. The book ends with Graham and his new wife, Stella, moving into and restoring the decayed mansion where the original KKK had held its secret meetings. By having the newlyweds occupy and revitalize the Inwood plantation, Dixon allows the Klan symbolically to live on after the close of his trilogy.

In Charles W. Chesnutt's 1901 novel, *The Marrow of Tradition,* a small scene takes place that presumably would have both arrested Thomas Dixon's attention and horrified him. As the three white leaders plot the political coup that will overthrow the town of Wellington's black leadership, General Belmont reads aloud an advertisement from the town's African American newspaper that promises to lighten blacks' skin and hair: " 'Kinky, curly hair made straight by one application of our specific. Our face bleach will turn the skin of a black or brown person four or five shades lighter, and of a mulatto perfectly white. When you get the color you wish, stop using the preparation.' Just look at those heads! — 'Before using' and 'After using.' We'd better hurry, or there'll be no negroes to disfranchise!' "[21] The general's worry about having black persons to disfranchise follows from a certain panic that whiteness may be imitable, or, worse, that there is no essence there to imitate, only an arbitrary color line that can potentially be crossed.[22] Worried that blacks will "all be white" (84), the general fears the end of racial division. Indeed, this particular anxiety is (almost) realized later in the novel, when Jerry, a black butler, appears with a "black face [that] is splotched with brown and yellow patches, and . . . hair [that] shines as though [he] had fallen head-foremost into a firkin of butter" (243). By having the whitening agent deface rather than transform Jerry in this painful scene of tragicomedy, Chesnutt metaphorically represents the high and dangerous stakes of skin color at the turn of the century. Moreover, he symbolically depicts the psychic anguish at issue in attempting to gain the privileges of whiteness by bleaching one's skin while living in an apartheid culture whose dominant white faction would nonetheless redraw the arbitrary line of whiteness wherever necessary to maintain exclusive rights to the advantages of white skin.[23]

Yet what Jerry represents in *Marrow* is the attempt to *become* white, not necessarily the attempt to obliterate the boundary between black and white, General Belmont's fears notwithstanding. In his Reconstruction trilogy, on the other hand, Dixon imagines what from his point of view is an even more disastrous possibility, that is, that the United States would become "the new 'Mulatto' nation" (*LS* 81), as a character in *Spots* puts it. Indeed, Reverend Durham, the moral spokesman of *Spots,* repeats no less than six times at key points in that novel that "nationality demands solidarity. And you can never get solidarity in a nation of equal rights out of two hostile races that do not intermarry. *In a Democracy you cannot build a nation inside of a nation of two antagonistic races; and therefore the future American must be either an Anglo-Saxon or a Mulatto*" (*LS* 336, emphasis original). The nightmare is, of course, that the future will be one of racial mixing unless the seemingly inevitable race war develops, affording whites the opportunity to expunge blacks from America (*LS* 338). Lest readers miss his point about contemporary America and race mixing, Dixon conjures up what he regards as the danger of miscegenation—or, according to *Spots,* "Africanisation," since "amalgamation simply mean[s] Africanisation" (*LS* 386)—with particular clarity in *The Clansman,* a text in which a mulatto woman makes a rare appearance in his fiction. In that novel, Austin Stoneman (Thaddeus Stevens) keeps a mulatto mistress who becomes the de facto "first lady of the land" after Abraham Lincoln's assassination (*C* 91). Further, we learn at the novel's close that Stoneman imposed Reconstruction's "reign of terror" (*C* 17) on the South as part of his "dream of lifting her to [his social] level" (*C* 371). In Dixon, the horrors of Reconstruction follow from the unfortunate fact of previous race mixing that created the "yellow vampire" (*C* 371) who figuratively sucks the lifeblood from the national body politic. But even worse is Stoneman's subsequent and misguided attempt to create a social parity between blacks and whites by squashing the white South beneath his iron rule. Operating from the "one drop" rule of racial identity (*LS* 338), in which a supposed single drop of "black" blood makes one black, Dixon makes racially mixed persons the particular target of his vitriol because anything less than complete separation threatens "the foundation of racial life and of civilisation" (*LS* 336) by making America's future "mulatto" (*LS* 81). It is, then, a particular anxiety about the merging of America's black and white races during the time in which he is writing as well as in the future that provokes Dixon's ire. This, in turn, leads him to return to the scene of Reconstruction to show that the social anarchy created by postwar miscegenation, and still bedeviling America in 1900, was a direct product of Reconstruction's political "spirit of anarchy" (*LS* 94).

Yet, if anxiety about racial mixing makes Dixon return to Reconstruction in order to reconsider citizenship and the "future American" (*LS* 387), it is important to realize that his viewpoint, though probably representative of the culture at large, was not uncontested in the early twentieth century. Charles Chesnutt, in a series of three articles also entitled "The Future American" that appeared in 1900, shortly before Dixon began to write *The Leopard's Spots*, offered a strikingly counter racial theory. However, in a rhetorical move that exemplifies the severely debilitated form of turn-of-the-century racial discourse, Chesnutt, even as his writing opposes Dixon's ideology, also presumes the basic terms of Dixon's arguments about skin color. Arguing that racial amalgamation should be state policy rather than officially proscribed, as it still was in the South of 1900, Chesnutt, anticipating Dixon's Reverend Durham, recognized that "there can manifestly be no such thing as a peaceful and progressive civilization in a nation divided by two warring races."[24] And since, as Dixon would have agreed, "homogeneity of type, at least in externals, is a necessary condition of harmonious social progress," Chesnutt advocated state-sponsored miscegenation that would eventually erase color differences. With the achievement of color homogeneity, "there would be no inferior race to domineer over; there would be no superior race to oppress those who differed from them in racial externals. The inevitable social struggle, which in one form or another, seems to be one of the conditions of progress, would proceed along other lines than those of race."[25]

Chesnutt's straightforward elimination of racial categories via a government-sponsored campaign of racial mixing has a certain rigorous logic to it, though one imagines that gender, class, or sexual difference would too easily become the "other lines" along which discrimination would be articulated.

[109]

Yet his bravery in advocating such a program in 1900, albeit in a Boston newspaper, is rather remarkable. This is true even though Chesnutt, as a very fair-skinned but legally "black" man who enjoyed a high degree of class privilege, would have had good reason to muse on the deconstruction of race, both in his journalism and, more famously, in novels such as *Marrow, The House Behind the Cedars,* and *Paul Marchand.* In fact, one of the interesting aspects of Chesnutt's articles is precisely the somewhat self-interested recognition that prejudice would find other routes of least resistance, such as class discrimination, if color difference were eliminated. But reading Dixon makes it clear that race trumps class (or anything else) every time, which is why Dixon so obsessively returns to a castigation of mulattos as he works to shore up the boundaries of whiteness and citizenship in his trilogy. And the place that Dixon found most amenable for such racialized nation-work was Reconstruction, where he could imaginatively redraw the "new map of the world [that] had been made" by the Civil War (*LS* 4).

Reconstruction, Anarchy, and the
Ku Klux Klan's New America

The Leopard's Spots was, among other things, an intentional riposte to Harriet Beecher Stowe's *Uncle Tom's Cabin,* a novel whose own plotline concerning black emigration to Liberia entangles it firmly in questions of citizenship and racial politics. In particular, Dixon resuscitates the fiendish slave owner Simon Legree from his apparent death near the end of Stowe's novel, only to refashion him for his own politico-racial agenda. In *The Leopard's Spots,* Legree introduces a key theme in Dixon's writing, the contradictory danger and opportunity provided by disguises and concealed identities. When the Civil War came, Legree avoided military service on either side by cross-dressing as an immigrant German woman, "a sister just from the old country" (*LS* 86). At the war's end, Legree readopts masculine attire, becomes "a violent Union man" (*LS* 86), and wins election to the North Carolina legislature as part of what Dixon calls the wholesale fraud of the 1868 post–Reconstruction Act election. From his position as speaker of the state House of Representatives, Legree "cover[s] the South with the desolation of anarchy" (*LS* 196) until the state is "redeemed." Fleeing to Wall Street after being exiled from the South, Legree buys a seat on the stock exchange with the millions he has embezzled from the state government and becomes "one of the most daring and successful of a group of robbers who preyed on the industries of the nation" (*LS* 164).

In *Spots,* unmasking a cross-dressing scalawag (i.e., a Union-supporting southerner) such as Legree reveals a robber baron. Of course, despite his long residence in the South, Legree is not exactly a scalawag either, since, according to Stowe's novel, he was born and raised in New England.[26] That Legree is from the North adds symbolic weight to Dixon's characterization of him as a "distinguished ruffian whose cruelty to his slaves had made him unique in infamy in the annals of the South" (*LS* 86). Legree thus becomes in *Spots* the antithesis of the "true" southern slaveholder, such as Charlie Gaston's father, whose brand of ownership could inspire a slave to "kill many Yankees in the war" (*LS* 104). Moreover, by transforming Legree into an embezzling northern capitalist, Dixon takes his place in a long line of southern apologists for slavery, including John C. Calhoun and George Fitzhugh, who emphasized the comparatively worse inhumanity and barbarity of northern capitalism. This specific twist would also have had particular resonance with Dixon's initial audience, as the book first appeared during an especially intense period of antimonopoly sentiment in America.

Resuscitating Legree from the "rumours of his death" (*LS* 85) in Stowe's novel allows Dixon to blame transplanted northerners like Legree for the excesses of slavery that resulted in the Civil War. Yet it is Dixon's use of disguises and feigned identities in his depiction of Legree — first as a woman and then as a staunchly loyal unionist — that makes the evil former slave owner an especially important character in his work. The varied identities of Legree anticipate Dixon's much more sinister anxiety about black Union soldiers in *The Clansman*. In that novel, immediately after the book's first intimation concerning black rapists, readers are introduced to Gus, the former slave who ultimately becomes the text's requisite rapist. But before the rape reveals the "truth" of his identity, Dixon represents Gus as "a member of the company of negro troops, [who] parades . . . every day to show off his uniform" (*C* 191). As the southern culture is explained to Gus by Austin Stoneman's henchman, the "white trash" of the South "are not even citizens of the Nation," while Gus, because he "wear[s the United States's] uniform," is "not only their equal" but "their master" (*C* 205). As Dixon makes clear by evoking rape immediately before introducing Gus, the problem with Gus in this scene is not that his uniform symbolically represents the conquering, even imperialistic, army of the North. On the contrary, Dixon consciously leaves space in his narratives to praise the "genuine Yankee soldier" (*LS* 85) whose whiteness will ultimately transcend the cultural distinctions encoded in the differences of military uniforms. The Yankee uniform, however, allows Gus illegitimately to act like a citizen; the Yankee blue literally shrouds his black rapist identity in the cloak of nationhood.

Dixon's dilemma is thus that the military-issue blue uniform, and the concomitant fact that it can be worn by persons of the wrong color, separates whites from each other. His complaint is not with a reconstructed United States or with nationhood per se. Indeed, Dixon does not want the South to be its own autonomous country; his novels' former Confederate soldiers realize "that the everlasting question of a divided Union was settled and settled forever. There was now to be one country and one flag, and deep down in their souls they were content with it" (*LS* 34). Instead, Dixon's quandary is how to stabilize the categories of race and then rewrite racial prerogative as the key to national citizenship, which is why *The Leopard's Spots* obsessively returns to the question of whether "the future American [will] be an Anglo-Saxon or a Mulatto" (*LS* 161). In the logic of Dixon's texts, Gus has to be made a rapist to underscore the earlier mistaken identification of him as a model citizen attired in the state's official uniform. Moreover, this necessary erasure of inauthentic black citizen-soldiers from the national body politic explains why the execution of Gus and his rapist henchmen, which "struck terror to the heart of every negro" (*C* 352), is immediately followed by a scene of rapprochement between Klan members and Yankee soldiers. The Klan's leader, Ben Cameron, "wheeled his men, galloped in front of the [Union] camp, drew them up at dress parade, and saluted. A low word of command from a trooper, and the Westerners quickly formed in ranks, returned the salute, and cheered" (*C* 352–53). With the "wild cheer [that breaks] from the soldiers" (*C* 352), the Klan and the Union army unite as members of the same white nation over the dead "Captain of the African Guards lying in his full uniform" (*C* 327).

The acts of naming Gus as a rapist rather than a citizen-soldier and then lynching him unite the nation's official military with the South's paramilitary Klan in *The Clansman*. But the anxiety about attributing the proper nomenclature to persons and events that is seen in the characterizations of Legree and Gus pervades Dixon's entire trilogy. This is why Thaddeus Stevens, leader of the postwar Radical Republicans, becomes in *The Leopard's Spots* Austin Stoneman, "an anarchist" who "has obtained the dictatorship of a great Constitutional Government" (*LS* 96). And though Eric Foner's 1988 synthetic history of Reconstruction identifies Stevens as a "racial egalitarian" driven by "the utopian vision of a nation whose citizens enjoyed equality of civil and political rights,"[27] Dixon's Stevens/Stoneman brandishes "social dynamite" (*LS* 98) and masterminds the "conspirators" seeking racial vengeance against the South (*LS* 34).

Published within two decades of the Haymarket bombing and in the immediate aftermath of the anarchist Leon Czolgosz's assassination of President William McKinley, Dixon's depiction of Stevens as the anarchic Austin

Stoneman places the congressman outside the symbolic national body politic. Furthermore, Dixon applies the period's racist coding to his physical description of Stoneman; referring to Stoneman's "huge ape-like arm" (*C* 133),
he correlates the congressman's political bestiality with the supposed beast-
liness of blacks. Rather than seeking to reunite the nation on terms of racial
equality, then, Stoneman becomes the clandestine organizer of black organizations (*C* 207) that Dixon describes as "oath-bound secret societies" who
are "armed to the teeth" and "terrorising the country, stealing, burning and
murdering" (*LS* 101).

Dixon's description of blacks bound together by "secrecy and ritual"
(*C* 206) and executing surprise raids on the local population bears a surprising resemblance to the rhetoric about secret terrorist cells that saturated both
popular and official commentary about anarchists in the 1880s. Dixon thus
rewrites the discourse of northern class politics that coalesced around terms
such as "anarchy," "dynamite," "class," and "terror" in the 1880s into the language of racial politics. By making blacks into terrorists, Dixon also metaphorically identifies them as threats to the stability of the national order. Specifically rewriting class as race, Dixon's texts work to mobilize the nationalist
and xenophobic sentiment that was so critical during the Haymarket era and
then redirect that exclusionary energy into the nationalist politics for a new
century: white supremacy.

Yet, if Dixon manages to translate historical organizations such as the black
Union Leagues into clandestine terrorist groups,[28] he also faced the seemingly paradoxical task of depicting the rampant and illegal murder of thousands of African Americans in such a way that these murders did not themselves have the taint of terrorism.[29] To solve this dilemma, Dixon parcels the
Klan's actions off from the roguish (if nonetheless justified, in his view) lynch
mobs. This is why *The Leopard's Spots*'s hero, Charlie Gaston, is "by Dick's
side begging for a fair trial for him" (*LS* 382) at the very moment that a member of the mob strikes the match to burn Dick alive as retribution for raping
a young white girl. The mob, which "seemed to melt into a great crawling,
swaying creature, half reptile, half beast, half dragon, half man, with a thousand legs, and a thousand eyes" (*LS* 384), comes, as Sandra Gunning has suggested, a bit too close to the purported barbarism of the black beast whom it
set out to punish.[30] Thus, while the mob in Dixon's fiction represents a beast-
like savagery, the Klan is paradoxically figured as the opposite of anarchy or
savagery, becoming instead a highly codified, quasi-legal institution.

Of course, it comes as no surprise that Dixon's fictitious glorification of
the Klan does not tally with the historical record of an organization that con-
ducted what has been called the only successful terrorist campaign in Ameri-

can history.[31] The historical Ku Klux Klan was formed in Tennessee by six Confederate officers immediately after the Civil War and had outposts in all southern states by 1868.[32] Nevertheless, the Klan possessed neither an orderly structure nor a stable and hierarchical regional leadership. Violence, primarily against the freed slaves, but also against immigrant northerners, Union-supporting southerners, and interracial couples, was generally ad hoc and executed by local groups on their own initiative. The Klan's activity was most violent and regular in southern communities where there existed little or no differences in economic status between blacks and whites. This pattern underscored the Klan's goal of regulating black citizens' newly acquired social status by attempting to reimpose the deferential social standards that existed during slavery. Moreover, while contemporary commentators routinely pinned the Klan's activities on the South's poorer whites, Klan membership appears to have regularly crossed class lines. Leadership, especially, was generally provided by an area's more "respectable citizens," often the local law enforcement officers, who subsequently either offered rationalizations for the KKK's brutality or simply refused to take legal action against it. Indeed, the Klan's victims were bereft of effective juridical recourse until as late as 1871 because the Klan's crimes were "offenses against state and local law," leaving the federal government without jurisdiction and protective power.[33] In April 1871, however, Congress passed the Ku Klux Klan Act, which for the first time in American history held that crimes committed by individuals were offenses subject to federal law. By placing violence that infringed upon a person's civil or political rights within the purview of the federal government, the juridical changes brought by the act, according to an editorial in *The Nation*, "not only increase[d] the power of the central government, but they arm[ed] it with jurisdiction over a class of cases of which it has never hitherto had, and never pretended to have, any jurisdiction whatever."[34] The Ku Klux Klan Act did not bring large numbers of southern Klansmen to justice, but the suggestion that the federal government was willing to exert its legal and punitive authority did produce a dramatic, if temporary, decline in southern violence after 1871. Yet the reality that the Klan's support among local citizens prevented the Reconstruction governments from suppressing it without federal intervention also meant that the Klan accomplished one of its primary goals: to demonstrate the illegitimacy of the Reconstruction regime.

In Dixon's fiction, this perceived illegitimacy of the Reconstruction government becomes the key to the surprisingly nationalist twist that he gives to his depiction of the Ku Klux Klan. Dixon's appeal to notions of nationhood has been noted previously by critics such as Walter Benn Michaels. Michaels labels *The Clansman* an "anti-imperialist novel" and suggests that implicit discussions of the issues raised by turn-of-the-century American imperialism can be found in the novel's return to Reconstruction. This narrative move "placed anti-imperialism at the heart of an emerging discourse of American racial and national identity."[35] Michaels can identify *The Clansman* as an anti-imperialist novel because he reads it as Dixon's narrative of the South fending off a conquering empire, the North.

There is a certain amount of evidence for Michaels's position. For instance, *The Leopard's Spots* translates the Reconstruction government's lack of local support into a regime that is "corrupt and degraded" and a "conspiracy against human progress" (*LS* 109, 196). It deceitfully bilks millions of dollars from North Carolina's treasury and supports the "Negro reign of terror" (*C* 362). And with Austin Stoneman as the supreme architect of the "Black Plague of Reconstruction" (*C* 179), the Constitution, for those Reconstruction governments, represents only "a league with death and a covenant with hell" (*C* 42). However, what Michaels obscures in his provocative claim that "Dixon actually imagines no preexisting state to be saved from the empire by the Klan," instead "creat[ing] it out of resistance to the empire,"[36] is precisely that the Klan in Dixon does believe in the founding principles of the American republic. That is, as Dixon tells us in a crucial scene where he has the Klan list its "patriotic" purposes, a key objective of the "Invisible Empire" is "to protect and defend the Constitution of the United States, and all the laws passed in conformity thereto" (*C* 320–21). Dixon's KKK does not create the state ex nihilo, as Michaels suggests, but instead fights against what Dixon regards as the abrogation of the American nation's (racist) ideals. Rather than establishing a new state with rights parceled out according to skin color, the objective of Dixon's Klan is to restore order to what he terms the "anarchy" of Reconstruction (*LS* 196) by adhering ever more faithfully to the color privilege that is, in fact, built into the nation's founding legal document.[37] The Klan is thus already an arm of the government, a faithful public servant composed of what *The Traitor*'s dedication identifies as "citizens of the Invisible Empire" who possess a greater commitment to the ideals of the republic than any agency in Washington.

As the enshrouded and unidentifiable "citizens" of an "Invisible Empire," Ku Klux Klan members would seem to have a strange relationship to a nation-defining Constitution, a quintessentially public document. On the other hand, however, the white-males-only anonymity of the Klan bears an eerie resemblance to the ideal citizen envisioned by the eighteenth-century framers of America's Constitution. As Lauren Berlant and several other theorists of the Constitution have argued, the American subject is granted the privilege of suppressing his specific historical situation—his race and gender—under the abstract personhood that the constitutional framers envisioned as the unit of membership in the national public sphere. The implicit whiteness and male gender of the originary citizen is protected and subsumed under an abstract national identity, what Berlant terms a "prophylaxis for the person." One effect of this process is that the implicitly white and male model citizen appears as the Constitution's disembodied "person" while retaining a cultural and political authority.[38]

While the Constitution produced a theoretically abstract form of citizenship, identity in Dixon's novels bears a certain similarity to this abstraction in that, as Walter Benn Michaels points out, it "is always fundamentally spiritual."[39] Moreover, if the American Constitution envisaged an abstract or theoretically "disembodied" citizen, the Klan's white sheets, which in Dixon symbolize the Klan's connection to those men who "led our Revolution" (*C* 342), become the guarantor of a protected and similarly invisible citizenship in the appropriately named "Invisible Empire." Yet that membership in the KKK, like the implicit white citizenship created by the Constitution, paradoxically hinges on the materiality of the white male body. And lest readers agree with *The Leopard's Spots*'s scalawag governor, who deems the Klan simply a lawless band of "conspirators against the Union" (*LS* 160), Dixon makes it clear that the revolutionary lineage of the KKK specifically signifies its fidelity to the nation whose principles have been abrogated by the Reconstruction governments. This lineage and faithful adherence to the Constitution explain how Dixon can label Ben Cameron a "successful revolutionist" in *The Clansman* (374). For Dixon, the KKK is the terrorist arm of a besieged state seeking to escape the power of an unjust occupier. Moreover, Dixon explicitly disavows the notion of a small, conspiratorial cabal, instead describing the Klan as "the resistless movement of a race, not of any man or leader of men" (*C* 341). Complementing this emphasis on mass rather than individual personhood, when the Klan rides, it is "utterly impossible to recognise a man or a horse, so complete was the simple disguise of the white sheet" (*LS* 153).

Deindividualizing Klan members by making them indistinguishable, the privacy afforded by the white sheets makes it possible for Dixon both to applaud the Klan as "the white terror" (*LS* 152), "shrouded in a mantle of darkness" (*C* 341), and to regard it as a specifically *public* extension of the Constitution.[40] That is, if the Klan's strikes, which are unprovoked, unannounced, and under cover of darkness, appear to be those of the prototypical privacy-seeking terrorist, the other element essential to the Klan's terror in Dixon is its resolute publicity. All white people, "fused in the white heat of one sublime thought" (*C* 343), already know who belongs to the Klan. In fact, at the height of the historic Klan in the late 1860s, leading southern citizens regularly chose the victims and also participated in the savage raids right along with poorer whites to whom the violence was more commonly attributed.[41] Dixon's intervention into constitutional notions of citizenship in the Reconstruction trilogy is thus to fashion the privilege of citizenship in his "Invisible Empire" according to the abstraction favored by the American Constitution, while making that ideal citizen a vengeful and, paradoxically, already-known terrorist.

Indeed, as Richard Rubenstein has argued about terrorist groups in general, and the Ku Klux Klan in particular, they are most effective when they have a network of grassroots support in which sympathizers furnish protection and other necessities.[42] In the case of the historic Klan, this support included not only the collusion of southern towns' "best citizens" and its poorer white farmers, but also white women who sewed the Klan's costumes and local merchants who attempted to cash in on the Klan's aura by utilizing the KKK's name and imagery to market their products.[43] In Dixon's fiction, then, it is precisely by making the Klan members citizen-terrorists and leaders of the local white population that he attempts to draw an ideological line of separation between the violence of the KKK and the violence of the freed slaves' very similar-sounding "oath-bound secret societies" that are "terrorising the country" during Reconstruction (*LS* 101). As citizens and the recognized representatives of other citizens, Klan members become the semi-official and public paramilitary arm of the government. The "African" regime (*LS* 196), on the other hand, is basely illegitimate. Turning to the Constitution, or, as Charlie Gaston in *The Leopard's Spots* puts it, "return[ing] to the sanity of the founders of this republic," Dixon is thus able to regard the legal history of the postwar period as a fatally flawed attempt to "make men out of paper" (*LS* 442).

But if Dixon's complaint against the postwar constitutional amendments — "making men out of paper" — seems to be an incoherent criticism, given the fact that the United States was in a sense "made" by writing and paper in the Declaration of Independence and Constitution, his cynical response is to find the true germ of America in the "heritage of centuries of heroic blood from the martyrs of old Scotland," who "walked in chains to the stake with songs on their lips" (*C* 101). Appropriating the contemporary discourse of lynching and stake burning to reveal the difference between the latter-day, inauthentic, "paper" citizens of America and the country's "true" racial lineage, Dixon transforms the U.S. Constitution and the KKK's white sheets into contemporary symbols of the Scottish clans' quest for freedom. In his racialist view, this can only mean that the postwar amendments designed to bring some degree of racial equity to America were a fundamental misreading of the nation's heritage.

The point of Dixon's fondness for the Constitution and his return to the era of Reconstruction from his writerly position at the turn of the century is to disavow the mob violence of lynching.[44] There would have been good reason to distance one's self from this violence, even from Dixon's highly racist point of view. Historian Joel Williamson reports that an average of 138 persons were lynched each year in the southern states during the 1890s, with blacks comprising 75 percent of victims. The first decade of the twentieth century witnessed a small decline in the number of lynchings, but the percentage of black victims increased to 90. In fact, in the years between 1885 and 1907, there were more persons lynched in the United States than legally executed. In 1892, the statistical height of lynching, there were twice as many lynchings as executions.[45]

The barbarity of mob lynching obviously exceeds the phenomenon's chilling historical statistics. The 1893 ritualized burning of Henry Smith in Paris, Texas, can, perhaps, synecdochically represent the thousands of other victims. Accused of raping and murdering a three-year-old white girl, Smith was subjected to stomach-turning cruelty and torture. After his capture, he was tied to a chair that had been mounted atop a wagon and driven around the town of Paris so that the thousands of people who had been brought in by special excursion trains could see and taunt him. When finally placed upon a raised platform to be murdered before the massive crowd of witnesses, Smith was bound to a stake and tortured with hot irons over every part of his body until, once he appeared to be dead, his body was set afire. During all this, an entrepreneurial photographer took pictures of the event to sell as souvenirs, and, reportedly, a "graphophone recording" was made of the whole grisly affair.[46]

In the face of such mob violence, which appeared more anarchic than any act ever committed by the self-proclaimed anarchists of the late nineteenth century, Dixon disclaimed the mob in *The Leopard's Spots* and concocted his Constitution-protecting Ku Klux Klan in *The Clansman*. But if the white sheets signal the Klan's fidelity to the Constitution, those sheets nonetheless create a quandary similar to that presented by Gus's wearing of the Yankee uniform. That is, as the trilogy's last book, *The Traitor*, makes clear, the white disguise can easily conceal the identity of a scoundrel performing unauthorized attacks in the Klan's name. Taking up its narrative plotline after "redemption" of North Carolina's government in the 1870 state elections, the Klan is dissolved early in *The Traitor* in order to spare its members "persecution, exile, imprisonment and death" (*T* 54) resulting from the Ku Klux Klan Act of 1871. But a "wildcat Klan" quickly emerges, leading to the rapid "degradation of the Klan into an engine of personal vengeance and criminal folly" and "covering the name of the Ku Klux Klan with infamy" (*T* 58, 95, 97). Under command of the reckless and unscrupulous Steve Hoyle, the new Klan "whip[s] scalawag politicians night after night" and terrorizes freed slaves for all sorts of slights, "real or fancied." And crucially, this new Klan does not confine its violence to racial politics but also whips a white man as punishment for spousal abuse and "tar[s] and feather[s] a white girl of low origin" (*T* 96). In *The Clansman,* on the other hand, the KKK confines itself to punishing politicians and performing the highly ritualistic and orderly (but offstage) execution of Gus.

The "reign of folly and terror" (*T* 96) perpetrated by Dixon's rogue Klan is especially interesting because it actually mirrors the actions of the historical KKK. Like *The Traitor*'s "wildcat Klan," the Reconstruction-era Klan itself regularly raped black women and terrorized lower-class white women of "bad character" with whippings and even sexual mutilation.[47] Not surprisingly, Dixon's desire to rewrite the KKK as the official terrorist wing of an apartheid state leads him to separate violence that cannot be regarded as explicit punishment of black rapists away from the "real" Klan and link it to the Klan impersonators. Furthermore, Dixon rhetorically connects the lawless acts of blacks during Reconstruction with the new Klan's violent activities. Both conjure up for him the French "reign of terror," and both receive similar punishments from the real Klan. In *Traitor,* the outlaw Klan members are "given forty lashes" and left "gagged and bleeding dangling by their arms from the limbs of the trees" (*T* 109). The key difference here is, of course, that white men are strung up by their arms rather than their necks. Yet the point of meting out versions of the same punishment to Klan impersonators and black rapists is to reinforce the idea that the Klan, for Dixon, is, paradoxically enough, truly committed to "Law and Order" (*LS* 151). The Reconstruction governments and lawless Klan impostors, on the other hand, stand squarely "in violation of the Constitution" (*T* 330).

The message of *The Traitor* is thus that the Klan's white sheets ultimately prove no more effective than the Yankee uniform as a way of demarcating the nation's true citizens. Susceptible to being worn by the wrong persons, the white sheets have to be discarded and the Klan disbanded. Dixon, however, makes what would appear to be the death knell for the Klan into an opportunity to rejuvenate the white race. John Graham, hero of *The Traitor,* in a gesture meant to indicate his devotion to Stella, his love interest, violates the Klan's supreme law. By taking her to the decayed and abandoned mansion that serves as the KKK's "council chamber" and showing her "the guarded secrets of the Invisible Empire, its signs, passwords, ritual and secret oath," Graham commits an act that necessarily signs his own death warrant at the hands of the Klan (*T* 229–30). But that retributive violence never comes to pass. Graham is soon captured by the U.S. Army and sent to prison until he is pardoned by the "little politicians" who, finally, cower before a Supreme Court that would strike down their "venomous Conspiracy Acts" that stand "in violation of the Constitution of the Republic" (*T* 330). Crucially, Graham's disclosing the Klan's secrets to Stella sealed her love for him. The book's closing scene finds them living happily with their children in the restored mansion where the Klan had formerly met, with John Graham having abandoned the law and gone into textile manufacturing. Graham's abandonment of the Klan's principles thus makes possible a new form of southern capitalism and the reproduction of white children, who are themselves sanctified as the proper "future American" by living in the very place from which the real Klan had launched its raids as the "sole guardians of white civilisation" (*T* 230).

Imperial Adventures, Class Politics, and the Reuniting of White America

Dixon's Klan in *The Clansman* and in *The Traitor* is a middle-class organization. This creates an ideological problem for his texts in the form of economically disenfranchised poor whites, such as Allan McLeod in *The Leopard's Spots* or Steven Hoyle in *The Traitor*, who inevitably become—aside from the mandatory black rapists—the books' political villains. Of course, one of Dixon's primary answers to the problem of disunited whites is the invention of the black rapist. And when he does mention class issues that could potentially separate whites, he suppresses any discussion of postbellum realities such as the crop lien system that smothered the economic hopes of blacks and whites alike.[48] Moreover, as I noted earlier, Martha Hodes's research into Klan activities has shown that violence against lower-class white women was also a regular part of the Klan's behavior. Yet for Dixon, rape serves precisely to paper over all the economic differences that divided southern whites. In *The Clansman,* for instance, the rape victim is a young woman from the middle class, but significantly, the young victim in *The Leopard's Spots* is the daughter of a poor farmer and belongs to the lower class of whites. The rape and murder of a poor white child directly leads to the elision of class difference, since "in a moment the white race had fused into a homogenous mass of love, sympathy, hate and revenge. The rich and the poor, the learned and the ignorant, the banker and the blacksmith, the great and the small, they were all one now" (*LS* 372).

But while Dixon notoriously preyed on the period's hysteria about black male sexuality and helped create the new ideological figure of the black male rapist, he also recalibrated or provided new meanings for certain powerful late-nineteenth-century ideas that were already in circulation. Specifically, in the last third of the nineteenth century, it was regularly asserted that the Civil War had finally solved the nation versus section dilemma that had haunted American politics for a century. Dixon's ideological move in his trilogy is to accept that America was "one country now" (*LS* 79), but rather than acknowledging the nationalization of citizenship and rights guaranteed by the postwar amendments, he nationalizes what he regards as the southern point of view. Aside from the black rapist, his primary tools for making this ideological pirouette come in his fictionalization of America's turn-of-the-century imperialism and his depiction of southern capitalism.

In Dixon's version of the Spanish-American War, America's first overseas war, though "we feared the gulf between the rich and the poor had become impassable . . . once more we showed the world that classes and clothes are but thin disguises that hide the eternal childhood of the soul" (*LS* 410). The divisiveness of religion in American life falls by the wayside too, as "we saw our Catholic regiments march forth to that war with . . . the flag of our country above them, going forth to fight an army that had been blessed by the Pope of Rome" (*LS* 409–10). And the South, by supplying many of the short war's heroes, produced an "America, united at last and invincible," thus "re-unit[ing] the Anglo-Saxon race" (*LS* 412). With this reuniting of America's white citizens "into one homogenous mass," the "Negro ceased that moment to be a ward of the nation" (*LS* 413).

Tempered by the white heat of war (and, more cynically, we might add, the yellow journalism of Hearst and Pulitzer), white Americans in Dixon overcome the economic divisiveness that had grown out of the severe depression of the 1890s and finally take up the "white man's burden," a phrase Dixon appropriates for the subtitle of *The Leopard's Spots*. Yet, if class status and clothing provide only a meager disguise for what Dixon identifies as the commonality of the soul, this commonality is only made evident in his work by shared skin color. Furthermore, this narrative line glosses over the very important fact that it was not at all clear in the 1890s who qualified as "white" in the United States. That decade witnessed the emergence of America's second great wave of immigration, which, unlike earlier moments, was composed largely of southeastern European and Jewish immigrants. And though the Progressive Era rhetoric of "Americanization" was emerging by this time—

and is even reflected in *The Traitor* in a southern Jew who supports the Klan because he, too, has known oppression (*T* 107)—the question of whether or not Jews, Italians, Greeks, and Slavs were entitled to the prerogatives of whiteness was not settled. Dixon casts aside these issues, however, because the thrust of his narrative is to rewrite the southern view of race relations as the dominant national view. In Dixon, this remaking of the South as the nation itself works to undo the damage wrought by the unconstitutional Reconstruction governments, which had strayed from what he regards as the principles of the Constitution. In short, making war abroad and "wip[ing] the empire of Spain from the map of the Western world" (*LS* 409) reunite formerly class-divided whites and make it apparent that, as he had been in the South since Reconstruction, "the Negro was an impossibility in the newborn unity of national life" (*LS* 413).

This programmatic interest in excising African Americans from the national body politic, which is heightened by American imperialism in Dixon's fiction, explains why the chapter in *Spots* immediately following his depiction of the Spanish-American War is titled "Another Declaration of Independence." In that chapter, Dixon, like Charles Chesnutt in *The Marrow of Tradition* but with a radically different agenda, implicitly returns to the 1898 Wilmington riot and fictionalizes it. In Dixon's account, the local black newspaper "publishe[s] an editorial defaming the virtue" of white women. In response, Charlie Gaston becomes chairman of a "committee of twenty-five" that forces the town's leading black citizens to flee for their lives (*LS* 415–16). These events conform to what happened in Wilmington before the riot, but Dixon makes a crucial change in his delineation of its immediate cause. In Dixon's version, the riot is instigated by a regiment of black soldiers who have been stationed at a town named Independence, North Carolina, throughout the war, and specifically by a black soldier who bumps into a white girl on the sidewalk and is consequently beaten to death by her escort (*LS* 414). As in Reconstruction, then, the American military uniform provokes a crisis at the turn of the century by disguising the true nature of "Negro troops" (*LS* 414). American foreign wars and the renewed specter of black troops thus make possible the reinvigoration of the Declaration of Independence in the symbolically named Independence, North Carolina, a town that "boasted the first declaration of independence from Great Britain" and "whose ancestors had been leaders in the great Revolution" (*LS* 414–15). In Dixon, however, the Declaration is figuratively rewritten; no longer needing to free themselves from British rule, American citizens now "issue a second Declaration of Independence" that frees them from "Negro Anarchist[s]" and black claims to the rights of citizenship (*LS* 415–16).

Igniting a "race fire" (*LS* 419), the revolution at Independence rings the death knell for "fusion politics" in *The Leopard's Spots*. In Dixon's book, as in North Carolina history, the "fusion" ticket—an alliance of Populists and Democrats on the national level and, simultaneously, a paradoxical alliance of Republicans, Populist farmers, and blacks in the racially organized southern political landscape—had managed significant victories in the state elections of 1894 and 1896.[49] The short-lived coalition was undermined, however, by the divisiveness of race in the South and the violent disfranchisement of blacks under Jim Crow. In *Spots*, the end of "African" rule at Independence propels Charlie Gaston into the governor's mansion on a one-plank Democratic white supremacist platform. From then on, as in the earlier Redemption-era South, "every discordant element of the old South's furious political passions was now melted into harmonious unity. . . . Secessionist and Unionist now clasped hands. . . . Henceforth there could be but one issue—Are you a White Man or a Negro?" (*LS* 161). The point for Dixon is that eliminating the fusion politics that had temporarily threatened to rewrite the political map of the South, much as a "new map of the world had been made" by the Civil War (*LS* 4), makes possible the fusion of the white race across economic, religious, and regional differences. Complementing his repeated invocation of black male rape, Dixon, by making politics hinge on the singular plank of race, essentially replaces political difference with racial difference.[50]

Just as the Yankee uniforms and Klan sheets had to be disclaimed because they could disguise the wrong person, Dixon thus eliminates the ambiguity and potential exploitability of political alliances. Tying citizenship to whiteness via the "second Declaration of Independence" is not, however, where Dixon finishes his Reconstruction trilogy. With southern blacks disfranchised and essentially rendered noncitizens, southern whites turn their attention to economics. If, as Charlie Gaston tells his father-in-law in *The Leopard's Spots*, "the people of the South had to go into politics instead of business on account of the enfranchisement of the Negro" (*LS* 283)—and Gaston stays in politics as governor of North Carolina—it is his campaign of disfranchisement in that novel that makes it safe for John Graham, his novelistic descendent in *The Traitor*, to abandon politics for business. And in Dixon's vision, while imperialism and African American disfranchisement made possible the reuniting of a white race that had been torn asunder by the Civil War, it is when the South can finally turn to the development of industry and manufacturing that the North and South are firmly cemented in a bond of white supremacy.

But as with Dixon's depiction of the Spanish-American War, which convinced the North to follow the South's lead on the "Negro question," one of Dixon's primary purposes in fictionalizing the economics of the New South is specifically to make the rest of the nation more like the South rather than vice versa. For this purpose, Dixon returns to the narrative thread devoted to Simon Legree in *The Leopard's Spots*. After Legree is forced out of the South, he parleys his seat on the Wall Street stock exchange into "fifty millions of dollars" (*LS* 403) and ownership of several factories. From this mighty position, Legree lures other "petty millionaire[s]" into "speculative trap[s]" and financially crushes them (*LS* 405). But even worse than his financial despotism, Legree "has murdered the souls of many innocent girls in these mills" (*LS* 404). Indeed, with such unlimited power at his disposal, his "chances for debauchery and cruelty are limitless" (*LS* 405). Again the point is that industrial capitalism in the North far exceeds the barbarity of anything in the history of slavery. But in making the sexual abuse of young women the linchpin of this message, Dixon, without acknowledging it, pulls a page out of slavery's history. As is now widely known, the rape of female slaves was one of the more common and nefarious abuses of slavery. In sexualizing industrial capitalism, Dixon inadvertently conjures up the evils of slavery.

Yet, wary of readers making a connection between race slavery and the working conditions of industrial capitalism, Dixon is also quick to appropriate the late-nineteenth-century discourse of "wage-slavery" for his own purposes. Lifting Stowe's combative mulatto character, George Harris, from *Uncle Tom's Cabin*, Dixon sends him around the North looking for factory work. But in a series of scenes strangely reminiscent of Frederick Douglass's antebellum autobiography, northern white workers threaten to strike rather than work side by side with a black man. And significantly, rather than regarding blacks as similarly oppressed workers, a meeting of unionized socialists in *Spots* refuse Harris because "the Negro can under-live us." Moreover, slavery, in their view, "was a mild form of servitude in which the Negro had plenty to eat and wear," and, in fact, "slavery was never firmly established until the chattel form was abandoned for the wage system in 1865" (*LS* 400–401). Though it is true that, historically speaking, racial divisiveness kept most working-class radicals and African Americans apart during the nineteenth century,[51] Dixon's purpose here is to make the North follow the South's lead in its rejection of black citizens. Returning briefly to the North, then, Dixon finds confirmation both that northern industry exceeds southern slavery in cruelty and that, even more important, as with the Spanish-American War, rejection of African American citizens transgresses class lines, uniting all whites in a fever of racial antipathy. The stage is thus set for Dixon to valorize the manufacturing progress of the so-called New South.

[124]

In *The Clansman*, however, it is not a southerner who introduces manufacturing to the South. Instead, it is Phil Stoneman, son of the notorious Austin Stoneman, leader of the congressional Radical Republicans. But Phil Stoneman is no carpetbagger looking to mine southern industry for easy profits that can be channeled directly back to the North. On the contrary, he represents another example of the postwar reunion of North and South over the bodies of dead blacks. Convinced that rampaging blacks are pillaging the white South, he asks Ben Cameron to let him join the Klan (*C* 337). Moreover, he falls in love with a southern belle and, in a scene staged to inspire whites to reunite and exclude blacks, we are told that Stoneman and Cameron "were as much alike as twins" (*C* 8).

Dixon's decision to advance the cause of manufacturing via Stoneman's character is crucial precisely because Phil Stoneman, who is instantly accepted by all southerners because he "ha[s] no axe to grind" (*C* 210), contradicts the historical reality of much postwar economic development in the southern Piedmont region. Many of Dixon's contemporaries, as well as subsequent historians, viewed the New South's emergent economy as essentially "colonial" because it paid extremely low wages and produced raw products for distant markets where the more profitable finishing took place.[52] Dixon's Stoneman, however, whose southern sympathies make him "feel closer than a brother" to Cameron (*C* 225), unlike the Yankees who want to build a cotton mill in Chesnutt's *The Marrow of Tradition*, desires only to settle down in the South, marry, and leave his profits in the region.

In *The Clansman*, Stoneman has to become southern in disposition before the South can be introduced to manufacturing. Significantly, Dixon returns to this idea at the close of the trilogy's last novel, which finds John Graham returning from prison not to reorganize the Klan but to "beg[i]n the manufacture of cotton goods" (*T* 331). Dixon's repeated emphasis on the importance of textile manufacturing places him squarely in the tradition of economic boosterism that was rampant throughout the South at the turn of the century. The textile industry was indeed integral to the region's development, but far more southern industrial workers found themselves in mines or forests than inside factories. Those extraction industries ultimately failed to produce the widespread economic development that other regions of the country were experiencing at the time,[53] although they did produce the conditions for the particular form of southern class violence that I will examine in Chapter 5. But Dixon's fictional focus on the textile industry signifies more than a simple repetition of the southern boosters' economic optimism. By locating John Graham's textile factories where Inwood's "wide acres of forest extend to the river" (*T* 331), Dixon evokes the pastoral image of the antebellum South, and placing them at Inwood, the previous meeting spot of the Klan, ensures that southern manufacturing does not become a capitulation to the ways of the North. Instead, both in location and in product, Dixon's cotton mills maintain the heritage of the slave South by reinventing a small class of white owners who preserve their grip on power by becoming industrialists. Moreover, in a deft turn, the South in Dixon becomes an anticipatory bulwark "against the possible day when a flood of foreign anarchy threatens the foundations of the Republic" (*LS* 337). The political economy represented in the turn to textile manufacturing that ends Dixon's trilogy thus imagines the South as the preserver of the nation's integrity, much as the Klan, earlier in the trilogy, had reached back to the founding document of the Constitution to reaffirm America's whiteness after the Civil War. The mills at Inwood make the turn to manufacturing into a phenomenon that continues the specifically racialized legacy of the Klan while also foreshadowing its rebirth in the 1920s, when its violence would be directed at both African Americans and natives of those countries believed responsible for "the flood of anarchy."

Ida B. Wells and the Rewriting of America's "National Crime"

A fair amount of Dixon's energy in his trilogy is devoted to his self-authorization. That is, Dixon peppers his books' prefatory remarks with phrases such as "true story" and "authentic records." I have suggested that one way to grasp the ideological architecture of Dixon's racism is to look both at the ways he appropriates the rhetoric of other discourses, such as class strife, and at how he refashions the historical activities of the Ku Klux Klan into actions that defend the nation against imaginary black rapists. But another lens through which to view the racialized nation-work of Dixon's prose is the writing of his contemporary, Ida B. Wells. Like Dixon, Wells felt obligated to vouch continually for the authenticity of her writing. Of course, Wells's depiction of events is mediated by writing and ideological imperatives in a way that Dixon's also is, though her version of the era's racial violence is certainly a more accurate description. Further, her antilynching pamphlets highlight the ways in which a flexible rhetoric of racial terrorism within what each author identified as an accurate portrayal of social conditions served in both their accounts of lynching to delineate the ideological contours of the American nation's political economy.

My analysis of Wells's use of a discourse of nationhood in her writing departs from earlier important studies of her work, such as Hazel Carby's *Reconstructing Womanhood* and Paula Giddings's *When and Where I Enter.* Among other things, these accounts of Wells seek to reconstruct her turn-of-the-century work for a contemporary audience along an axis of gender. Carby, for instance, consciously seeks to counter those discussions of Wells, such as Thomas C. Holt's, that see her as a "lonely warrior" without a movement behind her whose work pales in comparison to that of W. E. B. Du Bois or Booker T. Washington. As Carby flamboyantly states the case, Wells was "an 'uppity' black woman with an analysis of the relationship among political terrorism, economic oppression, and conventional codes of sexuality and morality that has still to be surpassed in its incisive condemnation of the patriarchal manipulation of race and gender."[54]

Carby's analysis is penetrating with regard both to Wells and to the subtle gender biases that often still undergird contemporary scholarly investigations, such as those that see the public work of a Du Bois or Washington as *necessarily* more historically important than the different form of public work carried on by Wells. Further, recent work by Patricia Schechter has brilliantly theorized the role that both expressing and suppressing intense anger played in Wells's public persona.[55] This is certainly a crucial project in the ongoing reconstruction of American literary and cultural studies. Yet, too often, Wells's fascinating life and biography have taken precedence over analysis of her writing. Carby's discussion, for instance, does dwell to some extent on Wells's writing, but she frames her discussion within the context of Wells's life history so that the writing itself almost seems an explanation of Wells's biography. Of course, for a writer such as Wells whose work was so finely calibrated with her life, it is neither possible nor desirable to cleave her writing from her life. However, Wells's writing will sustain analysis not just for what she does, which has been aptly analyzed by Carby, but also for the rhetorical terms that were available to her to construct her argument.[56] Writing shortly after the incidents at Haymarket in which ideas of "Americanness" proved so decisive, and during the period when this country was celebrating the four-hundredth anniversary of its "discovery" by Columbus, Wells turned to notions of nationhood, citizenship, and anarchy as the primary discursive structures for the arguments by which she attempted to unite the North and South against lynching.

Wells's preferred methodology in *Southern Horrors* and *A Red Record* is to relentlessly deconstruct the claims of lynching's apologists. While most white Americans acquiesced in Dixon's justification of lynching as a punishment for black men's sexual assaults upon white women, Wells used the lynching statistics compiled by the *Chicago Tribune* to demonstrate that most lynchings did not even involve the charge of rape. Moreover, she unearthed evidence suggesting the falseness of accusations ranging from thieving and arson to rape that were routinely used as excuses for murdering black men. Wells also recounts stories of consensual interracial sexual relations "as a defense for the Afro-Americans Sampsons who suffer themselves to be betrayed by white Delilahs" (*SH* 53). But significantly, she does not end *Southern Horrors* with an account of a black man's lynching derived from the local white papers, as is her custom throughout her other writings.

Instead, *Horrors* closes with an account of men who "legally (?) hung poor little thirteen year old Mildrey Brown at Columbia, S.C., Oct. 7th, on the circumstantial evidence that she poisoned a white infant" (*SH* 71). Wells's insertion of the ironizing question mark after the word "legally" is a local occurrence of a wider strategy in her texts. At other points, she rhetorically asks if black men "always rape (?) white women" (*SH* 53) and marvels that "Southern States have legally (?) disfranchised the Afro-American" (*SH* 60). By drawing on the reports of white newspapers to ward off charges of bias, but then inserting these parenthetical question marks at key moments of those accounts, Wells subverted the seeming objectivity of the white papers' accounts, thereby making space for her alternative interpretation of lynching.[57] Further, Wells's ending *Horrors* with a lynched black girl jars uneasily against the dominant image of the mythological black male rapist's worst atrocity, the rape of a child. It was for this crime, for instance, that Henry Smith was tortured and burned alive in Paris, Texas, on a platform to which had been nailed a crudely lettered sign declaring "JUSTICE."[58] Substituting the body of a "legally (?)" murdered black child for the image of the black rapist, Wells mocks the idea that lynching can ever represent justice. Lynching especially could not represent the "justice for all" encoded in the American Pledge of Allegiance, a nationalist narrative that Francis Bellamy wrote the same year Wells published *Horrors* in preparation for the quadricentennial celebration of Columbus's voyage. Additionally, as Sandra Gunning has written, ending with Mildrey Brown's lynching is part of Wells's repudiation of the idea that lynching is always a punishment for the rape of white women. Wells's dramatic ending to *Southern Horrors* thus serves as a bitter comment on the reduction of all lynched bodies to the "obliterating stereotype" of the black rapist."[59]

By closing *Southern Horrors* with the lynched body of a black female, Wells also metaphorically returns readers to the pamphlet's opening. There Wells reprints her notorious editorial, first published in Memphis on 21 May 1892, in which, as a response to several recent lynchings, she argued that "nobody in this section of the country believes the old thread-bare lie that negro men rape white women" (*SH* 52). Several white papers had answered Wells's article with their own inflammatory editorials, informing Memphis's black citizens that it was "the duty of those whom *he* has attacked to tie the wretch who utters these calumnies to a stake . . . brand him in the forehead with a hot iron and perform upon him a surgical operation with a pair of tailor's shears" (*SH* 52, my emphasis). Wells's article was published in her Memphis newspaper, *Free Speech,* whose title consciously invoked the First Amendment to the Constitution. For a black-owned newspaper in the 1890s, such purposeful appropriation of the Constitution's First Amendment would also have conjured up the postwar amendments, which made blacks citizens and provided black men (if not black women) with a democracy's most fundamental right, the elective franchise. Taking a page from Thomas Dixon, the white newspapers' response denied the right of free speech to black Americans, thus also figuratively denying them the protection of the Constitution and even the designation of "citizen." Wells, aware of the constitutional irony at stake in the denial of "free speech" to black Americans, goes on to refer to those men who plan her lynching specifically as Memphis's "leading citizens" (*SH* 52).

The importance of Wells's ironically invoking the rights of citizenship here becomes even more apparent when we juxtapose this scene with her account of an Alabama lynching in *A Red Record.* In that case, when it became known that a black man was the father of a white woman's baby, he was lynched, despite the openly acknowledged fact that the relationship had been going on for over a year. Significantly, a message pinned to the corpse read "This the work of one hundred best citizens of the South Side" (*RR* 125). Simone Davis incisively suggests that Wells documents lynchers' penchant for writing on the bodies of dead black men to underscore her paramount rejection of the notion that whites lynch blacks in moments of high passion stemming from assaults on white women. Instead, the messages are calculated to send an "economically motivated, political message" to other African Americans.[60] Furthermore, in a historical episode that anticipates Dixon's turn-of-the-century fiction, the lynchers' specific identification of themselves as "citizens" reveals their fusion of citizenship and whiteness over a black man's dead body. Wells's alternative invocation of citizenship represents her attempt to use the powerful idea of citizenship itself to suggest that the legal form of membership in the American republic had become synonymous with barbaric violence in the 1890s.

If citizenship becomes an ideologically weighted term in the rhetoric of both Wells and lynching parties, that citizenship is also gendered. When Wells wrote her editorial in *Free Speech* questioning the bevy of rape charges leveled against African American men and thereby implying that white women often had consensual sex with black men, Memphis's white journalists could only imagine her as a black male rapist whom they would castrate with "tailor's shears" if possible. Wells is thus doubly erased along axes of gender and race in their riposte. The white response registers the invisibility of black women in a political climate that did not sanction political rights for any women and thus made it unimaginable that Wells's editorial could have been penned by other than a man. Moreover, in assuming that Wells was a black man, the white journalist's threat of lynching exemplifies the violent disfranchisement of black males under Jim Crow. As Wells put it, the South's "white citizens are wedded to any method however revolting, any measure however extreme, for the subjugation of the young manhood of the race. They have cheated him out of his ballot, deprived him of civil rights or redress therefor [*sic*] in the civil courts, robbed him of the fruits of his labor, and are still murdering, burning and lynching him" (*SH* 66). In this passage, Wells uses the language of matrimony to suggest that the whites-only matrimonial bond of the post-Reconstruction era, in which interracial marriages were legally proscribed, was in reality a thin cover for what white men were actually "wedded" to: the "revolting" violence of political disfranchisement.

That "revolting" violence directed against young black men also leads Wells to identify lynching as the "blot of a national crime" that causes America to stand "condemned before the world with a series of crimes so peculiarly national" (*RR* 81–82). By labeling lynching as a "peculiarly national" crime, Wells also conjures up the image of slavery, the so-called peculiar institution. In Wells's formulation, the nation itself, which bears responsibility for the "national crime" of lynching, comes to stand in for the antebellum "institution" of slavery in much the same way that the neo-slavery of Wells's own Jim Crow era had supplanted the chattel slavery of the prewar years. Indeed, Wells is referring specifically to the neoslavery of the post-Reconstruction era in her catalogue of the various violences directed against the "young manhood of the race." Besides outright violence, a series of poll taxes, literacy tests, and grandfather clauses that would have also prevented most poor whites from voting if the measures were equally applied had stripped black males' franchise from them.[61] An additional barrage of post-Reconstruction Supreme Court decisions had so thoroughly constricted the protections of federal citizenship that African Americans had largely been deprived of legal redress in the court system.[62] Meanwhile, the emergent system of sharecropping and the crop lien system that developed alongside it robbed the erstwhile slaves of the economic autonomy that freedom had promised.[63] The result of all this, for Wells, was a realization that America at the turn of the century was regressing in practice and sometimes in law back to behaviors that presumably had been abandoned with the death of America's "peculiar institution."

Indeed, by the time Wells was writing, some fifteen to twenty years after the demise of Reconstruction, lynch mobs no longer felt it necessary to conduct their raids under cover of night while wearing white sheets. Violence against black bodies had gone public, a fact documented by Wells's reprinting of press report after press report detailing public, festival-like, daylight lynchings that had become the terrible norm rather than the aberration by the mid-1890s. This development suggests the extent to which the post-Reconstruction North had acquiesced to the South's solution to the "Negro problem," as those persons bent on terrorizing African Americans no longer felt any need for the anonymity of darkness. And the reason that lynch mobs felt they could act with such impunity, Wells suggests in *A Red Record,* was that the "press and even the pulpit, in the main either by silence or open apology, have condoned and encouraged this state of anarchy" (*RR* 91). Evoking both the psychological and the nationalist meanings of "state," Wells argues that the American republic itself had degenerated into a system of lawlessness that enjoyed widespread tacit, and even openly declared, support.

The discursive web conjured up by what Wells elsewhere identified as America's support for "a system of anarchy and outlawry" (*RR* 75) throughout the 1880s and 1890s rhetorically hearkens back to the anarchist movements of the postwar period. For Wells's readers, as with Dixon's, the mention of anarchy would have brought to mind images of dynamite-wielding terrorists. But what is interesting here is that the anarchists of the 1880s, at least those in Chicago where Wells would go to live after the turn of the century, had put their faith in the belief that a violent cataclysm would usher in an era of widespread peace. The unfortunate irony is that the anarchists believed that violence could be a progressive act, while the violence of anarchic lynch mobs was fundamentally regressive in its attempt to force America back to the social order of slavery. Yet, if Wells problematically links the postwar anarchist movement with the lawlessness of lynch mobs, this was nonetheless a dramatic ploy on her part. The image of the Haymarket anarchists was so strong in the public mind in the last decade of the nineteenth century that to mention anarchy was also inevitably to relive the Haymarket bombing. Indirectly invoking Haymarket, then, Wells's *A Red Record* suggests that the American people, who so violently castigated Chicago's anarchists, were actually in support of a racialized anarchy, if not the anarchy of class violence. But for Wells, race and economics could not be so easily separated, precisely because she went to such pains to explain how a southern economic system that had lost slavery used the mythology of rape to regain control over the bodies of black men.[64] The anarchy of the South, according to Wells, was the effect of whites' attempts to regain their vested economic interests.

While anarchy suggested extreme political disorder and barbarism for Wells's contemporaries, Africa, then being subjugated by European imperialism, represented a corollary barbarism along a racial axis. Recognizing this, Wells not only suggested that America was really more like the dreaded anarchists than it dared to acknowledge, she also reversed the trope of barbarism to demonstrate that it was the United States that was bereft of civilization, not Africa. Had lynchings occurred "in the wilds of interior Africa," she writes, "the whole of Christendom would be roused, to devise ways and means to put a stop to it." But "American civilization" simply allowed these atrocities "to be passed by unnoticed, to be denied or condoned as the requirements of any future emergency might determine" (*RR* 112, 154). Invoking Africa, Wells also invokes colonialism and uses the barbarism of lynching to deconstruct the notion that Americans and Europeans could be bringing "civilization" to the "darker races" of the world.[65]

Implicitly chastising "the whole of Christendom," Wells also asks readers to recognize the racial blind spots that have often characterized American religion. In this, she looks backward to Frederick Douglass's *Narrative* and its stinging condemnation of American religion's hypocritical attitudes toward slavery. But Wells's mention of Christendom also reaches out to a writer contemporary with her, Mark Twain, whose essay "The United States of Lyncherdom" I alluded to in this chapter's title. In that short piece, Twain, with the biting sarcasm that characterizes his later work, laments the fact that in 1901 lynching spread to his native Missouri. Twain's wry suggestion is that perhaps the only hope for America is to bring religious missionaries working in China home to the United States, especially since in China "almost every convert runs a risk of catching our civilization. We ought to be careful. We ought to think twice before we encourage a risk like that; for, *once civilized, China can never be uncivilized again*. . . . Our missionaries will find that we have a field for them. . . . We implore them to come back and help us in our need. Patriotism imposes this duty on them. Our country is worse off than China."[66]

Twain's ironic comment on the danger of "civilizing" China can also stand as a final comment on Thomas Dixon, whose work is evoked by Wells's comments on religion and colonialism as well. As I noted earlier, Dixon subtitled his best-selling *Leopard's Spots* "A Romance of the White Man's Burden." The "white man's burden," as Wells and Twain demonstrated, was not the responsibility of "civilizing" people of color throughout the world, but rather to bring to fruition the civilizing promises of the Civil War amendments. Moreover, if one believes in the social power of literature, then it is impossible not to believe as well that the racist venom that suffused Dixon's wildly popular Reconstruction trilogy exacerbated the racial terrorism directed against African American citizens at the turn of the century. Had Wells lived in a racial climate in which her work could have found outlets other than only black-owned newspapers, and had Twain's essay, written in 1901 but not published until 1923, seemed more publishable, perhaps the racial violence of the early twentieth century would not have been so unimaginably widespread—nor so deadly.

CHAPTER FOUR

This Firm of Men-Killers

Jack London and the Incorporation of Terrorism

In the novels and essays of Thomas Dixon and Ida B. Wells, the nation-state becomes a key axis on which to plot their ideas concerning terrorism. Dixon astonishingly imagines the Ku Klux Klan as the protector of the American Constitution against the sexual terrorism of former slaves and their northern sponsors, worries that without such violence the United States will become a nation of mulattos, and even sees the KKK as a line of defense against the intrusion of anarchist foreigners. Wells, taking to heart Dixon's desire for the Klan to be truly representative of the United States, chastises her readers for their complicity in the "national crime" of rampaging violence against black men, women, and children. For both of these writers, and despite their striking dissimilarities, calibrating the relationship between the state and terrorism—including attacks against the state by subversives and conceptions of the nation itself as a terrorist enterprise—proves integral to comprehending spontaneous political violence at the turn of the century. But while Dixon and Wells recognized that the ambiguities of statehood were an essential grid for depicting racial violence in this era, questions about the nature of governments' involvement with terrorism were by no means restricted to race relations.

To take but two global examples from the period, during the abortive Russian revolution of 1905, the radical Socialist Revolutionary Party committed persistent and deadly terrorist assaults against the czarist regime's officials and administrators. Meanwhile, the government simultaneously harassed and murdered the political insurgents. And halfway across the world in Idaho, on 30 December of that same year, a homemade bomb rigged to a latch exploded when former governor Frank Steunenberg opened the gate to his lawn, gruesomely ending his life. Idaho officials responded to Steunenberg's assassination by illegally kidnapping and detaining for over a year three leaders of the militant Western Federation of Miners (WFM), including the era's most famous labor radical, William "Big Bill" Haywood.

Despite their clear differences of cultural and historical context, the geographically disparate episodes of political violence in Russia and Idaho exemplify a fluidity between—and the difficulty of separating—instances of political terrorism directed against a state and violence that is specifically authorized by a nation or government. While the assassinations of czarist officials and Governor Steunenberg have been considered terrorist attacks against the governments of Russia and Idaho, the states' actions in these episodes also look very much like the acts of terrorists. In particular, the Idaho officials' illegal kidnapping and detention of the WFM officers, who were in Colorado at the time of the murder, marked the breakdown of any adherence to jurisprudence by the government. Considered undesirable citizens because of their radical opinions, Haywood and his cohorts were covertly abducted and imprisoned despite being uninvolved with the Steunenberg assassination, suggesting, as had the trial of the Chicago Haymarket anarchists twenty years earlier, that any American citizen caught holding the wrong opinions could be judged responsible for criminal offenses he or she never committed. And if these acts of violence can at least initially point out the slipperiness between state and antistate terror, the extravagant scenarios spun out to explain Steunenberg's assassination also demonstrate in particularly dramatic form how terrorist events accrue cultural meaning through always interested narratives and rhetorical strategies.

These examples of political violence concisely evoke a cluster of issues that comprise my central concerns in this chapter, including the murky relationship between state and antistate terror, the blend of fact and fiction in accounts of terrorism, and, especially in the Idaho case, the complicity of state and capitalist violence. Equally important, these events are curiously and intriguingly linked by the figure of Progressive Era American novelist Jack London. The Russian revolutionaries' tactics played a decisive role in London's intellectual and philosophical development, convincing him that terrorism was sometimes a legitimate tactic in the class struggle.[1] London also responded to the kidnapping of Haywood with an outraged article condemning the state's patently illegal response to an illegal murder, followed shortly thereafter by his apocalyptic novel of state violence, *The Iron Heel*. And in 1910, London wrote approximately 120 pages of a novel titled *The Assassination Bureau, Ltd.*, in which he imagined an elite and clandestine business firm of terrorists systematically righting America's wrongs by killing those "criminals" whom the law protects, such as unscrupulous capitalists, crooked cops, and corrupt judges.

London, however, despaired at his inability to imagine a satisfactory ending to *Assassination Bureau*'s inquiry into the philosophical legitimacy of violence and left the manuscript languishing among his unpublished papers when he died in 1916. The subsequent publishing history of the novel is one of those historical coincidences that, to the paranoid, can look like conspiratorial truth. *Bureau* was not published until 1963, shortly before President Kennedy was assassinated.[2] As Donald Pease has aptly demonstrated, the text's premise of an extralegal agency secretly controlling society eerily corroborated the surfeit of conspiracy theories that materialized after Kennedy's tragic murder.[3] But if Jack London provides an unexpected link between different forms of terrorism in the early twentieth century and Kennedy's 1963 assassination, this is due to more than just the long delay and coincidental timing of *The Assassination Bureau*'s publication. The key element is London's sustained interest in terrorists throughout his most productive and successful decade, 1900 to 1910. London's critics, however, have traditionally focused either on his glamorous authorial persona[4] or on what Earle Labor has termed his "Northland Saga,"[5] that impressive body of fiction that grew out of his experience in the Klondike gold rush; even those scholars attentive to his admittedly inconsistent socialism and class radicalism have consistently overlooked London's interest in terrorist violence.

Yet London repeatedly invoked terrorists as a subject in his short stories, novels, and nonfiction, thereby participating in the discursive construction of an American terrorist identity that had been emerging in American culture since the Haymarket trial in the 1880s. London's major fictional depiction of terrorists comes in *The Assassination Bureau,* but his interest in terrorists — as both literary and historical figures — repeatedly surfaces throughout the century's first decade. In 1901, he published "The Minions of Midas"; in 1902, "The League of the Old Men"; 1906 saw his vitriolic reaction to the Haywood kidnapping; in 1908, he published the short story, "Goliah," as well as his more well-known apocalyptic novel, *The Iron Heel.* And he wrote the ill-fated *Assassination Bureau* in 1910. Throughout these strikingly different writings, which range from the violent dystopia of *The Iron Heel* to the aged Indians who assassinate encroaching white traders in "Old Men" and the farcically comic, good-hearted terrorist of "Goliah," London consistently grapples with the relationship between terrorism and what he often referred to as the "capitalist organization" — the thoroughly intertwined and tightly coiled strands of capitalism, the legal system, and the state in modern America.

By focusing in his journalism and fiction on the simultaneous emergence of modern terrorism and corporate capitalism in the United States, London suggests that understanding these historical phenomena is contingent upon theorizing where and how they are similar, as well as how American ideology works to make them appear entirely separate and antithetical. In London's writing, the terrorist, conventionally understood as the embodiment of chaos, the prototypical outsider and threat to the forces of law and society, emerges as a figure that specifically questions and worries distinctions between order and disorder in Progressive Era America. To be more precise, London does not represent terrorists as a chaotic threat against the dominant order. Instead he repeatedly imagines rational, orderly, businesslike terrorists, a reversal he complements throughout his writing with depictions of a bureaucratic nation-state that, despite a formal organization embodied in its police, judges, and elected officials, is at the root of the Progressive Era's roiling labor and political disorders. The figure of the terrorist in London's work provides a means to analyze the discursive and ideological production of law and order, as well as the cultural construction of chaos or lawlessness. Furthermore, his construction of a terrorist identity also attends to the political consequences of such dualisms, and, crucially, how such distinctions were contradicted, contested, and muddied during the first decades of the twentieth century.

Dynamite and the State's Business

Frank Steunenberg was the first American assassinated by dynamite.[6] His murder and the ensuing kidnapping of three WFM officers were events replete with shocking lawbreaking by state officials and fantastic cloak-and-dagger intrigue. Committed by a drifter named Harry Orchard who possessed vague ties to the WFM, the bombing came after years of protracted and often violent struggle between the WFM and the mining corporations, which had been supported by Steunenberg's administration in the 1890s. Orchard was easily fingered for the crime, since he had carelessly left crumbs of dynamite sprinkled across his hotel room's floor and burglar's tools in his trunk. Orchard, however, was also explicitly encouraged to link Bill Haywood, Charles Moyer, and George Pettibone with the assassination by the state of Idaho's primary investigator in the case, James McParland.

McParland, who had been tapped to lead the investigation by Idaho governor Frank Gooding, was head of the Pinkerton Detective Agency's Denver bureau. As chief of the Denver office for the decade leading up to the Haywood affair, McParland had succeeded in placing dozens of spies inside the WFM who had attempted to undermine Haywood's authority within the organization. But McParland had earned a reputation as an antiunion detective decades before, when he had gone incognito and infiltrated an Irish coal miners' underground organization in rural Pennsylvania. Working under the alias James McKenna, McParland lived among the miners for years and assumed a leadership position in their militant labor union, only to come out of his disguise and dramatically emerge as the state's star witness in the 1876 trials of the radical "Molly Maguires" for sabotage and assassination. Because of the wide press coverage given to McParland's trial testimony, in which he swore that he had been present at the planning of many union-authorized assassinations, and the popular success of Allan Pinkerton's account of McParland's infiltration in his 1878 dime novel, *The Molly Maguires and the Detectives,* the Mollies' trials yoked labor violence and trade unionism in the public mind for decades to come.[7]

When greeted with the opportunity presented by the Steunenberg case yet again to undermine labor, McParland seized it. His initial ploy was to have Harry Orchard transferred from the small-town jail where he was being held to the state penitentiary's death row. Orchard was placed in solitary confinement, and McParland deviously ordered the prison guards to stare at him incessantly, but without saying a word. After leaving him in his cell and feeding him little for several weeks, McParland finally invited the prisoner to enjoy a sumptuous lunch and fine cigars with him in the warden's office. Orchard could escape the hangman's rope, McParland informed him, only by implicating the WFM union leaders in a confession. Orchard complied, and the state of Idaho rewarded him by transferring him yet again, this time to a private bungalow in the prison yard. There he entertained and was congratulated by Idaho's governor and the prosecuting attorneys in the Steunenberg case. Orchard continued to live in his private house within the prison's confines until he died in 1954.

With Orchard's confession in hand, McParland convinced the local district attorney to issue a warrant for the arrest of Haywood, Moyer, and Pettibone. Significantly, though, none of the men were in Idaho, and since none of them had even been in Idaho at the time of the assassination, they could not legally be considered fugitives from justice and extradited from Colorado. McParland nevertheless produced bogus extradition papers stating that the men had been present at Steunenberg's assassination and were now on the run in Colorado. Taking his perjured extradition warrant to Colorado,

McParland met with Colorado's governor, a state supreme court justice, and a prominent mine manager. In this meeting, the famous detective divulged a plan to abduct the WFM officers and then ferry them aboard a specially chartered train to Idaho. But with no legal arrest warrant and no extradition hearing, the capture of the WFM officers would be a patently unlawful kidnapping.

McParland's plan worked to perfection. Haywood, found in a brothel and arrested without a warrant or extradition papers, was sped to Idaho along with Moyer and Pettibone aboard the specially prepared train. Making no stops until it was safely out of Colorado for fear of being served with a habeas corpus writ that would free the unlawfully incarcerated prisoners, the train soon reached Boise where Haywood was dumped on the death row recently vacated by Harry Orchard. Noting the arrest of the labor radicals, no less a personage than President Theodore Roosevelt quickly denounced the men as "undesirable citizens." He also asserted that "the Western Federation of Miners is a body just like the Molly Maguires of Pennsylvania,"[8] thereby connecting the three men to the image of violent labor radicals popularized decades earlier in the coal mines of Pennsylvania. Meanwhile, the U.S. Supreme Court acknowledged the illegality of their kidnapping but, unfathomably, ruled that they could be lawfully prosecuted since they were now in the state that had indicted them, regardless of how they came to be there.[9] Thus branded illegitimate Americans by the president and shrugged off by the Supreme Court, the three convicts were left to languish in prison for over a year until their case finally came to trial in the summer of 1907. The jury, however, faced with the holes in Orchard's testimony that had been pointed out by famed defense attorney Clarence Darrow, ultimately, and to many court watchers' surprise, acquitted the prisoners of the conspiracy charge.

While Haywood and the others waited in prison for their trial, their plight became a cause célèbre among radicals and socialists worldwide, including Jack London. London contributed money to the prisoners' defense fund and gave a fiery speech at a February 1907 rally commemorating the first anniversary of the kidnapping.[10] But the point where I want to pick up London's involvement in the case is with the article that he published in the *Chicago Daily Socialist* in November 1906. Titling his article "Something Rotten in Idaho," London begins his indictment of the state's actions by decrying the collusion between the mainstream press and the prosecution:

Up in the State of Idaho, at the present moment, are three men lying in jail. Their names are Moyer, Haywood, and Pettibone. They are charged with the murder of Governor Steunenberg. Incidentally they are charged with thirty, sixty or seventy other atrocious murders. Not alone are they labor leaders and murderers, but they are anarchists. . . . These men will surely be hanged. The foregoing epitomises the information and beliefs possessed by the average farmer, lawyer, professor, clergyman and businessman in the United States. His belief is based upon the information he has gained by reading the newspapers.[11]

London's sense that the press was working hand in hand with the state foreshadows an important theme in his apocalyptic novel of failed revolution, *The Iron Heel,* a text he began writing the same year he published the article on the Idaho case. In *The Iron Heel,* London imagines a society in which the "press of the United States" is, as his revolutionary hero, Ernest Everhard, puts it, "a parasitic growth that battens on the capitalist class. Its function is to serve the established by moulding public opinion, and right well it serves it."[12] In other words, what London recognized in the Steunenberg case, and would shortly thereafter fictionalize, was the ability of "print-capitalism"— that knotty conjunction of modern forms of capitalism and the media—to construct a public consciousness from individuals' solitary acts of reading.

I take the phrase "print-capitalism" from Benedict Anderson's analysis of newspapers in his foundational study of nationalism, *Imagined Communities,* in which he suggests that no "more vivid figure" for the imaginary creation of a public community exists than newspaper readers. Though privately reading, such readers cannot but be aware that their private act is being performed by countless others "of whose existence [they are] confident, yet of whose identity [they have] not the slightest notion," producing a "remarkable confidence of community in anonymity."[13] While Anderson succinctly describes the media's role in producing a public, London's article elaborates on the highly charged political stakes of this rhetorical creation of the public sphere. London demonstrates here an understanding that language represents an important site of political struggle and that competing ways of providing meaning for material conditions (such as the Steunenberg assassination or the definition of "terrorist") result from social power struggles fought within and through language. This is why London notes that most depictions of Haywood and the others do not identify them as just "murderers," but also as "anarchists." In post-Haymarket America, "anarchist" retained a sense of conspiratorial and terroristic violence. Moreover, the putative link between the two cases was only strengthened by the fact that dynamite was the specific device used in both Haymarket and the Steunenberg assassination.

London himself makes the connection between the falsely convicted Haymarket anarchists and the Steunenberg case concrete, but not in the way we might expect. Asking rhetorically if the mine owners are "law abiding citizens," London argues that "'to hell with the Constitution' was their clearly enunciated statement." He also offers a comparison: "In Chicago a few years ago some men were hanged for uttering incendiary language not half so violent as this. But they were workingmen. The mine owners of Colorado and Idaho are the chief executives, or capitalists. They will not be hanged." Rather than compare the illegalities suffered by the Haymarket anarchists and the WFM officers, London articulates the legal double standard that brought the anarchists to the gallows while providing the mine owners "full liberty . . . to hang some other men whom they do not like . . . for the sake of a few millions of dollars."[14] By focusing on this legal double standard, London is highlighting the discursive and contingent construction of criminality. Fully supported by the official state apparatus, the capitalists, according to London, are regarded as defenders of the public order even as they infringe on the WFM officers' constitutional rights.

With this indictment of the collusion between the "capitalist organization" and the legal system, London's "Something Rotten" ranks as one of his most convincing pieces of working-class propaganda. Moreover, London directly links this connivance to actions performed in the name of the state of Idaho that are essentially acts of state-authorized terrorism directed against the WFM officers and intended to coerce that organization into ceasing its radical agitation. He writes, "Moyer, Haywood, and Pettibone . . . are at present in jail in the State of Idaho because of the perpetration of lawless acts by officers of the law, from the chief of the state executives down to the petty deputy chiefs — and this in collusion with mine owners' associations and railroad companies. . . . It is conspiracy and violation of law on the part of the very men who claim that they are trying to bring punishment for conspiracy and violation of law."[15] By invoking the word "conspiracy" in his description of the Idaho politicians' actions, London turns the tables on usual distinctions between terrorists and the upholders of the law. The government, argues London, is just as likely as any other criminal to hatch secretive plans for committing "lawless acts" against American citizens. The only difference is the balance of power. In other words, the government, grounded in the discourses of law and citizenship that underpinned President Roosevelt's denunciation and the Supreme Court's evasion, is able to produce the cultural knowledge and commonsense definitions that imagine terrorism specifically as illegal violence against the state. Government violence, from this point of view, is simply maintaining the social order.

The need to regulate, explain, or neutralize disparate forms of subjectivity (such as radical, leftist, or insurgent) in the interests of existing power relations is fought at the level of the sign and realized through a discourse of terrorism that imagines terrorists as pathological killers, labor radicals, or unwanted immigrants. This discourse of political violence is itself, as we have seen, entrenched in and constructed from the powerful institutions of government and law. Yet the very organization of such a discursive formation also implies the possibility for subverting or reconstituting this dominant image. To put this point in more concrete historical terms, London, by arguing that the state is more conspiratorial, more violent, and less respectful of the law than the so-called criminals, opened the possibility of reconceptualizing dominant or commonsense notions concerning who embodied order and who represented disorder in Progressive Era America. In his analysis, the state itself becomes a chaotic entity in which jurisprudence is not respected and, depending upon the political climate, any citizen can become the victim of political violence. In London's account of the Steunenberg assassination, then, we cannot simply say that the state becomes the terrorist. Rather, the point of his analysis is both to lay bare the entrenched power interests that preserve binaries such as "government vs. anarchy" or "terrorism vs. Law" and to call into question the effect that such discourses had for the way capitalism, labor unions, and violence would be understood "by the average farmer, lawyer, professor, clergyman and businessman in the United States."[16]

While London, in his writing concerning the 1905 Steunenberg assassination, strove to identify and interrogate the very real material consequences that can follow from the ephemerality of language, naming, and representation, he also issued that year a direct judgment on the efficacy of terrorism as political strategy. Speaking to a businessman's club in Stockton, California, London claimed as his brothers the Russian revolutionaries who had managed several successful terrorist attacks against czarist officials.[17] And in "Revolution," an essay that he frequently delivered as a speech for the Socialist Party between 1905 and 1909, London again offered his support to the assassins: "In Russia . . . the government executes the revolutionists. The revolutionists kill the officers of the government. The revolutionists meet legal murder with assassination. Now here arises a particularly significant phase which would be well for the rulers to consider. Let me make it concrete. I am a revolutionist. Yet I am a fairly sane and normal individual. I speak, and I *think*, of these assassins in Russia as 'my comrades.' So do all the comrades in America, and all the 7,000,000 comrades in the world. . . . We do back up the assassinations by our comrades in Russia."[18] London here supports the use of violence to coerce the czarist regime, refusing either to rebuke the Russian terrorists or to see their actions as well-meaning but misguided. Moreover, he offers a version of the Russian political climate in which the czarist government's assaults on the revolutionaries exist in a reciprocal relationship with the terrorists' assassination of government officials. But in using the curious phrase "legal murder" to describe the government's actions, London, as he did in "Something Rotten," again suggests that the difference between the state's and the revolutionaries' violent actions is merely semantic—that what counts as legitimate violence hinges on the power of discursive institutions such as the law or the government to define the social order.

Coming only half a decade after the Secret Service had uncovered a plot purportedly planning the assassinations of several Western rulers, some of whom had already succumbed to terrorist attacks, including Austria's empress and the king of Italy,[19] and only four years after Leon Czolgosz had assassinated President McKinley, London's oft-repeated espousal of revolutionary terrorism during his 1905 lecture tour resulted in a significant backlash. Some public libraries withdrew all his books from their shelves, and Yale's Woolsey Hall was closed to student-initiated events for years after London raised a surprisingly boisterous furor among the 2,800 students gathered to hear him speak.[20] But perhaps what auditors of his "Revolution" speech found most disquieting was not simply his support of political violence, but London's claim that he is a "fairly sane and normal" person and yet a "revolutionist" who supports the terrorists. By proposing that terrorism can appear rational to "sane and normal" persons, London implicitly argues against the common stereotype, current in his day and ours, of the terrorist as a "ruffian of feeble brain" whose violence is strictly caused by "insanity."[21] Or, in the more scientific, if tautological, vocabulary of a contemporary scholar, "terrorists are driven to commit acts of violence as a consequence of psychological forces, and . . . their special psycho-logic is constructed to rationalize acts they are psychologically compelled to commit."[22] Instead, London suggests that even the most extreme and violent behavior may proceed from a strategic and calculated choice among available political alternatives.[23] London is here fighting a political and ideological battle through language. He recognized that if revolutionary violence is dismissed as only the work of killers possessing a deviant "psycho-logic," then their complaints and arguments against society's injustices will likewise be dismissed as "the ravings of madmen."[24]

While London's rhetoric in "Revolution" demonstrates his recognition of the political implications that follow from how the connotation of "terrorists" is inflected and accented, he also moves his discussion away from the specific conditions of the Russian empire. By both warning "rulers" in general, rather than only Russia's czarist regime, and claiming a worldwide likemindedness of "7,000,000 comrades" who support the revolutionaries' terrorism, London implicitly suggests that terroristic violence could have a political usefulness against oppression elsewhere in the world. This vision of popularly supported terrorists deeply enmeshed in the social fabric is particularly intriguing because it radically differs from the remarks on terrorists by a powerful contemporary Marxist, Vladimir Lenin. In *What Is to Be Done?*, his classic theoretical work outlining the principles of a revolutionary socialist party, Lenin argued that "terrorists bow to the spontaneity of the passionate indignation of intellectuals, who lack the ability or opportunity to connect the revolutionary struggle and the working-class movement into an integral whole. It is difficult indeed for those who have lost their belief, or who have never believed, that this is possible, to find some outlet for their indignation and revolutionary energy other than terror."[25] According to Lenin, terrorism is the violence of intellectuals who find themselves alienated from the working class and who have lost faith in workers' revolutionary potential. Although, as Richard E. Rubenstein has written, the Socialist Revolutionaries whom Lenin critiqued—and London supported—believed that the proletariat would overthrow the czarist regime after terrorist attacks had sufficiently weakened the morale and efficiency of the state,[26] Lenin warned elsewhere that terrorism "is *not connected in any way* with work among the masses, for the masses, or together with the masses" and that "the terrorism of the Socialist Revolutionaries is nothing else than *single combat.*"[27] For Lenin, terrorism merely distracts from the time and energy that should be devoted to organizing workers into a revolutionary body and therefore fails to contribute to a workers' uprising.

Though London in 1905 was certainly unaware of Lenin's writings and has never been recognized as a rigorous or even consistent socialist thinker, the disparity between his thinking on terrorists and the classic Marxist position espoused by Lenin highlights London's own attempts to reimagine the dominant notions of terrorists. In other words, if, from a capitalist point of view such as the Idaho mine owners', terrorists are considered an alien graft on the dominant order that must be removed, Lenin, from an opposing political position, also dubs them alien threats to insurgent political movements. But London, alternatively, sought a rational and socially progressive logic underwriting the actions of terrorists (who were routinely presumed to be psychopathic) specifically to question the presumed rationality of the social order. For him, terrorists must be something other than maniacal murderers or hopelessly disconnected intellectuals. And it is precisely this notion that London elaborates with the fictional portrayal of his rational terrorist-philosopher, Ernest Everhard, in *The Iron Heel.*

Terrorism and the "Capitalist Organization"

In 1906, while Haywood and his cohorts were awaiting trial in Idaho, London was hard at work on *The Iron Heel*. His letters throughout that year record his hopes for the book and his progress on it. As he wrote the novel, London enthused to potential publishers that "it certainly deals with the live things of to-day."[28] Shortly before Macmillan issued the book, London exclaimed to his publisher that with "the general situation in the United States for the past year . . . the public is just ripe to boost *The Iron Heel* along into large sales. As I say, and as I repeat, this is the psychological moment for *The Iron Heel* to appear."[29] The Idaho trial that had gripped the nation with the fear of dynamite and class violence, as well as the financial panic of 1907, had convinced the always sales-minded London that the time was propitious for his massively violent novel of socialist revolt against the entangled forces of government and capitalism. Of course, as London later bemoaned, his pre-publication exuberance was not justified by the book's sales figures or critical reception: "It was a labor of love and a dead failure as a book," London wrote to a friend. "The book buying public would have nothing to do with it and I got nothing but knocks from the socialists."[30]

London's apocalyptic novel of failed revolution against a brutal capitalist state did not endear him to the mainstream book-buying public or to American socialists, who in 1908 still largely held that socialism would progress through the ballot box. Yet *The Iron Heel* provides a compelling analysis of the relays between an American terrorist subjectivity, capitalism, the state, and matters of representation and publicity in the era of emergent corporate capitalism. Moreover, by offering this meditation within a narrative that also depicts a revolutionary underground honeycombed with spies and counterspies who commit terrorism both against and for the government, London fictionalizes the concern with the discursive construction of legality and criminality that had animated his rage in the "Something Rotten in Idaho" article.

London constructed *The Iron Heel*'s narrative so that it is both dystopian and utopian, backward looking and forward looking. *The Iron Heel* purports to be a transcription of the "Everhard Manuscript," a memoir written by Avis Everhard in 1932 in the final days leading up to a second massive but unsuccessful revolt against a ruthless capitalist class known as the Oligarchy or the Iron Heel. The action of the memoir, however, only includes events up through the dramatic failure of the socialists' first revolt in late 1917, which was led by Avis's heroic husband, the political revolutionary and occasional terrorist, Ernest Everhard. After the failure of the second insurrection in 1932, the manuscript was lost for seven centuries, during which time a socialist revolution finally overthrew the Oligarchy and established the utopian "Brotherhood of Man." The actual present of the novel is thus set in the year 419 B.O.M. (Brotherhood of Man), and the manuscript is presented along with footnotes appended by historian Anthony Meredith that correct, clarify, or expand upon Avis's narrative. *The Iron Heel* therefore offers two narrative points of view and two moments in time as reference points. It is only by combining the manuscript's information with the footnotes that we learn the entire history of the Oligarchy and Everhard's unsuccessful uprising against it.

One of the more chilling aspects of London's narrative is the Iron Heel's method of coercion. London adumbrates our own day's fascination with conspiracy. He imagines that "it is the brain of the Plutocracy that controls the government, and this brain consists of seven small and powerful groups of men. And do not forget that these groups are working to-day practically in unison" (424). Yet these conspirators, and the Iron Heel over which they preside, do not simply or violently grind all members of society mercilessly into the ground. Instead, they operate by a much subtler system of reward and coercion for brain workers and important political figures that is coupled with a harsh abandonment of regular laborers: "No one to-day is a free agent. We are all caught up in the wheels and cogs of the industrial machine" (358) in one way or another, Ernest tells Avis soon after they meet.

London's understanding of just how all persons are enmeshed in the "industrial machine" can be fleshed out through the neo-Marxist concepts of "regime of accumulation" and "mode of regulation." These Althusserian theoretical models of the economy represent attempts to provide supple explorations of the Marxist base and superstructure formulation without reducing the latter to either a redundant version of the former or simple false consciousness. A regime of accumulation, according to Martyn J. Lee, refers to the types and organization of both the productive forces and the social conditions that govern the reproduction of labor-power in a particular historical period. The complementary mode of regulation, in which London's novel is most interested, comprises the institutions, systems, and techniques that either encourage or coerce citizens to conform to the prevailing regime of accumulation. A mode of regulation provides a social architecture that includes such things as large-scale state policies and economic programs, but its support of the regime of accumulation also extends beyond these direct components of economic life. It includes the more ephemeral and intricate components of social life, including language, aesthetic practices, cultural values, and belief systems.[31]

In *The Iron Heel,* London brilliantly outlines how the Oligarchy's regime of accumulation is buttressed by a particular mode of regulation. Uninterested in a notion of workers' false consciousness, London instead zeros in on how the ruling plutocracy justifies its actions to itself. In one of the novel's typical Edward Bellamy–like moments of exposition, Ernest instructs Avis, "When they want to do a thing, in business of course, they must wait till there arises in their brains, somehow, a religious, or ethical, or scientific, or philosophic, concept that the thing is right" (365). Provocatively, London moves beyond the notion of conspiracy here; instead he is after something much more subtle as he ponders how individuals can contort their thinking and actually believe that their pernicious actions are benevolent, even in the face of anguished suffering. Indeed, this ability to justify their actions extends right down to the level of individual language. When Avis separately interviews two female Oligarchs whose husbands own a mill in which workers suffer particularly harrowing accidents, the women independently "talked in the same large ways about policy, and the duties and responsibilities of the rich." What is most striking is that the wealthy women unknowingly deliver their opinions "in almost identically the same language" (366), suggesting the extent to which their subjectivity is inscribed by the ideology of their class.

While members of the Oligarchy, "drunk with conviction of the superiority of their class" (367), individually manage to convince themselves that their actions are beneficial for society, this uniformity is complemented by the ruling class members' behavior with each other. The Oligarchy absolutely sticks together. Judges and lawyers on important cases belong to the same men's clubs, live in the same exclusive neighborhoods, and their wives shop together and frequently entertain each other's families (354). Moreover, the principal newspaper editors are "all solid with the corporations," and reporters are discouraged if they try to write anything against the capitalist Oligarchy (363). Further, as Ernest chastises a gathering of ministers and academics: "You herd with the capitalist class . . . that pays you, that feeds you, that puts the very clothes on your backs. . . . And in return you preach to your employers the brands of metaphysics that are especially acceptable to them," those that "do not menace the established order of society" (335).

While the Oligarchy allows subservient knowledge workers to keep their jobs and awards them for reinforcing the hegemonic structures of the Iron Heel in their pulpits and classrooms, it takes a more nefarious approach with those in its own ranks who dare to assail the dominant order. Bishop Morehouse, who decries the organized church's platitudes after Ernest shows him the true suffering of the poor, is removed from his congregation and placed in an insane asylum. And Avis's father, who defiantly publishes an intriguingly prescient monograph on the corporate takeover of American universities, has his book suppressed, is forced into retirement from his job at Berkeley, and has his home and valuable corporate stock stripped from him. One widely reprinted editorial cartoon even portrays him waving a red flag and leading a mob of long-haired radicals who clutch dynamite bombs in their hands. By subjecting Avis's mild-mannered, professorial father to his era's usual way of lampooning and discrediting those persons with subversive or merely oppositional ideas, London fictionalizes the similar caricaturization of the Haymarket anarchists a few decades earlier. And even more pointedly, the press's treatment of Avis's father dramatizes in exaggerated form the logic behind Theodore Roosevelt's dubbing Haywood and his codefendants "undesirable citizens" at the same time that London was writing his novel. Through these sometimes subtle and sometimes more directly vicious means, the Oligarchy manufactures consent, makes the capitalist order appear natural, and snuffs out dissent when it does flare up.

The Oligarchy also extends these methods into the classes of society that labor under the Iron Heel. In a "tacit conspiracy" (364) against all workers, the Oligarchy uses a "divide and conquer" strategy with the nation's labor force. The ruling class subsidizes the unions of skilled workers who are essential to the major industries. By increasing wages and shortening hours, the Iron Heel assures that "membership in these unions will become like seats in Paradise" (466). Less important unions and unskilled workers, on the other hand, are routinely allowed to suffer abuses and accidents in unsafe factories "in order that a larger dividend might be paid" (360) to stockholders.[32] And should workers attempt to gain compensation for their injuries through the court system, the utter complicity of capitalists, lawyers, and judges stymies them every time. Instituting this castelike division of labor, the Oligarchy rewards its immediate inferiors and counts on them to suppress any murmurings of revolt long before they reach the privileged neighborhoods and workplaces of the Oligarchs.

Depicting both the small brain trust controlling the Oligarchy and the much wider, much more supple dissemination of a hegemonic ideology, London thus imagines a ruling class that combines readers' common desire for conspiratorial answers to complex social problems with a nuanced understanding of how social dominance is fabricated and maintained. Yet, critically, he also imagines a state that willingly resorts to terrorizing the citizens whom it deems unworthy of such soft coercion. Recalling the logic of his remarks about the Russian revolution, and thereby implicitly calibrating the relationship of state terror to insurgent antistate terrorism, London writes that regularly and without notice the Oligarchy snatches revolutionaries from their homes and murders them. "Without warning, without trace," Anthony Meredith informs us in a footnote, "men and women . . . disappeared and were seen no more, their ends shrouded in mystery" (503). The Oligarchy complements these discriminate assassinations with a random extermination of innocent citizens on a colossal scale. "In mobs composed wholly of themselves," the state's agents provocateurs act as saboteurs who "fire and loot buildings and factories" in order to prompt riots and mob violence that can then be savagely suppressed (479–80). Indeed, "eleven thousand men, women, and children were shot down on the streets of Sacramento" after the Iron Heel's agents provoked a riot (480). The Oligarchy's intent to crush any resistance by slaughtering 11,000 citizens surely rates as one of the most incredible instances of state-authorized terror in American literature, and London's gruesome foresight here has been remarked upon often by commentators who see in the Oligarchy's tactics a portent of Stalin's terror in the Soviet Union and fascism in Germany and Italy.[33]

Though London anticipates later twentieth-century atrocities, his depiction of the Iron Heel's brutality also reminds us that, historically, terror has more often been the chosen weapon of the powerful, not the weak. It may be worth recalling that the *Oxford English Dictionary* defines the original usage of "terrorism" as "government by intimidation as directed and carried out by the party in power in France during the Revolution of 1789–94." London's future-oriented text, in its juxtaposition of revolutionaries' violence and the state terror of the Oligarchy, neatly telescopes the slippages and revisions that concepts of terrorism underwent over the course of the nineteenth century as the term's connotations moved closer to the notion of insurgent political violence that we generally recognize today as terrorism. But while London's juxtaposition concisely evokes the changing ideas of terrorism over the nineteenth century, his depiction of the state's mobilizing its massive resources to produce widespread terror among the populace also works to defamiliarize what was already by 1907 the increasingly constricted sense of the term as applicable only to fanatical revolutionaries. In London's portrayal of America during the twentieth century's first three decades, terror is state policy.

London depicts a terroristic state partly because his book entered into a lively, ongoing debate at the time of its publication over the role of violence in revolutionary politics. American socialists were riven over the issue of whether they could succeed in America simply by the electoral process or if violence would be necessary to overcome an inherently violent capitalist state. The right wing of the Socialist Party argued for the efficacy of the ballot box, while the left wing suggested the inevitability of violence. The split helped lead to the 1905 founding of the leftist, polyglot Industrial

Workers of the World and the 1913 ousting of IWW founder Haywood from the Socialist Party.[34]

In London's *The Iron Heel* all the socialists, with the crucial exception of Everhard, maintain what the narrative views as a misplaced faith in the ballot box. London dramatizes this errant belief in the political process when he has over fifty socialists, including Everhard, elected to Congress. Somewhat to their surprise, they are allowed to take their seats in the legislature. But of course it is a setup. While Everhard has the floor in the midst of a debate, someone from the gallery hurls a bomb onto the floor of the legislature. Immediately, blame falls on Everhard, and, since they were surely part of a widespread plot, all socialist congressmen are arrested and imprisoned for "terroristic tactics" (490). As Avis narrates, however, no socialist had a "hand in the affair," while "there is evidence to show that the Iron Heel was responsible for the act" (489–90). In a footnote, Anthony Meredith confirms her suspicion, and, with his access to historical evidence, identifies the agent provocateur whom the Iron Heel had forced to throw the bomb that could then be blamed on the socialists.

The point, of course, is that socialists cannot trust the ballot box because the government will always in one way or another deal them a rigged hand from the outset. But London, via Anthony Meredith's historical footnotes, does more than simply identify the bomb thrower. Meredith draws historical equivalencies between the government's framing of Everhard and "the ferocious and wanton judicial murder of the innocent and so-called Haymarket Anarchists in Chicago," as well as the frame-up and trial of Moyer, Haywood, and Pettibone (492). London combines the imaginative dimension of fiction and the intellectual heft of scholarly footnotes both to invoke and to solve Progressive Era leftists' favorite duo of government-authorized miscarriages of justice, Haymarket and the WFM trial. Linking the Haymarket bombing and the Steunenberg assassination to Iron Heel–sponsored terrorism in the U.S. Congress, London elides the differences between these three events and boils them all down to what he depicts as the very real government plots against the imaginary cabals of dissident Americans.

In *The Iron Heel*'s congressional bombing, Everhard and his colleagues were, true to form for the Oligarchy, not convicted without witness testimony and a trial. Yet London does not simply imagine a scenario of trumped-up evidence. Instead, among Everhard's fellow representatives, "at the trial, and still with honest belief, several testified to having seen Ernest prepare to throw the bomb, and that it exploded prematurely." But "of course they saw nothing of the sort. In the fevered imagination of fear they thought they saw, that was all" (490). As with the mill owners' wives, the congressmen who actually believe that they witnessed Everhard throw the bomb speak volumes about the interpellation of individuals into a dominant ideology. In the face of Everhard's own testimony that, were he going to throw a bomb, it would certainly be much more powerful than the "feeble little squib" that exploded in Congress (490), the congressmen fall back on what they "know" about radical politicians. The Iron Heel does not have to coerce testimony because the combination of panic and "common sense" ensures that citizens will see things that simply never existed and startlingly fail to notice the real perpetrator throwing a bomb from the spectators' gallery.

Confronted with the Oligarchy's overwhelming control of cultural knowledge and common sense, Everhard is not simply "a revolutionist" (358). He is also specifically a writing revolutionist who is "hard at work on a new book entitled 'Philosophy and Revolution'" (340). The significance of this coincidence demonstrates London's abstract recognition that representation is integral to questions of how class politics and violence are understood. But this moment also extends beyond *The Iron Heel*, for London's characterization of his proletarian hero as a writer is somewhat autobiographical. In a 1909 article London defended his choice to devote time to writing over more direct involvement in strikes and pickets by arguing that "in five days, I write an article on socialism. I publish it in an American bourgeois magazine with half a million circulation. Each copy is circulated to an average of five readers. In five days I have added two and a half million [persons]."[35] In his more explicitly political life, London thus recognized that in an era of mass communication and large aggregations of capital, he could trade on his famous name in order to publish socialist tracts in the most unlikely of places. But more crucially, he understood that this was a worthwhile use of his time because influencing how insurgent political ideologies would be understood in the United States depended to a large extent on the ability to control their representation and the discourse about them.

In *The Iron Heel*, Everhard is a working-class philosopher who takes his turn on the soapboxes (338), yet he argues that the Iron Heel's viselike grasp on power cannot be overcome with rhetoric alone. Accordingly, he also masterminds and commits terrorist acts. In what Anthony Meredith regards as his "greatest achievement," Ernest organizes the "Fighting Groups," which are modeled on Russian revolutionary terrorists and covertly assassinate the Oligarchy's agents in a "strange and awful and subterranean" warfare (483–84). Additionally, midway through the novel, when the Oligarchy abandons its more subtle methods of controlling society's key institutions in favor of brutal suppression of the masses, Ernest cautions politically naive fellow socialists: "Do you know where you can get plenty of lead? When it comes to powder, chemical mixtures are better than mechanical mixtures, you take my word" (476). Everhard's invocation of the efficacy of "chemical mixtures" places him squarely within a terrorist discourse extolling the value of chemical explosives that stretches back through the Haymarket years to Alfred Nobel's invention of dynamite in the 1860s. By depicting Everhard as a proponent of chemical explosives, London touched the rawest nerve of his contemporary readers, who had been badly shaken by radicals and anarchists' dynamite threats and bombings over the past few decades. But since London couples Everhard's enthusiasm for "chemical mixtures" with a predilection for producing scholarly monographs on philosophy and revolution, Everhard's character should be regarded as an attempt by London to reimagine the dominant representation of political terrorists. Everhard, that is, presents the figure of a rational terrorist who belies the stereotype of a crazed dynamiter most commonly associated with the use of chemical explosives.

The keys to understanding Everhard's form of revolutionary violence and terrorism are organization and strategy. In a highly provocative argument, Arthur Redding has written that Everhard's revolution is threatened from below as much as from above, that the "promised order" of the revolution must be purified of both the chaotically violent masses and the capitalists' formal and informal armies.[36] London's revulsion at the sordid lumpen proletariat in his writing as well as his personal life has been well documented; throughout his life he feared slipping back into the lower class from which he had emerged.[37] In *The Iron Heel*, this repugnance takes the form of what Redding has shrewdly identified as a "frenzy of hyperdiscrimination," since London repeatedly reinforces the distinctions between the revolutionaries and the loathsome masses on whose behalf they are purportedly fighting. Ultimately, Redding argues, London's book is a dramatic attempt "to purge violence, embodied as the dread and contaminating other, from revolution itself."[38] Though Redding persuasively portrays London's recoiling in horror from the violence unleashed by revolution, I think instead that London does not so much recoil from violence as imagine key forms of it that must be harnessed and systematized so as to contain the more anarchic violence of the proletariat.

This is why London, for instance, has Avis and Anthony Meredith go into such detailed descriptions and analysis of a character who is only mentioned very briefly in the narrative, the "gentle-souled terrorist," Biedenbach (500). And though, as Meredith explains, no record of Biedenbach can be found in any historical document other than the Everhard manuscript, a later excavation of Avis's longtime hideout finds artifacts that she attributed to him and confirms his existence (500–501). London has Meredith prove the historical existence of Biedenbach in order to give the gloss of historical validation to the terrorist activities of the revolutionaries. More precisely, he pauses over Biedenbach to highlight the differences between the planned revolutionary terrorism of the socialists and the disorganized, unprincipled, roguish violence of the terrorists who spring into existence after the first planned revolt is horrifically suppressed in the "Chicago Commune." As Avis somewhat petulantly comments, many distressed comrades responded to the utter decimation of their revolt by resorting to "terroristic tactics" (552). And as for other terrorist organizations, she writes that "these misguided people sacrificed their own lives wantonly, very often made our own plans go astray, and retarded our organization" (552–53). Similarly, Avis tells the unfortunate story of a maimed worker whose tragic amputation in the mills was responsible for her own revolutionary conversion: "He became an anarchist—not a philosophic anarchist, but a mere animal" who "blew the Pertonwaithe palace into atoms" (505). In *The Iron Heel*, the disorganized or merely vengeful violence of terrorists is counterproductive precisely because it is merely reactive, untheorized, and helter-skelter. For terrorism to be validated in the novel as a legitimate revolutionary force, it has to be a conscious part of a strategic plan that combines calculated acts of violence with attempts to win the public's hearts and minds.

Yet, while London works hard to maintain a fire wall between Everhard's systematic terrorism and other forms of terror, this logic nonetheless threatens to implode in his actual portrayal of terrorist activity in the novel. Indeed, the state disguises its agents specifically as revolutionary saboteurs and manages to honeycomb the revolutionaries' organization with double agents. With the Iron Heel's agents actually committing terrorist acts against the state, London's depiction of early-twentieth-century America elides any apparent differences between terrorism against and terrorism by the state. As they permeate Everhard's revolutionary network, the Iron Heel's agents engage in "warfare dark and devious, replete with intrigue and conspiracy, plot and counterplot" that regularly ends in "death, violent and terrible" (484). But like the Oligarchy's moles and secret agents, Ernest and Avis also take on "dual rôle[s]" as "accredited international sp[ies] of the Iron Heel" and "manage a few important things for the Revolution" (508) while working as double agents. As double agents who even go so far as to become "agents-provocateurs . . . ostensibly serving the Iron Heel," but who are "secretly working with all [their] might for the Cause," Ernest and Avis find themselves "in both camps at the same time" (523), their espionage activities parallel and even inseparable from the behavior of the Iron Heel's own operatives. Thus imagining a modern capitalist state whose agents impersonate terrorists and whose antagonists pretend to be state agents, London reduces terrorism and state actions to the same cataclysmic cycles of violence. Ultimately, in this confusion of state operatives and terrorists, London pushed the logic of the Haywood-Moyer-Pettibone kidnapping and trial to its decisive and deadly conclusion, one in which the acts of the state and those opposing it could not be separated.[39]

If, on the one hand, London worked so hard to keep his revolutionaries pristine and separate from the threats of both the upper and lower classes, his text, on the other hand, is everywhere shot through with the ideological contradictions enacted by the violent similarities in the Oligarchy's and socialists' techniques. The novel thus not only offers an allegory of failed revolution in America and a fictional examination of the incoherencies at stake in reified notions of law and terrorism but also suggests that the advanced industrial capitalist state reduces everything in its horizon to one cultural logic. That logic, however, is not the ubiquity of capitalist exchange that horrified Marx. For London, all entities under capitalism, whether supporting or contesting the state, must deal in political violence.

Corporate Terrorism

When London returned to the fiction of terrorism with *The Assassination Bureau* in 1910, *The Iron Heel*'s implied logic concerning the ubiquity of violence in the capitalist state proved pivotal to his thinking. In *The Assassination Bureau,* London takes the alchemy of violence and capitalist enterprise that he saw at the heart of America and reconfigured it specifically as a corporate terrorist enterprise. But while *Bureau* portrays a close-knit connection between capitalism and a terrorist identity, that novel does not represent the only or even first time that London imagined a business of terror. "The Minions of Midas," published in 1901 by *Pearson's* magazine, depicts an extortionist-terrorist enterprise. Elaborately plotted in terms of its form, this short story consists of facsimiles of seven extortion letters from the Minions addressed to their victim, Eban Hale, "Money Baron," all framed by an explanatory letter from Hale's personal secretary and sent to the story's first-person narrator.[40] The self-named Minions have, after making a "thorough study of economics, decided to enter upon this business" of terror. Foreshadowing the Iron Heel's monopoly on positions of wealth and power, the Minions are convinced that the "great trusts and business combinations" have prevented them from assuming the places "which [their] intellects qualify [them] to occupy" because they "are of the unwashed" and "without capital" (435–36). To alleviate their poverty, the Minions repeatedly send letters demanding $20 million from Hale, who continually refuses to capitulate. As they had promised, the Minions proceed to kill innocent and arbitrary victims from various social strata after each letter, giving Hale shorter and shorter notice before each crime is committed.

As we shall see, the Minions, a "business proposition" (436) whose shadowy and furtive members remain unknown to Hale and the police throughout the story, anticipate the corporate and bureaucratic structure of London's more developed *Assassination Bureau.* But "The Minions of Midas" also establishes other key links between terrorism and capitalism, such as the reason these savvy terrorists give for choosing their jingoistic name or "official seal" (436). In the last lines of their first letter to Hale, they impishly indicate that "some day, to protect ourselves against competitors, we shall copyright it" (436). In the years around 1900, copyrighted brand names and trademarks emerged as a potent force in American corporate capitalism as manufacturers sought to stimulate and control consumer demand in a market flooded by the ever-increasing volume of production. To take but one of many possible examples, in 1899, the year before London wrote "Minions," the National Biscuit Company initiated the first million-dollar advertising campaign designed to launch a new product, the enticingly named Uneeda Biscuit soda cracker. Almost instantly, James Beniger writes, Uneeda became a household word, and the power of brand names and trademarks was firmly established.[41]

At a basic level, London's copyright-conscious terrorists are simply toying with a new corporate strategy. But at a more abstract level, London succinctly indicates an important similarity that knits together the concurrent development of corporate capitalism and modern terrorism. The trademark or brand name deployed in massive ad campaigns was an integral element in turn-of-the-century capitalism's attempt to utilize evolving communication technologies such as the new mass-circulation dailies and low-priced magazines, while those same new forms of communication were instrumental in the rise of modern terrorism. Arguing for such a connection between modern terrorism and the 1881 perfection of the rotary press, Alex P. Schmid and Janny de Graaf suggest that the late-nineteenth-century mass press provided much publicity for terrorists and their actions and consequently contributed to terrorism's early development.[42] In short, modern terrorism could hardly have arisen without the simultaneous emergence of the mass press that, coincidentally, also played a pivotal role in corporate capitalism's development during this period.

In "The Minions of Midas," London deepens our understanding of the relationship between capitalism and terrorism by illustrating the pivotal role that communication technology plays in each. Unlike the utterly repressive

[155]

and dystopian Iron Heel, the terrorists depicted in this more "realistic" short story depend on the newspaper to disseminate knowledge of their killings. Hale's assistant, though not believing the Minions' first warning that a random workman will be killed if Hale failed to surrender the $20 million, "turn[s] involuntarily to the morning paper" where he finds confirmation of the murder (437). With each random outrage, the press coverage becomes greater until the "papers teemed with glaring . . . headlines" complaining about the inability of the police to protect the citizenry (439). Finally, under mounting pressure, both Hale and his assistant commit suicide because the Minions' continual threats and acts of random terror convince them that "society is shaken to its foundations. . . . Law and order have failed" (443).

London's "Minions of Midas" concisely demonstrates the central role the media plays in linking modern terrorists with their immediate victims, the public at large, and the person whom they hope to coerce with their violence. Moreover, the resolution of his story—the suicides of Hale and his assistant because of their lost faith in "law and order"—represents London's theorization of terrorism's symbolic violence. That is, the Minions choose targets because they symbolize what American culture generally holds dear (young mothers, babies, and the elderly are all among their victims) rather than because they bear any personal grudge, since their terrorist organization seeks to persuade Hale that the government is powerless to protect him from their extortion. In this regard it is critical that the Minions first threaten and then succeed in killing the head police investigator while he is on the phone to Hale. Murdering the inspector in the police station, the very symbol of law and order, emblematizes the state's vulnerability. And when citizens believe they are unsheltered by the forces of order, then indeed "society is shaken to its foundations."

While the Minions choose targets for their symbolic resonance, they also employ strategies intended to undermine, rather than directly attack, the state's own organizations and favored systems. As Jonathan Auerbach has pointed out, the Minions, despite their protestations to the contrary, do not engage in a battle between separate economic classes but rather emerge as capitalism's double.[43] They form a business organization to combat the inequalities generated by American corporate capitalism, use the U.S. government's mail system to deliver their extortion letters, and depend on the antiterrorist *Morning Blazer* newspaper's need to sell papers to distribute information about their acts. In sum, they repeatedly appropriate elements of the systems and organizations they are protesting in order to coerce Hale into capitulating to their demands. Using the state's structures against itself particularly terrifies because it suggests that the state can no longer control its own domain—that terror is woven into the very fabric of the state. As the Minions inform Hale, "*We are part and parcel of your possessions*" (442, emphasis original).

This scenario in "Minions" is particularly interesting because of its historical analogues in which the mail, the media, capitalism, and terrorism have comprised a circuit suggesting that terrorism is "part and parcel" of the United States. Before America's frightening experience with anthrax-laced letters in October 2001, Theodore Kaczynski, the so-called Unabomber, provided another example. Throughout the 1980s and 1990s he used the U.S. Postal Service to send his letter bombs and ultimately convinced the *New York Times* and *Washington Post* to jointly publish his manifesto-like screed against technology and leftists in the *Post*. But the Unabomber was not the first American to orchestrate a concentrated campaign of terror through the normally innocuous mail system. In April 1919 a bomb was discovered in the mail of Seattle's mayor, who had been crisscrossing the country whipping up the notorious "Red Scare" of 1919. The next day, dynamite exploded in the home of a Georgia senator who had advocated restricting immigration. And this was only the beginning. In total, thirty-eight package bombs were found that spring, working their way through the mails to various capitalists and government officials, including J. P. Morgan, John D. Rockefeller, and Attorney General A. Mitchell Palmer (conductor of the notorious 1919–20 "Palmer Raids," in which hundreds of leading radicals, including Emma Goldman, were illegally detained or deported). The bombings appeared to confirm a prediction made in the *New York Times* the previous New Year's Day, after "infernal machines" destroyed the homes of a Pennsylvania Supreme Court judge, a superintendent of police, and a Chamber of Commerce president, that those particular attacks heralded "the start of terrorist plots planned to reach from one end of the country to the other."[44] When the mail bombings were followed in early June 1919 by a coordinated dynamite attack in which explosions occurred simultaneously at the residences of prominent government officials and capitalists in eight major cities, it appeared that a nationwide terrorist conspiracy was truly afoot.[45]

The mail bombings were widely reported in the press, and speculation was rampant concerning who could be responsible, with most commentators pointing at various immigrants or labor radicals and villainizing them as dangerous threats to American democracy. The *New York Times* reported the mail bombing campaign as "a bold plot against the American Government and the forces of law and order,"[46] while its editorialists charged that "Bolsheviki, anarchists, and I.W.W.'s are pointed out by all the indications as the men who intended to assassinate by bombs so many officials," thereby "seek[ing] the overthrow of American institutions and of American society."[47] In these accounts, anarchist, IWW member, and Bolshevik are all interchangeable, with each term mobilized to construct an image of American law and order under attack by terroristic foreigners who are dangerously and hopelessly un-American.

While this strident rhetoric strove to create an explicit image of the terrorists as foreign radicals — even though, or perhaps because, the police were unsuccessful in apprehending the responsible parties — the mail bombers' actual methods created an uncanny image of terrorists as a fundamental element of American capitalism, thereby recalling the Minions' warning to Eban Hale that they are "part and parcel" of his domain. To make the bombs look like a package from Gimbels department store, the terrorists forged the Gimbels name on high-quality wrapping paper, penciled the word "Novelty" next to the logo, and sealed each end with a small, ornate piece of red, scalloped paper.[48] In this way, the architects of the campaign attempted to capitalize on Gimbels's common practice of sending out free novelties, thus also appropriating one of corporate capitalism's favorite gimmicks — the complimentary promotional item. Moreover, making the bombs appear to come from Gimbels also suggested that capitalism bore its violent destruction within itself, much as the Minions of Midas claimed that they had inevitably been created in a violent reaction to the inexorable forces of capitalism.

Nearly ten years after "Minions," when London returned to a direct consideration of business and terrorism in *The Assassination Bureau*, this unique twist on the common Marxist idea that capitalism harbors its own self-destructive energy spectacularly reemerged in the Minions' corporate descendent, the Assassination Bureau. *Bureau*, however, occupies a strange position in the London canon as the rare novel left unfinished at the author's death in 1916. Although London's motto was "never revise, never rewrite,"[49] this one novel had him stymied. London, who routinely complained of his struggle to imagine plot scenarios,[50] had purchased the idea for this story of secretly plotting terrorists from a young Sinclair Lewis in 1910, only to become disillusioned with the novel shortly thereafter. As he wrote to Lewis, "I have 20,000 words done on the *Assassination Bureau*, and for the first time in my life am stuck and disgusted. I haven't done my best by it, and cannot make up my mind whether or not to go ahead with it."[51] Despite, or perhaps because of, this position in the corpus of a writer who notoriously tried to sell everything he could and who measured his output in the terms of sheer quantity (he claimed to write 1,000 words a day, day in and day out),[52] *The Assassination Bureau* has been almost completely ignored by London's critics and biographers.

The novel itself, set in 1911, tells the story of Ivan Dragomiloff, a Russian émigré and former terrorist who now lives a dual life in New York. Publicly, he owns a profitable import-export business trading in Russian goods, while privately he masterminds the Assassination Bureau, Inc. The bureau, organized as a corporation and staffed by carefully trained killers—all of whom, interestingly enough, are former academics—actively solicits the business of terrorist organizations, anarchist groups, and anyone else who bears a murderous grudge. For a fee, based on a sliding scale of charges, the bureau will assassinate anyone. But there is one twist. All proposed murders must be carefully studied and approved by Dragomiloff, who will only warrant killings that narrow what he perceives to be the gap between America's juridical ideals and its actual juridical procedures, in which the crimes of the powerful are ignored or concealed. The smooth, machinelike efficiency of the organization is halted one day, however, by a progressive reformer, Winter Hall, who discovers the existence of the bureau and vows to destroy it. Hall meets with Dragomiloff and convinces him that the bureau's form of social work is actually regressive for society as a whole, whereupon Dragomiloff promptly and surprisingly decides to disband his organization and, stranger yet, takes a contract out on himself. A lethal cat-and-mouse game ensues, in which Dragomiloff kills the members of his firm while they try to assassinate him. But at this point, London, unable to reverse the entropic direction in which he had taken his plot and worried that the story had become "farcical," simply broke off his narration and planned instead to set sail on a six-month sea adventure,[53] leaving the novel unfinished and unpublished.

When London begins his story, Dragomiloff has been in the assassination business in America for eleven years,[54] but he was a committed terrorist long before immigrating to the United States. As a "young Bakuninite in Russia" (46) who had been "inoculated with radical ideas and joined the Young Russians" (44–45) while a college student, Dragomiloff had been "in prison several times" and escaped the country just as he was about to be shipped to Siberia because his "latest conspiracy had leaked" (45) to the czarist government. Faced with Siberia, Dragomiloff managed to flee Russia by assuming the identity of his brother-in-law, Sergius Constantine, "a pronounced conservative" who had conveniently just died of smallpox, and who "was buried under [Dragomiloff's] name" (45). By having Dragomiloff assume his conservative brother-in-law's name and identity to escape the Russian state police, London proposes a fluid relationship between businessmen and terrorists that he will return to throughout the narrative. It is as Sergius Constantine that Dragomiloff builds a prosperous importing business in New York, while, as Ivan Dragomiloff, he applies the same business strategies of organization, record keeping, and a pragmatic concern with the fiscal bottom line to his international terrorist corporation. Ironically, as a successful businessman, Dragomiloff/Constantine assumes his supporting role in the "capitalist organization"—that intimate relationship between capitalism and the state that London identified and condemned in his piece on the Haywood kidnapping and in *The Iron Heel*—just as certainly as the "pronounced conservative" Constantine supported the Russian state before his untimely death.

Before he fled Russia, Dragomiloff, as a follower of Mikhail Bakunin, Russia's principal theorist of anarchism and terrorism in the late nineteenth century, would have found himself at the center of a heated controversy between Bakunin and Karl Marx concerning the philosophy of workers' insurrections. In brief, Bakunin believed terrorists could provide an incipient workers' revolt a much needed shove to set it in motion, while Marx, like Lenin some decades later, thought terrorism a distraction from the effort to build a collective consciousness among workers. Bakunin, whom Marx expelled from the First International in 1872 and who has been called "the prophet . . . of terrorist amoralism" and "guerrilla insurrectionism,"[55] produced a founding document of modern terrorism in his 1869 manifesto, "Revolution, Terrorism, Banditry." He wrote, "The healthy, uncorrupted mind of youth must grasp the fact that it is considerably more humane to stab and strangle dozens, nay hundreds, of hated beings than to join with them to share in systematic *legal* acts of murder . . . by all the people of standing who, directly or indirectly, oppress those who have no standing!"[56] The phrase "legal acts of murder" intriguingly prefigures London's words concerning the Russian revolutionaries' terrorist acts committed some thirty years after Bakunin published his defense of terror. London's repetition in "Revolution" of Bakunin's phrasing most likely was not a conscious act. I would suggest, however, that his condemnation of the czarist regime's "legal murder" does put him in dialogue with Bakunin's particular way of thinking about or theorizing the state's methods of legitimating its actions and policies through a discursive naturalization of existing power relations. And in Dragomiloff's Assassination Bureau, which specializes in the murder of "people of standing who, directly or indirectly, oppress those who have no standing," London fictionalizes and exports Bakunin's theorization of subversive violence from Russia to America.

When Dragomiloff slipped out of Russia at the turn of the century, he would have found himself part of a massive wave of immigrants moving from Russia and southeastern Europe to the United States. With Dragomiloff's immigrant status, the connections between discourses of terrorism and national identity that proved so vital to understanding the construction of terrorists in the Haymarket affair of 1886 again emerge. In *The Assassination Bureau,* however, London imagines Dragomiloff neither as the immigrant heir to the American revolutionary tradition (as the Haymarket anarchists characterized themselves) nor as a menacing foreign threat to American democracy (as the anarchists' opponents depicted them). Rather, Ivan and his daughter, Grunya, could be the official representatives of Progressive Era Americanization programs. They both speak English that is "without accent" (10), and she performs "settlement work" among more recent immigrants on New York's East Side (12–13).

As thoroughly assimilated immigrants without any obvious trace of their Russian heritage, Ivan and Grunya represent one important way that questions of identity and nationality were negotiated via the ideology of Americanization during the Progressive Era. Indeed, at nearly the same time that London was writing his novel, Henry Ford aggressively promoted the abandonment of a previous national identity in favor of the adopted American identity that Ivan and Grunya outwardly embody. In the 1910s Ford, who bears responsibility for a number of bizarre events in American history, demanded that his immigrant employees participate in his English School. During the graduation ceremonies, the workers disembarked from a simulated immigrant ship dressed in clothes intended to signify their foreignness and holding signs indicating their countries of origin. After being made to "represent" themselves in this way, the employees disappeared into a gigantic replica of a melting pot, which the teachers pretended to stir vigorously with huge ladles, and then emerged a few minutes later dressed in "American" clothing and holding an American flag.[57] In its exaggerated attempt to dramatize the Americanization process, Ford's tableau aptly demonstrates the intense preoccupation with national identity and rituals of citizenship during the twentieth century's opening decades.

Yet London's representation of Ivan and Grunya gives the lie to the rhetoric of Americanization that Ford's English School so beautifully emblematized. Despite her Americanized appearance and speech, Grunya remains a "philosophic anarchist" (14) committed to dismantling the U.S. government, while it is precisely Dragomiloff's identity as an American businessman that makes his other terrorist self possible. In Dragomiloff, then, London imagines the worst nightmare for the proponents of Americanization, since his Russian-American businessman-terrorist refuses to abandon one identity for another. Moreover, by creating a figure who slides easily between identities, London again undermines the discursive formations that create and reify polarized identities in the interest of existing power relations. In other words, London's Americanized businessman-terrorist breaks down the "us vs. them" binary that is explicit in Ford's tableau and that, crucially, was also routinely used to characterize political violence in the interest of making a dominant social order appear natural, correct, and under siege by outsiders (think, for instance, of Roosevelt's attempt to cast insurgent American labor radicals out of the body politic by condemning them as "undesirable citizens").

Since London's text pivots on Dragomiloff's unstable identities, it is also particularly appropriate that the Russian immigrant founds an import-export business when he arrives in New York. The question of borders and identity is no more clearly at issue than in an import-export corporation, where commodities are classified by their ability to represent the culture of the country where they were produced. But if importers such as S. Constantine and Company depend for their livelihood on carefully demarcated borders between countries, at the turn of the century they were also the primary beneficiaries of American imperialists' transgression and dissolution of national boundaries. The sharp spike in the volume of international commerce brought about by American imperialism also triggered a rebound in manufacturing after the depressed 1890s, which in turn stimulated both the immigrant rush into American factories and the concerns that we have seen about American identity. Likewise, expansion of overseas trade also produced the middle-class taste for the exotic and foreign goods in which import houses such as Sergius Constantine's trafficked.[58] Indeed, ironically but perhaps not surprisingly, the penchant for exotic fashions emerged at exactly the same time that Americans such as Henry Ford were in an uproar about immigrant workers failing to assume "American" customs, dress, and speech. By placing Dragomiloff and his corporate disguise at the epicenter of this conflicted discourse on cultural borders, commerce, and identity, London underscores the highly politicized character and incoherence of all reified identities, such as "American" or "terrorist." He also suggests that Dragomiloff's other import, Bakunin-inspired terrorism, should be understood in terms analogous to, rather than distinct from, his simultaneous career as a businessman.

In fact, when Dragomiloff moves from being a young revolutionary terrorist in Russia to a businessman in the United States, he does not leave behind his violent inclinations for helping social justice along. Rather, he makes them more systematic by organizing a multinational corporation, a "firm of men-killers" (23) specializing in assassinations and numbering corrupt labor union bosses, underhanded financiers, a "Cotton King," abusive husbands, and assorted societal gadflies among its many victims (20–24). Years in the planning stages before it was ever realized as a financially successful enterprise, Dragomiloff's Assassination Bureau is an exceptionally well-organized company. It operates by strictly codified procedures, including full payment in advance and the return of all fees plus 5 percent interest should the bureau fail after a full year to assassinate its target, an occurrence that has never come to pass (5–7). The firm also has routine methods for recruiting potential members and for soliciting clients. Moreover, Dragomiloff caters to the interests and needs of his clients by offering a sliding scale of charges. Anarchists, for instance, receive the "biggest cut-rate" (7) offered by the bureau because they are generally poor, while the cost of specific victims, which ranges from "half a million" for a king of England to "anywhere between seventy-five and a hundred thousand dollars" for "little second- and third-rate kings" and "fifty thousand" for a police chief (5), is determined by a given victim's "position and influence" in society (31).

By going to such lengths to detail the commercial aspects of Dragomiloff's sophisticated conspiratorial organization, London imagines a "firm of men-killers" that mobilizes the organizing principles of capitalism that he railed against so vehemently in his "Something Rotten in Idaho." The implications that follow from London's tale of capitalistic terrorism are twofold. On the one hand, London's depiction registers his intuitive grasp of corporate capitalism's hegemonic role in modern America. Put more concretely, London's representation of the terrorist business fictionalizes how the capitalist state elicits consent by establishing its interests as the interests of its subjects, even those who wish to oppose it. Providing Dragomiloff with the structure and logic of his entrepreneurial assassinations, capitalism reproduces itself through the Russian-born terrorist even as he coordinates the removal of its worst abusers. Yet, as Raymond Williams has written, while "hegemony . . . by definition . . . is always dominant, it is never either total or exclusive"; "it is also continually resisted, limited, altered, challenged by pressures not at all its own."[59] According to Williams, who is following Antonio Gramsci here, hegemony is a constantly fluctuating practice that favors generating consent over active coercion and therefore never simply squashes all resistance.[60] Similar to *The Iron Heel*'s confusion of state and antistate terrorists, London's latter novel itself exemplifies this formulation of hegemony's pressures and its cleavages. While his depiction of Dragomiloff's enterprise registers the reach of capital's dominating influence, his conception of the rational and systematic terrorist also offers a point of resistance. London's fictional representation hearkens back to his defense of the Russian terrorists' rationality and additionally moves the discourse of terrorism away from the rhetoric of insanity that is exemplified by the *North American Review* and *Living Age* articles noted earlier. Moreover, by creating a terrorist who is also a capitalist, London's novel evokes those capitalists and state officials who acted like terrorists in the kidnapping of the WFM labor leaders. Consistently representing and tallying these moments where the boundaries of reified identities are blurred, London thus repeatedly undermines easy distinctions between law and violence, order and disorder, government and anarchy.

Such ideologically loaded dualisms are challenged not only by London's portrait of a capitalist terrorist identity, but also by his thorough delineation of the structural organization of Dragomiloff's enterprise. Specifically, the business of terror in London's novel is carefully organized along the lines of a bureaucratic corporate model. Each member has a precise and limited role in the business. Dragomiloff, for one, "spend[s] no time drumming up trade" and "never execute[s]" since that "is not [his] branch." He merely judges the merits of a potential job, and that only "locally" (28). In addition to this strict regimentation according to both expertise and geography, the members usually remain anonymous to Dragomiloff. "I rarely see them," he says at one point, "unless they rise in the organization, and by the same token very few of them ever see me" (29). Though this anonymity may be a necessary arrangement in a business where betrayal to the authorities would be catastrophic, it also suggests an intriguing link between the veiled and secret world of terrorists and the labyrinthian bureaucracies of modern corporate capitalism that were developing shortly before and during the period in which London wrote. New layers of middle management and the increasing priority placed upon organization and job specialization in America's bureaucratic business enterprises occluded the public's ability to see and understand the inner workings of business;[61] this obscurity, ambiguity, and attention to administrative details is mirrored in the clandestine workings of London's imagined conspiratorial terrorist group.

The significance of this parallel can be illuminated by the work of Max Weber, one of the first to attempt to theorize the role of bureaucracy in modern culture. In his posthumously published *Economy and Society*, Weber argues that bureaucratization means that "individual performances are allocated to functionaries who have specialized training and who by constant practice increase their expertise." And, most crucially, "this superiority of the professional insider every bureaucracy seeks further to increase through the means of *keeping secret* its knowledge and intentions. Bureaucratic administration always tends to exclude the public, to hide its knowledge and action from criticism as well as it can."[62] Bureaucracies, whether they be found in the elaborate corporate trusts that so frustrated reformers during the historical moment in which London wrote his novel or in an imagined Assassination Bureau, both further their goals through hidden knowledge, covert schemes, and specialized job descriptions.

In fact, with Weber's analysis of bureaucracies' secretive nature in mind, I would argue that London's particular depiction specifically evokes the conspiratorial and ruthless bureaucracies of the era's notoriously veiled corporate trusts. These Byzantine organizations were denounced repeatedly at the turn of the twentieth century for their covert machinations and mind-boggling intricacies. As *The Nation* editorialized in 1887, the trust "is bound by no law. There are no limitations upon it, not even those of time and space. Neither the public nor the shareholders can call it to account. It has no fixed abode, no place of meeting, no books of account that anybody can demand access to. . . . It may oppress the public without fear of the State because there is nothing for the State to lay hold of."[63] The "Trust Problem," as it was known during the Progressive Era, presented to reformers the difficulty of penetrating intricate yet highly clandestine organizations that appeared to be controlling large segments of American business and society—organizations that, aside from their less violent methods, were not all that different from Dragomiloff's Assassination Bureau. London's 1910 novel thus also recalls and modifies the bureaucratic, capitalist Oligarchy of *The Iron Heel*, for now the capitalist organization itself figures specifically as the incubator of substate terrorism.

The effect of London's "bureaucratization of assassination," then, is not only to diffuse personal responsibility for murder throughout the "bureaucratic rationale" of the agency's organization, thus "effectively reduc[ing] its political meaning to zero,"[64] but also to suggest that the secretive and well-organized nature of bureaucratic organizations makes them, because of their very structure, particularly amenable to menacing and clandestine ends.[65] Whereas corporate trusts' labyrinthian design made it difficult to track their activities, the Assassination Bureau, which operates "outside the law" (8) and whose only product is murder, makes explicit and deadly the often extralegal activities of corporate bureaucracies. Indeed, it is the bureau's "numerous" agents (5) and meticulous processing of its executions through a carefully demarcated chain of command that underpin the firm's flawless record, thereby assuring that no contract goes unfulfilled while the police "never g[e]t a clue" (20). Moreover, the inner workings of the bureau itself provide a nefarious twist on the notion of employee allegiance that, according to Alan Trachtenberg, emerged at the turn of the century as a particularly desirable and rewardable trait within corporate America.[66] Dragomiloff's "organization for assassination" (20) guarantees fidelity through its own murderous incentive, as any member who proves disloyal to the firm's principles and business strategies unfailingly suffers execution.

Thus understood alongside the era's secretive and well-oiled business machinery, it is the Assassination Bureau's recapitulation of the period's fascination with the pursuit of efficiency that, in particular, signals London's attempt to redefine the conventional notion of terrorists that I discussed earlier.[67] On the novel's opening page, for instance, we learn that Dragomiloff's office is kept "in scrupulous order and advertised a presiding genius that was the soul of system" (1). Moreover, Dragomiloff likes to compare his organization to the "anarchists" (5) and other "terrorists" (2) who contract for his services: "You anarchists are poor operators," he tells one client, because "whenever you try your hand you bungle it or get caught" (5). As Ivan is also fond of pointing out, "Usually the person or personage they try to kill gets off unscathed" while his bureau has never failed because the "organization is as near perfect as the mind of man can make it" (30). What Dragomiloff dislikes about his less organized clients is precisely their inefficient operation and, from his administrative point of view, bungling conspiracies. By bringing corporate planners and bureaucratic functionaries' favorite tool — the "organization chart" explicitly coupling particular duties with specific employees — to the business of terrorism, Dragomiloff metaphorically serves as yet another relay between bureaucratic management, corporate capitalism, and the usually hidden sphere of terrorists. In Dragomiloff capitalism, terrorism, and bureaucratic organizations all point to and indicate one another.

That Dragomiloff is appalled by the procedures yet sympathetic to the politics of the terrorists and anarchists who solicit his business is also especially intriguing insofar as this dynamic almost exactly recapitulates an introduction that London wrote for Alexander Berkman's *Prison Memoirs of an Anarchist* only a few months after he had abandoned *The Assassination Bureau.* During the violent strike at the Carnegie Steel Company's Homestead mills in 1892, Berkman had unsuccessfully attempted to assassinate Henry C. Frick, Carnegie's chairman of the board. Berkman, who spent fourteen years in prison for his crime, wrote his autobiography after his release and solicited London to write an introduction. London wrote the preface, but Berkman rejected it because of its unflattering characterization of the would-be assassin. In the introduction, which was finally published in 1989, London calls Berkman "my brother" but dismisses his "terroristic deed" by arguing that "it must be granted that the anarchists do not know how to kill" because of "a fatal inefficiency." And Berkman in particular "was too much the fevered thinker, too little the practical man" even to "realize that a well nourished revolutionist was a more efficient revolutionist."[68]

Since this censure of Berkman's inefficiency repeats the novelistic depiction of the inept anarchists who contract with the Assassination Bureau, London seems to be drawing an ideological line between what he regards as the ineffectual and unconsidered tactics of anarchists and Dragomiloff's orderly attempts to enact the conditions for a more just society through a systematic use of violence. Repeatedly considering different ways of using violence to remake society, London tosses aside anarchic violence and posits that the Assassination Bureau's mimicry of the "specialized training" and "expertise"[69] of the state's bureaucratic functionaries works most effectively. Specifically, such imitation turns the predominant qualities of the modern state—its order and systematic functioning—upon itself. Thus imagining a clandestine and fully developed corporation that systematically eliminates the "criminals" whose offenses are ordinarily concealed by the machinery of the state apparatus, London implicates modern America's corporate economy itself in the violence that the state reserves the right, in cases such as the kidnapping of Bill Haywood, either to criminalize or to overlook.

While the Assassination Bureau mimics the state in its particular bureaucratic form and structure, Dragomiloff also positively usurps the state's right to define, judge, and sentence criminal behavior as his agency strives for greater social justice. In this, London's novel works to rearticulate that conjunction of capitalism and the state that was at stake in the Haywood-Moyer case. The Assassination Bureau, for instance, when defining who counts as a criminal, "demand[s] a moral sanction for all [its] transactions" (7), and a contract is never entered into until Dragomiloff is "satisfied that it is socially justifiable" (4). In fact, the bureau members, all former academics who still spend much time producing scholarship and discussing the moral virtues of assassination, conduct their business with "the strictest honesty" (8) because they "are all rather fanatical when it comes to ethics" (28). As Dragomiloff puts it, "We have the sanction of right in all that we do. . . . We have our own code of right, and our own law" because "nothing that is not founded on right can endure" (28–29).

By imagining a for-profit Assassination Bureau that places itself above the law and regards its own assassinations as a more equitable distribution of justice than that offered by the state itself, London's novel fundamentally asks what grants the government authority to take its citizens' lives. Probing the political or ideological motivations that undergird a formal juridical system, London suggests that America's laws are more committed to protecting the powerful than dispensing impartial justice. This is why, at the opening of the novel, Dragomiloff accepts a commission to assassinate a "chief of police" whose "officers gave perjured testimony on the witness stand" (3–4) against the "terrorists" of the "Caroline Warfield group" (9). Thus contrasting his depiction of the assassins who have made a "fetish of ethics" (82) with this portrayal of corruption in Chief of Police McDuffy—whose occupation theoretically embodies the state's legal impartiality—London again recalls his writing concerning the unlawful police actions in the Haywood-Moyer case and the assassinations of Russia's 1905 revolution. Similarly, *The Assassination Bureau*'s depiction of a cultural terrain where law is a shield protecting the guilty and assassins plot murder in order to produce a more equitable society highlights the ambiguity and difficulty involved in evaluating both political violence in itself and the cultural discourses that produce notions of terrorists and criminals.

Since Dragomiloff so heartily professes his belief in the social utility of his organization, the novel's plot initially appears to spin violently out of control when he suddenly becomes convinced that his firm is actually harmful for society and should be dissolved. Faced with the arguments of Winter Hall, a young reformer bent on destroying the bureau, that "the time had come in the evolution of society when society, as a whole, must work out its own salvation," Dragomiloff does "not deny that he played the part of the man on horseback, who thought for society, and drove society; but he did deny, and emphatically, that society as a whole was able to manage itself" (36–37). But after several days of pitched rhetorical battle, Dragomiloff accepts Hall's argument: "'I see, now,' he said, 'that I failed to lay sufficient stress on the social factors. The assassinations have not been so much intrinsically wrong as socially wrong. . . . As between individuals, they have not been wrong at all. But individuals are not individuals alone. They are parts of complexes of individuals. There was where I erred. . . . I was not justified'" (37). Dragomiloff in this scene plays out a well-known tension in London's work between his fascination with the Nietzschean Superman who can forcefully bend others to his will and a faith in a more socialistic organization of society.[70] The chief's epiphany here serves—as London often claimed *The Sea-Wolf* and *Martin Eden* also served—as an indictment of individualism.[71] Unlike Ernest Everhard, who was heavily engaged in socialist politics, or the WFM leaders, who were part of a large labor union, or even the Russian revolutionaries, who enjoyed the support of "7,000,000 comrades," Dragomiloff is not part of a widespread movement. Accordingly, like Wolf Larsen and Martin Eden, he must be shown the error of his individualistic ways. As we have seen before, London repeatedly needs to imagine political violence as part of a large movement to right society's ills rather than the rogue violence of disillusioned murderers, in part due to his commitment to socialism and in part because he is attempting to rethink the dominant discourse of terrorism.

But Dragomiloff does not simply decide to disband his organization; he underscores his new outlook by taking a contract out on himself. When London was writing the novel, it was this decision and the almost farcical chase scenes that ensue from it that produced his disillusion with *Bureau* and his uncharacteristic inability to see the work through to its end. This unexpected plot twist confounded London and perhaps suggests the extent to which he remained unsure about the political effects unleashed by his conception of a socially progressive terrorist corporation. Yet the plot is nonetheless consistent with London's overall suspicion toward the discursive construction of law, order, and the distribution of power within society. Indeed, this particular plot twist demonstrates in exaggerated form the sheer power of language to construct a terrorist identity, since it is the chief's own definition of an enemy of the state that, when convincingly applied to himself, recasts him from the subject to the object of terrorism, thereafter hounded as a criminal by the bureau because of his own decree. Because of his actions Ivan becomes both a judge and a criminal, thus metaphorically effacing any difference between the embodiment of the state and its adversaries. Moreover, while on the run he takes every opportunity to kill his former employees, bringing his organization to its demise by assassinating the assassins. Ivan's murders, which are justified in his mind for the same reasons that he sanctioned earlier assassinations, reduce criminal and state violence to two sides of the same coin.[72] Whether devising an Assassination Bureau to close the state's juridical loopholes or destroying the bureau by murdering its members, Ivan makes criminality, law, and terror into reversible, contingent, and ultimately indivisible concepts.

For London, then, in his journalism as well as his fiction, the advanced capitalist state in America is unimaginable without an accompanying discourse of terrorism. But this is not simply because terrorism is the chosen form of resistance by those excluded from capitalism's bounty; rather, for London, terror is a fundamental and constituent element of America's identity at the turn of the twentieth century. His construction of a terrorist subjectivity emerges from this central insight, as he depicts at one moment a state that kidnaps and coerces its adversaries and at another moment terrorists who are surprisingly astute capitalists usurping the state's prerogatives. London constructs a contingent and contradictory terrorist subjectivity, thereby refusing to reify an image of terrorists in line with the frequent equivalence drawn at the turn of the century between "terrorist" and "anarchist," in which both terms imply a dangerously un-American radicalism. Ultimately, London's multiple terrorist subjectivities probe the theoretical coherence and implications of the discursive boundary separating licit and proscribed violence, as he questions whether terrorism and order might be inseverable or even indistinguishable in early-twentieth-century American culture.

CHAPTER FIVE

Sabotage

Class Antagonism and the Fantasies of Violence

In 1880s Chicago, as we have seen, one of the citizenry's most predominant anxieties was that an indistinguishable person blending unobserved into the crowd might, in fact, be a terrorist. As Lyman Abbott had warned, the then-new invention of dynamite was particularly fearsome precisely because its compact size made it possible for someone to carry a bomb undetected "in a carpet-bag." Abbott worried that disaffected members of the working class, believing that "property is theft," would resort to clandestine attacks against persons and structures that both facilitated and symbolized the synergy between capitalism and the state in industrial America.[1] By the first decade of the twentieth century, Abbott's worries about the anonymity of the potentially dangerous individual and the massive power that could be wielded by a terrorist, as well as the discomfort created by the possible disjuncture between a person's public identity and violent private desires, had been all too familiar to Americans for twenty-some years.

Then, on 1 October 1910, the "crime of the century" occurred, pulled off by James McNamara, who had been crisscrossing the country carrying dynamite in a valise and setting off explosions for several years. Around 1:00 A.M. on that October morning, dynamite planted in a nearby alley destroyed the *Los Angeles Times* newspaper offices and printing plant.[2] The *Times* bombing culminated a series of spectacular explosions at various building sites and industrial complexes between 1905 and 1911 and resulted in two lengthy trials tying it to the radical International Association of Bridge and Structural Iron Workers (IABSIW) trade union. Like the Haymarket and Steunenberg bombings before it, the destruction of the *Times* sparked the production of reams of paper. Memoirs, confessions of reluctant dynamiters, diatribes, and analyses by commentators of every political persuasion appeared in the years immediately following the bombing. All these texts attempted in one way or another to make sense of the ideological and material ties between clandestine acts of terrorist violence, industrial capitalism, and the state—the same issues that Abbott had worried about in 1885.

An article by Walter V. Woehlke entitled "Terrorism in America," which appeared in *Outlook* magazine in the wake of the *Times* dynamiting trial, exemplifies the key issues raised by this flood of writing. Woehlke's first line immediately asks, "Why do trade unions resort to violence, bloodshed, and destruction of property to win strikes?"[3] Reiterating 1880s Haymarket-style fear about violence directed toward the agents of capitalism, Woehlke instantly equates terrorism with the action of labor unions. And not surprisingly, the primary evidence in his condemnation of the "nitroglycerine and gas-pipe habit" includes the leaders of the Western Federation of Miners who were charged with Frank Steunenberg's 1905 assassination and the Chicago anarchists convicted for the Haymarket bombing.[4] Bringing his discussion up to date, Woehlke then discusses industrial sabotage, including the tale of a duped manufacturer who hired a man because he swore he did not belong to a union, only to have the worker sabotage a large piece of expensive machinery within a few hours of being employed. As Woehlke then asks, "Does this damaging of property differ from the crimes of the McNamaras in any manner except in degree? Black hatred is engendered by the relentless, unceasing struggle to unionize or disunionize the industries. The atmosphere of shops, factories, labor headquarters, and employers' offices is charged with it. Terrorism and murder are growing out of it."[5] Woehlke is representative of many early-twentieth-century commentators when he writes that terrorism is something that grows out of the conflict between labor and capital, and, more precisely, that it is an action labor unions do *to* capitalist owners in an effort to coerce them. Yet, in his hardly acknowledged but nonetheless visible recognition that the "unceasing struggle" is two-sided, that owners fought as hard with various methods to "disunionize" employees as those workers fought to organize, there lies a crucial conundrum that runs throughout the period's debates about outbursts of class violence. Woehlke's statement here can be read as suggesting that "terrorism and murder" emerge from directives issued in "employers' offices" as much as from "labor headquarters," even though the entire thrust of his article is to uncover the terrorism specifically of labor unions.

In the 1910s, dominant ideas concerning "terrorism," much like Woehlke's, held that it was organized labor's unfortunate principal occupation, indeed that terrorism was precisely the illegitimate activity labor union members pursued instead of being responsible, hard-working, faithful employees. For both unionists and capitalists these debates over violence and labor often focused on sabotage—what it was and was not, whether it was violent or nonviolent, whether it included violence against persons or only property destruction, who engaged in it and who did not, whether or not it was effective, and what types of fear it produced. These arguments took shape in many forms of cultural representation, including the news media, pamphlets, memoirs, histories, songs, and poetry. In this chapter, I suggest that sabotage became such a preoccupying issue in the twentieth century's first decades not simply because it was one of the more dramatic components of the seemingly interminable conflict between capital and labor, though it certainly was that. Rather, the specter of sabotage crystallized many of the issues raised by the slippage, seen in Woehlke's "Terrorism in America" article, between the stated idea that terrorism is the work of labor unions and the implicitly raised but unacknowledged possibility that it may be a more fraught and complex phenomenon and may come from more sources than disgruntled workers. I focus on three overlapping case studies, including the accounts that emerged after the 1910 *Los Angeles Times* bombing, contemporary discussions of sabotage linked to the radical Industrial Workers of the World labor union, and the poetry of Covington Hall, a labor activist affiliated with the IWW. Sabotage emerged as such an explosive and divisive issue, I argue, specifically because of the ideological contradictions the concept embodied for contemporary audiences. Notions of sabotage threatened to implode all divisions between private desires and public actions, between who is a terrorist and who is not, and between what constitutes violence and nonviolence in the capitalist state.

The Career Dynamiter and the National Dynamite Plot

The bombing of the *Los Angeles Times* building in October 1910 was both a likely and an unlikely capstone to the rash of explosions that had plagued bridge-building and steel firms for several years. In August 1905, the IABSIW went on strike against the massive American Bridge Company because that company had subcontracted work to a firm that used nonunion labor. Over the next year, the strike spread to other firms and hardened over the conflicting desires of building firms to employ nonunion labor, the so-called open shop, and the union's attempt to make union affiliation requisite for employment, a labor arrangement known as a closed shop.[6] Between the summer of 1905 and September 1911, a staggering eighty-six structural steel jobs were bombed or damaged in some way. Over those years, the saboteurs packed

300–400 pounds of nitroglycerine and 2,000 pounds of dynamite into suitcases, transported these bombs on ordinary passenger trains, and checked them along with other baggage in railway stations and hotels.[7] This mass movement of bombs was all done, as one commentator put it, "to the imminent peril of thousands of innocent men, women and children. A heavy jolt in coupling, a slight accident and a train would have been blown to pieces on the rails."[8]

Ortie McManigal, who would later confess to dozens of bombings, was directly responsible for transporting many of those concealed bombs. Traveling anonymously from city to city on the train, McManigal embodied the era's classic fears of terrorist violence. With his suitcases full of explosives, McManigal often acted as an innocuous tourist after he reached the places where he intended to plant a bomb. On one mission, during which he blew up the Llewellyn Iron Works in Los Angeles on Christmas Day 1910, McManigal spent Christmas Eve on an excursion around the city, even posing for pictures with other sightseers at San Gabriel mission.[9] Moreover, McManigal routinely sent his wife in Chicago a souvenir spoon from wherever he happened to be completing a dynamiting assignment.[10] The peripatetic dynamiter's tourism and souvenir hunting were bizarre and fascinating attempts to maintain domesticity and normalcy, even as he traveled about the country wreaking havoc.

Posing for photographs with other tourists or buying collectibles for his wife, McManigal also embodied the uncanny form of near yet far intimacy in modern mass culture that pioneering sociologist George Simmel accounted for in his theorization of "the stranger" in urban society during this same period. As McManigal stood in the railway station shop buying spoons while holding luggage with enough dynamite to destroy whole city blocks, he was at once the same as and radically dissimilar from his fellow travelers. Or, as Simmel puts it in his description of the stranger, McManigal's strangeness was not generated by his dynamite-wielding otherness, but by his close proximity that was nevertheless unapproachable, a recognizable, safe-looking, yet distinct and unknowable presence. For Simmel, strangeness is produced "by the fact that similarity, harmony, and nearness are accompanied by the feeling that they are not really the unique property of this particular relationship: they are something more general, something which potentially prevails between the partners and an indeterminate number of others."[11] The terrorist endlessly exploits this generalized similarity of mass culture; indeed, a large part of the fear generated by terrorists is this exact propensity to blend into crowds, to be unrecognizable despite their destructive intentions. This nefarious twist on the stranger/tourist was a source of continual fascination when the IABSIW was finally brought to trial for the dynamite conspiracy, as McManigal literally embodied the terrible possibility inherent in the bland indistinguishability of modern mass culture.[12] A potentially deadly sightseer, McManigal ironically used tourism's conveyances and infrastructure (trains, bridges, hotels) to arrive at places where he would bomb other bridges, railroad tracks, and hotels, only then to go out and again melt into the crowd as a tourist.

Between 1905 and 1911, when McManigal was crossing the country buying spoons and blowing up construction sites, he was taking direct orders from the Structural Iron Workers' union headquarters in Indianapolis, specifically from the union's secretary, John J. McNamara. The Iron Workers were convinced, and with good reason, that the National Erectors Association (NEA), a band of steel construction corporations, wanted to extirpate labor unions and operate solely on an open shop basis. The use of dynamite was designed to intimidate corporations and contractors by convincing them that their worksites would be destroyed and employees endangered unless jobs were awarded to unionized firms. Not coincidentally, it also added much to the cost of jobs, as NEA firms were forced to implement antiterrorist measures, including extra lighting, barbed wire, and armed patrols, at their worksites.[13]

In the summer of 1910, James B. McNamara, brother of IABSIW secretary John McNamara, and a man who himself had performed several dynamitings, was sent to Los Angeles, one of the strongest open shop cities in the country. That open shop attitude was personified most fervently by Harrison Gray Otis, owner and publisher of the *Los Angeles Times*. As McManigal later described the bombing of Otis's newspaper, McNamara filled a suitcase with twenty pounds of nitrogelatine and placed it among some of the *Times*'s flammable ink barrels.[14] The blast and resulting fire destroyed large sections of the building, caused over $500,000 in damage, and, tragically, killed twenty workers. Later that same day, unexploded bombs were also found in suitcases at the homes of Otis and Felix J. Zeehandelaar, a prominent antiunion Los Angeles businessman. The bomb found at Zeehandelaar's residence ultimately led William J. Burns, head of the Burns National Detective Agency, to link the Los Angeles bombings with an unexploded bomb found some time earlier at a nonunion construction site. Burns, who had been tapped by the mayor of Los Angeles to head the city's investigation of the *Times* bombing, had, independent of that assignment, also contracted with several steel corporations to investigate the long series of bombings against their properties.[15]

Burns caught up with and arrested James McNamara and McManigal on

11 April 1911. McManigal quickly turned state's evidence, and the trial of the McNamara brothers for the *Times* explosion began the following autumn. Not surprisingly, much like the Haywood-Moyer-Pettibone trial, the McNamara case became a cause célèbre. All the usual suspects weighed in with opinions, including, again, Theodore Roosevelt, and, from his Idaho jail cell, Harry Orchard. Both men denounced the dynamiters.[16] On the other hand, Samuel Gompers, president of the American Federation of Labor, threw his support behind the McNamaras, arguing that they were being scapegoated and falsely accused.[17] Bill Haywood threatened a nationwide general strike to support the accused men. Thousands of dollars were raised for their defense, and Clarence Darrow, in a reprise of Haywood's trial, agreed to defend the two brothers. The McNamaras initially pleaded "Not Guilty," only to shock almost all spectators by reversing their plea to "Guilty" well after the trial was under way. John McNamara was sentenced to fifteen years, and James McNamara was ordered to serve a life sentence. Additionally, the *Times* trial led to the even more dramatic 1912 trial and convictions of nearly forty union leaders associated with the IABSIW on the charge of conspiring to transport explosives on passenger trains across state lines.[18]

Yet, even to this day, it remains something of a mystery as to why the *Times* was targeted following the earlier destruction of so many construction sites. Even though the *Times* exemplified business corporations' widespread desire during this period to maintain an open shop, the bombing was in many ways strikingly dissimilar to the earlier assaults. It was not aimed at a steel erection company, and, much more important, it was the only attack during the six-year bombing spree that involved a large loss of life. Taking the lives of twenty innocent victims, the *Times* blast was a marked departure from the earlier attacks against unoccupied structures. In some ways, both in our own time and at the turn of the twentieth century, this distinction is the difference between sabotage and terrorism. Whereas sabotage is often believed to be aimed at the crippling of machinery, terrorism is thought to be random, indiscriminate, and unpredictable violence against people. But more often in the early twentieth century, and as we will especially see in discussions of the IWW and sabotage, the relationship of sabotage to terrorism, and any supposed differences between them, was cloudy at best. Woehlke's "Terrorism in America" article, for instance, specifically argued that the "damaging of property" differed only in "degree" from the *Times* bombing, and that both were species of terrorism. For another editorialist writing in *Outlook* magazine, the destruction of the *Times* simply represented "the crowning crime" of the "hired assassins."[19] William J. Burns's memoir of the case, *The Masked War*, repeatedly calls the dynamite attacks a "reign of terror" and, in a familiar trope, states that "the war with dynamite was a war of Anarchy against the established form of government of this country."[20]

Those commentators who deemed the bombings to be the work of terrorists proceeded to a certain extent from clearly identifiable ideological grounds. The discursive power to label an action terrorism often makes it easier to win the hearts and minds of the public, a truism both at the turn of the twentieth century and now. However, beyond the ideological imperatives that buttressed this act of labeling, theoretically important connections exist between the earlier bombings and the *Times* blast. Terrorism is not limited to actions that are necessarily and definitely intended to kill people. The mere threat of horrific mass violence—the possibility, for example, that the bombing of a construction site was actually a botched attempt to take lives, or that the bombing of inanimate structures is only a harbinger of worse violence to come—creates the dread inherent to terrorism. Indeed, the true terror of the six-year rash of bombings against inanimate metal and concrete was not that they had killed people, but, terribly, that they had not, that there existed the possibility that the bombing campaign could change direction and suddenly be aimed at targets more likely to produce death in addition to or instead of material destruction. The bombings against structures always harbored the possibility that they were mere prelude to even more awful attacks. In this manner, terrorism circumscribes individual citizens' behaviors, as some actions become too risky or dangerous. As Joseba Zulaika and William A. Douglass have suggested, "In the terrorism framework it is this very anticipation which translates into the tension inspired by imagined terror, the most terrifying of its possible guises."[21]

This potential threat explains why the memoirs of the bombing campaign obsessively return to the idea that death was often narrowly averted in the years leading up to the *Times* explosion. In Burns's and McManigal's accounts, night watchmen constantly, and mostly through sheer luck, escape explosions. Burns also writes that an October 1911 attempt to dynamite a bridge near Santa Barbara only minutes before President Taft's train crossed it narrowly failed.[22] These accounts of near misses and fortunate escapes all point to a cluster of key theoretical issues at stake in comprehending early-twentieth-century discourse about terrorism, including the sheer unknowability of when terrorists might strike, the ways in which an action always potentially presupposes an even worse calamity, and the uneasy fear that more violence is always just around the corner.

Yet we must also ask exactly what the Iron Workers were assaulting when they placed their dynamite. If, at a direct level, they were attacking the debilitating labor policies of the open shop, at another level their violent outbursts raise more fundamental questions concerning the relationship between violence enacted against structures, against bodies, against corporations, and against the American government. How, for instance, is terrorizing capitalist employers similar to or different from terrorizing a populace or a nation? Burns saliently raised this point in a *New York Times* interview when he posited that IABSIW headquarters in Indianapolis was "the centre of a band of dynamiters who had terrorized employers throughout the country," ultimately leaving steel construction industry moguls little reason to believe that "the United States was a free country."[23]

Of course, Burns was ignoring the fact that America hardly seemed to be a free country during this period from the standpoint of workers either. The Progressive Era saw the Sherman Anti-Trust Act turned against workers' organizations and unions as corporate America sought relief from union pressure in the courts.[24] The irony of the Sherman Anti-Trust Act being brandished against unions stung the Structural Iron Workers particularly hard. Their employers, banded together in the NEA, formed one arm of the United States Steel Corporation, or the "Steel Trust," as U.S. Steel and its associated firms were popularly known. The IABSIW, in fact, firmly believed that the NEA was "merely an offshoot of the Steel Trust . . . a limb of the biggest kind of big business . . . [that] has been warring on union labor for years."[25] Indeed, the Steel Trust sat at the epicenter of open shop industrial politics, since it forcefully opposed unions and instructed subsidiary firms to take a similar hard line against organized labor.

The IABSIW's desperation arising from its relatively weak position led it to embark upon clandestine violence. But one major problem the Iron Workers union faced in its struggle with corporate America was the fact that, while the "gigantic trust" of steel companies in many ways had all the rights of a singular person, it lacked an individual body that could be eliminated. To put this idea in concrete historical terms, nearly fifty years before the IABSIW bombings, the passage of the Fourteenth Amendment in 1868 proscribed states from depriving any person of life, liberty, or property without due process of law and from denying any person the equal protection of their laws. The legislation had been drafted to protect the emancipated slaves, but it was couched in an inclusive language of universal rights and privileges that corporate lawyers successfully mobilized to persuade the courts that corporations should also be considered as persons within the amendment's broad language.[26] But if the corporation is understood as a person, it is curiously disembodied, since there is no single material form, except for the paper on which it is chartered, that can be connected to the corporation's person. Figured as a person in legal discourse and constructed as an entity by money and exchange, the disembodied corporation, the person without a body, is part of a cultural network in which a particular mode of representation (charters, stocks, and other signifiers) is correlated in a circular fashion with a discourse of the body and economics.

In the Structural Iron Workers' campaign against the Steel Trust and its open shop companies, attacks against NEA properties became, by extension, attacks against the government that had created a disembodied but rights-possessing corporate enemy. Thus, while William Burns's claim that the dynamite campaign was an assault against "the established form of government of this country" was largely intended simply to tar the IABSIW with the well-worn brush of un-American and disloyal radicalism,[27] he may nonetheless have been more accurate than he was aware. In many ways during the Progressive Era, through both the creation and the interpretation of laws, it did seem that government, business, and the nation-state formed a triangular relationship that excluded labor. Moreover, if American legal theory had created a corporate entity that, in the IABSIW's words, "know[s] neither body nor soul,"[28] the widespread and variously located assaults throughout the country had a surprisingly apt logic. They theoretically underscored the union's dismayed recognition that the corporate body existed only as a government-authorized, atomized, and inanimate fiction, but a fiction nevertheless capable of wielding rights and powers that seemingly far outstripped those accorded to working-class persons.

Yet, if American legal theory produced a situation in which the massive trusts and their disembodied corporate persons were buttressed by governmental ideology and actions, massacring twenty innocent workers in the *Times* building hardly seems like an appropriate or even effective way to strike a blow at that perceived symbiosis. After the bombing, commentators routinely remarked upon the harrowing fact that the terrorists committed "the treacherous assassination of fellow-laborers — for it was the linotype workers, machinists, printers, compositors, and telegraphers, as well as the newspaper writers, whose lives were sacrificed in the explosion," not the owners or large-scale capitalists.[29] Moreover, it was claimed, the McNamaras cared "no more for the destruction of innocent human lives than a boy would care about killing flies."[30] James McNamara reportedly "express[ed] disappointment that the loss of life had not included others who escaped," even though he was a printer himself.[31] In his confession, Ortie McManigal also reported that John McNamara responded with indifference to the deaths in Los Angeles, suggesting that it "will make them sit up and take notice." McManigal added that as the dynamite campaign drew to a close, McNamara simply wanted to kill people and wreak havoc.[32]

There is reason to doubt the veracity of McManigal's memoir, since his confession to Burns gained his freedom relatively soon after the conclusion of the trials.[33] Suspicion also existed at the time that he might have actually been an agent provocateur in Burns's employ who orchestrated bombings that could then be pinned on labor unions.[34] Additionally, James McNamara's confession, certainly another highly self-interested document, claimed that he "did not intend to murder" anyone and that a technical glitch in the *Times* bomb caused it to go off at the wrong time.[35] The relationship between truth and falsehood in all these statements is impossible to ascertain, but, more important, it is also somewhat beside the point. Nan Enstad, in a different context, has noted that historical sources must be evaluated as representations of the past, rather than as unmediated or transparent descriptions of events.[36] McNamara's statement was no doubt an appeal for leniency, and the other statements about his bloodlust are significant not for what they can tell us about him, but instead for their role in the ideological creation of a terrorist figure during this period. Called upon to imagine a person capable of such atrocity, McManigal responded in predictable form by plotting out the dimensions of what he and other commentators at the time imagined as a terrorist subjectivity. The reputed and incomprehensibly violent attitude toward innocent victims ascribed to the McNamaras served as a way to channel, focus, and ultimately deny the much more pervasive and wholesale violence enacted in different forms by both capital and labor in the early twentieth century.

But whatever the logic behind the memoirs' depictions of a terrorist, the victims' innocence was a key element in contemporary accounts of the *Times* bombing. With the deaths of twenty workers who just happened to be working the night shift at the plant, the bombing was seen as a terrible chance occurrence. Only days after the *Times* bombing, nonunion workers at the nearby Llewellyn Iron Works were subsequently thrown into a panic when a ticking device thought to be a bomb was discovered. The object turned out to be only a decoy, presumably placed on the company's grounds to frighten the workers.[37] In addition, then, to the cultural production of a terrorist figure that is worked out in the postbombing literature, the *Times* bombing and the bomb scare at the Llewellyn factory signify the dangerous choreography of chance and innocence that is a key component of terrorism. On the one hand, from the Structural Iron Workers' viewpoint, nobody working at a nonunion plant was exactly innocent, for workers and managers alike at those sites, regardless of personal actions, participated in a general devaluation of labor and compromised the struggle for unionization and better working conditions. Yet it was the seemingly random killing of those twenty workers that

made the *Times* bombing appear so purposeless to its interpreters and commentators. And it was precisely this purposelessness, insofar as the victims
had done nothing concrete to those who pursued such atrocious and deadly
action against them, that created the terror and apprehension in the populace
evinced by the edgy workers at the Llewellyn Iron Works. As one historian
has put it, Los Angeles was gripped by a "panicky feeling," "uneasiness," and
"tenseness" in the wake of the bombing.[38]

The most terrifying aspect of the *Times* bombing, however, may not have
been the seeming randomness, but the fact that apparent indiscrimination
existed simultaneously with a certain selectivity. As Zulaika and Douglass
argue about terrorism more generally, it "appears to be simultaneously both
selective and indiscriminate, and its efficiency derives precisely from such
confusion of target categories."[39] In the case of the IABSIW, the type of target
the union aimed at was fairly predictable, as it was always an open shop corporation. But there was always considerable randomness within this class of
targets, and the expansion of the dynamitings to the *Times,* which was similar in policy but extremely different in its product, exponentially increased
the terror. After the *Times* bombing, it appeared that any open shop concern
would do, or even, when the bomb was placed at prominent businessman
Felix Zeehandelaar's home, that any procapitalism person of symbolic value
could make a fitting target. The terror of the *Times* bombing, and the reason
for the vast outpouring of verbiage to explain it, was not simply the astonishing loss of life. It was also the manner in which the event embodied the
deadly play of innocence, chance, and sudden death that is the tragic mark
of terrorism.

At the trials, when Ortie McManigal turned state's evidence against the
McNamara brothers, he became the prosecution's star witness against these
forms of seemingly random violence. McManigal recounted that he was committing bombings elsewhere in the country even as James McNamara was in
Los Angeles dynamiting the *Times.* John McNamara, the mastermind behind
most of the bombings, had ordered the concurrent assaults so that, even if
one dynamiter was caught, "he would have the other man loose, so he could
keep up the noise; and so that when there would be an explosion in the west,
there would be an echo in the east; and when an explosion happened in the
east, there would be an echo in the west; so as to keep them guessing as to
who it was."[40] McManigal also testified that John McNamara was planning
an even more aggressive dynamite campaign at the time he was apprehended.
The Structural Iron Workers' leader had envisioned a corps of eight to ten
men, scattered around the country, who would use signals to synchronize
their explosions.[41] Moreover, according to William J. Burns, in a scenario

that equaled the terror of Jack London's then recently published *Iron Heel,* John McNamara had hatched a conspiracy to blow up Los Angeles's water works, electricity plants, and public buildings. The alleged plot metamorphosed into larger and larger attacks, including a plan to shatter Detroit with multiple simultaneous explosions, blowing up the Panama Canal, and even stealing the gate receipts of the recently opened Indianapolis Motor Speedway.[42] Yet Sidney Fine, the most prominent historian of the conflict between the National Erectors Association and the Structural Iron Workers, has quite rightly pointed out that there is little if any corroboration of these allegations, produced originally by McManigal and echoed by Burns.[43]

But again, what is interesting about these statements made by key actors in the dynamite conspiracy cannot be boiled down to a debate about their truthfulness and reliability as historical evidence. Instead, Burns's and McManigal's remarks demonstrate how terrorism discourse is, ironically not unlike capitalism itself, dead if it is not growing. That is, acts labeled terrorism inevitably gain discursive momentum and spiral into larger and larger phenomena, ultimately making the aggrandizing rhetoric of both terrorists and their commentators into part of the machinery of terror. In the *Times* case, dynamiting a building signaled apparently inevitable and random outbursts of destruction throughout that city and other metropolitan areas. It also harbingered possible assaults on two potent early-twentieth-century symbols of the American nation, the then nearly completed Panama Canal and the Indianapolis Speedway. In the rhetoric of terrorism, material conditions mix indiscriminately with fantasy as threats provoke responses, violence prompts retribution, and heated rhetoric on both sides legitimates further violence.

Yet, if all this action churned around McManigal, he was a somewhat anomalous terrorist. His memoir, for instance, hardly depicts a man characterized by a terrorist's supposed transcendent faith in his cause. Instead, he claims to have been coerced by union strongmen because, through "an accidental training," he happened to learn the use of dynamite while working in a quarry.[44] McManigal subsequently becomes a mere "instrument of destruction," a "tool," and the union's "slave." Claiming his own lack of agency with these mechanical and racialized metaphors, the itinerant dynamiter becomes simply an extension of the dynamite he used to set his explosions. Interestingly, McManigal imagines himself as apart from a cabal in which, initially at least, he would appear to occupy a central place. His story is replete with bizarre moments where he tries to blend into the urban background and hide from union leaders, only to be ferreted out by the union's "evil genius."[45]

McManigal's strange confession thus demonstrates not only his own presumed reluctance, but also the way in which the imaginative rhetoric associated with terrorism always seems to envision a dangerous cabal elsewhere —in this case an imaginative dimension that extended even to the perpetrator of the violence.[46] That is, the rhetoric diagnosing terrorism thrives on the idea that a shadowy conspiracy is secretly orchestrating events from some obscure and clandestine location. As one commentator at the time put it, "The 'direct action' brought to light by the case against the McNamaras and the men 'higher up' . . . was action planned with devilish ingenuity, secretly perfected, and directed by an 'inner circle' of intellectually alert, exceptionally able, entirely unscrupulous individuals."[47] In this description, even the scare quotes placed around significant and evidently widely unknown phrases is meant to signal the difference and strangeness of the McNamaras, a strangeness that evidently necessitates a unique, insider's idiom in order to comprehend it. Crucially, this distancing effect serves as a way to control and displace cultural issues raised by violent acts, even in those instances, such as the McNamaras, when a cabal is actually at work. Violence always becomes something "they" do from under cover of darkness, thus obscuring, in the case of the Structural Iron Workers in particular, the less immediate but still pervasive aggression enacted upon the union in the form of corporations' blacklists, harassment of labor agitators, and firing of union members.

The image of a cabal elsewhere radically separates "them" from "us," but this idea is repeatedly belied in the case of the IABSIW. John J. McNamara was not simply an alienated radical, but also an attorney. More diabolically, his union's Indianapolis business office was not merely the usual mundane place of paper shuffling and record keeping, but a secret cache for dynamite as well.[48] Furthermore, McManigal posed as a traveling salesman on his dynamiting expeditions,[49] and reporters at the time almost invariably remarked upon his continual reference to his explosions as "jobs." The dynamiter additionally reports in his memoir that he coded his reports in the idiom of American capitalism. Telegraphing updates to his bosses, McManigal on one occasion wired "Sold Stock Boston (with date), Hoboken, (with date)" to confirm explosions in those cities.[50] The point, then, is that as much as McManigal sought to distance himself from the McNamaras, and commentators at the time sought to distance American ideals from the IABSIW, at every turn the IABSIW undermined those reputed dissimilarities. By using the tropes of capitalism and appearing in some of its customary places and guises, the dynamite conspirators held out at every moment the unthinkable possibility that violence was endemically American after all. Both the large amount and the form of rhetoric produced at the time to separate union violence from the ideological construct of "America" stands as testimony to Americans' intense need to imagine otherwise.

The Sabo-Tabby, the Wooden Shoe,
and Those "Bomb-Throwing I Won't Works"

In the wake of the *Times* bombing, the McNamaras' surprising confession, and the spectacular conspiracy trial of over three dozen labor leaders, sabotage loomed large in the American cultural imagination. The *Outlook,* for instance, offered an essay defining sabotage as "the deliberate scientific destruction of public property." Making the *Outlook*'s coded anxiety about dynamite explicit, the *Independent,* in a flashback to the type of rhetoric that followed the Haymarket tragedy, worried that the McNamaras would inspire others to use dynamite, leading to "nothing less than the overthrow of civilization." Similarly, the *Century* intoned that sabotage is "damaging to the essential foundations of law and order" and, echoing Philip Sheridan's remarks from twenty-five years earlier, suggested that "under modern conditions, the priceless treasures of the ages, the costly buildings reared to beauty and service, and the structures which are the instruments of commerce and industry, are all at the mercy of individual and collective sabotage."[51]

In these articles, sabotage becomes a synonym for terrorism and an assault on the established order. The threat and seeming ubiquity of sabotage undergirded calls for the suppression of labor activists, while the mythic power that it apparently possessed was clearly echoed in the exaggerated claims put forth in this reportage. Thorstein Veblen remarked as much at the time, arguing that "the sinister meaning which is often attached to the word in American usage" occurred because opponents of unions' demands had wrested control of the term's meaning and used it to slander labor.[52] Veblen was justifiably distressed that the word had come to connote simply and only destructive violence, since, as we will see, sabotage just as often entailed nonviolent acts committed by workers to further their goals. But the point of the argument about sabotage at the turn of the century was precisely the fact that for so many persons it did, unequivocally, equate to catastrophic terrorism. This was a cultural reality that one labor union in particular, the radical Industrial Workers of the World, disparaged and dissented from but also notoriously sought to manipulate.

No labor organization in the first decades of the twentieth century aroused the suspicion and fear of random violence more than the iww, "those bomb-throwing I Won't Works," as they were sometimes derided.[53] The iww, which had been founded in 1905 but only began to have a large—and therefore threatening—cultural presence in the 1910s, was frequently and directly tied to violent sabotage. In an inflammatory rhetorical flourish regularly reproduced in other magazines, the *Literary Digest* lumped the iww with "anarchists, Bolsheviki . . . and other extreme radicals [who] have for some time been frenziedly 'whooping it up' for revolution, terrorism, destruction and general Hades and chaos in this country." Another article informed readers that "sabotage . . . designates the chief means whereby the I.W.W. hope to gain their ends . . . destruction apparently playing a large part in the scheme of the I.W.W.-ite for achieving his peculiar brand of paradise." In the *Forum*, Lewis Allen Browne echoed these ideas, stated that "the majority of those in America who come within the classification of American Bolsheviki are I.W.W. members," and then enumerated a laundry list of purported iww sabotage efforts.[54]

The peculiar and excessive amount of vitriol directed toward iww members, or Wobblies, as they were popularly known, offers a fair measurement of the threat seemingly posed by this radical union. The Wobblies sought to organize supposedly unorganizable workers—the "timber beasts" of the great Northwest, migrant farm workers, miners, blacks, Asians, Jews, and the unskilled, low-skilled, and often immigrant industrial workers left behind by the "craft union" organizational program of the more respectable AFL. And if its goal of organizing America's disinherited was not enough, the iww also aimed at nothing less than a revolution of the working class that would rise up and abolish capitalism. Further, the iww vigorously eschewed politics, arguing that the ballot box was ineffective and pointless until workers controlled the means of production. As the Wobblies abandoned American shibboleths, reached out to the unskilled masses, refused to recognize the right to private property, and shunned politics, they appeared ideologically, and sometimes literally, too foreign, too incomprehensible, and too outrageous for most Americans. As iww poet and organizer Arturo Giovannitti put it in an article commissioned by the *Independent*, apparently to provide its readership an up-close glimpse of the iww strangeness, "We have nothing in common with you, we do not recognize the 'public,' the 'people,' the 'nation,' Christendom or humanity—we know only the working class."[55] It is small wonder that so many mainstream commentators sought to defuse the Wobblies' threat by characterizing them as radical bomb throwers whom America desperately needed to suppress.

While the possibility, and apparent inevitability, of sabotage prompted a denunciatory, ritualistic cavalcade of attacks upon the iww in the mass media, the panic engendered by the McNamaras' 1911 confession also produced division on the American left, particularly within the Socialist Party. The party's right wing, hoping to progress in the United States through the ballot box, accused the left wing, which included the iww, of "advocat[ing] terrorism and murder."[56] At its 1912 convention, the party amended its constitution to read that any member opposing political action or advocating sabotage would be expelled.[57] Ultimately, this internecine fight resulted in the expulsion of IWW leader Bill Haywood from the party in February 1913 and snapped the ties between the Socialists and Wobblies. Of course, it also pleased members of the mainstream press, who were glad to learn that socialism "rejects the theory that the lawless shall gain power by intimidation and terrorism."[58]

Indeed, the IWW did court a reputation for violence in the years around the McNamara debacle. Until the time of his death in San Quentin prison, the union maintained a bond with James McNamara and consistently supplied him with tobacco money.[59] More significantly, immediately following Haywood's expulsion from the Socialist Party, delegates at the IWW's 1913 convention adopted a resolution stating that while the employing class instigates violence, if that dominant class decides "that violence will be the arbiter of the [wage] question, then we shall cheerfully accept their decision and meet them to the best of our ability — and we do not fear the result."[60] Though this resolution placed the onus upon owners by portraying the IWW in a purely defensive position, it also made it clear that the Wobblies would not shy away from violence.

Wobbly rhetoric was often even more directly confrontational and violent. Vincent St. John, a founding member and general organizer of the IWW from 1908 to 1915, sometimes espoused personal violence and destruction of property if such actions would hasten the revolution. Other leaders admitted that they would willingly dynamite factories in the course of a strike. James Thompson also growled at the government's Commission on Industrial Relations, "I not only believe in destruction of property, but I believe in the destruction of human life if it will save human life."[61] And in his widely circulated pamphlet of 1912, *Direct Action and Sabotage,* IWW founding member William E. Trautman held that the suppression of free speech bred justifiably violent responses. He argued further that militant organizations cannot always "refrain from the use of violent and destructive methods."[62]

Yet, despite calls for violence and the generalized rhetoric of destruction that filled IWW publications, the National Civil Liberties Bureau noted in 1919 that not a single charge of violence had been proved against the union.[63] A thorough study issued in 1939 by Eldridge F. Dowell of Johns Hopkins elaborated on these findings, stating that the IWW definitely and publicly advocated sabotage, but no IWW saboteur had ever been caught or convicted.[64] These findings are fascinating, given the way the reputation for violent acts has consistently shadowed the IWW for nearly a century. Fred Thompson, the unofficial house historian of the IWW, offered one explanation in 1955. He argued that the linkage of the Wobblies with sabotage at least partially resulted from overly enthusiastic soapbox orators, who found that talking about sabotage and violence gave their listeners a vicarious thrill and incidentally helped to sell IWW newspapers as well.[65] Thompson is surely right in his criticism of those ubiquitous soapbox orators during the IWW's salad days, but they served an important purpose in the union by providing isolated workers in western mining and timber towns with potentially new ways of thinking about their subjectivity as workers. And when those soapboxers were aggressively silenced by local authorities, as was often the case, they provided opportunities for reflection on the American legal system, on who counted as a citizen deserving of protection under the Bill of Rights and who did not, and on what could be done about that situation.

It is also true, however, that sabotage signified more in the Wobbly lexicon than simply violence against property and persons. Sabotage was one form among many of what the IWW termed "direct action," which was understood to be the conscientious withdrawal of efficiency on the part of workers. Direct action was anything done at the point of production to hinder capitalists' objectives and assist in the wage struggle. Thus the electoral process or the boycotting of goods, for instance, were indirect and therefore less effective acts. Examples of nonviolent direct actions included soldiering on the job, working slowly, misdirecting shipments or bills of lading, exposing company secrets or owners' bad-faith practices toward consumers, and even working strictly according to rules, thereby shunning initiative or ingenuity. Bill Haywood was even fond of pointing out that "we strike with our hands in our pockets. We have a new kind of violence—the havoc we raise with money by laying down our tools."[66] Haywood is referring to the much discussed "folded arms" strategy, whereby workers would cause production to grind to a halt simply by removing their labor power. According to William Trautman, no violence was needed when all workers quit work together.[67] In other words, as the IWW newspaper, *Solidarity,* intriguingly editorialized, "Our dynamite is mental."[68] Despite what appears to be the naïveté of Trautman and Haywood's faith that *all* workers would come out on strike together, thus resisting the crippling ethnic and race-baiting policies owners routinely used to impede workers' collective actions, the IWW's faith in what its leaders depicted as the almost magical, massive general strike that would overturn capitalism eloquently testifies to the union's dream of creating a more equitable existence for the world's most disenfranchised workers.

Yet what is ultimately most important for understanding how terrorism and sabotage were configured and intellectually processed during this era is precisely the way Wobbly rhetoric tiptoed around calls for extreme violence and assertions that sabotage was nonviolent, often even in the same piece.

Thus, in famed organizer Elizabeth Gurley Flynn's pamphlet entitled *Sabotage,* she claims both that "sabotage is not physical violence" and, in an extremely fierce closing flourish, that "sabotage is a shining sword. It pierces the nerve centers of capitalism, stabs at its hearts and stomachs, tears at the vitals of its economic system."[69] It must have been a very small mental leap indeed for the original readers of such words to imaginatively substitute the bodies of capitalists for Flynn's abstract "economic system."

In this rhetorical situation in which violence is everywhere called forth and anticipated but seemingly rarely practiced, IWW discourse prompts consideration of the cultural role occupied by threats and public depictions of violence, the role of language in social change, and how the forms that this imaginative dimension took could have affected both working-class subjectivity and the cultural image of a terrorist. Not coincidentally, as several scholars have remarked, one of the IWW's most enduring and important legacies in this regard lies in the vast array of propaganda, songs, poems, and cartoons created by the many talented artists and writers associated with the union. In particular, the cultural production of the IWW repeatedly threatens to undermine any simple binary between words and deeds. The art's quality of being threateningly belligerent while simultaneously just representation and therefore "not real" expressed the Wobblies' sophisticated understanding of how language itself, even — or especially — in the absence of actual violence, can at once intimidate antagonists with the promise of seemingly inevitable bloodshed and offer sites of collectivity and solidarity to working-class readers and viewers.

The Wobblies were undoubtedly one of the earliest radical organizations in America to use art routinely for political purposes. Their particular methods and foci emerged as a way to reach the often formally uneducated, immigrant, and itinerant workers they hoped to organize into the One Big Union. Their cartoons, poetry, and songs never operated in a separate realm of artistic production that was removed from the grubbiness of everyday life; instead, they regarded their art as a crucial intervention into how citizens understood labor, capitalism, and violence. A poem appearing in the widely read western IWW newspaper, the *Industrial Worker,* can exemplify the role of poetry in the union:

> *S*oap stops water from making steam in boilers.
> *A*safetida keeps patrons from struck theatres.
> *B*y working slow profits are greatly reduced.
> *O*il containing emery makes machinery strike.
> *T*elling trade secrets wins battles for workers.

*A*ccidents often are an aid in winning strikes.
*G*uerilla warfare always gets the bosses' goat.
*E*nds that are revolutionary justify the means.[70]

A poem for largely uneducated audiences, this acrostic delights in its clev-
erness as it spells out "sabotage" with the first letter of each line. Yet it also
rather openly calls for acts of sabotage and, more important, provides examples and ideas while predicting the results. As far removed as possible
from the aesthetic concerns of high modernism with which it is contemporary, this 1913 poem is didactic, referential, and explicitly aimed at forming a
working-class consciousness.

Wanting to reach the masses, iww artists also used "cultural guerrilla"
tactics as they regularly parodied, imitated, and borrowed from other well-
known cultural texts and institutions.[71] They famously revised tunes made
popular by the Salvation Army, often substituting their own radical lyrics and
singing the new songs to the tune of religious standards. Thus "Take It to the
Lord in Prayer" became "Dump the Bosses Off Your Back," the ever-popular
"Onward, Christian Soldiers" became "Onward, One Big Union!," and
"Sweet Bye and Bye" was transformed into "The Preacher and the Slave."
Joe Hill, the most famous Wobbly bard, satirized Salvation Army preachers
for offering only promises of a reward in heaven to starving workers:

Long-haired preachers come out every night,
Try to tell you what's wrong and what's right;
But when asked how 'bout something to eat
They will answer with voices so sweet:
You will eat, bye and bye,
In that glorious land above the sky;
Work and pray, live on hay,
You'll get pie in the sky when you die.

(ll. 1–8)[72]

Dubbed the "starvation army" by Wobblies, the mildly reformist Salvation
Army preachers and brass bands provided the main competition for iww
street corner orators.[73] Wobbly parody in this case offered a readily recognizable tune that could be picked up quickly by potential members, while
explicitly decrying the Salvation Army's woefully inadequate charity.

In addition to parodying established cultural forms, the iww created a
unique language of violence. For instance, the anonymous poet, Shorty, published "The Kitten in the Wheat" in a 1917 issue of *Solidarity*, the mouthpiece
of the iww in the eastern United States:

A sab-cat and a wobbly band,
   A rebel song or two;
And then we'll show the Parasites
   Just what the cat can do.

.   .   .   .

The sab-cat purred and twitched her tail
   As happy as could be
They'd better not throw "wobs" in jail
   And leave the kitten free.

.   .   .   .

The sab-cat purred and twitched her tail
   And winked the other way;
Our boys shall never rot in jail,
   Or else the Plutes will PAY.

               (ll. 1–4, 9–12, 17–20)[74]

Just as the fear of gang signs and symbols occupies a significant place in our contemporary cultural imagination, especially if those symbols are seemingly expressed in graffiti that is indecipherable to the uninitiated, the peculiar linguistic features of Wobbly poetry raised alarms in the mainstream media. The *Literary Digest,* for example, ran something of an exposé of IWW symbols in 1919 and included this poem by Shorty as a prime example of Wobbly symbology. The language and context of the poem is fear-inducing both in its initially mysterious idiom and in what it actually calls for. Like much Wobbly poetry, it was printed without attribution, thus adhering to the IWW's idea of collectivity, while also presenting a threat in the sheer anonymity of the poet. He or she could be any employee, anywhere. As Walter Woehlke's article, "Terrorism in America," pointed out, and as Walker Smith also warned, saboteurs could easily gain work by posing as scabs or purportedly loyal employees.[75] Or, according to Wobbly poet, editor, and cartoonist Ralph Chaplin's "That Sabo-Tabby Kitten": "On every wheel that turns I'm riding, / No one knows, though, where I'm hiding" (ll. 21–22).[76] Sabotage apparently could come from anywhere at any time; the only thing future victims could count on was its pervasiveness and inevitability. In Chaplin's and Shorty's poems, the "kitten in the wheat" and the "sab-cat" recall the famed symbol of the black cat, with its back arched and claws extended, that the IWW reproduced again and again throughout the 1910s to signify sabotage.[77] The "'wobs'" are, of course, IWW members, and, in a self-referential moment, it is a rebellious song that stokes workers' ire and courage. The "kitten" left free is the vengeance-seeking saboteur, as Shorty employs the mercantile language of capitalism to describe the potential violence enacted upon the owners. And the "Plutes" and "Parasites" who will pay are those much-maligned capitalists.

Also pervasive in Wobbly iconography was the image of a wooden shoe symbolizing sabotage. In the oft-reprinted "Rebel's Toast," Joe Hill advised fellow workers that

> If Freedom's road seems rough and hard,
> And strewn with rocks and thorns,
> Then put your wooden shoes on, pard,
> And you won't hurt your corns.
>
> (ll. 1–4)[78]

In the same vein, and similar to hundreds of other cartoons produced in IWW literature during this period, a political cartoon published by the *Industrial Worker* in February 1913 depicts a laborer kicking off his wooden shoe smack into the nose of a top-hatted capitalist. "SABOTAGE" is printed across the shoe. As he is struck, the capitalist spills his money bags, loses his top hat, sees stars, and will presumably also lose the factory that is depicted in the background of this confrontation (see figure 5.1).[79] The wooden shoe loomed so large in Wobbly iconography because the term "sabotage" itself derived from the French word *sabot,* or wooden shoe. Origins of the connection between wooden shoes and labor violence are hazy, however, with some early-twentieth-century writers arguing that the term "sabotage" derived from nineteenth-century French workers' practice of fouling machinery with their wooden shoes. Others argued that the term originated with the clumsy work of wooden-shooed peasants brought to the city as strikebreakers; the term thus denoted legitimate workers' practice of "working slow" to anger bosses, much as their scab counterparts inadvertently had done.[80]

The wooden shoe, the sabo-tabby, and the words that clustered around these images were only the most famous examples of the IWW's special idiom. The reward in heaven promised by the Salvation Army for docile submission in the present was simply "pie in the sky." IWW soapboxers also derided as "sharks" the often exploitative employment agents whom western timber workers were forced to utilize to obtain work. And laborers unable to see the light and join the union were either "blockheads" or "Scissor Bills." As Joe Hill wrote,

> Don't try to talk your union dope to Scissor Bill,
> He says he never organized and never will.
> He always will be satisfied until he's dead,
> With coffee and a doughnut and a lousy old bed.

FIGURE 5.1. "Direct Action Makes Capitalism See Stars."
Industrial Worker, 6 February 1913.

And Bill, he says, he gets rewarded thousand fold,
When he gets up to heaven on the streets of gold.
(ll. 21–26)[81]

As Van Wienen has suggested, Dick Hebdige's pioneering book, *Subculture,* though written about the punks, mods, and teddy boys of 1970s British youth culture, can nonetheless help theorize the Wobblies' methods and position in American cultural production. Hebdige argues that repudiating the implicitly governing cultural codes of a society—in the case of the Wobblies, refusing to accept the usual definition of a "good worker" or scorning the seemingly benevolent and innocuous "Starvation Army"—has a subversive value that can demystify what passes as the common sense of a society. Taking place at the level of signification, this refusal to play by the rules of a given society challenges myths of cultural unity and consensus.[82] Renaming capitalism's cast of characters as Scissor Bills, Sharks, Sabcats, and Plutes, the Wobblies sought to build a distinctly oppositional subculture that rejected as capitalist mythology the idea that capital and labor could ever have the same interest at heart. Moreover, as with any exclusionary device, the unique and creative idiom of the Wobblies served an inclusive function as well. For workers in the know, IWW slang offered opportunities for solidarity, collective winks and grins, and sensations of numerical strength. And perhaps this was most so when mainstream periodicals like the *Literary Digest* printed studious, serious exposés of Wobbly language. Interpreting that idiom for their readers, these periodicals found themselves able to respond only with the solemnity and unease produced by being outside the linguistic boundaries of a joking and punning yet threatening subculture.

Creating a bewildering miscellany of neologisms and refashioned familiar words, the Wobblies consciously exploited the ephemerality of language—its openness to change, shifts in meaning, and counterhegemonic possibilities—to frighten and irritate capitalist America. Ralph Chaplin testified concerning this idea during the IWW's trial under the Espionage Act passed in 1917. As he explained his deployment of the popular image of impending foul luck, the black cat, Chaplin suggested that sabotage was used to make capitalists wary of possible misdeeds.[83] For Chaplin, sabotage is more mental than physical; in addition to the terrorism of physical assault, sabotage suggests the tingling apprehension and terror aroused by living in a society where violence seems likely.

One highly important way that the IWW treaded this line between language and action was the mass production of their stickerettes. Dubbed "silent agitators" to signify their mute but real effects, these gum-backed stickers manipulated the artificiality of that binary by combining the feigning yet menacing attributes of language with the possibility of real violence. Stickers, however, had been used previously by Wobblies, especially to agitate for the eight-hour workday. In 1911 the *Industrial Worker* advertised these early prototypes and offered 1,000 stickers for $1. In its ads, the newspaper punningly and rhetorically asked readers, "Are you a sticker?," thus linking workers' sense of personal identity to the protest offered by the stickers.[84] Just as a sticker pasted in a prominent location incessantly offers its message to all passersby, the newspaper encouraged its readers to be similarly indefatigable voices against capitalist oppression. A few years later, in 1915, the IWW launched its much more ambitious stickerettes. Printed in the Wobblies' favored red and black, the stickerettes ranged in size from two square inches to nearly three by four inches and prominently featured IWW artwork, slogans, and propaganda. In the initial printing of 500,000 stickers, eleven different designs were available, with the wooden shoe and black cat often featured, as were depictions of Scissor Bills and other calls for workers' solidarity.[85]

One popular stickerette depicted a giant wooden shoe crushing a top-hatted capitalist, while the sun, shining in the background, is marked "IWW" (see figure 5.2). SABOTAGE is printed prominently across the sticker's width,

FIGURE 5.2. IWW stickerette. Black and white on a red background.
Courtesy of the Washington State Historical Society, Tacoma.

and an oft-quoted saying by Bill Haywood rounds out the image: "Sabotage means to push back, pull out or break off the fangs of Capitalism." Another favorite sticker portrayed a blood red moon, overlaid by the hissing black cat with claws extended, tail puffed up, and back arched forebodingly (see figure 5.3). The accompanying text reads "BEWARE" at the top and "SABOTAGE" at the bottom and between this offered an additional warning: "Good Pay or Bum Work / I.W.W. / One Big Union / We Never Forget." A third sticker pictured a giant worker shod in sabots and clutching entire ships and factories (see figure 5.4). "SOLIDARITY / Takes the Whole Works / Join the / One Big Union" was its particular message.

With their visually striking graphics and catchy, jingoistic axioms, the stickerettes redeployed the techniques of mass capitalism, such as advertisements, catchphrases, and market saturation, for "illegitimate," revolutionary ends. Indeed, when asked at the IWW's federal trial to explain his creation of

FIGURE 5.3. IWW stickerette. Black and white overlaying a red moon.
Courtesy of the Washington State Historical Society, Tacoma.

FIGURE 5.4. IWW stickerette. Black and white on a red background.
Courtesy of the Washington State Historical Society, Tacoma.

the stickerettes, Ralph Chaplin testified that he had been directly inspired by commercial advertising. Furthermore, the stickerettes were strikingly modern, even a bit ahead of their time, in their form and style. They appealed to workers' fantasies and bosses' fears by offering workers indirectly referential images that catered to dreams of power and hopes for greater stature. Alternatively, with stickers deriding Scissor Bills, the Wobblies anticipated other modern advertising practices by mocking certain behaviors, pointing out imperfections, and appealing to social shame.[86] Not unlike Listerine or the deodorant Odo-ro-no, which presented minor personal dramas of social inadequacy in their print advertisements, the IWW stickerettes allowed viewers to vicariously experience social stigmatization, only to be saved from despair by the wonder-working cure of the One Big Union. In short, the IWW appropriated the tools of American capitalism then being developed to teach citizens the pleasures of mass consumption and reformulated those techniques to help the most disenfranchised workers imagine new, more empowered identities.

Combining the logic of mass advertising and political campaigns, the IWW's repeated use of certain key slogans or mottoes forms a particularly striking aspect of the stickerettes. Political slogans had been around for decades in America, but this was the era in which corporate capitalism realized the similar power of brand names, trademarks, and jingles. The Wobbly slogans both combine and extend the mnemonic and propagandistic aspects of commercial and political advertisements that, as we saw in the last chapter, Jack London so convincingly mimicked in "The Minions of Midas." The IWW stickerettes function more in the way that Jean-Jacques Lecercle has theorized slogans. Lecercle posits that a slogan's work is not simply to represent a cultural situation independent of that slogan. Rather, a slogan helps to create new states of affairs by naming them, that is, by "nam[ing] the unnamed and so far unnameable." Slogans create and make visible the links between language and material actions by providing names and ideas about situations that do not necessarily yet exist. Slogans are therefore both predictive and corrective, as they foresee new possibilities and can also update available language by wrenching it into accord with historical change.[87] For the IWW, those stickerette slogans, which depicted the idea of a unified working class existing in revolutionary opposition to capitalism, aimed to bring that militant working class into existence explicitly by utilizing the peculiar, threatening, and divisive Wobbly idiom. The stickerettes simultaneously imagined the possibility of and created the aggressive and redoubtable One Big Union.

Featuring giant workers, claiming to "never forget" past wrongs, employing their unique, menacing symbology, and obliquely calling for violence, the stickerettes, like most Wobbly art, danced around the line between violence and nonviolence. With their empowering depictions and poaching raids on capitalist techniques, these small gum-backed stamps, not surprisingly, became incredibly popular. Much as the temporary vogue of sporting buttons with "Undesirable Citizen" emblazoned across them became a faddish protest during the 1907 Haywood-Moyer-Pettibone trial, the stickerette craze reached such heights that the journal *Solidarity* proclaimed May Day 1917 "Stickerette Day." Entitled "Stick 'Em Up," a song penned by Shorty, author of "The Kitten in the Wheat," announced,

Now all the bosses and their stools will think they're out of luck
To see the spots of black and red where Stickerettes are stuck;
And after they have scratched them off and shook their fists and swore
They'll turn around to find again about a dozen more.

Upon the back of every truck, on packages and cards,
Upon the boats and in the mines and in the railroad yards,
From Maine to California and even further yet,
No matter where you look you'll see a little Stickerette![88]

Shorty's poem imagines the United States covered by stickerettes and implicitly covered by Wobblies as well. Harassed by IWW members and sympathizers who seem to emerge from nowhere only to slide back under cover, bosses in all industries are plagued by the annoying stickers with their threatening messages. Shorty's poem also raises another key aspect of Wobbly philosophy that the stickerettes embodied, and which was pure anathema to the American public: the refusal to recognize private property. As Walker Smith's 1913 pamphlet, *Sabotage,* put it, "Sabotage is a direct application of the idea that property has no rights that its creators are bound to respect"; in fact, sabotage "destroy[s] the 'property illusion.'"[89]

Along these lines, the stickerettes are analogous to the later twentieth-century phenomenon of graffiti. Like graffiti artists, who referred to their practice of painting subway trains in the 1970s as "bombing" them, the stickerettes combined powerlessness and puissance. A harassing but perhaps inconsequential gesture, the mass pasting of stickerettes at worksites and public places nonetheless could tap into the IWW's enemies' potential fears of the unknown and uncertainties about what the reputedly terroristic IWW might be planning. As depicted in Shorty's poem, the stickerettes became so popular for some and irritating for others because they were edgy, hinted at violence, and, like the fear created by more violent terrorist acts, embodied an unpredictable yet reliable quality in their seeming inevitability.

While the stickerettes offered Wobbly sympathizers a mostly innocent way to harass their bosses that nevertheless harbored threats of violence, pamphlet literature written by IWW members simultaneously strove to explain and justify both nonviolent and violent forms of sabotage. Sabotage was regularly designated guerrilla warfare in which the ends justify the means.[90] Echoing the nineteenth-century Russian terrorist theorists, pamphleteers argued further that individual acts of sabotage "shatter the stability of capitalist absolute control of the job" and "awaken a portion of the workers from their lethargy."[91] Elizabeth Gurley Flynn claimed that, despite conventional wisdom, sabotage is courageous rather than cowardly, a courage measured for her by the paucity of sabotage's critics who would be brave enough to try it.[92] Walker Smith also argued that workers' present powerlessness necessitated sabotage, arguing that it would be suicide to act as if they possessed the might for open battle. Sabotage, he wrote, "is the smokeless powder of the social war. It scores a hit, while its source is seldom detected. It is so universally feared by the employers that they do not even desire that it be condemned for fear [the] slave class may learn still more its great value."[93] Indeed, Smith, in yet another reproduction of a plotline from Henry James's *The Princess Casamassima* and simultaneous anticipation of our own day's debate over publicizing terrorist acts, notes that capitalists would often rather hush up events than risk publicizing their vulnerability and encouraging similar attacks.

Salvatore Salerno, in his highly lucid analysis of sabotage and attempt to justify its use in our own day, has argued that IWW sabotage has "absolutely nothing to do with any form of life-threatening 'terrorism' or personal injury."[94] Yet the pamphlets written by IWW members suggest a cultural situation more complex than Salerno identifies in his understandable desire to distance the IWW from terrorism. Discussions of sabotage, as emblematized by Smith's evocative "smokeless powder," often reproduced and manipulated what we can by this point recognize as the characteristic rhetoric of terrorism. Sabotage, for Smith, implies dynamite, while determining where the violence originated is nearly impossible; potential violence remains everywhere and nowhere at once. Further, it is often up to daring, individual saboteurs to awaken the masses and frighten capitalists. As for the morality of sabotage, Smith argues that "morals today are based upon private property" and are therefore irrelevant to the propertyless toilers. But the issue was in fact moot: "The question is not, Is sabotage immoral? — but, Does sabotage get the goods?" Smith asked rhetorically.[95]

While the IWW's pamphleteers readily produced extremely violent rhetoric and justifications of sabotage, they complemented this with a rejection of conventional definitions of key American concepts and tried to substitute their own meanings. William Trautman argued that violent direct actions are not inherently evil but instead are to be considered either "social" or "anti-social," according to whether they have progressive or debilitating results for the working class.[96] And to the oft-repeated claims that sabotage was destroying civilization, Smith fumed, "Civilization is a lie"[97] because it was built upon the labor of an exploited working class. As pamphlet writers frequently pointed out, one of the most egregious forms of this exploitation was the sabotage that capitalists themselves regularly practiced. Infiltrating worker organizations with spies and agents provocateurs and, more harmful to the public, illegally adulterating foodstuffs and other products were primary forms of capitalist sabotage decried in IWW pamphlets. For instance, in her discussion of the IWW-led 1913 Paterson silk strike, Flynn carefully explained that silk makers routinely mixed impurities into raw silk to increase the amount of finished silk produced. The process, ironically, was called "dynamiting silk."[98] Additionally, according to Trautman, workers were forced by their bosses to practice sabotage against consumers on a daily basis, but if workers used nonviolent "open mouth" sabotage to publicize their employers' deceptions, they were regarded as criminals.[99] Trautman's point here is to overlay his argument justifying workers' sabotage with an ancillary but equally important struggle within language itself for control over the terms of cultural debate. As much as they were explaining acts of sabotage and at times calling for it, Smith, Trautman, and Flynn were also trying to exercise power through language. Attempting to make sabotage mean only what they wanted it to connote, the IWW writers aimed to sound both violent and nonviolent, to threaten the capitalist class, embolden the working class, and, ultimately, to make sabotage into an heroic act of class defiance.

Covington Hall: Wobbly Poet of Visionary Violence

In May 1913 the *Industrial Worker* printed an article claiming that Covington Hall "personifies the poetic spirit of the revolution better than any man in the movement today, barring none." Hall possessed "true poetic power, united with the historical culture of the scholar, and the fiery zeal of the revolutionist."[100] At that time Hall, a newspaper editor, publicist, and poet, belonged to the IWW-affiliated Brotherhood of Timber Workers (BTW). While IWW pamphleteers tiptoed along the line between violence and nonviolence,

violence as a galvanizing revolutionary force seemed literally to swirl around Hall's larger than life persona. Indeed, a lead article in a January 1913 issue of the *Industrial Worker* detailed how the "degenerate scum that forms the Burns Detective Agency," who had only recently wrapped up their operations in the *Los Angeles Times* bombing case, were plotting to murder Hall.[101] For his part, not only was Covington Hall among the most prolific of iww poets, but, more important, his poetry's frequent return to violence offers a compelling account of the extraordinary role that sabotage sometimes played in activist-minded literature during this turbulent era.

The BTW, with which Hall was deeply engaged, was a radical, broad-based, astonishingly racial-and-gender inclusive union of impoverished, downtrodden lumber workers. Formed in 1910, the BTW combated the systematic legal and extralegal oppression of the southern lumber trust in Louisiana and Texas. Long hours of dangerous work, Taylorist work practices, irregular pay periods, payment in company "scrip" rather than cash when compensation was doled out, and forced deep-woods residence in company towns with only company stores and company houses all stoked workers' anger. "Yellow-dog" contracts banning union membership and blacklisting of known union employees further rankled the "timber beasts" and spurred the often violent outbursts between workers and the Southern Lumber Operators' Association.[102]

While editing the BTW's official journal, *The Lumberjack,* and his own briefly published serial, aptly titled *Rebellion: Made up of Dreams and Dynamite,* Hall regularly called for sabotage against the lumber trust. One scholar has argued that the BTW probably encouraged sabotage more than any other iww union, and Hall even organized what has been called a "secret terrorist organization."[103] On the other hand, BTW members, including Hall and founder Ed Lehman, were themselves frequently the victims of beatings, shootings, and other sometimes clandestine and sometimes open violence. Similar to the circumstances surrounding the Western Federation of Miners in Steunenberg's 1905 assassination, this aspect of the BTW's battle with corporate capitalism troubles any easy definition of a terrorist in industrializing America. Hall's voluminous poetry, which at its best infuses a haunting lyricism with a committed revolutionary fervor and a fury at inequity, demonstrates the fantastic—meaning both "fantasy" and "awesome"—hope that desperate and disempowered laborers placed in sabotage and clandestine violence as they struggled against corporate and industrial capitalism. Hall's work as an editor, activist, and poet underscores the crucial role that artistic production played in fomenting dissent, creating alternatives to capitalism in the twentieth century's early decades, imagining sabotage as a dramatic equalizer in the struggle against emerging corporate hegemony, and problematizing any simple definition of terrorist.

During the BTW's battles with the corporate employers, the lumber trust hired detectives from the Burns agency, the same firm then investigating the steel erector association bombings, to identify men who secretly belonged to the union. As in the steel erector industries, blacklists and corporate spies were repeatedly used by the lumber trust throughout the struggle with the BTW in the early 1910s. Even more harrowing, on 7 July 1912, as BTW organizer A. L. Emerson spoke at a Grabow, Louisiana, rally protesting the use of replacement workers at a timber mill, company gunmen started shooting at the crowd from hidden locations within surrounding buildings. In this dreadful repetition of the scene at Haymarket nearly thirty years earlier, four people were killed and over forty injured in the ensuing gun battle. Emerson and other BTW members were put on trial but eventually acquitted.[104] In addition to this ambush, company owners used a form of violence made popular in other parts of the country where the IWW was attempting to organize workers: they viciously attacked the BTW with so-called law and order leagues, often made up of a town's leading citizens. One leader of a "good citizens league," E. I. Kellie, who was also a candidate for Congress, wrote to the head of the lumber trust that he and some of the "boys" had forced the IWW out of town. Kellie's group also warned the Wobblies that they "were the law and we would not allow no one to speak here that preached their doctrine. Kellie's 'Old Ku Klux Klan' are not dead, they were only sleeping and were thoroughly aroused the other night."[105] Similarly, the Merryville, Louisiana, Good Citizens' League lashed out at the BTW in February 1913. With the local lumber company's director in charge, the league ransacked union offices, attacked several Wobblies, and forcibly led them out of town, while also pausing to burn the soup kitchen run by female BTW members.[106]

With powerful citizens orchestrating violent raids on undesirable residents, the southern lumber wars recall the "capitalist organization" against which Jack London railed. Further, by consciously invoking the Ku Klux Klan, the timber conflict of the early 1910s inevitably prompts comparisons to the historic KKK of the 1860s and to its later fictional incarnation at the turn of the century in Thomas Dixon's fiction. Like the KKK, the chief citizens of the southern mill towns engaged in a propaganda battle with the BTW by attempting to convince the local populace that the IWW reds were the true agents of violence. Lumber barons frequently characterized BTW members as violent terrorists in the local media. Moreover, as Hall details in his memoir, the Burns agency went so far as to distribute a counterfeit IWW leaflet describing violence the Wobblies wanted to enact. Hall, not surprisingly, fought propaganda with humor and quickly penned a parody of the circular, *All About Bums, the Big Sensation.*[107]

Hall responded with satire and verbal mockery, prime weapons of Wobblies and the dispossessed more generally. Even so, at stake in this repartee was a larger cultural struggle over who had the power to designate terrorists and victims. A BTW leaflet, printed after the corporate attack on the Grabow workers' rally, fumed that the lumber trust "still cries for blood, still strives to make its terror terrorize, still demands that more murder be done."[108] But despite these rhetorical efforts, in neither the era of the historic KKK nor in its rhetorical reinvention in 1910s Louisiana could recently freed black Americans and impoverished radical workers be considered the victims of terrorism. In the high-stakes game of naming "terrorism," a person is only understood as a victim if he or she ideologically counts as a citizen in whom the state takes full concern and an active interest. The lumber trust, embodying corporate capitalism and enjoying the legal and forceful backing of the state, thus strove to identify itself as the victim under attack by rogue workers espousing and performing sabotage and other physical violence. Repeating rhetoric from an earlier era that successfully labeled disempowered black men as rapists who terrorize white women, even as those men were victimized by nighttime Klan raids, the lumber trust used the gravitas granted by the state to beat, harass, and murder IWW members while shouting "terrorist threat."

The noxious idiom of the KKK was not the sole property of the lumber barons, however. In 1913 Hall imagined an intensely secretive and combative organization of workers, which he deemed the "Clans of Toil." Hall even suggested that southern workers organize their militancy along the same lines as the KKK, including the notorious white sheets. Yet, as David Roediger has explained, Hall was also the leading voice calling for black-white unity in the BTW and in the South generally in the struggle against capitalism. His choice of names here thus seems a remarkable blind spot for a racially conscious labor agitator working so soon after the KKK's demise. Indeed, the year before Hall organized his Clan in 1916, D. W. Griffith had premiered *Birth of a Nation,* his movie version of Thomas Dixon's *The Clansman.* What Hall idolized in the Ku Klux Klan, though, was not its obvious racism, but rather its rebellion against rule imposed by outsiders. This is not to excuse Hall, for it is remarkable that he could have ever expected black southerners to be able to identify with a secretive organization modeled on the historic Klan.[109] In Hall's invocation of the Klan and frequent romanticization of it in his poetry, we again see the flexibility of metaphors of violence. Like "terrorism" itself, the Klan became an elastic metaphor of power that could be used to describe either the clandestine violence of a town's "best citizens" or the rebellion of disenfranchised "timber beasts."

While Hall's Clan represented the possibility of violent retribution, he did not shy away from more direct calls for sabotage in his editorials and in what he chose to publish in his capacity as an iww newspaper editor. As editor of *The Lumberjack,* for instance, Hall published a poem entitled "Saw Mill 'Accidents,'" written by "the Wooden Shoe Kid."[110] After detailing several cases of industrial sabotage, including broken saws, malfunctioning steam boilers, and incorrectly shipped merchandise, the poem's narrator opines that workers "'awake at last, / Have donned their wooden shoes'" (ll. 25–26) and warns the boss, "'If you don't come clean, fast, / You'll get a case of blues'" (ll. 27–28). Covington Hall also filed a report with the *Industrial Worker* describing sabotage in the southern timber region: "Trees began to show a tendency for absorbing spikes into their interior against which the saws protested by going up in the air," and "the flanges on the car wheels break off on the curves and all the logs go back into the woods instead of going to the mills as they should."[111] During the Merryville strike, in which Hall was heavily involved, another *Industrial Worker* editorial noted that "an engine, with a few cars of scabs, and gunmen, was proceeding lawfully on its ladylike way from the woods to town . . . when lo! and behold, a giant pine at [the] side of the tracks suddenly grew tired of standing, and resolved at this psychological moment to utilize the slowly moving engine directly under it as a pillow, which it did, amid rending of iron and steel. . . . We strikers are at a loss (?) to account for all these immoral, not to say unladylike, actions on the part of the bosses' sacred property. How sad it is, when even inanimate machines strike on their generous (?) employers. It's a damn shame!"[112]

These reports back to the iww from the southern timber wars describe the sabotage and implicitly encourage more but claim the violence only indirectly. Rather than make an outright claim of responsibility, Hall and other writers rhetorically suggested that even nature chose to sabotage the lumber companies. Some trees suddenly absorb spikes, while others decide to fall down and treat carloads of scabs as pillows. Feigning disbelief, the workers strike a pose of outrage as trees and inanimate objects rebel at being "property," much as the southern timber beasts were rebelling at feeling themselves to be the property, or wage-slaves, of the lumber corporations. This writer also distinctly genders the actions of his report, spoofing the patriarchal code of southern womanhood that equates subservience and morality with "ladylike" behavior while also equating rebellion with manhood. This is not surprising in the early-twentieth-century South, but it is unfortunately ironic since the women of the BTW were full voting members and played very important organizational roles within the union. The writer does, however, pay probably unintentional homage to one militant southern woman. *The Industrial Worker*'s editorialist employs the same strategy of marking irony and satire with interposed question marks that Ida B. Wells used in her own struggle against the KKK's ability to dominate societal understanding of southern black men.[113]

During the strike at Merryville, the *Industrial Worker* printed another poem that picked up on the violence implicit in the notion of trees falling on a carload of company employees:

> *S*cabs!
> *A*ttention
> *B*rotherhood of Timber Workers
> *O*n strike at Merryville, La.
> *T*ake warning!
> *A*merican Lumber Co.
> *G*oing crazy.
> *E*verybody's doin' it!
>   Doin' what? Nathin'.[114]

Like the *Industrial Worker* "sabotage" acrostic discussed earlier, this elliptical and confrontational poem threatens company scabs both directly and indirectly. Without ever naming the violence that could befall them, it announces the BTW's anger and admonishes lumber company employees to "take warning!" The poem also suggests that the BTW is going berserk, that "everybody" is offering wild and unpredictable reprisals against the American Lumber Company and its strike-replacement employees. And then, in a move highly characteristic of the rhetoric of violence, the speaker winks and claims that nothing is happening: no plots, no violence, no sabotage.

This idea of acting "crazy," going berserk, and wildly threatening scabs is absolutely integral to Covington Hall's most powerful poetry as well. He frequently gives this notion of outrageous unpredictability a twist by dwelling on the roles that madness, dreaming, and fantasies can play in radical dissent. For instance, in June 1916 Hall published "Us the Hoboes and Dreamers" in his own journal, *Rebellion: Made Up of Dreams and Dynamite.* When he reprinted this poem in later years, he would add an identifying epigraph: "Written when we Lumberjacks, Sodbusters, Hoboes and Dreamers were fighting the Lumber Barons of Louisiana and Texas, with our backs to the wall, back in 1910–14."[115] The poem starts chillingly, as the solidarity-minded narrator announces, "We shall laugh to scorn your power that now holds the South in awe" (l. 1). Celebrating the muscle of America's most dispossessed citizens, the poem then becomes one of the most vicious in Hall's oeuvre. It also continues in the second person, purposefully making the reader the recipient of the threat rather than a mere observer. The speaker promises to "trample on your customs," to "spit upon your law," and to "set our sisters on you" (ll. 2, 9). The speaker also promises that the assaults will come without warning from under cover of darkness: "We shall steal up through the darkness, we shall prowl the wood and town, / Till they waken to their power and arise and ride you down" (ll. 19–20). In these lines, Hall's speaker embraces one of the classic fantasies of violence, as he imagines that a surprising, violent act can awaken the sleeping masses and inspire a widespread class revolt. Warning that "we shall strike when least expected" (l. 27), the narrator threatens:

> We shall use your guile against you, all the cunning you have taught,
> All the wisdom of the serpent to attain the ending sought.
>
> We shall come as comes the cyclone — in the stillness we shall form —
> From the calm your terror fashioned we shall hurl on you the storm.
>
> (ll. 23–26)

In these key lines, the narrator claims that working-class violence is merely an example of applying what the workers have been taught. Faced with years of being cheated and tricked, they put those "cunning" lessons to full use by plotting diabolical violence. Phrased in this way, responsibility for a sudden and violent uprising shifts to the owning classes, who have precipitated such retribution with years of slyly manipulating workers. In a move characteristic of many Hall poems that celebrate Lucifer as the first true rebel, and which carries a distant echo of Milton's Satan, Hall also evokes the biblical serpent as a cunning deliverer. Moreover, this poem's original readers would have recognized in the serpent an allusion to Hall's favorite symbol of sabotage. Again and again in the magazines he edited, Hall featured drawings and cartoons in which a fanged serpent metaphorically represented sabotage. And in this poem, perhaps most ominously, it is exactly when the dominant classes believe they have completely extinguished the fire of potential revolt, when the "terror" of oppression has stifled dissent, that Hall promises rebellion like a "cyclone" that seems to come from nowhere and everywhere at once.

Hall's poem "The Madman's Boast" similarly employs the second-person address, and this time makes the "you" of the poem those persons who rail against the IWW.[116] In the epigraph, Hall identifies the poem as a "reply to those who have so often raged: 'All IWWs are crazy! You included!'" Drawing readers into the poem and making them think consciously about their own subject position in the class struggle, the speaker opens by asking, "What know you of madness, you whose minds have never gone astray?" (l. 1). In other words, the IWW's tactics only seem "crazy" to those persons who have never felt the mind-twisting sting of poverty or class oppression. But in true Wobbly style, the speaker then confronts his audience directly: "What! how dare you call me crazy? You who drudge down in the plain, / Far beneath the dazzling empire of the man you call insane!" (ll. 5–6). In this poem, it is the ability to dream, to extend the thought of how things could be well beyond the reality of how they are, that provides entrance into a "dazzling empire" but also causes those whose thinking is convention-bound by the logic of capitalism to label the speaker "insane."

Hall echoed this idea in prose. In 1925 he published "In Defense of Dreaming," arguing that it is through the "power to dream, to imagine beyond things as they are to things as they ought to be, that man has developed power to overcome adverse environments." He also admonished readers that "not until they begin to dream of better bread and higher liberty do they become 'dangerous citizens' and a hopeful sign."[117] In both his prose and poetry, Hall articulates a classic double bind: it is not until the downtrodden classes begin to dream the impossible that they have any hope, but that is also the exact moment when forces of the status quo will label them insane or crazy. Hall's poetic version of this sentiment undoes this double bind in "The Madman's Boast" by rhetorically turning the tables:

> You! 'tis you who are the madman! You whose eyes are on the ground,
> Kneeling with Ahriman's angels, with the gyves of custom bound!
> You who never knew the ecstasy and never felt the pain
> Of the souls who roam the empire of the man you call insane.
>
> (ll. 17–20)

In this final stanza Hall, as in many of his other poems, invokes religion, though not a Christian religion in this example. In the ancient Persian religion of Zoroastrianism, Ahriman is the spirit of darkness and evil and the archenemy of the Supreme Being, Ahura Mazda. Further, the speaker claims that being fettered by "custom" is the true definition of madness and suggests that the only path to the "dazzling empire" is the mixture of pleasure and pain that comes when one's mind has "gone astray," leaving behind conventional ideas.

Redefining words to highlight the way language ideologically serves as either confining or liberatory also plays a role in other poems by Hall, such as in "A Hymn to Hate."[118] Showing William Blake's influence, the poem operates in a series of binaries:

O thou, twin-born with Love from Beauty's line,
Her alter ego and, like her, divine,

. . . .

To thee whose fructifying kiss, O Hate,
So oft hath 'couraged men to challenge fate!

(ll. 1–2, 5–6)

Like madness in the previous poem and "love" in this verse, "hate" is god-like, rather than a poisonous emotion. "Thou art not evil—thou art good and fair! / To thee we owe the strength of our despair," the narrator continues (ll. 7–8). Hate turns out to be a highly productive, "good" emotion precisely because it prompts people to resist their apparent destiny and to imagine different and better lives for themselves. Indeed, "It is because Toil's legions know thee not, / Theirs is the burden's brunt, the bitter lot" (ll. 19–20). Hate is beautiful because it is the catalyst for undoing tyranny.

Yet, in "A Hymn to Hate" and in similar poems such as "A May Day Prayer," wherein he pleads, "Lord, give us 'Bitter Men!' / . . . / Men who speak the Naked Truth, who spit forth Searing Words straight into the 'fatted faces of Respectability'" (ll. 1, 5), Hall recognizes that his other poems' emphasis on violence is not self-sustaining.[119] That is, as much as he seems to call for violence to start a revolution and longs for the bitterness and hatred that can prompt that violence, Hall realizes that violence must be accompanied by changes in thinking. It is "bitter men" who speak the truth to power and thereby encourage other working-class people to believe as well. Hate and bitterness are beautiful to Hall because they are symptomatic of a rupture in dominant ideology that goes far beyond the mild dissent that, in his mind, America's dominant ideology allows so that it can be claimed that America is a free country where all citizens have the right to protest. The anguish, fury, and searing images of Hall's poetry derive from his belief that a revolution in thought and language is a necessary accompaniment to an economic and social revolution. Thus, as he puts it in "A Hymn to Hate," " 'Tis not till slavery's hated by the slaves— / 'Tis only then Truth rises from her graves—" (ll. 13–14). Using the popular metaphor of slavery to describe the debilitated condition of the working class, Hall claims that the first step to liberation is learning to see through the ideological myth that tells impoverished members of the working class to be good, unquestioning workers who place their faith in capitalism and obey their bosses (to be "Scissor Bills," in Wobbly shorthand). Only then will the "Truth" of a new language and a corrected way of understanding the world emerge from the "grave" in which industrial capitalism has buried it.

This realization that the thinking of the working class has to be refashioned explains the prominent and varied role that dreaming plays in much of Hall's poetry. The very short, four-line "Experto Credite" admonishes readers that there are "thoughts we cannot stifle" and "dreams that will not die," even "though we know the triumph never by us shall be won" (ll. 1, 4).[120] While "Experto Credite" suggests that the revolution remains far in the future, "The Dreamer's Faith" meditates directly on the difficulty of trying to change the way things are presently and bemoans the uncertainty of such questing.[121] Figuring "the Land of Dreaming" (l. 5) as a vast, uncharted territory in which explorers are often lost and bewildered, Hall agonizes that

> There all things change forever, and no things there endure;
> Its boundaries and landmarks forever ever shift,
> And they who travel therein oft many days must drift.
>
> (ll. 6–8)

And even if the dreamer should light upon the correct path, Hall suggests that he or she may often go unrecognized. His poem "The Dreamer" eulogizes a forgotten visionary to whom the world is nonetheless indebted, "For he beheld the Vision when the World-eye still was dim" (l. 14).[122] Yet, despite these difficulties, the poem "The Guarders of the Word" eloquently expresses Hall's reverence for the role dreamers play in revolutionary thinking:

> It is the Dreamers, whom no idols awe, —
> Love's Lucifers who mercify the Law;
>
> . . . .
>
> 'Tis they who bolden Fearful Souls to dare,
> Forbidden Fruit to eat, — the Cage forswear.
> (ll. 17–18, 23–24)[123]

As in other poems, Hall's speaker unconventionally and blasphemously puts his faith in Lucifer rather than God, as he makes "Lucifers" his heroes and yokes them directly to "Love." Refashioning religion further, these Lucifers are the "Dreamers" who manage to resist idolatry, rather than exemplifying brazen images themselves. And in a blasphemous riff on the story of Eden that metaphorically equates Adam and Eve with contemporary wage-slaves, eating the forbidden fruit results not in banishment, but in revolt and deliverance from "the cage" that imprisons them. Similar to other poems in which he imagines Jesus Christ as an oppressed worker, and akin to the IWW's rhetorical battles with the Salvation Army, in this poem Hall implies that conventional understandings of religion are used to oppress the working class. This also makes Hall the direct rhetorical descendent of antebellum African

American writers, such as Frederick Douglass, who excoriated southern biblical interpretations that upheld slavery. Hall's revisionist understanding of the Bible is of course far removed from any conventional biblical exegesis, including Douglass's, but for Hall that extreme, radical reinterpretation exemplifies the severe oppression of workers brought on by conventional wisdom. In addition to this revisionary religious thinking, in this poem Hall again demonstrates his penchant for refashioning the dominant vocabulary as a crucial component of recalibrating beliefs. Somewhat crudely, he concocts a new word in "mercify." But if his creation of new words seems poetically lacking, it nonetheless underscores the idea that the current vocabulary is inadequate to represent revolutionary change. New words and a new language are needed.

For Hall, the working-class consciousness of the producing class is always under the threat of erasure by the ideological mystifications of capitalism. Violence is therefore not only defensible but necessary if the oppressed classes are ever going to rise up and aggressively take what is rightfully theirs. Writing during a period of intense, multifaceted struggle that witnessed the IABSIW bombings and threats made by and against the IWW, Hall cannot imagine workers freeing themselves from the grip of exploitative corporate capital without resorting to violence. But because violence without a concomitant transformation in the consciousness of both workers and owners is ultimately self-defeating, he frequently returns to the power of dreaming, freshly created idioms, and revisions of religious and national myths.

Hall's nearly forgotten poetry thus highlights the artistic response to oppressive conditions that existed alongside the very real violence of the Iron Workers and the feigning violence of the IWW. Indeed, in his memoir written much later in life, Hall relates how the Iron Workers' bombing of the *Times* seemed, in that turbulent era, to be one among a growing number of cultural symptoms that portended impending revolution.[124] But more important than Hall's incorrect assessment of revolution's inevitability, his surreally violent poetry, along with the national dynamite conspiracy and the torrent of dramatic verbiage inspired by the Wobblies' own provocative art forms, expresses the cultural fears and fantasies that sabotage evoked. The rhetoric deployed at the time to make sense of cataclysmic violence lays bare the inner workings of an American culture equally enthralled with and alienated by terrorism.

After 9/11

I have argued in this book that a particular way of imagining certain acts of violence as "terrorism" emerged in the decades around the turn of the twentieth century, and that the imaginative dimensions of terrorism in this period, as well as its closely related material history, were intimately connected to the way industrial capitalism evolved and was narrated for Americans. Except for revisions, I finished writing before the tragic attacks on the World Trade Center and the Pentagon on 11 September 2001 made terrorism a daily, household word in the United States and a live, serious fear for perhaps the first time in nearly a century. But if the history I have mapped out makes it clear that past Americans also felt the unnerving and paralyzing fear of terrorism, the tragedy and magnitude of the events of 9/11 are vastly different in many significant ways. The horror of that day and its incessantly replayed, traumatizing images retain a vividness and a rawness that overwhelm the usual refuge of cultural historians—the anesthetizing effects of time and space. This terrible resistance on the part of 9/11 to studied analysis also has a certain sour irony to it, since so many words, from the commercial-free days of the nonstop newscasts in the immediate aftermath to the daily Pentagon briefings that narrated the war in Afghanistan, have, inevitably, flowed from dozens of sources in order to provide a blueprint for psychically processing such an atrocity. Terrorism is word *and* deed, symbol *and* substance, a form of action whose sheer outrageousness may awe us into silence, but which also compels us to attempt to regain our mental balance by groping toward a narrative structure in which the tragic events can be understood, even if they still make no sense to us.

One implicit argument of this book has been that the United States has had a long and pervasive amnesia about different acts and forms of terrorism in its history. Most Americans have never heard of the 1886 Haymarket bombing, or can only dimly recall its historical significance, and certainly are not aware that the 11 September disaster involving foreign terrorists, sudden, catastrophic attacks without a public claim of responsibility, and a media frenzy are also the key elements of a paradigm fully established in the aftermath of that 1886 tragedy. The 1905 assassination of former Idaho governor Frank Steunenberg with dynamite, the bombing of the *Los Angeles Times* building in 1910, and the 1920 explosion on Wall Street are also widely forgotten. The same is generally true for the thousands of black men and women lynched in the South, as well as for the much more recent rash of bombings perpetrated by the Weather Underground in the early 1970s. And though it remains underreported, clinics that perform abortions have been forced to become one of the most highly garrisoned public spaces in America due to their long history of bombings, bomb threats, and anthrax scares. Even the 1993 World Trade Center and 1995 Oklahoma City bombings have largely faded from our national consciousness.

This absence in our nation's historical memory is now filled by 9/11. From now on in American history, there will always be a terrible moment that can be pointed to as the day that terrorism was brought to the United States. Indeed, it is already widely agreed that America and the world have entered a decidedly new and different era. Sociologist Norman Denzin notes concisely that "the world changed on September 11, 2001," historian John Lewis Gaddis suggests that the collapse of the World Trade Center ended the post–Cold War era, and, in the intellectual sphere, academic e-mail listservs in the days after the attacks pondered whether this all meant the end of postmodernism.[1] Yet it is also important to note that commentators with a different frame of reference have questioned this logic. Noam Chomsky, one of America's great dissenters, recalls this country's long and frequently ugly record of using clandestine and often massive force throughout the world and argues that the most salient "new" aspect of the post-9/11 world is that, for the first time, the violence was directed at the United States. Political historian Niall Ferguson also suggests that the true novelty of 9/11 rests specifically in the combination of several different actions, including air piracy and attacks against urban centers, that have twentieth-century precedents.[2]

Almost certainly, though, Americans will remember 9/11 as a day that changed their world. And it will have changed it, or at least their perception of the world, which largely amounts to the same thing. The attacks of that day have already, for most Americans, become something like a hyperterrorist event that has occluded, amazing as it is to write this, other, more "mundane" forms of terrorism that were occurring before 9/11 and that are still occurring now. Threats and bombings at women's reproductive centers are one example, but, even more, before 9/11 terrorism to most Americans more than likely connoted a Palestinian suicide bomber blowing him- or herself up in an Israeli public space. Terrorism in Americans' minds might also have included Israel's programmatic assassinations of Palestinian leaders and other strikes against Palestinians performed with American-made missiles and fighter jets. All these forms of violence are, of course, still going on, even worsening, but the sheer atrocity of 9/11 has dramatically shifted the context in which American leaders and citizens understand them.

Notions of terrorism are always politically interested, and 9/11's effect on the way Americans calibrate ideas about terror, self-defense, and national boundaries has made analyzing other conflicts on their own terms and within their own contexts extremely difficult. And beyond the ways in which the tragedy has colored the American government's views on long-standing disputes, the meanings of terrorism have proliferated in other specific and politicized directions after 9/11. In February 2002 the House of Representatives Committee on Resources subpoenaed the former spokesperson of the Earth Liberation Front to testify immediately after the Federal Bureau of Investigation designated that organization as the largest and most active U.S.-based terrorist group. Further, in a back to the future reprise of the 1980s, in the early months of 2002 President Bush declined requests to use the American military to assist the Colombian government in its ongoing struggle with leftist insurgents, only to reverse course and send troops later that year. Advocates argued that the intervention was necessary to prevent Colombia from becoming an incubator of terrorist groups. It is not surprising that part of 9/11's discursive fallout has been this invocation of terrorism to buttress political arguments and ratchet up their appeals for urgent action. Yet, as fears of terrorism are mobilized to underwrite varied and contradictory political desires, we are also left wondering what particularities, contexts, and smaller-scale forms of violence are obscured by such wide-brush invocations of terrorist threats.

For many Americans, the most frightening aspect of 9/11 was the skyjacking (a surprisingly dusty-sounding term, intriguingly little-used in connection with the 9/11 attacks) of passenger jets. How, we wonder, could that most tedious form of travel, in which we zip along at 600 miles per hour while remaining so boringly immobile, have been transformed into such a cataclysmic weapon of mass destruction? In the terrifying scenario of 9/11, "our" modern technology has been turned against us, and the things that could be conceived of as weapons mutated disastrously. Beyond the stunning transformation of passenger jets into deadly missiles, we also were faced with the fact that the prosaic credit card has made it possible to access vast sums of money for nefarious purposes, and that other people's credit cards can now be stolen via the World Wide Web. Even certain computer games, the supposed province of politically disinterested young Americans, came under suspicion because it was soon realized that a few flight simulator programs are realistic enough to provide the feel of a real aircraft cockpit. In addition to these technological components of 9/11's tragedy, we are left with the realization that the engineering wonder inherent to our modern, space-eating skyscrapers also proved to be a site of dismaying vulnerability.

This sense of outrage concerning illegitimate uses of technology is, however, like terrorism in America, hardly new. The scale and magnitude are clearly different, but in the late nineteenth century, dynamite was itself a technology put to both socially sanctioned and dangerous, illicit uses. For instance, nitroglycerine, dynamite's key component, was essential in the creation of America's built environment during that period, especially in the construction of the transcontinental railroad during the 1860s. Of course, buried within that frequently celebrated history of railroad building lie the tragic deaths of hundreds of mostly immigrant workers who lost their lives during the push to complete the railway. But those deaths were and have been largely ignored, since dynamite played a socially legitimated role as a modernizing force. At the same time, however, late-nineteenth-century radicals publicly preached dynamite's awesome power in America's cities and exhorted listeners and readers to commit acts of terrorism against wealthy citizens. And when "dynamite outrages" did occur in America and in Europe at the turn of the century, commentators at the time viewed such bombings as the hideous and illegitimate corollary to the social progress that dynamite also made possible via the construction of a modern infrastructure. This country, then, has certainly previously felt the fear that important, modern technologies could be transformed into dangerous weapons.

In addition to the very real fear provoked by the awful revision of technology's intended uses 100 years ago as well as today, one reason we find this particular aspect of terrorism so riveting is that it provides us with a site to anchor our panic and our outrage. While terrorism achieves its effects by convincing citizens that their government is powerless to protect them against a shadowy foe, we tend to focus on technology as a locus of our fears because we can imagine it as something tangible that the government can protect. We may not be able to rid the world of people who wish to do us harm, but perhaps, with enough "human intelligence" (to use the spy world's double-edged phrase), we can safeguard our airplanes, our credit cards, or our nuclear power plants. We focus on technology, then, not only because its illegitimate usage at the hands of terrorists offers the most damning evidence of our vulnerability and lack of agency, our inability to control our lives, but because it can nevertheless be imagined as a tangible site that we can ultimately learn to protect.

Another role played by technology in the period immediately following 9/11 was the saturating coverage by the mass media. In the days after the attacks, we collectively watched video images of the planes veering into the twin towers again and again, a ceaseless repetition punctuated only by the even more difficult to watch scenes of grieving loved ones. Never before have so many of us wished so fervently to return to the banality of commercials and network sitcoms. In this regard, it has long been a chestnut of terrorism studies that the mass media and terrorism thrive off one another, that terrorists gain publicity for their causes via the media. In the events of 9/11, though, media coverage went beyond this symbiotic relationship, as the sheer magnitude of the bombings—what Nayan Chanda and Strobe Talbott have gruesomely termed "mass murder as performance art"[3]—intersected with the spectacle-addicted logic of most contemporary mass media. This intense media coverage was certainly warranted, as we all struggled to learn what had happened and to put the events into some kind of context. But the media again proved itself extraordinarily capable of circulating the most violent, even emotionally manipulative, images while offering an unfortunate dearth of historically informed, contextualized analysis of terrorism, of America's complicated history in the Middle East, of our "drug war's" paradoxical relationship with the Taliban, or even of America's earlier covert military training and outfitting of the mujahideen's resistance to the Soviet invasion of Afghanistan during the 1980s.[4]

Yet, despite television's saturation coverage, one important item was missing in the postbombing news, an item media coverage and terrorist fiction over the years have taught us to expect in terrorist events. There was no claim of responsibility. Though Osama bin Laden was quickly identified as a prime suspect, no acknowledgment was forthcoming from him or anyone else. Perhaps bin Laden thought that the United States might have taken seriously his 1998 fatwa calling upon all Muslims to kill Americans and that he therefore needed to make no claim. Or perhaps bin Laden knew that he would be instantly suspected and eventually face military retaliation and so chose to restrict his public statements to praise of the terrorists broadcast over the Arabic-language Al-Jazeerah network, a forum which, unlike American media coverage, might have been more conducive to the reciprocal relationship between terrorism and the media that is often postulated.

Whatever the reasons behind no one taking direct, public responsibility for the bombings and the related lack of a statement articulating specific grievances to which the attacks could, theoretically, bring attention, this absence has meant that Western commentators have not had to evaluate any such statements. Instead, the inevitable struggle in language for how we understand sudden violence has operated entirely on a level in which we project meanings onto the tragedy. In this vein, commentators have frequently argued that the attacks were aimed at Western capitalism and at the United States in particular because it is the engine driving economic globalization.[5] That the World Trade Center was a primary target certainly lends symbolic weight to this interpretation, since crashing planes into, for instance, the Statue of Liberty in New York's harbor would have sent a vastly different message.

Intriguingly, the paradigm emphasizing bin Laden and Al Qaeda's anger at Western capitalism has meant, like ideas about terrorism 100 years ago, that terrorism and capitalism are again intertwined in the narratives mobilized to explain mass violence. As in the decades around 1900, thinking about sudden cataclysmic violence means thinking about the economy. For the most part, though, this line of thought has taken a rather narrow form. Despite the nearly paralyzing complexity of the American economy's role in Middle Eastern history and contemporary politics, this particular element of the present-day interaction between terror and capitalism has gone largely undertheorized. Instead, and though a few commentators have robustly critiqued the fact that in contemporary American society freedom has been reduced to "the freedom to consume as one chooses,"[6] an uncritical celebration of capitalism has been a strong component of American discourse since the 9/11 attacks. Unlike past wars, in which Americans were admonished to conserve, this time we have been incessantly instructed to buy things. From the stories circulating immediately after the attacks about people buying stocks as a patriotic gesture to the sudden appearance of flags in the display windows of every store in our malls and printed on our ubiquitous credit card solicitations, patriotism in this war has been equated with consumer culture. Planting vegetables in the victory garden has been replaced by a shopping trip.

Our leaders' encouragement to consume as usual, even while the nation is at war, may cause some to wonder about the possible roles post-9/11 terrorist discourse will play in the ideological maintenance of neoliberal capitalism in the global political economy. That is, whether or not the attacks were intended as a purposeful assault on America's role in economic globalization, it is worth pondering the cultural effects generated by our leaders' drawing together market capitalism and the war on terrorism as they have explained how we should cope with this tragedy. Of course, admonitions to go about our normal lives and to try to resist being crippled by the fear of terrorism are necessary and important. But at the least, as patriotism is fastened onto everyday consumerism, this rhetoric exemplifies another incursion of market logic into the way we are encouraged to understand nonmarket activities.

Furthermore, contemporary dissenters from capitalist orthodoxy have decried the effects of neoliberal economics, especially the frequent conflation of market capitalism and democracy, as they have unfolded in the globalization of the capitalist economy. The critics of globalization and neoliberalism argue that the emphasis on foreign trade and investment as the recipe for world development results in a disastrous reduction in public spending on social services, a de-unionization of workforces at home and abroad, environmental degradation, and immense transfers of wealth to relatively few corporations coupled with an increase in poverty for workers in poorer countries, as well as an increasingly naturalized ethos of corporate capitalism. Globalization's defenders, on the other hand, contend that free trade and privatization will bring stability and ultimate prosperity to developing countries. While the final outcomes of our increasingly interdependent and global economies remain arguable, we might well pause to consider whether what we have been told will be a long and drawn-out war against terrorism may draw attention away from the more immediate social dilemmas that are accompanying economic, corporate globalization, as well as how intimately we would like the civic obligations and rewards of patriotism to be linked to the consumer culture of market capitalism.

As with the earlier period examined in this book, the contemporary forms of capitalism are undoubtedly entangled with the way we should make sense of 11 September's atrocity and our response to it. It is also extremely important, again as at the turn of the twentieth century, to conceptualize how this central component intersects with other elements of the tragedy. For instance, while condemning the assaults as an attack against "our" capitalist way of life may seem clarifying, it also terribly and misleadingly simplifies matters. Bin Laden, for instance, has previously served notice that he is fighting against what he considers the corrupt or inadequately Islamic regimes of the Middle East and their supporters, as well as the Israeli occupation of Palestine, not Western capitalism per se. His statements of hatred also extend to the American military's "defiling" sacred Islamic spaces in Saudi Arabia. While bin Laden's actions have not helped the poor and oppressed citizens of the Middle East on whose behalf he has in the past claimed to act, his reasoning certainly goes deeper than any straightforward or simple attack on capitalism and "our way of life." To see these atrocities in such terms may offer us the psychological relief of believing that bin Laden simply refuses to acknowledge modernity or is even insane, but it also prevents us from at least questioning the global effects of American capitalism, as well as past American policies that helped to create a bin Laden and his terrorist network.[7] Religion, capitalism, international politics — all are complex and internally riven components of our current crisis that cannot be wedged into a single, decontextualized narrative line describing an attack on our economy, and, by extension, our freedom.

But instead of making judgments based on the troubling complexities of actual historical conditions, our leaders, our news analysts, and our cultural commentators have tended to deal in abstractions and absolutist rhetoric. Francis Fukuyama's 1992 thesis regarding the triumph of liberal democracy in *The End of History and the Last Man* is out; Samuel Huntington's 1996 argument in *The Clash of Civilizations and the Remaking of World Order* is in. The American president and his advisors speak of evildoers, eradicating evil from the world, smoking terrorists out of their caves, good versus evil, being either "for" or "against" terrorism, and wanting bin Laden dead or alive. This absolutist and apocalyptic rhetoric is, again, not new to America's discursive history with terrorism. While nothing can explain away the gross indifference to human life that undergirds the 9/11 assault, such rhetoric reduces unspeakable violence to the simple workings of a familiar, but impoverished, narrative plot that fails to explain much at all about the world we now inhabit.

Although such abstractions and absolutist rhetoric have been the mainstay of much commentary since the attacks, this binary logic fails to surprise for reasons that go beyond policy makers and pundits' desire to simplify America's past and future. It is not surprising because terrorism itself deals in such abstractions. As a form of violence that enacts physical harm upon innocent but symbolically rich victims in order to exact a psychological blow upon others, terrorism is already mind-numbingly abstract. Such displaced violence seems even more predisposed than other forms of aggression to inciting absolutist abstractions that masquerade as explanations. Sudden, massive violence of the kind that struck the United States on 11 September exacerbates our tendency to reach for simple binaries that we can rally around but that will ultimately fail us. Such absolutist statements are in many ways precatory interpretations of 9/11's tragedy that long for a simpler world and even try to will that world into existence through such dichotomous pronouncements. Indeed, what is so striking about the months since the attacks is the stark realization that we apparently possess very few narratives to make sense of indiscriminate and large-scale violence. As we look back at the period studied in this book through the now inevitable lens of 11 September, the realization that, in our past and in our present, we have such a paucity of non-absolutist tropes with which to understand each other is, perhaps, the most frightening bellwether for our collective future.

Notes

Introduction

1. Howells, *Rise of Silas Lapham*, 171–72.

2. Qtd. in Lynn, *William Dean Howells*, 280, emphasis original.

3. See "Textual Variations: The Dynamite Passages," in Howells, *Rise of Silas Lapham*, 341–42.

4. Howells's involvement with Haymarket has been given a comprehensive treatment in Cady, *Realist at War*, 67–80; Garlin, *William Dean Howells;* and Howard A. Wilson, "William Dean Howells's Unpublished Letters."

5. "Red Plot Seen in Blast," *New York Times*, 17 September 1920, 2; "2 Messengers Killed with $170,000 in Bonds," *New York Times*, 17 September 1920, 5.

6. "Palmer Comes Here to Direct Inquiry," *New York Times*, 18 September 1920, 1.

7. "Red Plot Seen in Blast," 1.

8. Schmid, *Political Terrorism*, 64–67.

9. For a survey of influential and competing definitions, especially useful are Laqueur, *Age of Terrorism;* Harmon, *Terrorism Today;* and Rubenstein, *Alchemists of Revolution*. Additionally, James Der Derian, drawing on Paul Virilio's theories regarding the omnipresence of war and media in contemporary culture, offers a fascinating deconstructive reading of terrorism as such into eight "formations" blending both sign systems and material actions (*Antidiplomacy*, chap. 5). Bruce Hoffman's *Inside Terrorism* analyzes the implications of different governmental agencies' definitions of terrorism. Edward Said brilliantly explicates the essentialism and xenophobia that undergird much Western discourse about terrorists and terrorism in "The Essential Terrorist." For an important analysis of the connections between state and antistate terrorism, see Chomsky's *The Culture of Terrorism* and Chomsky and Herman, *The Washington Connection*. For an excellent metadiscursive analysis of the cultural narratives that both constitute "terrorism" as a particular type of violence and seek to explicate it, see Zulaika and Douglass, *Terror and Taboo*.

10. Wilkinson, "Terrorism," 189.

11. "Notice to Our Readers," *The Alarm*, 8 October 1886, unnumbered page.

12. Nobel's great technological advance was to stabilize nitroglycerine. Nitroglycerine, or "blasting oil," had been invented some time earlier but was dangerously

unstable and therefore difficult to use or even transport in its liquid form. Nobel mixed a particularly fine, porous, and powdery dirt found along the banks of the Elbe River with the liquid blasting agent. The absorbent earth solidified the explosive and made its handling almost risk-free without diminishing its power. Nobel named this potent combination of earth and nitroglycerine "dynamite" (Fant, *Alfred Nobel*, 93–94). Dynamite simultaneously revolutionized both the possibilities for the construction of a built environment and the possibilities for its violent destruction. In 1880s Chicago, for example, radical newspapers routinely published directions on how to make dynamite, often suggesting that nitroglycerine could be mixed with the sawdust that was always readily available due to the wood-frame construction around Chicago.

13. Qtd. in "The Butchers of Men," *The Alarm*, 15 November 1884, 1, emphasis original, and again in "Dynamite," *The Alarm*, 6 December 1884, 1.

14. The relationship of assassination to terrorism is particularly complex. Because terrorist violence is generally both seemingly random and apparently purposeless (in that the victims are "innocent" and not being singled out for punishment), even as it is nonetheless perceived as having a political motivation, the planned killing of a particular individual rather than an indiscriminate victim pressures any theoretical boundary between assassination and terrorism. According to Martha Crenshaw Hutchinson, assassinations may function as a form of terrorism "only if they are facets of a broader strategy. When such acts of violence accomplish in themselves the total objective of the assassin or the saboteur, their political significance is limited" (*Revolutionary Terrorism*, 20). That is, terrorism generates fear precisely by not being a discrete killing, by harboring the likelihood that more assassinations are to follow. But beyond this, terrorist violence is symbolic; by killing one victim, it means to coerce others. And here is where assassination bleeds into the category of terror, since the assassination of an important individual can generate the publicity and fear that is integral to modern terrorism.

15. As Alfred McClung Lee reported long ago, the 1880 census recorded over 3.1 million telegraphic messages sent by the press in that year, which translated into almost one million newspaper columns, largely for Associated Press affiliates; by 1885 the United Press disseminated an average of 17,500 words per day from New York to seventy other cities, and by 1886 it had organized a complex telegraphic circuit spanning over 2,600 miles between Chicago and San Francisco (Alfred McClung Lee, *The Daily Newspaper in America*, 512, 515). See also Blondheim's highly interesting discussion of the nationalization of news in his *News over the Wires*, esp. chap. 8.

16. Martin A. Miller, "Intellectual Origins of Modern Terrorism," 43–45.

17. The scholarly literature on the relationship between terrorism and the mass media is, of course, voluminous. Especially useful are Weimann and Winn, *Theater of Terror;* Paletz and Schmid, *Terrorism and the Media;* Nacos, *Terrorism and the Media;* and Dobkin, *Tales of Terror.* A more populist gauge of the relationship be-

tween terrorism and the mass media was articulated in 1984 by news anchorman Ted Koppel, who himself rose to national prominence during the 1979–81 Iran hostage crisis: "The media, particularly television, and terrorists need one another," Koppel intoned in an interview with *Harper's* magazine. He continued with the assertion that "they have what is fundamentally a symbiotic relationship" (qtd. in Kubiak, *Stages of Terror*, 1).

18. Schmid and de Graaf, *Violence as Communication*, 10.

19. Johns, *Man Who Shot McKinley*, 123.

20. Crenshaw, "Relating Terrorism to Historical Contexts," 20. Margaret Scanlan also insightfully notes that if "terrorists succeed when they seize headlines," this largely means "that they and their causes are understood in terms set by popular journalism" (*Plotting Terror*, 5).

21. Indeed, as I explore in Chapter 5, one of the worst acts of terrorism in American history, the 1910 bombing of the *Los Angeles Times* building, was directed against a significant representative of the media. That bombing, which was embedded in other simmering disagreements about the social organization of capitalism, makes it clear that terrorists' employment of the media for publicity is only one among many variables necessary for theorizing political violence.

22. Zulaika and Douglass, *Terror and Taboo*, 4.

23. As the *New York Times* editorialized, "In the aftermath of the [Oklahoma City] explosion, the gutted building and the cars burning in the streets were more reminiscent of war-torn Beirut than a city in America's heartland" ("Savagery in Oklahoma City," *New York Times*, 20 April 1995, A22). Likewise, survivors, witnesses, and Oklahoma City's citizens repeated a similarly shocked refrain that would soon be reiterated again and again in the media's coverage of this new "terror in the heartland": "This does not happen here. It happens in countries so far away, so different, they might as well be on the dark side of the moon" (Rick Bragg, "In Shock, Loathing, Denial: 'This Doesn't Happen Here,'" *New York Times*, 20 April 1995, 1).

24. On the political and ideological stakes of identifying the attacks as terrorism, war, hijacking, or crimes against humanity, see Chomsky, *9–11*, esp. 14–17.

25. "Rushing to Bash Outsiders," 70; Walter Goodman, "Wary Network Anchors Battle Dubious Scoops," *New York Times*, 20 April 1995, B12.

26. Among American novelists, DeLillo has provided the richest and most provocative investigation of late capitalism's intersection with modern terrorism. From the early novel *Players*, which hinges on a terrorist plot to blow up the New York Stock Exchange, through *The Names*, whose American businessmen skirt terrorist activities in foreign countries, up through *Libra*, which consistently imagines the Central Intelligence Agency as a terrorist arm of the U.S. government that also has deep business ties in the countries where it masterminds coups, and, most dramatically, in *Mao II*'s conflation of multinational capitalism and terrorist violence, DeLillo has repeatedly fictionalized and calibrated the finely meshed ties between covert political violence and a consumer society driven by market capitalism. See

also, especially, Peter Kramer's excellent 2001 novel, *Spectacular Happiness*, which imagines a handyman who starts blowing up Cape Cod trophy homes as a protest against private property and goes on to become a media celebrity.

27. Filmmaker John Waters brilliantly spoofs the intersection of corporate capitalism and terrorism in his 2000 film, *Cecil B. Demented*. In the film, desperate would-be independent filmmaker Cecil B. Demented and his gang of poorly paid theater workers/terrorists, the Sprocket Holes, kidnap famous Hollywood actress Honey Whitlock (Melanie Griffith). Whitlock, in a reprise of Patty Hearst's 1970s kidnapping, eventually sides with her captors, while the band of outlaws goes from multiplex to multiplex committing acts of terrorism against the corporate domination of the movie industry and filming the violence in real time.

28. Scanlan, *Plotting Terror*, 1; Said, "Essential Terrorist," 149.

29. Scanlan, "Language and the Politics of Despair," 182.

30. Preston, *Cobra Event*, 300–301. Testifying to the late-1990s currency of this theme, Robin Cook's 1999 best-selling medico-scientific thriller, *Vector*, constructs a similar plot around a demented worker's terroristic use of anthrax and rogue scientists from the former Soviet Union.

31. Der Derian, *Antidiplomacy*, 115. The phrase "spasmodic immediacy" is also Der Derian's (97).

32. On the Weather Underground, see Jacobs's fascinating *The Way the Wind Blew*.

33. Confino, *Daughter of a Revolutionary*, 230, emphasis original.

34. Laqueur, *Age of Terrorism*, 48; Martin A. Miller, "Intellectual Origins of Modern Terrorism," 42.

35. Zulaika and Douglass, *Terror and Taboo*, 33.

36. Rubenstein, *Alchemists of Revolution*, 8–9.

37. Bourdieu, *Outline of a Theory of Practice*, 79.

38. Martin A. Miller, "Intellectual Origins of Modern Terrorism," 42; Laqueur, *Age of Terrorism*, 48; Hoffman, *Inside Terrorism*, 17.

39. As Thomas Perry Thornton put it in a classic, if now somewhat dated, article, "Terror is a *symbolic* act designed to influence political behavior by extranormal means, entailing the use or threat of violence" ("Terror as a Weapon of Political Agitation," 73, my emphasis).

40. Schmid and de Graaf, *Violence as Communication*, 14–15.

41. Crenshaw, "Relating Terrorism to Historical Contexts," 4.

42. Schmid and de Graaf, *Violence as Communication*, 14.

43. Ibid., 14–15, my emphasis.

44. Zulaika and Douglass, *Terror and Taboo*, 67. As Zulaika and Douglass lament, "Among the various possible modes of formal argumentation within terrorism texts there is one that, for its very prevalence, deserves primary attention. This is the causal argument. It takes the form of the simple question: 'What are the *causes* of terrorism?' . . . This seemingly innocuous and even most scientific of questions gets formulated over and over again as a mantra, the quintessential research issue, the key

point of reference against which any analysis of terrorism must be measured" (ibid., emphasis original).

45. Feldman, *Formations of Violence*, 13–14, my emphasis.

46. Zulaika and Douglass, *Terror and Taboo*, 31–32, 65, 11.

47. Apter, "Political Violence in Analytical Perspective," 10–12. Within literary and critical theory, the relation of postmodernism to terrorism has also become of interest in recent years. Clair Wills, for instance, has written that there exists a "theory of narrative suggested by acts of political violence" ("Language Politics, Narrative, Political Violence," 46). For Wills, terrorism's dramatic rupture of the everyday norms of the commonsense and taken-for-granted rules for social behavior is a functional equivalent of postmodernism's rejection of Enlightenment rationality, though, paradoxically, terrorism remains committed "to the values of the European nation state" in its reliance "on the structures of symbolic representation" (ibid., 55). Wills is arguing here against Jean Baudrillard's notion that terrorism is antinarrative and therefore symptomatic of the end of a genuine social engagement. For Baudrillard, terrorism is "the only non-representative act." It is, perhaps not surprisingly, a "hyperreal act" that emerges from the vortex of a media-mad society: "Dedicated from the outset not to any representation or consciousness," terrorism is "senseless and indeterminate like the system it combats, . . . and for that matter a homologue deep down, of the silence and inertia of the masses" (Baudrillard, "In the Shadow of the Silent Majorities," 50–52). According to Baudrillard, terrorism is the representationally and politically null consequence of a citizenry that has been reduced by its mass-mediated culture to what, in another context, he ridicules as "a large soft body with many heads" ("Ecstasy of Communication," 129). In contrast to Wills, who sees linkages between terrorism's random and sudden explosions and the form of both literary and more properly social narratives, such as those that create, support, and rend asunder nation-states, Baudrillard's theory drains away from terrorism all notions of political engagement, including any idea that terrorist violence could induce citizens either to see it as a representation of their condition or as the sign of a peril that the government needs to stamp out.

48. The essays collected in *Class and Its Others,* edited by J. K. Gibson-Graham, Stephen A. Resnick, and Richard D. Wolff, especially Gibson-Graham, Resnick, and Wolff's "Introduction: Class in a Poststructuralist Frame," represent crucial recent theoretical attempts to, as they put it, develop a "political discourse that has a purchase on the dread and disavowed terrain of the economy" and to view the economy not as a preordained fact with certain built-in meanings, but "as a discursive terrain, a set of concepts, issues, contradictions, identities, and struggles" (1–2). I am suggesting that in the nineteenth century, terrorism was a constituent element of the economy's cultural terrain.

49. Trachtenberg, *Incorporation of America,* 99.

50. On the ideology of "free labor," see especially Eric Foner, *Free Soil, Free Labor, Free Men.*

51. Painter, *Standing at Armageddon,* xx.

52. Page Smith, *Rise of Industrial America,* 223.

53. *American Machinist* quoted in Daniel Nelson, *Managers and Workers,* 30; Asher, "Industrial Safety and Labor Relations," 115–16.

54. Braverman, *Labor and Monopoly Capital,* 133. Historical accounts detailing transformations in mechanical reproduction and distribution during this era begin with Siegfried Giedion's foundational and sweeping text, *Mechanization Takes Command,* and include, especially, Trachtenberg, *Incorporation of America,* esp. chap. 2; Chandler, *Visible Hand;* Beniger, *Control Revolution;* and Hounshell, *From the American System to Mass Production.*

55. Senate Committee on Education and Labor, *Relations between Labor and Capital,* 219.

56. McNeill, "Problem of To-Day," 460.

57. Parsons, *Famous Speeches,* 55.

58. Artaud quoted in Seltzer, *Bodies and Machines,* 172.

59. Philip S. Foner, *Autobiographies of the Haymarket Martyrs,* 164.

60. Clarke, *Effects of the Factory System,* 1, 73.

61. Yet, if terrorism appeared to many of its proponents to offer a compensatory agency or agency recovery, late-nineteenth-century terrorism's cultural commentators, when faced with the startling brutality of an act, tended to imagine complex conspiratorial plots that dissolved notions of individual actors into a deindividuated mass of conspirators. This tension between individual and conspiratorial explanations for what was conceived of at the time as working-class terrorism is taken up in Chapter 1.

62. Sklar, *Corporate Reconstruction,* 33.

63. On the fear of overproduction and the many possible solutions floated for it in the turn of the century's roiling economic milieu, see Sklar, *Corporate Reconstruction;* Dorfman, *Economic Mind in American Civilization;* and Ratner, Soltow, and Sylla, *Evolution of the American Economy,* chap. 12. On the period's emergent interest in solving overproduction by fostering mass consumption, see Chandler, *Visible Hand,* and Beniger, *Control Revolution.*

64. Sklar, *Corporate Reconstruction,* 15.

65. Michaels, *Gold Standard,* 187–206.

66. Lloyd, *Wealth against Commonwealth,* 519.

67. Qtd. in Jas. H. Davis, *Political Revelation,* 240.

68. Rapsher, "Dangerous 'Trusts,'" 509–11; Tourgée, "Anti-Trust Campaign," 36; Joseph Dana Miller, "Evils of Trusts," 621.

69. "Wages and Murder," *New York Tribune,* 27 April 1876, 4; Corbin, "Tyranny of Labor Organizations," 417.

Chapter One

1. Carl Smith, *Urban Disorder,* 123.

2. Indeed, one key prosecution witness, the aforementioned Seliger, admitted

on the witness stand that he had taken money from the police ("Trial of the Chicago Anarchists," 57).

Judge Joseph E. Gary's conduct at the trial exuded a clear favoritism toward the state, as he ruled almost all contested points in the prosecution's favor and permitted the state wide latitude in its arguments while holding the defense tightly in check. His administration of the trial, however, went beyond partisanship and was in fact downright bizarre. Gary's escapades in the courtroom demonstrate the extent to which the trial afforded the anarchists was a mere show trial. During the court proceedings, for instance, he routinely placed beautiful and luxuriously dressed young women on the bench with him, where they giggled, munched candy, and joked among themselves. One young woman also later asserted that Gary spent most of his time drawing pictures for her while arguments were in progress (Avrich, *Haymarket Tragedy*, 262–63).

3. On anarchist communal gatherings in Chicago, see Buhle, "Pessimists' Heresy," 104–5; Bruce C. Nelson, *Beyond the Martyrs*, esp. chaps. 5–6; and Avrich, *Haymarket Tragedy*, chap. 10. On the 1885 streetcar strike, see, in particular, Governor John P. Altgeld's fascinating discussion in his 1893 message pardoning the three living Haymarket defendants. Altgeld reproduces several letters from prominent citizens testifying to police brutality, especially on the part of Captain John Bonfield, who one year later would lead the police march to break up the Haymarket rally. Altgeld further posits that the Haymarket bomb was thrown by someone simply seeking revenge for earlier police brutality (*Reasons for Pardoning Fielden, Neebe, and Schwab*, 34–51).

4. Scott, "Recent Strikes," 357; Molineux quoted in Eugene E. Leach, "Literature of Riot Duty," 27; Abbott, "Danger Ahead," 54, 56.

5. Abbott, "Danger Ahead," 53.

6. For an excellent study that attempts to unpack the conundrum of an "organized mob" by focusing on riots in American history, see Gilje, *Rioting in America*. See also Eugene E. Leach, "Literature of Riot Duty."

7. Hay, *Bread-Winners*, 86.

8. Abbott, "Danger Ahead," 53.

9. On the prebombing history of inflammatory rhetoric and actions on the part of both the anarchists and the coalition of capitalists and authority figures who virulently opposed them, see Carl Smith, *Urban Disorder*, 101–18.

10. Schaack, *Anarchy and Anarchists*, 149, 184.

11. "That Infernal Machine," *Chicago Tribune*, 28 December 1885, 8. While the *Tribune* regarded "the affair as an insane freak of some socialistic crank," it also intriguingly reproduced its own version of the fusion between writing and terrorism: "The police," according to the article, were "determined to discover the author of the machine."

12. "Anarchy's Red Hand," *New York Times*, 5 May 1886, 1. Johann Most came to the United States in 1882 and filled his New York newspaper, *Freiheit*, with detailed descriptions of bomb-making while also advocating widespread, indiscriminate ter-

rorism. He was, in fact, frequently praised and reprinted by Chicago's anarchists. Most further summarized his instructions in an 1885 terrorist manual harrowingly entitled, *Revolutionary War Science: A Little Handbook of Instruction in the Use and Preparation of Nitroglycerine, Dynamite, Gun-Cotton, Fulminating Mercury, Bombs, Fuses, Poisons, etc., etc.*, which detailed how to organize small terrorist cells as well as methods for constructing and placing bombs for maximum efficacy. Among other things, Most's book also pioneered in the development of the letter bomb and in cloak-and-dagger techniques such as the use of invisible ink and communication via cipher and code names. Its contents were translated and serialized in Chicago's anarchist papers, and the manual itself was sold for a dime at the newspapers' offices and at anarchist meetings. On Most, see Avrich, *Haymarket Tragedy*, 163–73; Laqueur, *New Terrorism*, 13–15; and Martin A. Miller, "Intellectual Origins of Modern Terrorism," 43–45.

13. The Haymarket tragedy has, of course, always loomed as a milestone in histories of American labor, radicalism, and the politics of immigration. For instance, the bombing prompted this country's first major "Red Scare," which occurred in the immediate wake of the incident. Commentators have also generally agreed that the bombing and subsequent trial stalled American labor's burgeoning movement for an eight-hour workday and temporarily suspended the drive for unionization as well. Additionally, in *Urban Disorder and the Shape of Belief*, Carl Smith has brilliantly explained the Haymarket bomb and its aftermath in the context of late-nineteenth-century urbanization and Americans' attempts to define order and disorder in an industrializing culture. Despite the many fascinating stories and different aspects of Haymarket that scholars have identified, however, commentators have not remarked upon the fact that the bombing was also described at the time as the first outbreak of terrorist violence in the United States. In Smith's discussion of how the Haymarket radicals were perceived in the 1880s, for example, the word "terrorist" repeatedly crops up (*Urban Disorder*, 137, 138, 158, and as an illustration caption between 126 and 127), yet he never pauses to consider this particular estimation of the anarchists.

14. On the anarchists' characteristic rhetorical strategy of ironically reversing the accusations made against them, see ibid., 127–46.

15. While the English-language press universally condemned the anarchists, Bruce Nelson notes that many of America's foreign-language newspapers also denounced the defendants (*Beyond the Martyrs*, 195). Moreover, as Paul Avrich points out, Terence Powderly, leader of the Knights of Labor, made frenzied efforts to disassociate the Knights from the taint of radicalism (*Haymarket Tragedy*, 219–20), and Carl Smith adds that even pro-labor papers reviled the anarchists (*Urban Disorder*, 135). Among respectable public figures of the day, William Dean Howells, as I noted in the Introduction, was the only nationally known person who publicly questioned the anarchists' trial and convictions. The amount and severity of the abuse heaped on the popular Howells for his principled objections testify to the power of the nearly univocal disdain for any form of radicalism after the bombing.

16. Seltzer, *Serial Killers*, 1. Though Seltzer focuses on contemporary society, he dates the advent of this "wound culture" to the end of the nineteenth century (278).

17. Warner, "Mass Public and the Mass Subject," 250.

18. While I am suggesting that the Haymarket bombing and its aftermath provide a case study in the emergence of a modern cultural template for identifying certain acts as terrorism, I am not implying that either the word "terrorism" or a fear of conspiratorial labor violence was unknown previous to Haymarket. The violence of the Molly Maguires in the 1860s and 1870s, and their trials and executions in 1876 and 1877, which were widely reported and illustrated in the popular press, offer an important precedent.

The best work on the Mollies is Kevin Kenny's richly informative *Making Sense of the Molly Maguires*. Kenny combines astute analysis of historical evidence with a subtle reading of the nineteenth-century ideological forces that drove understandings of "Molly Maguirism." Yet, though Kenny frequently uses the words "terrorists" and "terrorism" to describe the Mollies and their violence, those assassinations, as he describes them, are best understood as highly sporadic vigilante justice doled out to avenge ethnic and other local grievances. Moreover, occurring in rural Pennsylvania's anthracite coal regions, the individual murders and beatings of the mine officials evoked a different form of fear in late-nineteenth-century citizens. Haymarket fused these earlier fears of wrathful vengeance and working-class conspiracy with the massive violence of dynamite exploding in an urban setting, which suddenly made it imaginable that a large number of random citizens could be both witnesses and victims of a large-scale atrocity at any given moment. However, the landmark trial of the Molly Maguires is significant for the manner in which its fabrication of an underground labor conspiracy served as a blueprint for later trials, including the Haymarket trial and the Western Federation of Miners trial in 1907, and also provided a benchmark with which some commentators could offhandedly equate and thereby denounce labor leaders.

19. *Anarchy at an End*, 63. The illustration originally appeared in the 15 May 1886 issue of *Graphic News* and, like many images of the bombing and its aftermath, was reproduced in numerous pamphlets and instant histories.

20. Carl Smith, *Urban Disorder*, 130.

21. A wide literature exists that analyzes the social impact these technological changes had on the news and its dissemination. See, for instance, Czitrom, *Media and the American Mind*, chap. 1; Schudson, *Discovering the News*, chaps. 2–3; and Blondheim, *News over the Wires*.

In some respects, the crucial role that the telegraph played in initial reports of the Chicago fire anticipated telegraphy's role in disseminating information about the bomb fifteen years later. See Pauly, "Great Chicago Fire," 677, and Carl Smith, *Urban Disorder*, 28–29. Smith notes the irony that telegraphy made it likely that Americans in far-flung places knew more about the fire while it was occurring than most Chicagoans.

22. Lum, *Concise History of the Great Trial*, 5.

23. "The Telegraph," 359. For a fascinating analysis of the telegraph's effect on what he terms "practical consciousness" or "the nature of awareness itself," see Carey, "Technology and Ideology."

24. The picture originally appeared in the 20 November 1887 issue of *Pictorial West* and was subsequently reproduced, among other places, in McLean, *Rise and Fall of Anarchy in America*, between pages 232 and 233.

25. See Francke, "Sensationalism and the Development of 19th-Century Reporting." On the *Gazette*'s use of extremely graphic illustrations to appeal to its readers' fantasies, nightmares, and desires, see Gorn, "Wicked World."

26. Seltzer, *Serial Killers*, 6.

27. McConnell, "Chicago Bomb Case," 734.

28. Carl Smith, *Urban Disorder*, 129.

29. Foster, "Death in America," 55.

30. The term is Seltzer's (*Serial Killers*, 34–38).

31. Edelman, *Constructing the Political Spectacle*, 31.

32. Ibid., 12.

33. Dwelling particularly on accounts of murder, Karen Halttunen's extremely insightful *Murder Most Foul* analyzes the focus on "body-horror" that increasingly undergirded accounts of violent crime and its pictorial representation throughout the nineteenth century. Similarly, David M. Stewart astutely attempts to trace the affective pleasures and enjoyment that nineteenth-century readers derived from the ubiquitous and often outrageous scenes of bodily violence and punishment in urban crime literature. See his "Cultural Work, City Crime."

34. McLean, *Rise and Fall of Anarchy in America*, 234–35.

35. Ibid., 231.

36. Foster, "Death in America," 42.

37. Lum, *Concise History of the Great Trial*, 172.

38. Hill, "Decisive Battles of the Law," 895.

39. Jeremy Green, "Disaster Footage," 575.

40. Schaack, *Anarchy and Anarchists*, 17–43. Subsequent page references are cited parenthetically in the text.

41. Apter, "Political Violence in Analytical Perspective," 13.

42. Hofstadter provides the classic statement on the history of American social and political paranoia in "The Paranoid Style in American Politics." The series of essays collected in the more recent volume, *Paranoia within Reason*, edited by George E. Marcus, extends Hofstadter's pioneering work into analyses of the ubiquity of conspiracy theories at the turn of the millennium.

On the fear of secret plots during the Revolutionary era, see Buel, *Securing the Revolution*, and Knox, *Conspiracy in American Politics*. On antebellum southern apprehensions concerning slave revolts, see Aptheker, *American Negro Slave Revolts;* Genovese, *From Rebellion to Revolution;* and, more recently, McKivigan and Harrold, *Antislavery Violence*.

43. Russell, "Haymarket and Afterwards," 405.

44. Qtd. in Avrich, *Haymarket Tragedy,* 222.

45. Frederick Ebersold, Schaack's police chief at the time of the investigation, told the *Chicago Times* in 1889 that the sedulous Schaack even went so far as to propose sending police agents out to form their own imitation anarchist cells that could then be broken up, with much publicity and fanfare, by other secret agents. See Donner, *Protectors of Privilege,* 15.

46. Avrich, *Haymarket Tragedy,* 223.

47. Donner, *Protectors of Privilege,* 14.

48. Joseba Zulaika and William A. Douglass have convincingly argued that such a rhetorical mélange of "fact" and "fiction" is typical of discussions about terrorism in general (*Terror and Taboo,* 4). But beyond this, the putatively ubiquitous conspiracy that Schaack and many others imagined as the source of the Haymarket bombing bizarrely—if only coincidentally—reproduced the plot of Émile Zola's 1885 novel, *Germinal.* Zola's book was, ironically enough, a particular favorite of America's anarchists, who translated, reprinted, and continually lauded it in their newspapers. In *Germinal,* the anarcho-terrorist Souvarine single-handedly destroys the mine where he works in a daring act of industrial terrorism. But the mining "Company had no idea who the real guilty party was; it came to suppose that there was a whole army of accomplices, since it seemed unbelievable that one lone man could have had the audacity and the strength to execute such a deed; and that in fact was the thought which obsessed the Company, this notion of a gradually growing threat to all of its pits" (477). As in Zola's fiction, Chicago's authorities, faced with a lack of knowledge and desiring to smash radicalism in the city, imagined the Haymarket bomb thrower as one point in a conspiratorial ring rather than as an individual agent. In Chicago, the "truth" put forth was indeed at least as strange as fiction, but more important, it again underscores how the sheer disruptive force of political violence often elicits the most complex and fantastic of possible explanations to account for its astonishing and shockingly random destruction.

49. Parsons, *Famous Speeches,* 78, 93, 95. Albert Parsons's brother later claimed to have evidence implicating the Pinkertons and further evidence showing that a *New York Star* reporter had been bribed to leave Chicago because he could prove a Pinkerton agent had thrown the bomb (Morn, *"The Eye that Never Sleeps,"* 99).

50. "Trial of the Chicago Anarchists," 313, 192, 33, 193, 83, 81. In his memoirs, the reporter Charles Edward Russell points out the dubiousness of this evidence. Many of the same bombs, he notes, were repeatedly planted and then "found" by the police (Russell, "Haymarket and Afterwards," 405).

51. On the *Tribune*'s role in the bomb scare, see, for instance, "Startling Evidence," *Chicago Tribune,* 11 May 1886, 2, and "The Dynamite Plot," *Chicago Tribune,* 24 May 1886, 1.

52. See "Anarchists Threaten Vengeance," *Chicago Tribune,* 3 November 1887, 2; "Running Down Rumors," *Chicago Tribune,* 8 November 1887, 1; and "Nervous at the Jail," *Chicago Tribune,* 10 November 1887, 3.

53. Russell, "Haymarket and Afterwards," 410.

54. Jones, *Autobiography of Mother Jones*, 22; Russell, "Haymarket and Afterwards," 411–12.

55. Russell, "Haymarket and Afterwards," 411.

56. "Bombs in Lingg's Cell," *Chicago Tribune*, 7 November 1887, 1. In Chicago's jittery state, these bombs appeared to be incontrovertible evidence of a terrorist conspiracy. But to the anarchists and their sympathizers who claimed that the police planted the explosives, the bombs represented just another conspiracy against them. As Lucy Parsons, Albert Parsons's wife, was quoted in the *Tribune* article detailing the cache of bombs found in Lingg's cell, "Of course the Police did it."

57. D. A. Miller, *Novel and the Police*, 164.

58. Richard Slotkin's groundbreaking *Regeneration through Violence* offered the initial and still most comprehensive account of how "the myth of regeneration through violence became the structuring metaphor of the American experience" more generally (5).

59. "Voice of the Press," *Chicago Tribune*, 9 May 1886, 6.

60. "The Un-Americanized Element," *Chicago Tribune*, 7 May 1886, 4; "Trial of the Chicago Anarchists," 175.

61. McLean, *Rise and Fall of Anarchy in America*, 12; "Trial of the Chicago Anarchists," 194.

62. "The Un-Americanized Element," 4; "Voice of the Press," 6.

63. "The Riot Comes to a Point," *Chicago Tribune*, 5 May 1886, 4.

64. "To the Workingmen of America," *The Alarm*, 4 October 1884, 3; Philip S. Foner, *Autobiographies of the Haymarket Martyrs*, 57; Parsons, *Famous Speeches*, 15.

65. "Enforce the Laws," *Chicago Tribune*, 5 May 1886, 4.

66. Writing in 1988 regarding American politics and Middle Eastern terrorism, Edward W. Said argued that this "denial and avoidance of history" is typical of terrorist discourse in late-twentieth-century America as well ("Essential Terrorist," 149).

67. Qtd. in Avrich, *Haymarket Tragedy*, 190.

68. Eric Sundquist has produced the fullest account of antebellum African Americans who imagined slave revolt as the truest expression of the Founding Fathers' ideas. See his *To Wake the Nations*, 27–134.

69. Carl Smith, *Urban Disorder*, 150. See also Slotkin, *Fatal Environment*, chap. 19. For a fascinating account of the links made between the urban and western frontiers in visual art of this period, see Nemerov, "Doing the 'Old America,'" esp. 297–303.

70. Editorial, *Chicago Tribune*, 9 May 1886, 4.

71. Carl Smith, *Urban Disorder*, 338.

72. State's Attorney Grinnell also made this point from the opposite direction at the trial when he compared the anarchists unfavorably to the Confederate rebellion: "The firing upon Fort Sumter was a terrible thing to our country, but it was open warfare. I think it was nothing compared with this insidious, infamous plot to ruin

our laws and our country secretly and in this cowardly way" ("Trial of the Chicago Anarchists," 29). The point, it would seem, is that those who are already ideologically identified as full citizens of the republic at least rebel openly, whereas one function of labeling anarchists and Indians as vile and sneaky cowards was to underscore the notion that they would never be allowed into the symbolic body politic.

73. Jacobson, *Whiteness of a Different Color*, 167. In addition to Jacobson's excellent study, the scholarly literature on the cultural construction of racial difference during the nineteenth century, particularly as it intersected with class distinction, has been voluminous in recent years. See especially Roediger's two volumes, *Wages of Whiteness* and *Towards the Abolition of Whiteness; Lott, Love and Theft;* and Saxton, *Rise and Fall of the White Republic*.

74. Doane, "Information, Crisis, Catastrophe," 233.

75. Dell, "Bomb-Talking," 74.

76. Derrida, "Signature Event Context," 12, emphasis original.

77. For details of this and other large demonstrations held in the years leading up to the Haymarket bombing, see Avrich, *Haymarket Tragedy*, 143–49, and Bruce C. Nelson, *Beyond the Martyrs,* chap. 6.

78. "They Want Blood," *Chicago Tribune,* 29 April 1885, 2.

79. Carl Smith, *Urban Disorder,* 115.

80. "The Butchers of Men," *The Alarm,* 15 November 1884, 1, emphasis original.

81. "Dynamite," *The Alarm,* 21 February 1885, 3.

82. "The Socialist," *The Alarm,* 25 October 1884, 2; "The Useless Classes," *The Alarm,* 1 November 1884, 2; "The Dynamite Terror," *The Alarm,* 21 February 1885, 2.

83. "Dynamite," *The Alarm,* 6 December 1884, 1. Joseph Conrad provided the most imaginative fictionalization of this trope in his 1907 novel, *The Secret Agent.* The anarchist professor in that book never leaves home without a bomb in his pocket, which keeps the police from approaching too closely.

84. Lucy Parsons, "A Word to Tramps," *The Alarm,* 4 October 1884, 1.

85. Qtd. in "Trial of the Chicago Anarchists," 86.

86. Most, "Advice for Terrorists," 104. Ironically, as far as is definitively known, this most extreme prophet of terror never actually engaged in a terrorist act himself. As with his less imaginative followers, dynamite for Most was almost as much a state of mind as a material fact.

87. Parsons, *Famous Speeches,* 82.

88. Zulaika and Douglass, *Terror and Taboo,* 76.

89. See Carl Smith, *Urban Disorder,* 115–18, and Avrich, *Haymarket Tragedy,* chap. 12.

90. Confino, *Daughter of a Revolutionary,* 230.

91. Qtd. in "Trial of the Chicago Anarchists," 108.

92. Parsons, *Famous Speeches,* 104.

93. Martin A. Miller, "Intellectual Origins of Modern Terrorism," 44, and Laqueur, *Age of Terrorism,* 56.

94. Avrich, *Haymarket Tragedy,* 171.

95. "The Anarchists' Record," *Chicago Tribune,* 12 November 1887, 9. Julius Lieske was beheaded in 1885 as punishment for assassinating Frankfurt-am-Main's chief of police (Avrich, *Haymarket Tragedy,* 172).

96. Parsons, *Famous Speeches,* 52.

97. "The Useless Classes," 2.

98. Avrich, *Haymarket Tragedy,* 173, and "They Want Blood."

Chapter Two

1. "Explosion on the Underground Railway," *London Times,* 31 October 1883, 10; "Explosion on the Metropolitan Railway," *London Times,* 3 January 1885, 5; "Dynamite Outrage at Victoria Station," *London Times,* 27 February 1884, 10; "Dynamite Outrages in London," *London Times,* 31 May 1884, 7.

2. Melchiori, *Terrorism in the Late Victorian Novel,* 1.

3. It is worth noting that, on the American side of the Atlantic, the conspiratorial imagination of Albert Parsons's *Alarm* hypothesized a police frame-up behind the London bombings: "The dynamite scare which has been going on in England for some time past, is likely to lead, eventually, to some very unexpected and very curious revelations. There is no doubt that the police force and especially the secret detective force of Scotland Yard is at the bottom of all the manipulations" ("Dynamite in London," *The Alarm,* 27 December 1884, 2).

4. Short, *Dynamite War,* 1. See esp. chaps. 1 and 7. Throughout the 1880s, however, the United States refused to turn over suspected terrorists to Great Britain for trial. It is a historical irony that at the turn of the twenty-first century America finds itself in a position in which it militarily and economically penalizes states that it believes harbor or train terrorists.

5. Melchiori, *Terrorism in the Late Victorian Novel,* 18.

6. Editorial, *London Times,* 15 December 1884, 9.

7. Melchiori, *Terrorism in the Late Victorian Novel,* 21.

8. Editorial, *London Times,* 26 January 1885, 9.

9. Harlow, *Thomas Sergeant Perry,* 318, emphasis original.

10. On this point, see Brodhead, *School of Hawthorne,* chap. 8.

11. Trilling, "*Princess Casamassima,*" 74; Cargill, "*Princess Casamassima,*" 97–105.

12. Stoehr, "Words and Deeds in *The Princess Casamassima,*" and Esch, "Promissory Notes," 319.

13. Seltzer, "*The Princess Casamassima,*" 97, 113.

14. Rowe, *Theoretical Dimensions of Henry James,* 165.

15. Blair, *Henry James and the Writing of Race and Nation,* chap. 3; Wendy Graham, *Henry James's Thwarted Love,* 179.

16. Sypher, *Wisps of Violence,* 27.

17. Ibid., 28.

18. Interpretations of the Princess have traditionally oscillated between a puni-

tive tone and sympathetic but nonplussed hand-wringing. On the side of those critics who condemn her, Donald David Stone identifies her as one of James's *"femme fatales"* (*Novelists in a Changing World,* 302); Lionel Trilling finds a self-hatred in her character and observes that "she constitutes a striking symbol of that powerful part of modern culture that exists by means of its claim to political innocence and by its false seriousness" (*"Princess Casamassima,"* 92). Irving Howe, on the other hand, praises the Princess as "the great triumph of the book" but goes on to claim, in a somewhat cryptic and backhanded recognition of the limits placed upon her in the culture of the 1880s, that she is "a woman who would be more than a woman" ("Henry James," 142).

19. Brodhead, *School of Hawthorne,* 143.

20. Edel and Powers, *Complete Notebooks of Henry James,* 20.

21. Sara Blair also draws this inference about the Princess en route to her argument about the "performative race work" of the novel (*Henry James and the Writing of Race and Nation,* 91–92).

22. Brodhead, *School of Hawthorne,* 144.

23. Edel, *Henry James Letters,* 28.

24. Ibid., 61.

25. James, preface to *The Princess Casamassima,* in *Art of the Novel,* 76.

26. Bell, *Meaning in Henry James,* 152–59.

27. Writers such as Peter Kropotkin, Sergey Nechayev, and the Haymarket anarchists regularly claimed that they had lost all faith in the word and that only violence could have a stable message, implying that the message of a bomb could be derived from a terrorist incident without ambiguity. But see the Introduction for a discussion of the ironies that are nonetheless implicit in such "propaganda by the deed."

28. James, preface to *The Princess Casamassima,* in *Art of the Novel,* 76, emphasis original.

29. James, preface to *The American,* in *Art of the Novel,* 31, emphasis original.

30. James, *Princess Casamassima,* 97. I have chosen to use the Penguin edition because it reprints the first (1886) edition of James's novel, rather than his revised New York edition of 1908. Subsequent page references are cited parenthetically in the text.

31. James's choice of artisanal rather than factory workers for Hyacinth and the book's other workers/anarchists has elicited much insightful commentary, starting with Lionel Trilling, who identified them as "an aristocracy of labor largely cut off from the mass of the workers" (*"Princess Casamassima,"* 71). More recently, using the scene in which Hyacinth takes his work home to bind a particularly beautiful book for the Princess, John Carlos Rowe has offered a brilliant riff on the woefully ironic way in which the "dignity and honor of the labor" became the reward for artisanal workers who were being squeezed out by mass production (*Theoretical Dimensions of Henry James,* 171). More critically, Mike Fischer indicts Hyacinth's pride in his finished product, arguing that Robinson "repeats the classic mistake of other artisans of his time" by reveling in individual virtuosity and forsaking community with

the mass of workers responsible for less glamorous tasks, such as making the book's paper and printing it ("Jamesian Revolution," 92).

32. See Scanlan, "Terrorism and the Realistic Novel," and Anesko, *"Friction with the Market,"* 109.

33. Schocket, "Undercover Explorations of the 'Other Half,'" 112.

34. Ibid., 120.

35. The Princess Casamassima and these nonfictional individuals share the trait of passing downward in the class system. While these narratives suggested the relative ease with which middle-class adventurers and social critics could insert themselves into the culture of the working classes, a far greater cause of anxiety in these decades was produced by the realization that mass production also made it possible for the lower classes to dress like and imitate wealthier persons. See Enstad's engaging *Ladies of Labor, Girls of Adventure.* This phenomenon was also dramatized at the turn of the century in a host of popular stories and essays appearing in newspapers and magazines, while the more canonical Theodore Dreiser made the signifying system of clothes and class identity a major concern in *Sister Carrie* and *An American Tragedy.*

36. Edel, *Henry James,* 318.

37. James, preface to *The Princess Casamassima,* in *Art of the Novel,* 59.

38. Edel, *Henry James Letters,* 97, 100, and Edel and Powers, *Complete Notebooks of Henry James,* 31.

39. Brodhead, *School of Hawthorne,* 157.

40. Zola, "Experimental Novel," 176.

41. Rowe, *Theoretical Dimensions of Henry James,* 181.

42. Much recent and valuable scholarly attention has been directed at deconstructing the nineteenth-century notion of "separate spheres" of men's and women's activities, which the Princess's desire to commit a public act of terrorism also contradicts. See, especially, the 1998 special issue of *American Literature,* titled "No More Separate Spheres!"; Davidson's "Preface: No More Separate Spheres!"; and Kerber's informative review essay, "Separate Spheres, Female Worlds, Woman's Place."

43. An article entitled "Russia" that appeared in the 14 October 1884 *London Times* offers a case in point. Describing an "important political trial of 14 Nihilists," the author quickly draws readers' attention to "three women, first the good-looking and remarkably intelligent Figner, *alias* Vera Filipava, who has been one of the moving spirits in nearly every plot and attempt at political assassination since 1878" (5).

44. On the gender anxiety produced by the "New Woman," the literature is lengthy. See especially Carroll Smith-Rosenberg's foundational work, "The New Woman as Androgyne," and Patricia Marks's study of popular culture's reactions to women's changing roles, *Bicycles, Bangs, and Bloomers.*

45. Carl Smith, *Urban Disorder,* 160–62.

46. Schaack, *Anarchy and Anarchists,* 207. For a detailed discussion of the derogatory racialization of anarchists that is also at stake here, see Chapter 1.

47. On Lucy Parsons's life, see Ashbaugh, *Lucy Parsons.*

48. "Subterranean Russia," 215; "The Attempted Assassination of Captain Katansky," *London Times*, 4 September 1884, 5.

49. Stepniak, "Female Nihilist," 501.

50. Ibid., 512.

51. Rowe, *Theoretical Dimensions of Henry James*, 172.

52. Ibid.

53. Stepniak, "Female Nihilist," 510.

54. For two important readings of *Princess* that closely examine the role of Hyacinth's spontaneous revolutionary vow, see Esch, "Promissory Notes," and Stoehr, "Words and Deeds."

55. James, *Roderick Hudson*, 317, 187. Subsequent page references are cited parenthetically in the text.

56. Wendy Graham, *Henry James's Thwarted Love*, 190.

57. Hugh Stevens has also added to interpretations of Hyacinth's sexuality by focusing, more than Graham, on the irreducible ambiguity at stake in James's bookbinder. For Stevens, the novel's "delicate young protoqueer" embodies the "discrepancies resulting from the circulation of same-sex desires in a social space in which such desires have no recognition" (Stevens, *Henry James and Sexuality*, 107, 104).

58. Sypher, *Wisps of Violence*, 28, 39.

59. Ibid., 28.

60. Warner, "Mass Public and the Mass Subject," 240–41.

61. John Carlos Rowe offers an alternative interpretation of Hoffendahl's invisibility. According to Rowe, as long as Hoffendahl's followers "are ordered to act as representatives of some invisible, latent order of things, then revolution becomes merely a version of 'radical chic,'" and the dissidents "represent nothing so much as the power of control, ideological repression, that not only permits them to exist but has in a very real sense 'invented' them as characters" (Rowe, *Theoretical Dimensions of Henry James*, 175). Operating from a Greenblattian notion that power is most effective when it produces its own subversive elements so as to contain them, Rowe, I think, misses the point of Hoffendahl's invisibility. Were Hoffendahl a visible antagonist, then he would not have the disconcerting power derived from his radical unpredictability. Invisibility is the source of the terrorist's power, not the mark of his or her co-optation by a cynical government apparatus.

62. The late 1996 takeover of the Japanese ambassador's residence in Lima, Peru, by the Túpac Amaru terrorist group provides a recent example of this phenomenon. After the residence was stormed and the rebels killed, the Peruvian government initially refused to release the bodies of the terrorists to their survivors for burial. Fearing that public display of the bodies would exacerbate a movement to martyr the dead terrorists, the government hoped to short-circuit the production of antigovernment narratives by keeping the bodies invisible to Peruvian citizens. See Calvin Sims, "Peru Hears Report Some Rebels Were Slain Trying to Surrender," *New York Times*, 25 April 1997, A1, and Diana Jean Schemo, "As a Rebel's Path Ends, Hard Turf but Soft Hearts," *New York Times*, 29 April 1997, A4.

Chapter Three

1. On this aptly named "decade of the bomb" in Europe, see Martin A. Miller, "Intellectual Origins of Modern Terrorism," 46–47.

2. James, *Princess Casamassima,* 243.

3. Qtd. in Roediger, "Strange Legacies," 95, emphasis original.

4. As Eric Foner has written, the 1872 Colfax, Louisiana, massacre exemplified the danger for blacks if they defended themselves. Blacks in Colfax, fearing that southern whites would use violence to "redeem" the local government, held the small town for three weeks until whites finally used rifles and a cannon to overpower them. Over fifty black citizens who had already surrendered were then massacred (Eric Foner, *Reconstruction,* 437).

Several decades after Colfax, however, W. E. B. Du Bois fictionalized a scenario in which blacks respond to lynching with dynamite in his underread 1928 novel, *Dark Princess.* In that book, a black Pullman porter is wrongly lynched after a wealthy white woman cries rape when her attempt to seduce him is unexpectedly interrupted. In response, a radical West Indian, Miguel Perigua, tells the book's black hero, Matthew Towns, that there is a "lynching belt" in the South, and "we'll blow it to hell with dynamite from airplanes" because "terrorism, revenge, is our program" (46). Perigua ultimately attempts to dynamite a specially chartered train carrying Klansmen to a national meeting but only succeeds in blowing himself up.

5. On the other hand, the reason southern whites did not turn to dynamite in their attacks against blacks is also a perplexing question, since dynamite was the sine qua non of weapons designed to terrorize in this period. However, because dynamite was the weapon that the country's least (economically) powerful citizens clung to with an incredible intensity in these years, it became, symbolically, the weapon of desperation wielded by the state's dispossessed. In Thomas Dixon's fiction, discussed below, the marauding whites, especially the Ku Klux Klan, were functioning as something like semiofficial agents of the state. This would make a turn to dynamite by the KKK, in Dixon at least, symbolically paradoxical if not incoherent.

6. Qtd. in Philip S. Foner, *American Socialism and Black Americans,* 81.

7. Ironically, in Henry James's *Princess Casamassima,* the principal revolutionary, Paul Muniment, works as a chemist, yet this whiff of a possible relation to bombmaking is left completely unelaborated. Though he is a close associate of the novel's chief terrorist, Diedrich Hoffendahl, Muniment is never connected in any way with the 1880s culture of bombs.

8. Qtd. in Philip S. Foner, *American Socialism and Black Americans,* 81.

9. Ibid., 80, my emphasis.

10. Roediger, "Strange Legacies," 95.

11. Vološinov, *Marxism and the Philosophy of Language,* 23, emphasis original. Of course, a word such as "terrorist"—and the words that cluster around it, such as "freedom fighter" or "criminal"—exemplifies Vološinov's point. The notion of a terrorist is a highly politicized identity that is claimed or unclaimed at particular his-

torical moments for specific and differing reasons and takes on its most contradictory senses in times of the greatest unrest.

12. Wells, *Southern Horrors,* 50. Subsequent page references are cited parenthetically in the text and are indicated by the abbreviation *SH.*

13. Dixon, *Leopard's Spots,* unnumbered prefatory page. Subsequent page references are cited parenthetically in the text and are indicated by the abbreviation *LS.*

14. Dixon, *Clansman,* 1. Subsequent page references are cited parenthetically in the text and are indicated by the abbreviation *C.*

15. Williamson, *Crucible of Race,* 141.

16. Wells, *Red Record,* 81. Subsequent page references are cited parenthetically in the text and are indicated by the abbreviation *RR.*

17. As Dixon wrote after he completed *The Leopard's Spots,* "I have made no effort to write literature. I had no ambition to shine as a literary gymnast. It has always seemed to me a waste of time to do such work. Every generation writes its own literature. My sole purpose in writing was to reach and influence with my argument the minds of millions. I had a message and I wrote it as vividly and simply as I knew how" (qtd. in Cook, *Thomas Dixon,* 52).

18. Dixon, it should be noted, would have denied this assertion. As he wrote in a 1905 *Saturday Evening Post* article, "I have for the Negro race only pity and sympathy. . . . As a friend of the Negro race I claim that he should have the opportunity for the highest, noblest and freest development of his full, rounded manhood. He has never had this opportunity in America, either North or South, and he never can have it. The forces against him are overwhelming" ("Booker T. Washington and the Negro," 1). Of course, it goes without saying that Dixon here omits the violent reasons behind that lack of opportunity. Dixon's articulation of his own position on racial matters was also strangely borne out on the cover of the first edition of *The Leopard's Spots.* When Doubleday printed a hangman's noose on the cover instead of the tobacco leaf against a red background that Dixon had designed, he was, astonishingly enough, shocked and horrified. He ordered the publisher to burn the 15,000 copies that had already been printed, but this could not be done because they had been sold in advance (Dickson, introduction to *The Reconstruction Trilogy,* xiii).

19. Cook, *Thomas Dixon,* 75.

20. Dixon, *Traitor,* 52. Subsequent page references are cited parenthetically in the text and are indicated by the abbreviation *T.*

21. Chesnutt, *Marrow of Tradition,* 84. Subsequent page references are cited parenthetically in the text. Chesnutt's Wellington riot fictionalizes the 1898 coup d'état in Wilmington, North Carolina. In the days leading up to the 10 November riot, Wilmington's white citizens had become incensed at an editorial written by Alexander Manly, the editor of a local black-owned newspaper. In response to racist propaganda describing the sexual threat black men purportedly posed for white women, Manly had suggested that interracial sexual relations were more often consensual. When the white Democratic Party then swept the elections on 8 November and "redeemed" the local government, Wilmington's inflamed and hostile white popula-

tion decided not to wait for the transfer of governmental power that would come in the spring. Manly's newspaper offices were burned by a mob, prominent African American citizens, including Manly, were forced to flee the town, the Republican mayor was compelled to resign, black-owned businesses and churches were destroyed, and several African Americans lost their lives. For further historical details of the Wilmington riot, see Prather, *We Have Taken a City*, and Sundquist, *To Wake the Nations*, 406–54.

22. Samira Kawash brilliantly theorizes the emptiness of race as either a biological or a cultural concept and suggests that race is instead an arbitrarily drawn line in her *Dislocating the Color Line*.

23. See, for instance, the 1898 Mississippi voting rights case, *Williams v. Mississippi*, in which the Supreme Court agreed that African Americans had certain definable and categorizable traits that went deeper than skin color.

24. SallyAnn Ferguson, "*MELUS* Forum: Charles W. Chesnutt's 'Future American,'" 107. Ferguson's article reprints all three of Chesnutt's articles, which originally appeared in the *Boston Evening Transcript*, 18 August 1900, 20; 25 August 1900, 15; and 1 September 1900, 24, respectively.

25. SallyAnn Ferguson, "*MELUS* Forum: Charles W. Chesnutt's 'Future American,'" 107, 99.

26. Stowe, *Uncle Tom's Cabin*, 398.

27. Eric Foner, *Reconstruction*, 230.

28. For a historical discussion of the Union Leagues, see ibid., esp. 281–345.

29. Writing concurrently with Dixon, Charles Chesnutt specifically describes the violent disfranchisement of blacks as "terrorism" in *Marrow of Tradition* (240).

30. Gunning, *Race, Rape, and Lynching*, 40.

31. Rubenstein, *Rebels in Eden*, 28.

32. Hodes, "Sexualization of Reconstruction Politics," 405. Hodes provides an excellent analysis of the intersection of sex and politics in the Reconstruction South, arguing for "a definition of politics that is broad enough to encompass traditional acts of citizenship and authority . . . and, at the same time, the power of sexual agency" (415). My account of the Ku Klux Klan is drawn largely from Eric Foner, *Reconstruction*, 425–59. On the KKK, see also Trelease, *White Terror*, and Wade, *Fiery Cross*.

33. Trelease, *White Terror*, 383.

34. Qtd. in Eric Foner, *Reconstruction*, 455.

35. Michaels, *Our America*, 16–17.

36. Ibid., 22–23.

37. Indeed, in 1790, as if to cement the color privilege of a Constitution that had already counted black slaves as only partial persons, the first Congress convened under the new Constitution voted that a person must be "white" in order to become a naturalized citizen of the United States (Roediger, *Towards the Abolition of Whiteness*, 181).

38. Berlant, "National Brands/National Body," 113. On the relationship between

the abstract white male body and citizenship, see also Young, "Polity and Group Difference," and Norton, *Reflections on Political Identity*.

39. Michaels, "Souls of White Folk," 190.

40. Though I am focusing on the vagaries of publicity and invisibility in Dixon's KKK, Judith Jackson Fossett offers a different and very incisive interpretation of a contradiction embodied in the surprising combination of "white" violence and "darkness" symbolized by the Klan's sheets. Fossett argues that the white sheets of the Klan are always already "corrupted" by blackness, since the cotton used in the disguises was most likely planted, harvested, and processed by southern blacks: "Despite its brighter-than-white appearance in the fields, cotton grown according to American agricultural, racial, and labor practices can *never be white*" ("[K]night Riders in [K]night Gowns," 42, emphasis original).

41. Eric Foner, *Reconstruction*, 432; Trelease, *White Terror*, 52.

42. Rubenstein, *Rebels in Eden*, 28.

43. Eric Foner, *Reconstruction*, 435.

44. I am not suggesting that, historically speaking, the KKK of the immediate postwar years was not itself also exemplary of some of the most egregious mob violence in American history. Rather, I am arguing that it is precisely in the discrepancy between the mob violence of the Klan and the very different manner in which Dixon depicts it that we can see the ideological architecture of his racial writing.

45. Williamson, *Crucible of Race*, 185. For the best explanatory study of lynching, which combines the quantitative analysis of the social sciences with a rhetorically sensitive qualitative analysis, see Tolnay and Beck, *Festival of Violence*. Tolnay and Beck's work fleshes out Williamson's point about executions. According to their research, southern blacks during the "lynching era" (as well as presently) were also far more likely to be legally executed than whites: 81 percent of legal executions in the South between 1882 and 1930 involved a black offender (*Festival of Violence*, 100). Though a causation is less easy to establish than the readily apparent correlation, it is within the domain of such statistics that the gruesome cultural work of Dixon's fiction is most apparent. That is, we should probably not be surprised at the grim overlap between "legal" and "illegal" murders of African Americans in an era in which Dixon's version of race relations reached best-seller status.

46. Williamson, *Crucible of Race*, 185–86.

47. Hodes, "Sexualization of Reconstruction Politics," 409–10.

48. Gunning, *Race, Rape, and Lynching*, 39.

49. McMath, *American Populism*, 205–6.

50. Michaels, *Our America*, 20.

51. As David Roediger has written, "Working class formation and the systematic development of a sense of whiteness went hand in hand for the US white working class" (*Wages of Whiteness*, 8).

52. Ayers, *Promise of the New South*, 105. See also Woodward's classic account of the South's colonial economy, *Origins of the New South*, and Wright, *Old South, New*

South. Furthermore, Covington Hall, the radical editor, poet, and Industrial Workers of the World organizer whose work I discuss in Chapter 5, regularly described the South as a foreign colony under control of the American government and, more particularly, government-backed corporations. As Hall put it in an article titled "Southern Conditions," written from the "colonized" South and published in the September 1919 *One Big Union Monthly,* "I see that the *The Monthly* wants news from all foreign countries, so I thought the editor might be interested in a few items from the strange Land of Dixie" (reprinted in Hall, *Labor Struggles in the Deep South,* 214).

53. Ayers, *Promise of the New South,* 105.

54. Holt, "Lonely Warrior"; Carby, *Reconstructing Womanhood,* 108.

55. See Schechter, "'All the Intensity of My Nature,'" and *Ida B. Wells-Barnett and American Reform.*

56. See, however, two excellent works that focus exclusively on, and offer incisive analyses of, Wells's rhetorical style. Shirley Wilson Logan explains how Wells marshals descriptive passages to achieve a "presence" in her antilynching writing (*"We Are Coming,"* chap. 4), and Simone W. Davis shows how Wells uses conventional binary oppositions prevalent in American culture in order to gain authority but also simultaneously undercuts such binaries to subvert the stereotypical ideologies they support ("'Weak Race'").

57. Schechter, "Unsettled Business," 293.

58. Wells herself details this crime in *A Red Record,* where she also writes that her research into the case indicated that Smith was mentally impaired (96).

59. Gunning, *Race, Rape, and Lynching,* 87.

60. Simone W. Davis, "'Weak Race,'" 83.

61. On the various methods used to prevent black men from voting, see Franklin and Moss, *From Slavery to Freedom,* 254–63.

62. Eric Foner, *Reconstruction,* 524–34.

63. Ibid., 404–9.

64. Carby, *Reconstructing Womanhood,* 112.

65. Gail Bederman provides a sophisticated analysis of how Wells's antilynching campaign links the trope of "civilization" and late-nineteenth-century anxieties about the demise of masculinity. See "'Civilization.'"

66. Twain, "United States of Lyncherdom," 678, emphasis original.

Chapter Four

1. Johnston, *Jack London,* 120.

2. Working from the unfinished manuscript and notes found among London's papers, Robert L. Fish completed *The Assassination Bureau* and published it along with "Jack London's Notes for the Completion of the Book" and the "Ending as Outlined by Charmian London" in the fall of 1963.

3. Pease, introduction to *The Assassination Bureau,* viii.

4. For a perceptive account of how London's biography has often overwhelmed critical interpretations of his work, see Auerbach, *Male Call,* 4–5.

5. Labor and Reesman, *Jack London,* 24.

6. Lukas, *Big Trouble,* 64. In addition to Lukas's sweeping book, which beautifully weaves Steunenberg's assassination into a rich tapestry of class antagonism and cultural history but, I believe, goes beyond its evidence in implying the WFM defendants' guilt, my account of the assassination and subsequent trial are drawn from Carlson, *Roughneck,* 86–135, and Dubofsky, *We Shall Be All,* 96–105. For generally anti-Haywood, anti-WFM versions of the assassination and trial, see Grover, *Debaters and Dynamiters,* and Holbrook, *Rocky Mountain Revolution.*

7. On the Molly Maguires and McParland's involvement with them, see Kenny's brilliant *Making Sense of the Molly Maguires.*

8. Qtd. in Carlson, *Roughneck,* 108.

9. Supreme Court Justice Joseph McKenna was the lone dissenter. He wrote that "kidnapping is a crime, pure and simple. . . . All of the officers of the law are supposed to be on guard against it. But how is it when the law becomes the kidnapper, when the officers of the law, using its forms and exerting its power, become abductors?" (*Pettibone v. Nichols,* 218).

10. Philip S. Foner, *Jack London,* 86.

11. London, "Something Rotten in Idaho," 407.

12. London, *Iron Heel,* 397. Subsequent page references are cited parenthetically in the text.

13. Anderson, *Imagined Communities,* 35–36.

14. London, "Something Rotten in Idaho," 409–10.

15. Ibid., 410, 407–8.

16. Ibid., 407.

17. Philip S. Foner, *Jack London,* 68.

18. London, "Revolution," 1150, emphasis original.

19. Lukas, *Big Trouble,* 62.

20. Johnston, *Jack London,* 116.

21. The two quoted phrases are from, respectively, "Real Anarchist," 780, and Oswald, "Assassination Mania," 314.

22. Post, "Terrorist Psycho-logic," 25.

23. For a theoretical analysis proposing terrorism as a strategic choice, see Crenshaw, "Logic of Terrorism."

24. Oswald, "Assassination Mania," 315.

25. Lenin, *What Is to Be Done?,* 75.

26. Rubenstein, *Alchemists of Revolution,* 171.

27. Lenin, "Why the Social Democrats Must Declare War," 210, emphasis original.

28. Labor, Leitz, and Shepard, *Letters of Jack London,* 2:676.

29. Ibid., 728.

30. Qtd. in Johnston, *Jack London*, 140.

31. Martyn J. Lee, *Consumer Culture Reborn*, 68–72. See also Aglietta, *Theory of Capitalist Regulation*.

32. Like many elements of *The Iron Heel*, this aspect can be read somewhat allegorically in terms of the era's conflict between the radical, generally itinerant, often unskilled, uneducated, and immigrant members of the Industrial Workers of the World, which aimed to organize all producers regardless of skill, race, or gender, and the generally more respectable members of the American Federation of Labor (AFL), which sought to protect some workers' privilege at the expense of others by organizing along strict craft lines. Perhaps not surprisingly, *The Iron Heel* was wildly popular among IWW members, who routinely denigrated the AFL as the "American Separation of Labor." The IWW predicted disastrous results for the labor movement if it followed the AFL's path, and London's fiction appeared to justify such forebodings.

33. See Philip S. Foner, *Jack London*, 97; Lerner, introduction to *The Iron Heel*, ix–xi; and France, Preface to *The Iron Heel*.

34. See Chapter 5 for a discussion of the IWW and sabotage, as well as the schism within the Socialist Party that developed over this form of violence.

35. Qtd. in Johnston, *Jack London*, 130.

36. Redding, *Raids on Human Consciousness*, 111.

37. See Johnston, *Jack London*.

38. Redding, *Raids on Human Consciousness*, 109, 110.

39. In his introduction to London's *The Assassination Bureau*, Donald Pease finds that an "erasure of the differences between violent crime and the law" (xxvi) also runs throughout what, on first glance, seems to be that strikingly different novel. London's fascination with the cultural politics of violence, however, knits together his more famous dystopian novel and the seldom read *Bureau*.

40. London, "Minions of Midas," 435. Subsequent page references are cited parenthetically in the text.

41. Beniger, *Control Revolution*, 344–46.

42. Schmid and de Graaf, *Violence as Communication*, 9–14.

43. Auerbach, *Male Call*, 126.

44. "Scent Nation-Wide Terrorist Plot," *New York Times*, 1 January 1919, 13.

45. Reading the newspaper clippings following these bombings during the summer of 1919 is an object lesson in the history of Americans' anxiety about terrorism, for the press reports exude a sense that citizens were extremely fearful that more bombings could and almost certainly would occur anytime and anywhere. In this regard, they provide an important historical corrective to the reporting of terrorist outrages in America during the last several years, which all too often, and all too erroneously, focused on terrorism's supposed "newness," the sense that it had finally happened in America, where terrorism supposedly could not happen.

46. "Postal Officials Begin Wide Search," *New York Times*, 1 May 1919, 3.

47. "The Bomb Plot," *New York Times,* 2 May 1919, 12, and "The Bomb Conspirators," *New York Times,* 4 June 1919, 14.

48. The forged Gimbels wrappers were also responsible for one of the stranger elements of this case. The ornamental red paper used to seal the packages meant that the packages would have to go first class, but the bombers had not affixed sufficient postage for this. Consequently, fourteen of the bombs were later discovered in a New York post office, where the packages had been casually set aside for insufficient postage and therefore never sent through the mails. See "Bomb Plot."

49. Labor, Leitz, and Shepard, *Letters of Jack London,* 3:1384. On London's production, see also Christopher P. Wilson, *Labor of Words,* 96–101, and Auerbach, *Male Call.*

50. As London wrote to Elwyn Hoffman in 1900, "I'm damned if my stories just come to me. I had to work like the devil for the themes. Then, of course, it was easy to just write them down. Expression, you see — with me — is far easier than invention" (Labor, Leitz, and Shepard, *Letters of Jack London,* 1:194–95).

51. Ibid., 2:933.

52. Ibid., 3:1384.

53. Ibid., 2:1059.

54. London, *Assassination Bureau,* 26. Subsequent page references are cited parenthetically in the text.

55. Avrich, preface to *Bakunin on Anarchy,* xxv.

56. Bakunin, "Revolution, Terrorism, Banditry," 67–68, emphasis original.

57. Nye, *Henry Ford,* 71.

58. On the vogue of exoticism in the twentieth century's first decades, see William Leach, *Land of Desire,* 104–11.

59. Williams, *Marxism and Literature,* 112–13.

60. Generating consent is favored over coercion not least because the display of naked power, as in the government-sanctioned kidnapping of "Big Bill" Haywood and his cohorts, invites resistance, such as London's article and the groundswell of popular support for the illegally detained men.

61. Trachtenberg, *Incorporation of America,* 84.

62. Weber, *Economy and Society,* 975, 992, emphasis original.

63. "Trusts and Confidences," 380.

64. Pease, introduction to *The Assassination Bureau,* xxv.

65. In this regard, London's imagined Assassination Bureau not only evokes the corporate trusts of his era but also spectacularly prefigures the American Central Intelligence Agency (CIA) (ibid., xix). Created in 1947, the CIA has a long and by now well-documented history of coups, countercoups, and assassinations, all processed through a massive bureaucracy that has made it nearly impenetrable to external investigators over the last half-century. Indeed, it could even be argued that the CIA's history of covertly overthrowing governments thought hostile to American interests, such as in Iran and Guatemala during the 1950s, represents another

dimension of a terrorist identity in America that is explicitly tied to the bureaucratic nation-state.

Within the realm of fiction, Don DeLillo has made these connections between the state, the terrorist CIA, and corporations explicit. In *Libra,* his fictional account of John F. Kennedy's assassination, the CIA is routinely referred to as the "company." Furthermore, linking corporations with state terrorism, DeLillo writes that "when the Agency wanted to do something interesting in Kurdistan or Yemen, it filed for incorporation in Delaware. . . . Parmenter himself could not always tell where the Agency left off and the corporations began" (*Libra,* 125–26).

66. Trachtenberg, *Incorporation of America,* 84.

67. On the cult of efficiency in business, government, and literature during the Progressive Era, see Tichi, *Shifting Gears,* 75–96.

68. Labor and Leitz, "Jack London on Alexander Berkman," 451, 452, 454.

69. The quoted phrases are from Weber, *Economy and Society,* 975.

70. Concerning Nietzsche's influence on London, see Bridgwater, *Nietzsche in Anglosaxony,* 163–70, and Dunford, "Further Notes."

71. Labor, Leitz, and Shepard, *Letters of Jack London,* 3:1513.

72. Pease, introduction to *The Assassination Bureau,* xxiv, xxvi.

Chapter Five

1. Abbott, "Danger Ahead," 53, 54.

2. In November 1911, the *Times* erected a monument memorializing the bombing's "victims of conspiracy, dynamite and fire: The Crime of the Century" (Stimson, *Rise of the Labor Movement,* 366).

3. Woehlke, "Terrorism in America," 359.

4. Ibid., 362–63.

5. Ibid., 364.

6. Fine, "National Erectors' Association," 6.

7. Fine, *"Without Blare of Trumpets,"* 86–87.

8. Burns, *Masked War,* 41.

9. McManigal, *National Dynamite Plot,* 81.

10. "Dynamiting as a Profession," 600.

11. Simmel, "Stranger," 407.

12. In a lengthy essay written for *Survey* magazine at the close of the dynamite conspiracy trial, John A. Fitch exclaimed, in the familiar truth-is-stranger-than-fiction paradigm often used to process and make sense of mass violence, "Only corroborative evidence and the almost unbelievable acts of other defendants, proven to have taken place, would avail to convince one of the truth of [McManigal's] story which, had it been written out instead of lived, would have been too lacking in plausibility to find a publisher. Think of checking a suit case full of dynamite in a railroad station!" ("The Dynamite Case," 609).

13. Fine, *"Without Blare of Trumpets,"* 88.

14. McManigal, *National Dynamite Plot,* 76.

15. Fine, *"Without Blare of Trumpets,"* 97, 102.

16. In "Murder Is Murder," Roosevelt denounced the "cowardly infamy" of dynamite (13), while the *Independent* commissioned an article from the imprisoned Harry Orchard. Orchard's "Violence in Labor Disputes" lamented the conspiratorial ways of labor organizations and offered himself as a sad example of someone who unwittingly was trapped in the maelstrom of labor violence (389).

17. Almost immediately after the bombing, labor activists in Los Angeles put forth an alternative theory for the explosion. Noting that for several weeks prior to the blast *Times* employees had complained of gas leaks, and that workers had remarked upon especially severe gas odors on the night of the explosion, unionists argued that the blast was a tragic accident precipitated by Otis's negligence. Dubious labor leaders also pointed out that, in another suspicious circumstance, the *Times* lost no valuable records in the immense conflagration that followed the explosion. Moreover, no executives, managers, or editors had been in the building at the time of the explosion. These coincidences prompted some labor leaders to suggest that Otis had intentionally destroyed the building ("Concerning the 'Times' Explosion," *Industrial Worker,* 19 October 1910, 1; Stimson, *Rise of the Labor Movement,* 367–68; Adamic, *Dynamite,* 212).

18. For details on this trial, see Fine, *"Without Blare of Trumpets,"* 118–25.

19. Woehlke, "Terrorism in America," 364; "Government by Dynamite," 63.

20. Burns, *Masked War,* 15, 30, 31, 11.

21. Zulaika and Douglass, *Terror and Taboo,* 141.

22. Burns, *Masked War,* 40.

23. "Union Leaders Arrested for Bomb Outrage," *New York Times,* 23 April 1911, 1; Burns, *Masked War,* 30.

24. Shapiro, "McNamara Case," 71.

25. "More Los Angeles Police," *New York Times,* 25 April 1911, 2.

26. On the lengthy struggle to have corporations understood as legal persons, see Howard Jay Graham, *Everyman's Constitution,* chap. 9.

27. Burns, *Masked War,* 11.

28. Both this phrase and "gigantic trust," in the preceding paragraph, are from a January 1910 editorial in *Bridgemen's Magazine,* qtd. in Shapiro, "McNamara Case," 73.

29. "Black Hand Methods in Unionism," *New York Times,* 2 October 1910, 12.

30. "Dynamiting as a Profession," 600.

31. "Government by Dynamite," 63.

32. McManigal, *National Dynamite Plot,* 71, 86.

33. Adamic, *Dynamite,* 216.

34. Ibid., 246; McManigal, *National Dynamite Plot,* 90.

35. "James B. McNamara's Confession," *New York Times,* 2 December 1911, 1. In yet another fascinating instance of the repetitions and imitations that traverse the distance between representation and reality in the discourse of terrorism, this notion of

a terrorist bomb exploding at the wrong time has provided the fulcrum of two important novels written at either end of the twentieth century, Joseph Conrad's 1907 *The Secret Agent* and Doris Lessing's 1985 *The Good Terrorist*. In both books, the mistimed explosion underscores the naïveté of would-be terrorists who are essentially playing at being radicals. Paul Auster's 1992 novel, *Leviathan,* uses this trope somewhat differently, opening with a terrorist accidentally blowing himself up while making one of the bombs he uses to destroy small-town replicas of the Statue of Liberty throughout America. For Auster, the sheer materiality of the explosion sets off an existential meditation on male friendship, sexuality, and intimacy.

36. Enstad, "Fashioning Political Identities," 774.

37. "Believe Dynamite Launch Is Found," *New York Times,* 5 October 1910, 2.

38. Stimson, *Rise of the Labor Movement,* 375–76.

39. Zulaika and Douglass, *Terror and Taboo,* 130.

40. Qtd. in Fine, *"Without Blare of Trumpets,"* 98.

41. Ibid., 99.

42. Burns, *Masked War,* 299; "Burns, Here, Tells of Dynamite Plots," *New York Times,* 8 May 1911, 3; Fine, *"Without Blare of Trumpets,"* 99.

43. Fine, *"Without Blare of Trumpets,"* 99.

44. McManigal, *National Dynamite Plot,* 9.

45. Ibid., 9, 15, 29, 32.

46. For an elaboration of this idea, see Chapter 1's discussion of the Haymarket bombing.

47. "Direct Action," 420.

48. Fine, *"Without Blare of Trumpets,"* 109–10.

49. McManigal, *National Dynamite Plot,* 59.

50. Ibid., 36.

51. "Sabotage," 915; "Frankensteins of Civilization," 1434–35; "Lawlessness and Sabotage," 792.

52. Veblen, "On the Nature and Uses of Sabotage," 341.

53. Thompson, *The I.W.W.,* 80.

54. "Sabotage, 'Sab Cats,' and the 'One Big Union,'" 58; "What the I.W.W. Black Cat and Wooden Shoe Emblems Mean," 70; Browne, "Bolshevism in America," 710–13.

Within the literary realm, Eugene O'Neill ironically dramatized this supposed connection between the IWW and terrorism in his 1921 play, *The Hairy Ape.* In one scene, the befuddled protagonist, Yank, seeks out an IWW local assembly and offers his services as a saboteur of capitalism: "Dynamite! Blow it offen de oith—steel—all de cages—all de factories, steamers, buildings, jails—de Steel Trust and all dat makes it go." But Yank delivers his proposal so clumsily that the IWW members assume he must be an "agent provocator" sent by "Burns or Pinkerton"; one member even tells Yank, "You're such a bonehead I'll bet you're in the Secret Service" (158–59).

55. Giovannitti, "Syndicalism," 211.

56. Kipnis, *American Socialist Movement*, 392.

57. Ibid., 403.

58. "Trend," 909.

59. Thompson, *The I.W.W.*, 87–88.

60. Qtd. in ibid., 85.

61. Dubofsky, *We Shall Be All*, 160–63.

62. Trautman, *Direct Action and Sabotage*, 28, 32.

63. Kornbluh, *Rebel Voices*, 38.

64. Dowell, *History of Criminal Syndicalism Legislation in the United States*, 36.

65. Thompson, *The I.W.W.*, 86.

66. Qtd. in Dubofsky, *We Shall Be All*, 161.

67. Trautman, *Direct Action and Sabotage*, 54.

68. Qtd. in Dubofsky, *We Shall Be All*, 161.

69. Flynn, *Sabotage*, 95, 120.

70. *Industrial Worker*, 12 June 1913, 2.

71. Hampton, *Guerrilla Minstrels*, 61.

72. Joe Hill, "The Preacher and the Slave," *I.W.W. Songs*, 36.

73. Salerno, *Red November, Black November*, 130.

74. Shorty, "The Kitten in the Wheat," reprinted in Kornbluh, *Rebel Voices*, 61.

75. Walker C. Smith, *Sabotage*, 75.

76. Ralph Chaplin, "That Sabo-Tabby Kitten," reprinted in Kornbluh, *Rebel Voices*, 59.

77. In an interesting historical irony, an advertisement for "Cat's Paw" shoes appears on the same page as the *Literary Digest* article about IWW language. The advertisement features the Cat's Paw Shoe Company's symbol, an arched-back black cat, and also depicts a laborer standing on the skeleton of a half-built skyscraper. Inadvertently blending representations of two radical unions, the IABSIW and the IWW, the ad demonstrates the surprising continuities between capitalist advertising and revolutionary symbology in this era. For an informative discussion of the IWW's reciprocal relationship with capitalism, see Van Wienen, *Partisans and Poets*, 95–102.

78. Joe Hill, "The Rebel's Toast," reprinted in Kornbluh, *Rebel Voices*, 57.

79. The cartoon, "Direct Action Makes Capitalism See Stars," appeared on the front page of the 6 February 1913 issue of the *Industrial Worker*.

80. Salerno, introduction to *Direct Action and Sabotage*, 5.

81. Joe Hill, "Scissor Bill," *I.W.W. Songs*, 17.

82. Hebdige, *Subculture*, 1–19.

83. Van Wienen, *Partisans and Poets*, 89.

84. See *Industrial Worker*, 23 February 1911, 2, and 27 July 1911, 4.

85. Bubka, "Time to Organize!," 21.

86. Van Wienen, *Partisans and Poets*, 95–98.

87. Lecercle, *Violence of Language*, 211.

88. Shorty, "Stick 'Em Up: Song for Stickerette Day, 1917," *Solidarity*, 28 April 1917, 2.

89. Walker C. Smith, *Sabotage*, 67, 90.

90. Flynn, *Sabotage*, 94; Walker C. Smith, *Sabotage*, 71.

91. Trautman, *Direct Action and Sabotage*, 31; Walker C. Smith, *Sabotage*, 71.

92. Flynn, *Sabotage*, 117.

93. Walker C. Smith, *Sabotage*, 72.

94. Salerno, introduction to *Direct Action and Sabotage*, 1.

95. Walker C. Smith, *Sabotage*, 68.

96. Trautman, *Direct Action and Sabotage*, 31.

97. Walker C. Smith, *Sabotage*, 68.

98. Flynn, *Sabotage*, 100.

99. Trautman, *Direct Action and Sabotage*, 41–42.

100. "Covington Hall," *Industrial Worker*, 15 May 1913, 3.

101. "Burns' Defective Skunks Would Murder Covington Hall," *Industrial Worker*, 9 January 1913, 1+.

102. Ferrell and Ryan, "Brotherhood of Timber Workers," 55–57.

103. Roediger, *Towards the Abolition of Whiteness*, 168; Cary Nelson, *Repression and Recovery*, 62.

104. James R. Green, "Brotherhood of Timber Workers, 1910–1913," 176, 180–82.

105. Qtd. in ibid., 194.

106. Ibid., 197.

107. Hall, *Labor Struggles in the Deep South*, 152.

108. Reprinted in ibid., 143.

109. Roediger, *Towards the Abolition of Whiteness*, 155–56.

110. "Saw Mill 'Accidents,'" reprinted in Kornbluh, *Rebel Voices*, 56–57.

111. Covington Hall, "Rebels of the New South," *Industrial Worker*, 30 May 1912, 3.

112. "Strange Actions in the Southern Lumber Camps," *Industrial Worker*, 27 February 1913, 1, 4.

113. On Wells, see Chapter 3.

114. *Industrial Worker*, 26 December 1912, 8.

115. Hall, *Dreams and Dynamite*, 16–18.

116. Ibid., 51–52.

117. Covington Hall, "In Defense of Dreaming," 181.

118. Hall, *Dreams and Dynamite*, 32.

119. Hall, *Battle Hymns of Toil*, 93–94.

120. Ibid., 111.

121. Hall, *Rhymes of a Rebel*, unnumbered page.

122. Hall, *Songs of Love and Rebellion*, 15.

123. Hall, *Rhymes of a Rebel*, unnumbered page.

124. Hall, *Labor Struggles in the Deep South*, 121.

Epilogue

1. Denzin, "Cultural Studies in America," 5; Gaddis, "And Now This," 3.

2. Chomsky, *9–11*, 11–12; Niall Ferguson, "Clashing Civilizations or Mad Mullahs," 117.

3. Talbott and Chanda, introduction to *The Age of Terror*, xiii.

4. See also Douglas Kellner, who strongly condemns television coverage of the attacks. He argues that the "unrelenting war hysteria and utter failure to produce anything near a coherent analysis of what happened and reasonable response to the terrorist attacks put on display the frightening consequences of allowing corporate media institutions to hire ideologically compliant news teams that are not competent to deal with complex political events" ("September 11, Terrorism, and Blowback," 31).

5. As with so many other key components of 9/11, Chomsky is the most impassioned dissenter from this chorus of voices (*9–11*, 35).

6. Giroux, "Terrorism and the Fate of Democracy," 11.

7. Chomsky, *9–11*, 30–32.

Works Cited

Abbott, Lyman. "Danger Ahead." *Century* 31 (1885): 51–59.

Adamic, Louis. *Dynamite: The Story of Class Violence in America.* Rev. ed. New York: Viking Press, 1935.

Aglietta, Michel. *A Theory of Capitalist Regulation: The U.S. Experience.* Translated by David Fernbach. London: NLB, 1979.

Altgeld, John P. *Reasons for Pardoning Fielden, Neebe, and Schwab, the Haymarket Anarchists.* Chicago: Charles H. Kerr Publishing Company, 1986.

Anarchy at an End. Chicago: G. S. Baldwin, 1886.

Anderson, Benedict. *Imagined Communities: Reflections on the Origin and Spread of Nationalism.* Rev. ed. London: Verso, 1991.

Anesko, Michael. *"Friction with the Market": Henry James and the Profession of Authorship.* New York: Oxford University Press, 1986.

Apter, David E. "Political Violence in Analytical Perspective." In *The Legitimization of Violence,* edited by David E. Apter, 1–32. New York: New York University Press, 1997.

Aptheker, Herbert. *American Negro Slave Revolts.* New York: International Publishers, 1983.

Ashbaugh, Carolyn. *Lucy Parsons: American Revolutionary.* Chicago: Charles H. Kerr Publishing Company, 1976.

Asher, Robert. "Industrial Safety and Labor Relations in the United States, 1865–1917." In *Life and Labor: Dimensions of American Working-Class History,* edited by Charles Stephenson and Robert Asher, 115–30. Albany: State University of New York Press, 1986.

Auerbach, Jonathan. *Male Call: Becoming Jack London.* Durham: Duke University Press, 1996.

Avrich, Paul. *The Haymarket Tragedy.* Princeton: Princeton University Press, 1984.

———. Preface to *Bakunin on Anarchy,* by Mikhail Bakunin, edited and translated by Sam Dolgoff, xiii–xxvii. New York: Alfred A. Knopf, 1972.

Ayers, Edward L. *The Promise of the New South: Life after Reconstruction.* New York: Oxford University Press, 1992.

Bakunin, Mikhail. "Revolution, Terrorism, Banditry." In *The Terrorism Reader: A*

Historical Anthology, rev. ed., edited by Walter Laqueur and Yonah Alexander, 65–68. New York: New American Library, 1987.

Baudrillard, Jean. "The Ecstasy of Communication." Translated by John Johnston. In *The Anti-Aesthetic: Essays on Postmodern Culture,* edited by Hal Foster, 126–34. Seattle: Bay Press, 1983.

———. "In the Shadow of the Silent Majorities." In *In the Shadow of the Silent Majorities or, The End of the Social and Other Essays,* translated by Paul Foss, John Johnston, and Paul Patton, 1–61. New York: Semiotext(e), 1983.

Bederman, Gail. "'Civilization,' the Decline of Middle-Class Manliness, and Ida B. Wells's Antilynching Campaign (1892–94)." *Radical History Review* 52 (1992): 5–30.

Bell, Millicent. *Meaning in Henry James.* Cambridge: Harvard University Press, 1991.

Beniger, James R. *The Control Revolution: Technological and Economic Origins of the Information Society.* Cambridge: Harvard University Press, 1986.

Berlant, Lauren. "National Brands/National Body: *Imitation of Life.*" In *Comparative American Identities: Race, Sex, and Nationality in the Modern Text,* edited by Hortense J. Spillers, 110–40. New York: Routledge, 1991.

Blair, Sara. *Henry James and the Writing of Race and Nation.* Cambridge: Cambridge University Press, 1996.

Blondheim, Menahem. *News over the Wires: The Telegraph and the Flow of Public Information in America, 1844–1897.* Cambridge: Harvard University Press, 1994.

Bourdieu, Pierre. *Outline of a Theory of Practice.* Translated by Richard Nice. Cambridge: Cambridge University Press, 1977.

Braverman, Harry. *Labor and Monopoly Capital: The Degradation of Work in the Twentieth Century.* 1974. Reprint, with an introduction by John Bellamy Foster, New York: Monthly Review Press, 1998.

Bridgwater, Patrick. *Nietzsche in Anglosaxony: A Study of Nietzsche's Impact on English and American Literature.* Leicester: Leicester University Press, 1972.

Brodhead, Richard H. *The School of Hawthorne.* New York: Oxford University Press, 1986.

Browne, Lewis Allen. "Bolshevism in America." *Forum* 59 (1918): 703–17.

Bubka, Tony. "Time to Organize! The IWW Stickeretts." *American West* 5, no. 1 (1968): 21–22, 25–26.

Buel, Richard, Jr. *Securing the Revolution: Ideology in American Politics, 1789–1815.* Ithaca: Cornell University Press, 1972.

Buhle, Paul. "Pessimists' Heresy: Anarchism and American Labor." In *From the Knights of Labor to the New World Order: Essays on Labor and Culture,* 99–120. New York: Garland Publishing, 1997.

Burns, William J. *The Masked War: The Story of a Peril That Threatened the United States by the Man Who Uncovered the Dynamite Conspirators and Sent Them to Jail.* 1913. Reprint, New York: Arno Press, 1969.

Cady, Edwin H. *The Realist at War: The Mature Years, 1885–1920, of William Dean Howells.* Syracuse: Syracuse University Press, 1958.

Carby, Hazel V. *Reconstructing Womanhood: The Emergence of the Afro-American Woman Novelist.* New York: Oxford University Press, 1987.

Carey, James W. "Technology and Ideology: The Case of the Telegraph." In *Communication as Culture: Essays on Media and Society,* 201–30. Boston: Unwin Hyman, 1989.

Cargill, Oscar. "*The Princess Casamassima:* A Critical Reappraisal." *PMLA* 71 (1956): 97–117.

Carlson, Peter. *Roughneck: The Life and Times of Big Bill Haywood.* New York: W. W. Norton, 1983.

Chandler, Alfred D., Jr. *The Visible Hand: The Managerial Revolution in American Business.* Cambridge: Harvard University Press, 1977.

Chesnutt, Charles W. *The Marrow of Tradition.* New York: Penguin Books, 1993.

Chomsky, Noam. *The Culture of Terrorism.* Boston: South End Press, 1988.

———. *9–11.* New York: Seven Stories Press, 2001.

Chomsky, Noam, and Edward S. Herman. *The Washington Connection and Third World Fascism.* Vol. 1 of *The Political Economy of Human Rights.* Boston: South End Press, 1979.

Clarke, Allen. *The Effects of the Factory System.* London: Grant Richards, 1899.

Confino, Michael, ed. *Daughter of a Revolutionary: Natalie Herzen and the Bakunin-Nechayev Circle.* Translated by Hilary Sternberg and Lydia Bott. La Salle, Ill.: Library Press, 1973.

Cook, Raymond A. *Thomas Dixon.* New York: Twayne Publishers, 1974.

Corbin, Austin. "The Tyranny of Labor Organizations." *North American Review* 149 (1889): 413–20.

Crenshaw, Martha. "The Logic of Terrorism: Terrorist Behavior as a Product of Strategic Choice." In *Origins of Terrorism: Psychologies, Ideologies, Theologies, States of Mind,* edited by Walter Reich, 7–24. Cambridge: Cambridge University Press, 1990.

———. "Thoughts on Relating Terrorism to Historical Contexts." In *Terrorism in Context,* edited by Martha Crenshaw, 3–24. University Park: Pennsylvania State University Press, 1995.

Crenshaw Hutchinson, Martha. *Revolutionary Terrorism: The FLN in Algeria, 1954–1962.* Stanford: Hoover Institution Press, 1978.

Czitrom, Daniel J. *Media and the American Mind: From Morse to McLuhan.* Chapel Hill: University of North Carolina Press, 1982.

Davidson, Cathy N. "Preface: No More Separate Spheres!" *American Literature* 70 (1998): 443–63.

Davis, Jas. H. (Cyclone). *A Political Revelation.* Dallas: Advance Publishing Company, 1894.

Davis, Simone W. "The 'Weak Race' and the Winchester: Political Voices in the Pamphlets of Ida B. Wells-Barnett." *Legacy* 12, no. 2 (1995): 77–97.

DeLillo, Don. *Libra.* New York: Viking, 1988.

Dell, Floyd. "Bomb-Talking." In *Haymarket Scrapbook,* edited by Dave Roediger and Franklin Rosemont, 74. Chicago: Charles H. Kerr Publishing Company, 1986.

Denzin, Norman K. "Cultural Studies in America after September 11, 2001." *Cultural Studies Critical Methodologies* 2, no. 1 (2002): 5–8.

Der Derian, James. *Antidiplomacy: Spies, Terror, Speed, and War.* Cambridge, Mass.: Blackwell, 1992.

Derrida, Jacques. "Signature Event Context." Translated by Samuel Weber and Jeffrey Mehlman. In *Limited Inc,* 1–23. Evanston: Northwestern University Press, 1988.

Dickson, Sam. Introduction to *The Reconstruction Trilogy,* by Thomas Dixon Jr., ix–xx. Newport Beach, Calif.: Noontide Press, 1994.

"Direct Action." *Independent* 72 (1912): 419–20.

Dixon, Thomas, Jr. "Booker T. Washington and the Negro." *Saturday Evening Post* 178 (19 August 1905): 1–2.

———. *The Clansman: An Historical Romance of the Ku Klux Klan.* 1905. Reprint, Lexington: University Press of Kentucky, 1970.

———. *The Leopard's Spots: A Romance of the White Man's Burden—1865–1900.* New York: Doubleday, Page, 1902.

———. *The Traitor: A Story of the Fall of the Invisible Empire.* New York: Grosset and Dunlap, 1907.

Doane, Mary Ann. "Information, Crisis, Catastrophe." In *Logics of Television: Essays in Cultural Criticism,* edited by Patricia Mellencamp, 222–39. Bloomington: Indiana University Press, 1990.

Dobkin, Bethami A. *Tales of Terror: Television News and the Construction of the Terrorist Threat.* New York: Praeger, 1992.

Donner, Frank. *Protectors of Privilege: Red Squads and Police Repression in Urban America.* Berkeley: University of California Press, 1990.

Dorfman, Joseph. *The Economic Mind in American Civilization, 1865–1918.* Vol. 3. 1949. Reprint, New York: Augustus M. Kelley, 1969.

Dowell, Eldridge Foster. *A History of Criminal Syndicalism Legislation in the United States.* Baltimore: Johns Hopkins University Press, 1939.

Dubofsky, Melvyn. *We Shall Be All: A History of the Industrial Workers of the World.* 2d ed. Urbana: University of Illinois Press, 1988.

Du Bois, W. E. B. *Dark Princess: A Romance.* 1928. Reprint, with an introduction by Claudia Tate, Jackson: University Press of Mississippi, 1995.

Dunford, Michael. "Further Notes on Jack London's Introduction to the Philosophy of Friedrich Nietzsche." *Jack London Newsletter* 10 (1977): 39–42.

"Dynamiting as a Profession." *Outlook* 102 (1912): 600–601.

Edel, Leon. *Henry James: A Life.* New York: Harper and Row, 1985.

———, ed. *Henry James Letters.* Vol. 3. Cambridge: Harvard University Press, 1980.

Edel, Leon, and Lyall H. Powers, eds. *The Complete Notebooks of Henry James.* New York: Oxford University Press, 1987.

Edelman, Murray. *Constructing the Political Spectacle.* Chicago: University of Chicago Press, 1988.

Enstad, Nan. "Fashioning Political Identities: Cultural Studies and the Historical Construction of Political Subjects." *American Quarterly* 50 (1998): 745–82.

———. *Ladies of Labor, Girls of Adventure: Working Women, Popular Culture, and Labor Politics at the Turn of the Twentieth Century.* New York: Columbia University Press, 1999.

Esch, Deborah. "Promissory Notes: The Prescription of the Future in *The Princess Casamassima.*" *American Literary History* 1 (1989): 317–38.

Fant, Kenne. *Alfred Nobel: A Biography.* Translated by Marianne Ruuth. New York: Arcade Publishing, 1993.

Feldman, Allen. *Formations of Violence: The Narrative of the Body and Political Terror in Northern Ireland.* Chicago: University of Chicago Press, 1991.

Ferguson, Niall. "Clashing Civilizations or Mad Mullahs: The United States between Informal and Formal Empire." In *The Age of Terror: America and the World after September 11,* edited by Strobe Talbott and Nayan Chanda, 113–41. New York: Basic Books, 2001.

Ferguson, SallyAnn. "*MELUS* Forum: Charles W. Chesnutt's 'Future American.'" *MELUS* 15, no. 3 (1988): 95–107.

Ferrell, Jeff, and Kevin Ryan. "The Brotherhood of Timber Workers and the Southern Trust: Legal Repression and Worker Response." *Radical America* 19, no. 4 (1985): 55–74.

Fine, Sidney. "The National Erectors' Association and the Dynamiters." *Labor History* 32 (1991): 5–41.

———. *"Without Blare of Trumpets": Walter Drew, the National Erectors' Association, and the Open Shop Movement, 1903–57.* Ann Arbor: University of Michigan Press, 1995.

Fischer, Mike. "The Jamesian Revolution in *The Princess Casamassima:* A Lesson in Bookbinding." *Henry James Review* 9 (1988): 87–104.

Fitch, John A. "The Dynamite Case." *Survey* 29 (1913): 607–17.

Flynn, Elizabeth Gurley. *Sabotage: The Conscious Withdrawal of the Workers' Industrial Efficiency.* 1916. Reprinted in *Direct Action and Sabotage,* edited and with an introduction by Salvatore Salerno, 91–121. Chicago: Charles H. Kerr Publishing Company, 1997.

Foner, Eric. *Free Soil, Free Labor, Free Men: The Ideology of the Republican Party before the Civil War.* New York: Oxford University Press, 1970.

———. *Reconstruction: America's Unfinished Revolution, 1863–1877.* New York: Harper and Row, 1988.

Foner, Philip S. *American Socialism and Black Americans: From the Age of Jackson to World War II.* Westport, Conn.: Greenwood Press, 1977.

———. *Jack London: American Rebel.* New York: Citadel Press, 1947.

————, ed. *The Autobiographies of the Haymarket Martyrs.* New York: Humanities Press, 1969.

Fossett, Judith Jackson. "(K)night Riders in (K)night Gowns: The Ku Klux Klan, Race, and Constructions of Masculinity." In *Race Consciousness: African-American Studies for the New Century,* edited by Judith Jackson Fossett and Jeffrey A. Tucker, 35–49. New York: New York University Press, 1997.

Foster, Hal. "Death in America." *October* 75 (1996): 37–59.

France, Anatole. Preface to *The Iron Heel.* Translated by Jacqueline Tavernier-Courbin. In *Critical Essays on Jack London,* edited by Jacqueline Tavernier-Courbin, 35–37. Boston: G. K. Hall, 1983.

Francke, Warren. "Sensationalism and the Development of 19th-Century Reporting: The Broom Sweeps Sensory Details." *Journalism History* 12, no. 3–4 (1985): 80–85.

"The Frankensteins of Civilization." *Independent* 73 (1912): 1434–35.

Franklin, John Hope, and Alfred A. Moss Jr. *From Slavery to Freedom: A History of African Americans.* 7th ed. New York: McGraw-Hill, 1994.

Gaddis, John Lewis. "And Now This: Lessons from the Old Era for the New One." In *The Age of Terror: America and the World after September 11,* edited by Strobe Talbott and Nayan Chanda, 1–21. New York: Basic Books, 2001.

Garlin, Sender. *William Dean Howells and the Haymarket Era.* New York: American Institute for Marxist Studies, 1979.

Genovese, Eugene D. *From Rebellion to Revolution: Afro-American Slave Revolts in the Making of the Modern World.* Baton Rouge: Louisiana State University Press, 1979.

Gibson-Graham, J. K., Stephen A. Resnick, and Richard D. Wolff. "Introduction: Class in a Poststructuralist Frame." In *Class and Its Others,* edited by J. K. Gibson-Graham, Stephen A. Resnick, and Richard D. Wolff, 1–22. Minneapolis: University of Minnesota Press, 2000.

Giedion, Siegfried. *Mechanization Takes Command: A Contribution to Anonymous History.* New York: Oxford University Press, 1948.

Gilje, Paul A. *Rioting in America.* Bloomington: Indiana University Press, 1996.

Giovannitti, Arturo M. "Syndicalism—The Creed of Force." *Independent* 76 (1913): 209–11.

Giroux, Henry A. "Terrorism and the Fate of Democracy after September 11." *Cultural Studies Critical Methodologies* 2, no. 1 (2002): 9–14.

Gorn, Elliot J. "The Wicked World: The *National Police Gazette* and Gilded-Age America." In *The Culture of Crime,* edited by Craig L. LaMay and Everette E. Dennis, 9–21. New Brunswick: Transaction Publishers, 1995.

"Government by Dynamite." *Outlook* 103 (1913): 62–65.

Graham, Howard Jay. *Everyman's Constitution: Historical Essays on the Fourteenth Amendment, the "Conspiracy Theory," and American Constitutionalism.* Madison: State Historical Society of Wisconsin, 1968.

Graham, Wendy. *Henry James's Thwarted Love.* Stanford: Stanford University Press, 1999.

Green, James R. "The Brotherhood of Timber Workers, 1910–1913: A Radical Response to Industrial Capitalism in the Southern U.S.A." *Past and Present* 60 (1973): 161–200.

Green, Jeremy. "Disaster Footage: Spectacles of Violence in DeLillo's Fiction." *Modern Fiction Studies* 45 (1999): 571–99.

Grover, David H. *Debaters and Dynamiters: The Story of the Haywood Trial.* Corvallis: Oregon State University Press, 1964.

Gunning, Sandra. *Race, Rape, and Lynching: The Red Record of American Literature, 1890–1912.* New York: Oxford University Press, 1996.

Hall, Covington. *Battle Hymns of Toil.* Oklahoma City: General Welfare Reporter, 1946.

————. *Dreams and Dynamite: Selected Poems.* Edited by Dave Roediger. Chicago: Charles H. Kerr Publishing Company, 1985.

————. "In Defense of Dreaming." In *Free Spirits: Annals of the Insurgent Imagination,* edited by Paul Buhle et al., 181. San Francisco: City Light Books, 1982.

————. *Labor Struggles in the Deep South and Other Writings.* Edited by David R. Roediger. Chicago: Charles H. Kerr Publishing Company, 1999.

————. *Rhymes of a Rebel.* Newllano, La.: Llano Cooperative Printery, 1931.

————. *Songs of Love and Rebellion.* New Orleans: John J. Weihing Printing Company, 1915.

Halttunen, Karen. *Murder Most Foul: The Killer in the American Gothic Imagination.* Cambridge: Harvard University Press, 1998.

Hampton, Wayne. *Guerrilla Minstrels.* Knoxville: University of Tennessee Press, 1986.

Harlow, Virginia. *Thomas Sergeant Perry: A Biography.* Durham: Duke University Press, 1950.

Harmon, Christopher C. *Terrorism Today.* London: Frank Cass, 2000.

Hay, John. *The Bread-Winners.* 1883. Reprint, Ridgewood, N.J.: Gregg Press, 1967.

Hebdige, Dick. *Subculture: The Meaning of Style.* London: Methuen, 1979.

Hill, Frederick Trevor. "Decisive Battles of the Law: The Chicago Anarchists' Case." *Harper's Monthly Magazine* 114 (1907): 889–900.

Hodes, Martha. "The Sexualization of Reconstruction Politics: White Women and Black Men in the South after the Civil War." *Journal of the History of Sexuality* 3 (1993): 402–17.

Hoffman, Bruce. *Inside Terrorism.* New York: Columbia University Press, 1998.

Hofstadter, Richard. "The Paranoid Style in American Politics." In *The Paranoid Style in American Politics and Other Essays,* 3–40. New York: Alfred A. Knopf, 1966.

Holbrook, Stewart H. *The Rocky Mountain Revolution.* New York: Henry Holt, 1956.

Holt, Thomas C. "The Lonely Warrior: Ida B. Wells-Barnett and the Struggle for Black Leadership." In *Black Leaders of the Twentieth Century,* edited by John

Hope Franklin and August Meier, 39–61. Urbana: University of Illinois Press, 1982.

Hounshell, David A. *From the American System to Mass Production, 1800–1932: The Development of Manufacturing Technology in the United States.* Baltimore: Johns Hopkins University Press, 1984.

Howe, Irving. "Henry James: The Political Vocation." In *Politics and the Novel,* 139–56. New York: New American Library, 1987.

Howells, William Dean. *The Rise of Silas Lapham.* Edited by Don L. Cook. New York: W. W. Norton, 1982.

I.W.W. Songs: To Fan the Flames of Discontent. 19th ed. 1923. Reprint, Chicago: Charles H. Kerr Publishing Company, 1996.

Jacobs, Ron. *The Way the Wind Blew: A History of the Weather Underground.* London: Verso, 1997.

Jacobson, Matthew Frye. *Whiteness of a Different Color: European Immigrants and the Alchemy of Race.* Cambridge: Harvard University Press, 1998.

James, Henry. *The Art of the Novel.* Edited by R. P. Blackmur. New York: Charles Scribner's Sons, 1934.

———. *The Princess Casamassima.* New York: Penguin, 1987.

———. *Roderick Hudson.* New York: Penguin, 1986.

Johns, A. Wesley. *The Man Who Shot McKinley.* South Brunswick: A. S. Barnes, 1970.

Johnston, Carolyn. *Jack London—An American Radical?* Westport, Conn.: Greenwood Press, 1984.

Jones, Mary Harris. *The Autobiography of Mother Jones.* Edited by Mary Field Parton. Chicago: Charles H. Kerr Publishing Company, 1990.

Kawash, Samira. *Dislocating the Color Line: Identity, Hybridity, and Singularity in African-American Literature.* Stanford: Stanford University Press, 1997.

Kellner, Douglas. "September 11, Terrorism, and Blowback." *Cultural Studies Critical Methodologies* 2, no. 1 (2002): 27–39.

Kenny, Kevin. *Making Sense of the Molly Maguires.* New York: Oxford University Press, 1998.

Kerber, Linda K. "Separate Spheres, Female Worlds, Woman's Place: The Rhetoric of Women's History." *Journal of American History* 75 (1988): 9–39.

Kipnis, Ira. *The American Socialist Movement, 1897–1912.* New York: Columbia University Press, 1952.

Knox, Wendell J. *Conspiracy in American Politics, 1787–1815.* New York: Arno Press, 1972.

Kornbluh, Joyce L., ed. *Rebel Voices: An IWW Anthology.* Expanded ed. Chicago: Charles H. Kerr Publishing Company, 1998.

Kubiak, Anthony. *Stages of Terror: Terrorism, Ideology, and Coercion as Theatre History.* Bloomington: Indiana University Press, 1991.

Labor, Earle, and Robert C. Leitz III. "Jack London on Alexander Berkman: An Unpublished Introduction." *American Literature* 61 (1989): 447–56.

Labor, Earle, and Jeanne Campbell Reesman. *Jack London*. Rev. ed. New York: Twayne Publishers, 1994.

Labor, Earle, Robert C. Leitz III, and I. Milo Shepard, eds. *The Letters of Jack London*. 3 vols. Stanford: Stanford University Press, 1988.

Laqueur, Walter. *The Age of Terrorism*. Boston: Little, Brown, 1987.

————. *The New Terrorism: Fanaticism and the Arms of Mass Destruction*. New York: Oxford University Press, 1999.

"Lawlessness and Sabotage." *Century* 81 (1911): 791–92.

Leach, Eugene E. "The Literature of Riot Duty: Managing Class Conflict in the Streets, 1877–1927." *Radical History Review* 56 (1993): 23–50.

Leach, William. *Land of Desire: Merchants, Power, and the Rise of a New American Culture*. New York: Vintage Books, 1994.

Lecercle, Jean-Jacques. *The Violence of Language*. London: Routledge, 1990.

Lee, Alfred McClung. *The Daily Newspaper in America: The Evolution of a Social Instrument*. New York: Macmillan, 1937.

Lee, Martyn J. *Consumer Culture Reborn: The Cultural Politics of Consumption*. London: Routledge, 1993.

Lenin, V. I. *What Is to Be Done? Burning Questions of Our Movement*. New York: International Publishers, 1969.

————. "Why the Social Democrats Must Declare War on the SR.s." In *The Terrorism Reader: A Historical Anthology*, rev. ed., edited by Walter Laqueur and Yonah Alexander, 209–10. New York: New American Library, 1987.

Lerner, Max. Introduction to *The Iron Heel*, by Jack London, vii–xiii. New York: Macmillan, 1958.

Lloyd, Henry Demarest. *Wealth against Commonwealth*. New York: Harper and Brothers, 1899.

London, Jack. *The Assassination Bureau, Ltd.* New York: Penguin Books, 1994.

————. *The Iron Heel*. New York: Macmillan, 1908. Reprinted in *Novels and Social Writings*, by Jack London. New York: Library of America, 1982.

————. "The Minions of Midas." In *The Complete Short Stories of Jack London*, edited by Earle Labor, Robert C. Leitz III, and I. Milo Shepard, 433–44. Stanford: Stanford University Press, 1993.

————. "Revolution." In *Revolution and Other Essays*. New York: Macmillan, 1910. Reprinted in *Novels and Social Writings*, by Jack London. New York: Library of America, 1982.

————. "Something Rotten in Idaho." *Chicago Daily Socialist*, 4 November 1906. Reprinted in *Jack London: American Rebel*, edited by Philip S. Foner, 407–10. New York: Citadel Press, 1947.

Lott, Eric. *Love and Theft: Blackface Minstrelsy and the American Working Class*. New York: Oxford University Press, 1993.

Lukas, J. Anthony. *Big Trouble: A Murder in a Small Western Town Sets Off a Struggle for the Soul of America*. New York: Simon and Schuster, 1997.

Lum, Dyer D. *A Concise History of the Great Trial of the Chicago Anarchists in 1886.* Chicago: Socialistic Publishing Company, 1886.

Lynn, Kenneth S. *William Dean Howells: An American Life.* New York: Harcourt Brace Jovanovich, 1971.

Marcus, George E., ed. *Paranoia within Reason: A Casebook on Conspiracy as Explanation.* Chicago: University of Chicago Press, 1999.

Marks, Patricia. *Bicycles, Bangs, and Bloomers: The New Woman in the Popular Press.* Lexington: University Press of Kentucky, 1990.

McConnell, Samuel P. "The Chicago Bomb Case." *Harper's Monthly Magazine* 168 (1934): 730–39.

McKivigan, John R., and Stanley Harrold, eds. *Antislavery Violence: Sectional, Racial, and Cultural Conflict in Antebellum America.* Knoxville: University of Tennessee Press, 1999.

McLean, George N. *The Rise and Fall of Anarchy in America.* 1890. Reprint, New York: Haskell House Publishers, 1972.

McManigal, Ortie E. *The National Dynamite Plot.* Los Angeles: Neale Company, 1913.

McMath, Robert C., Jr. *American Populism: A Social History, 1877–1898.* New York: Hill and Wang, 1993.

McNeill, George E. "The Problem of To-Day." In *The Labor Movement: The Problem of To-Day,* edited by George E. McNeill, 454–69. 1887. Reprint, New York: Augustus M. Kelley, 1971.

Melchiori, Barbara Arnett. *Terrorism in the Late Victorian Novel.* London: Croon Helm, 1985.

Michaels, Walter Benn. *The Gold Standard and the Logic of Naturalism: American Literature at the Turn of the Century.* Berkeley: University of California Press, 1987.

———. *Our America: Nativism, Modernism, and Pluralism.* Durham: Duke University Press, 1995.

———. "The Souls of White Folk." In *Literature and the Body: Essays on Populations and Persons,* edited by Elaine Scarry, 185–209. Baltimore: Johns Hopkins University Press, 1988.

Miller, D. A. *The Novel and the Police.* Berkeley: University of California Press, 1988.

Miller, Joseph Dana. "The Evils of Trusts and Foolish Remedies." *The Arena* 23 (1900): 617–26.

Miller, Martin A. "The Intellectual Origins of Modern Terrorism in Europe." In *Terrorism in Context,* edited by Martha Crenshaw, 27–62. University Park: Pennsylvania State University Press, 1995.

Morn, Frank. *"The Eye That Never Sleeps": A History of the Pinkerton National Detective Agency.* Bloomington: Indiana University Press, 1982.

Most, John. "Advice for Terrorists." In *The Terrorism Reader: A Historical Anthology,* rev. ed., edited by Walter Laqueur and Yonah Alexander, 100–108. New York: New American Library, 1987.

Nacos, Brigitte L. *Terrorism and the Media: From the Iran Hostage Crisis to the World Trade Center Bombing*. New York: Columbia University Press, 1994.

Nelson, Bruce C. *Beyond the Martyrs: A Social History of Chicago's Anarchists, 1870–1900*. New Brunswick: Rutgers University Press, 1988.

Nelson, Cary. *Repression and Recovery: Modern American Poetry and the Politics of Cultural Memory, 1910–1945*. Madison: University of Wisconsin Press, 1989.

Nelson, Daniel. *Managers and Workers: Origins of the Twentieth-Century Factory System in the United States, 1880–1920*. 2d ed. Madison: University of Wisconsin Press, 1995.

Nemerov, Alex. "Doing the 'Old America': The Image of the American West, 1880–1920." In *The West as America: Reinterpreting Images of the Frontier, 1820–1920*, edited by William H. Truettner, 285–343. Washington, D.C.: Smithsonian Institution Press, 1991.

Norton, Anne. *Reflections on Political Identity*. Baltimore: Johns Hopkins University Press, 1988.

Nye, David E. *Henry Ford: "Ignorant Idealist"*. Port Washington, N.Y.: Kennikat Press, 1979.

O'Neill, Eugene. *The Hairy Ape*. 1922. Reprinted in *Complete Plays, 1920–1931*, by Eugene O'Neill. New York: Library of America, 1988.

Orchard, Harry. "Violence in Labor Disputes." *Independent* 72 (1912): 388–90.

Oswald, F. L. "The Assassination Mania: Its Social and Ethical Significance." *North American Review* 171 (1900): 314–19.

Painter, Nell Irvin. *Standing at Armageddon: The United States, 1877–1919*. New York: W. W. Norton, 1987.

Paletz, David L., and Alex P. Schmid, eds. *Terrorism and the Media*. Newbury Park, Calif.: Sage, 1992.

Parsons, Lucy E., ed. *The Famous Speeches of the Eight Chicago Anarchists in Court*. 1910. Reprint, New York: Arno Press, 1969.

Pauly, John J. "The Great Chicago Fire as a National Event." *American Quarterly* 36 (1984): 668–83.

Pease, Donald E. Introduction to *The Assassination Bureau, Ltd.*, by Jack London, vii–xxxii. New York: Penguin Books, 1994.

Pettibone v. Nichols. 203 *United States Reports*, 192–221. New York: Banks Law Publishing Company, 1907.

Post, Jerrold M. "Terrorist Psycho-logic: Terrorist Behavior as a Product of Psychological Forces." In *Origins of Terrorism: Psychologies, Ideologies, Theologies, States of Mind*, edited by Walter Reich, 25–40. Cambridge: Cambridge University Press, 1990.

Prather, H. Leon. *We Have Taken a City: Wilmington Racial Massacre and Coup of 1898*. Cranbury, N.J.: Associated University Press, 1984.

Preston, Richard. *The Cobra Event*. New York: Ballantine Books, 1997.

Rapsher, W. M. "Dangerous 'Trusts.'" *North American Review* 146 (1888): 509–14.

Ratner, Sidney, James H. Soltow, and Richard Sylla. *The Evolution of the American Economy: Growth, Welfare, and Decision Making.* New York: Basic Books, 1979.

"The Real Anarchist." *Living Age* 225 (1900): 780–88.

Redding, Arthur F. *Raids on Human Consciousness: Writing, Anarchism, and Violence.* Columbia: University of South Carolina Press, 1998.

Roediger, Dave. "Strange Legacies: The Black International and Black America." In *Haymarket Scrapbook,* edited by Dave Roediger and Franklin Rosemont, 93–96. Chicago: Charles H. Kerr Publishing Company, 1986.

Roediger, David R. *Towards the Abolition of Whiteness: Essays on Race, Politics, and Working Class History.* London: Verso, 1994.

———. *The Wages of Whiteness: Race and the Making of the American Working Class.* Rev. ed. London: Verso, 1999.

Roosevelt, Theodore. "Murder Is Murder." *Outlook* 98 (1911): 12–13.

Rowe, John Carlos. *The Theoretical Dimensions of Henry James.* Madison: University of Wisconsin Press, 1984.

Rubenstein, Richard E. *Alchemists of Revolution: Terrorism in the Modern World.* New York: Basic Books, 1987.

———. *Rebels in Eden: Mass Political Violence in the United States.* Boston: Little, Brown, 1970.

"Rushing to Bash Outsiders." *Time,* 1 May 1995, 70.

Russell, Charles Edward. "The Haymarket and Afterwards." *Appleton's Magazine* 10 (1907): 399–412.

"Sabotage." *Outlook* 98 (1911): 915–16.

"Sabotage, 'Sab Cats,' and the 'One Big Union.'" *Literary Digest* 64 (17 January 1920): 58–60.

Said, Edward. "The Essential Terrorist." In *Blaming the Victims: Spurious Scholarship and the Palestinian Question,* edited by Edward W. Said and Christopher Hitchens, 149–58. London: Verso, 1988.

Salerno, Salvatore. Introduction to *Direct Action and Sabotage,* edited by Salvatore Salerno, 1–18. Chicago: Charles H. Kerr Publishing Company, 1997.

———. *Red November, Black November: Culture and Community in the Industrial Workers of the World.* Albany: State University of New York Press, 1989.

Saxton, Alexander. *The Rise and Fall of the White Republic: Class Politics and Mass Culture in Nineteenth-Century America.* London: Verso, 1990.

Scanlan, Margaret. "Language and the Politics of Despair in Doris Lessing's *The Good Terrorist.*" *Novel* 23 (1990): 182–98.

———. *Plotting Terror: Novelists and Terrorists in Contemporary Fiction.* Charlottesville: University Press of Virginia, 2001.

———. "Terrorism and the Realistic Novel: Henry James and *The Princess Casamassima.*" *Texas Studies in Literature and Language* 34 (1992): 380–402.

Schaack, Michael J. *Anarchy and Anarchists: A History of the Red Terror and the Social Revolution in America and Europe.* Chicago: F. J. Schulte, 1889.

Schechter, Patricia A. "'All the Intensity of My Nature': Ida B. Wells, Anger, and Politics." *Radical History Review* 70 (1998): 48–77.

———. *Ida B. Wells-Barnett and American Reform, 1880–1930.* Chapel Hill: University of North Carolina Press, 2001.

———. "Unsettled Business: Ida B. Wells against Lynching, or, How Antilynching Got Its Gender." In *Under Sentence of Death: Lynching in the South,* edited by W. Fitzhugh Brundage, 292–317. Chapel Hill: University of North Carolina Press, 1997.

Schmid, Alex P. *Political Terrorism: A Research Guide to Concepts, Theories, Data Bases, and Literature.* Amsterdam: North-Holland, 1983.

Schmid, Alex P., and Janny de Graaf. *Violence as Communication: Insurgent Terrorism and the Western News Media.* London: Sage Press, 1982.

Schocket, Eric. "Undercover Explorations of the 'Other Half,' Or the Writer as Class Transvestite." *Representations* 64 (1998): 109–33.

Schudson, Michael. *Discovering the News: A Social History of American Newspapers.* New York: Basic Books, 1978.

Scott, Thomas A. "The Recent Strikes." *North American Review* 125 (1877): 351–62.

Seltzer, Mark. *Bodies and Machines.* New York: Routledge, 1992.

———. "*The Princess Casamassima:* Realism and the Fantasy of Surveillance." In *American Realism: New Essays,* edited by Eric J. Sundquist, 95–118. Baltimore: Johns Hopkins University Press, 1982.

———. *Serial Killers: Death and Life in America's Wound Culture.* New York: Routledge, 1998.

Shapiro, Herbert. "The McNamara Case: A Window on Class Antagonism in the Progressive Era." *Southern California Quarterly* 70 (1988): 69–95.

Short, K. R. M. *The Dynamite War: Irish-American Bombers in Victorian Britain.* Atlantic Highlands, N.J.: Humanities Press, 1979.

Simmel, Georg. "The Stranger." In *The Sociology of Georg Simmel,* translated and edited by Kurt H. Wolff, 402–8. New York: Free Press, 1950.

Sklar, Martin J. *The Corporate Reconstruction of American Capitalism, 1890–1916: The Market, the Law, and Politics.* Cambridge: Cambridge University Press, 1988.

Slotkin, Richard. *The Fatal Environment: The Myth of the Frontier in the Age of Industrialization, 1800–1890.* Middletown, Conn.: Wesleyan University Press, 1986.

———. *Regeneration through Violence: The Mythology of the American Frontier, 1600–1860.* Middletown, Conn.: Wesleyan University Press, 1973.

Smith, Carl. *Urban Disorder and the Shape of Belief: The Great Chicago Fire, the Haymarket Bomb, and the Model Town of Pullman.* Chicago: University of Chicago Press, 1995.

Smith, Page. *The Rise of Industrial America: A People's History of the Post-Reconstruction Era.* New York: Penguin, 1990.

Smith, Walker C. *Sabotage: Its History, Philosophy, and Function.* 1913. Reprinted in

Direct Action and Sabotage, edited and with an introduction by Salvatore Salerno, 57–90. Chicago: Charles H. Kerr Publishing Company, 1997.

Smith-Rosenberg, Carroll. "The New Woman as Androgyne: Social Disorder and Gender Crisis, 1870–1936." In *Disorderly Conduct: Visions of Gender in Victorian America,* 245–96. New York: Alfred A. Knopf, 1985.

Stepniak. "A Female Nihilist." *Cornhill* 50 (1884): 485–512.

Stevens, Hugh. *Henry James and Sexuality.* Cambridge: Cambridge University Press, 1998.

Stewart, David M. "Cultural Work, City Crime, Reading, Pleasure." *American Literary History* 9 (1997): 676–701.

Stimson, Grace Heilman. *Rise of the Labor Movement in Los Angeles.* Berkeley: University of California Press, 1955.

Stoehr, Taylor. "Words and Deeds in *The Princess Casamassima.*" *English Literary History* 37 (1970): 95–135.

Stone, Donald David. *Novelists in a Changing World: Meredith, James, and the Transformation of English Fiction in the 1880s.* Cambridge: Harvard University Press, 1972.

Stowe, Harriet Beecher. *Uncle Tom's Cabin.* New York: New American Library, 1981.

"Subterranean Russia." *Saturday Review of Politics, Literature, Science, and Art* 54 (12 August 1882): 214–15.

Sundquist, Eric J. *To Wake the Nations: Race in the Making of American Literature.* Cambridge: Harvard University Press, 1993.

Sypher, Eileen. *Wisps of Violence: Producing Public and Private Politics in the Turn-of-the-Century British Novel.* London: Verso, 1993.

Talbott, Strobe, and Nayan Chanda. Introduction to *The Age of Terror: America and the World after September 11,* edited by Strobe Talbott and Nayan Chanda, vii–xix. New York: Basic Books, 2001.

"The Telegraph." *Harper's Monthly Magazine* 47 (1873): 332–60.

Thompson, Fred. *The I.W.W.: Its First Fifty Years, 1905–1955.* Chicago: Industrial Workers of the World, 1955.

Thornton, Thomas Perry. "Terror as a Weapon of Political Agitation." In *Internal War: Problems and Approaches,* edited by Harry Eckstein, 71–99. Glencoe, N.Y.: Free Press, 1964.

Tichi, Cecelia. *Shifting Gears: Technology, Literature, Culture in Modernist America.* Chapel Hill: University of North Carolina Press, 1987.

Tolnay, Stewart E., and E. M. Beck. *A Festival of Violence: An Analysis of Southern Lynchings, 1882–1930.* Urbana: University of Illinois Press, 1995.

Tourgée, Albion W. "The Anti-Trust Campaign." *North American Review* 157 (1893): 30–41.

Trachtenberg, Alan. *The Incorporation of America: Culture and Society in the Gilded Age.* New York: Hill and Wang, 1982.

Trautman, William E. *Direct Action and Sabotage.* 1912. Reprinted in *Direct Action and Sabotage,* edited and with an introduction by Salvatore Salerno, 19–55. Chicago: Charles H. Kerr Publishing Company, 1997.

Trelease, Allen W. *White Terror: The Ku Klux Klan Conspiracy and Southern Reconstruction.* New York: Harper and Row, 1971.

"Trend." *Survey* 29 (1913): 909–10.

"The Trial of the Chicago Anarchists: August Spies, Michael Schwab, Samuel Fielden, Albert R. Parsons, Adolph Fischer, George Engel, Louis Lingg, and Oscar W. Neebe for Conspiracy and Murder. Chicago, Illinois, 1886." In *American State Trials,* vol. 12, edited by John D. Lawson, 1–319. St. Louis: F. H. Thomas Law Book Company, 1919.

Trilling, Lionel. *"The Princess Casamassima."* In *The Liberal Imagination: Essays on Literature and Society,* 58–92. New York: Viking, 1950.

"Trusts and Confidences." *The Nation* 44 (1887): 380–81.

Twain, Mark. "The United States of Lyncherdom." In *The Complete Essays of Mark Twain,* edited by Charles Neider, 673–79. Garden City, N.Y.: Doubleday, 1963.

U.S. Congress. Senate. Committee on Education and Labor. *Report of the Committee of the Senate upon the Relations between Labor and Capital.* Vol. 1. 48th Cong., 2d sess., 1883. Washington, D.C.: Government Printing Office, 1885.

Van Wienen, Mark W. *Partisans and Poets: The Political Work of American Poetry in the Great War.* Cambridge: Cambridge University Press, 1997.

Veblen, Thorstein. "On the Nature and Uses of Sabotage." *The Dial* 66 (1919): 341–46.

Vološinov, V. N. *Marxism and the Philosophy of Language.* Translated by Ladislav Matejka and I. R. Titunik. Cambridge: Harvard University Press, 1986.

Wade, Wyn Craig. *The Fiery Cross: The Ku Klux Klan in America.* London: Simon and Schuster, 1987.

Warner, Michael. "The Mass Public and the Mass Subject." In *The Phantom Public Sphere,* edited by Bruce Robbins, 234–56. Minneapolis: University of Minnesota Press, 1993.

Weber, Max. *Economy and Society: An Outline of Interpretive Sociology.* Edited by Guenther Roth and Claus Wittich. Berkeley: University of California Press, 1978.

Weimann, Gabriel, and Conrad Winn. *The Theater of Terror: Mass Media and International Terrorism.* New York: Longman, 1994.

Wells, Ida B. *A Red Record.* 1895. Reprinted in *Southern Horrors and Other Writings: The Anti-Lynching Campaign of Ida B. Wells, 1892–1900,* edited and with an introduction by Jacqueline Jones Royster. Boston: Bedford Books, 1997.

———. *Southern Horrors: Lynch Law in All Its Phases.* 1892. Reprinted in *Southern Horrors and Other Writings: The Anti-Lynching Campaign of Ida B. Wells, 1892–1900,* edited and with an introduction by Jacqueline Jones Royster. Boston: Bedford Books, 1997.

"What the I.W.W. Black Cat and Wooden Shoe Emblems Mean." *Literary Digest* 61 (19 April 1919): 70–75.

Wilkinson, Paul. "Terrorism." In *Ideas That Shape Politics,* edited by Michael Foley, 189–98. Manchester: Manchester University Press, 1994.

Williams, Raymond. *Marxism and Literature.* Oxford: Oxford University Press, 1977.

Williamson, Joel. *The Crucible of Race: Black-White Relations in the American South since Emancipation.* New York: Oxford University Press, 1984.

Wills, Clair. "Language Politics, Narrative, Political Violence." *Oxford Literary Review* 13, no. 1–2 (1991): 20–60.

Wilson, Christopher P. *The Labor of Words: Literary Professionalism in the Progressive Era.* Athens: University of Georgia Press, 1985.

Wilson, Howard A. "William Dean Howells's Unpublished Letters about the Haymarket Affair." *Journal of the Illinois State Historical Society* 56 (1963): 5–19.

Wilson Logan, Shirley. *"We Are Coming": The Persuasive Discourse of Nineteenth-Century Black Women.* Carbondale: Southern Illinois University Press, 1999.

Woehlke, Walter V. "Terrorism in America." *Outlook* 100 (1912): 359–67.

Woodward, C. Vann. *Origins of the New South, 1877–1913.* Baton Rouge: Louisiana State University Press, 1951.

Wright, Gavin. *Old South, New South: Revolutions in the Southern Economy since the Civil War.* New York: Basic Books, 1986.

Young, Iris Marion. "Polity and Group Difference: A Critique of the Ideal of Universal Citizenship." *Ethics* 99 (1989): 250–74.

Zola, Émile. "The Experimental Novel." In *Documents of Modern Literary Realism,* edited by George J. Becker, 162–96. Princeton: Princeton University Press, 1963.

———. *Germinal.* Translated by Peter Collier. Oxford: Oxford University Press, 1993.

Zulaika, Joseba, and William A. Douglass. *Terror and Taboo: The Follies, Fables, and Faces of Terrorism.* New York: Routledge, 1996.

Index